C++ PROGRAMMING
WITH DESIGN PATTERNS REVEALED

Tomasz Müldner
Acadia University

Addison
Wesley

Boston San Francisco New York
London Toronto Sydney Tokyo Singapore Madrid
Mexico City Munich Paris Cape Town Hong Kong Montreal

Senior Acquisitions Editor: Maite Suarez-Rivas
Project Editor: Katherine Harutunian
Executive Marketing Manager: Michael Hirsch
Production Supervisor: Marilyn Lloyd
Project Management: Pre-Press Company, Inc.
Copyeditor: Barbara McGowran
Proofreader: Pre-Press Company, Inc.
Text Design: Sandra Rigney
Composition and Art: Pre-Press Company, Inc.
Cover Design: Leslie Haimes
Design Manager: Gina Hagen
Prepress and Manufacturing: Hugh Crawford

Access the latest information about Addison-Wesley titles from our World Wide Web site:
http://www.aw.com/cs

Many of the designations used by manufacturers and sellers to distinguish their products are claimed as trade-marks. Where those designations appear in this book, and Addison-Wesley was aware of a trademark claim, the designations have been printed in initial caps or all caps.

The programs and applications presented in this book have been included for their instructional value. They have been tested with care, but are not guaranteed for any particular purpose. The publisher does not offer any warranties or representations, not does it accept any liabilities with respect to the programs or applications.

Library of Congress Cataloging-in-Publication Data

Müldner, Tomasz.
   C++ programming with design patterns revealed / Tomasz Müldner.
      p. cm.
   ISBN 0-201-72231-3 (pbk.)
      1. C++ (Computer program language) I. Title.
QA76.73.C153 M855 2002
005.13'3—dc21   2001045828

ISBN 0-201-72231-3
12345678910-HP-04030201

Dedication

To my family: Basia, Kasia, and Michał,
for their love and support

CONTENTS

Chapter 1
A Quick Tour of C++

Chapter 2
Procedural Programming

Chapter 3
Object-Based Programming, Part I　　63

Chapter 4
Object-Based Programming, Part II *133*

Chapter 5
Object-Oriented Programming, Part I *163*

Chapter 6
Object-Oriented Programming, Part II   *207*

Chapter 7
Introduction to Generic Programming:
Parameterized Types   *271*

Chapter 8
Generic Programming Using STL   *357*

Chapter 9
Miscellaneous Topics   *431*

PREFACE

C++ was designed by Bjarne Stroustrup of AT&T Bell Laboratories in the early 1980s. Since then, the language has gone through a process of many changes and standardizations and has gathered immense popularity. The final version of the standard, ISO/IEC 14882, was ratified in August 1998. A great deal of software is implemented in C++, and this language continues to be widely used for a variety of applications in both industry and research institutions. Therefore, it should not be surprising that as of today (middle of 2001), there are more than 400 books about this language.

Vision

So why yet another book on C++? First, many existing books on C++ are a thousand-plus pages long and can be overwhelming. If you are already familiar with the object-oriented philosophy, then it is possible to take advantage of your past knowledge and cover C++ in less than half this length. Second, we now have the commonly recognized ANSI C++ standard, which is not always reflected by all books. For example, new generic programming techniques are not covered in most of the existing books on C++. Third, our understanding of programming techniques has changed considerably, especially with the advent of design patterns and UML (Unified Modeling Language).

This book is called *C++ Programming with Design Patterns Revealed* because it is designed to demonstrate modern C++ programming techniques that make use of design patterns. In the past, many of the techniques used by C++ programmers were based on C techniques, resulting in programs that were not object oriented and not easy to maintain. Today, there are many new programming techniques available that allow us to take advantage of both the object-oriented constructs that C++ offers, and the high-level design concepts that are formulated as design patterns.

There are three important reasons why design patterns should be introduced *while* you are learning a programming language, rather than *after*. First, you can avoid viewing the statements of a programming language as the building blocks and instead apply patterns as mappings between a problem type and its effective solution. Second, you do not first learn low-level techniques, only then to be told that these techniques should not really be used. For example, you may initially learn to create objects using a particular technique that hard codes class names. Later on, you may discover that this technique makes it difficult to modify your programs, and you may find that using creational design patterns addresses this problem. Third, design patterns provide standard, language-independent thoroughly tested solutions. Usually, pattern books are designed for experienced programmers. I believe that learning a programming language first and patterns second is a major pedagogical mistake and instead propose that the two be integrated. Note that in addition to high-level design concepts, I also discuss idioms, which are constructs that describe techniques for expressing low-level ideas. Typically, these apply only to C++ and are not language independent.

Overview of the text

Each of the nine chapters starts with a preview, which briefly describes the topics discussed in that chapter, and ends with exercises. Chapter 1 provides a quick tour of C++. A rather short Chapter 2 describes issues related to functions that are not used in Java. Chapter 3 starts introducing concepts related to objects, and it concentrates on *object-based* programming (programming with classes but without inheritance). In this chapter, a number of programming idioms are introduced. Chapter 4 continues the discussion of object-based programming, and it introduces some basic UML notations. It discusses the composition of objects through delegation, as well as the management of the object-creational process. The first design pattern, the singleton, is presented in this chapter. Chapters 5 and 6 discuss *object-oriented* programming, using inheritance. In Chapter 5, some basic concepts are introduced, such as public inheritance, virtual functions, and abstract operations. The second design pattern, the template method, is described here. Chapter 6 provides a more detailed discussion of object-oriented programming. It begins with a description of how the object-creational process can be managed by using one more design pattern: the abstract factory. Next, this chapter compares inheritance, delegation, and multiple inheritance. Finally, this chapter talks about "programming to an interface" and introduces four more design patterns: the bridge, the prototype, the adapter, and the State. Examples of applications of these patterns are also provided in this chapter. Chapters 7 and 8 discuss concepts that are foreign to the typical Java programmer, namely, generic programming using templates. First, in Chapter 7, overloaded operators are introduced. Next, two more design patterns are described—the proxy and the iterator. Finally, the description of a template is provided. In order to document assumptions about type parameters, I use the notion of a "concept" and provide a listing of 11 concepts used throughout Chapters 7 and 8. Chapter 8 covers generic programming with the standard template library (STL). It describes all the basic components of generic programming: iterators, containers, algorithms, and adapters. Finally, Chapter 9 provides a description of various topics, such as details of I/O operations, pointers to members and their adapters, etc. Two more design patterns, the composite and the visitor, are also introduced in this chapter.

The Appendices contain a complete list of tables, figures, and examples that appear in the book (Appendix A), the list of idioms, patterns and concepts (Appendix B), the list of keywords (Appendix C), a description of numeric types (Appendix D), a list of string operations (Appendix E), an alphabetic summary of all standard generic algorithms (Appendix F), a list of header files (Appendix G), and finally a list of C++ compilers (Appendix H).

We made an early design decision to limit the size of the book to approximately 500 pages and cover only essential C++ constructs. At this point, you may wonder which topics are not covered in this book. First, I do not cover features of C++ that have been inherited from C and that are now *deprecated*, such as pointer arithmetic. Second, I do not cover object-oriented analysis and design and detailed use of UML—there are many excellent books that cover these topics. Third, I do not cover the details of debugging and testing techniques; again, there are many extensive and long books that deal with these topics (one of my favorite books in this area has more than one thousand pages). Fourth, I do not discuss non-portable techniques, in particular C++ applications that use graphical user interfaces, such as Microsoft Windows Visual C++. Although I do cover the basics of generic programming with the standard library, I do not provide fine-level details, such as implementing new library components (there are several recent books of the size of this book that concentrate just on these issues). Finally, I do not cover software engineering principles in detail, but I do refer to them.

Prerequisites

C++ Programming with Design Patterns Revealed is primarily designed for readers who know Java because many universities have recently changed their curricula to teach Java as the first programming language. The advantage of knowing Java is that you already understand various object-oriented concepts, such as classes and inheritance. You will still be able to learn C++ from this book even if you do not know Java, as long as you understand the principles of object-oriented programming (for example, you may know another object-oriented language, such as Eiffel). The C programming language is *not* a prerequisite for this book; although C++ is practically a superset of C, programming in C++ is very different from programming in C. (For those of you who know Java and would like to learn C, I recommend my other book, *C for Java Programmers*, published by Addison-Wesley.)

I also assume that you have some experience related to the conventional wisdom of program development: for example, the need for avoiding tricky and unreadable, or duplicate code. Since I assumed that you have knowledge of object-oriented programming, it would be silly not to trust that you have at least a basic understanding of these concepts (this understanding comes from reading "good" books and writing large programs—for a selection of some of my favorite books, please refer to the bibliography). In this book, I will concentrate on the proper use of C++ constructs—I will explain how these constructs can be used to write efficient, reliable, reusable, and modifiable programs.

Special Features

Important features of this book include:

- A complete coverage of ANSI C++
- 27 programming idioms
- 11 design patterns
- 27 tables comparing C++ and Java
- 60 figures, most of which show UML diagrams for examples in the text
- Over 30 examples of C++ programs
- Over 110 exercises.

You will be guided by specially marked sections of the text that present:

- programming style and guidelines
- advanced topics, which are essential but can be omitted in the first reading
- typical errors
- idioms
- design patterns
- modeling concepts.

Supplements

The complete code for all programs in this book, solutions to some exercises as well as PowerPoint or HTML files with the presentation based on the book are available from the Addison-Wesley web site: http://www.aw.com/cssupport. Instructors who adopt the book can obtain solutions to other exercises; please contact your Addison-Wesley sales representative or send email to aw.cse@awl.com.

Alternative Paths

Although the material in this text was designed to be used in a linear fashion, it can also be used in a different way. The various *miscellaneous topics* presented in Chapter 9 may be read earlier, if you desire. In particular, a detailed description of the I/O library presented in Section 9.2 requires only Section 2.4.6 as a prerequisite. Similarly:

- Section 9.3 on separate compilation and linking can be read after Section 2.8 on file organization
- Section 9.4 on generic pointers and pointers to functions can be read after Section 2.6 on pointers

- Section 9.5 on overloaded memory management can be read after Section 7.3.6
- Section 9.6 on debugging can be read after Section 5.13 on exceptions.

Although essential, some more advanced topics may be skipped: in particular, Chapter 1, which shows a quick tour of C++, Section 6.6, which presents the topic of programming to an interface, and some or all the presentation of STL in Chapter 8.

Notations

Most programming examples in this book are not necessarily complete, but they always include a reference to the file with the complete code listing, available on the Addison-Wesley web site http://www.aw.com/cs. For most programs, I will not show the conditional compilation guards introduced in Section 2.8.1 The following two lines, related to the use of the standard namespace introduced in Section 2.8.2, will also be omitted:

```
#include <iostream>
using namespace std;
```

If f is a function, then f() is used in the description even if f has parameters that are irrelevant for the discussion at hand; otherwise, I explicitly list parameters.

To denote the end of an example, I use ▶.

New terms appear in bold face. Code fragments appear in Courier font, for example find(). Incorrect expressions appear in Courier font, in italics; for example

```
if(x = 1) // assignment rather than comparison
```

Code that presents a C++ construct for the first time appears shaded.

In order to describe constructs that are syntactically identical, I will use a table with two columns; the construct appears in the left column, and a comment detailing its use in C++ appears in the right column. For example:

Construct	Comments about C++
/* ...*/	C++ does not provide a Java comment /* ...*/ used to create documentation

For constructs that are syntactically very similar but not identical in Java and C++, I will use a table with three columns: the Java construct appears in the leftmost column, the C++ construct appears in the middle column, and a comment detailing its use in C++ appears in the rightmost column. For example:

Java	C++	Comments about C++
| ```
class C {
 public static void
   main(String args[]) {
   . . .
 }
``` | ```
int main() {
   . . .
   return 0;
}
``` |    . . . |

Lack of a comment associated with a construct means that it is identical in Java and C++.

Acknowledgments

First and foremost, I would like to thank my wife Basia for her understanding, patience, and support. I would also like to thank my children, Kasia and Michał, both of whom graduated several years ago from the Computer Science program at Acadia University. Their critical comments were very useful for my previous book, and they also helped me a lot this time. The style, presentation, and explanation of various design patterns in this book would not be the same without Kasia's constructive criticism and suggestions. The first several chapters of this book were read by Curtis d'Entremont, who made a number of useful corrections and comments. Any remaining mistakes or omissions are wholly attributable to the author. Should you find any errors, please send email to tmuldner@ns.sympatico.ca. Several reviewers of the manuscript provided useful comments and suggestions:

Kenneth Basye, Harvard University Extension School
Bruce Char, Drexel University
Ron DiNapoli, Cornell University
Nigel Gwee, Louisiana State University
David Nicol, Dartmouth University
Randolph Odendahl, SUNY Oswego
Robert Pettus, University of South Carolina
Anne-Louise Radimsky, California State University, Sacramento
Steven Reiss, Brown University
Thomas Skinner, Boston University
Anurag Singla, Columbia University
Chris Wild, Old Dominion University

Finally, I am grateful to my editor Maite Suares-Rivas for her valuable input and for suggesting the "less-than-400-page book on C++", as well as Katherine Harutunian for her assistance during the production process.

Chapter **1**

A QUICK TOUR OF C++

1.1 *Preview*

This chapter gives you a brief tour of C++. I supplement this overview with two examples. You should be warned that C++ is a language rich in syntactic constructs (it has many keywords, some of them overloaded), and this tour is meant to provide only a general idea of what the language offers. I will provide more detailed explanations in subsequent chapters.

The first example is a program that prints `"Hello, world"`; it is followed by a description of some basic C++ constructs. The second example is a bit more complicated; it shows how to evaluate arithmetic expressions by using a stack. I provide two versions of this program: in the first version, the stack is defined as a class; in the second version, a built-in library stack container is used.

1.2 *First Example*

C++ programs consist of classes and stand-alone functions. Each program must contain a `main()` function, where the execution of the entire program starts. A very simple C++ program that prints `"Hello, world"` looks like this:

```
#include <iostream>
using namespace std;
int main() {
   cout << "Hello, world" << endl;
}
```

The first two lines are needed to use the standard input/output (I/O) library. The body of the main function consists of a single output statement that prints the "Hello, world" string, followed by the end-of-line character to the standard output stream signified by cout.

   This is a very simple example. I will describe more C++ constructs in the following sections to give you a better flavor of the language. The examples are meant as a general overview and so are not explained in detail. The goal of this chapter is to give you a high-level understanding of the differences between Java and C++. As promised, subsequent chapters will provide detailed explanations.

1.3   *Basic Constructs*

The Java programmer will find familiar syntax for variables, constants, comments and control structures, and classes, with a few minor syntactic details. For example, a two-dimensional point can be represented using the following class:

```
// class definition
class Point {
public:
  Point(double x, double y);                  // constructor
  double getX() const;                        // accessor (query)
  double getY() const;
private:
  double x_;
  double y_;
};
```

Functions that do not modify the state of the calling object, like the getX() function above, are called accessors, or queries, and are specified as const. Within a class, methods are merely declared. Complete definitions of class operations are *separate* from the class interface. For example, the operations of the Point class are defined as follows:

```
// Constructor definition: initializes an object

Point::Point(double x, double y) {           // note the use of Point::
  x_ = x;
  y_ = y;
}

// definitions of two accessors

double Point::getX() const {
  return x_;
```

```
}
double Point::getY() const {
  return y_;
}
```

C++ provides three kinds of variables:

- A *class variable,* whose value is the class object
- A *pointer variable,* whose value points to the class object
- A *reference variable*

For example:

```
Point x(1, 2);               // class variable
Point* p = new Point(3, 4);  // pointer
Point& r = x;                // reference (different than in Java)
```

Accessing class attributes is done using . for class variables and references, and ->
for pointers:

```
cout << x.getX();                        // output x coordinate
cout << p->getY();                       // output y coordinate
```

There is no built-in garbage collector, and one has to implement *explicit memory
deallocation* as needed. As an example, consider a class Segment, which contains
pointers to two previously defined Point objects:

```
class Segment {
public:
  Segment(double x1, double y1, double x2, double y2);

  ~Segment();                                       // destructor
  ...
private:
  Point* p_;
  Point* q_;
};
Segment::Segment(double x1, double y1, double x2, double y2) {
  p_ = new Point (x1, y1);
  q_ = new Point (x2, y2);
}
Segment::~Segment() {
  delete p_;                                // deallocate point p_
  delete q_;                                // deallocate point q_
}
```

The destructor ~Segment() is used to deallocate the memory used by the Point object and is implicitly called when any Segment object goes out of scope. Here is a simple example:

```
void foo() {
  Segment s(1, 2, 3, 4);
  ...
                    // when s goes out of scope, ~Segment() is called
                    // This destructor deallocates both points
}
```

1.4 *Inheritance*

C++ supports both single and multiple inheritance: A class may be derived either from a single base class or from several base classes. The language does not provide any syntax to define interfaces and abstract classes but does allow you to define abstract methods by using the = 0 syntax (see below). These methods have an *empty body*. An operation is polymorphic *only* when explicitly specified as virtual. The following example shows a function that is both virtual and abstract. This function is defined by the Point class and used to calculate the distance between two points:

```
class Point {              // abstract class; distance() is abstract
public:
  ...
  virtual double distance(const Point& p) const = 0;
  ...
protected:
  double x_;
  double y_;
};
```

The distance() function is *polymorphic* because it is specified as virtual, and it is *abstract* because its body is specified as = 0. When the class Point is extended, the body of distance() will be defined at some point in the inheritance hierarchy. The extended class is declared by specifying the base class as public (there are other options not discussed here). For example:

```
class PointAbsMetrics : public Point {          // no "extends"
public:
  virtual double distance(const Point& p) const;
  ...
};
```

```
double PointAbsMetrics::distance(const Point& p) const {
  return abs(x_ - p.x_) + abs(y_ - p.y_);
}
```

1.5 *Exceptions and Namespaces*

C++ provides exception-handling constructs but does not *force* you to use exceptions, instead allowing the use of other techniques that may be more appropriate or efficient for your particular application. To avoid name conflicts, C++ uses the namespace construct, which is similar to the Java package. For example, consider a collection of objects that have the following common interface:

```
class StrObjectIfc {                        // abstract
  virtual string getName() const = 0;       // accessor to get a string
};
```

The following collection consists of several classes, some of which represent exceptions. All these classes are stored in a single namespace:

```
namespace CollectionSpace {
  using namespace std;                       // import standard namespace

  // A class representing an exception thrown when
  //   a duplicate is to be added
  class DuplicateException : public exception {
  public:
    virtual const char* what() const throw();
    // does not throw anything
  };

  const char* DuplicateException::what() const throw() {
    return "Duplicate employee\n";
  }

  // A class representing an exception thrown when
  //    a collection is full.
  class FullCollectionException : public exception {
  public:
    virtual const char* what() const throw();
  };

  const char* FullCollectionException::what() const throw() {
    return "Full collection\n";
  }
```

```
// An interface representing a collection of objects;
//   each object has a unique string attribute.
class CollectionIfc { // abstract
public:
    static int max = 100;           // default size of this collection

    // add another element
    virtual void add(const StrObjectIfc&)
        throw (FullCollectionException, DuplicateException) = 0;

    // find an object given its attribute, return 0 if failed
    virtual StrObjectIfc* find(const string&) const = 0;
};

}
```

You can extend this namespace with various implementations of the abstract
CollectionIfc class; for example:

```
namespace CollectionSpace {                       // add to namespace

    class CollectionImpl : public CollectionIfc { //implements
    public:
        virtual void add(const StrObjectIfc&)
            throw (FullCollectionException, DuplicateException);
        virtual StrObjectIfc* find(const string&) const;
    };

}
```

For example, the client may use this namespace to create a class to represent a company as follows (here I show only one function, which is used to hire a new employee):

```
using namespace CollectionSpace;
class Company {
public:
    Company();
    void hire(const string& name)
        throw (DuplicateException, FullCollectionException);
    ~Company();
private:
    CollectionIfc* staff_;
};

Company::Company() {
    staff_ = new CollectionImpl();
}
```

```
void Company::hire(const string& name)
    throw (DuplicateException, FullCollectionException) {
  staff_.add(name);
}

Company::~Company() {
  delete staff_;
}
```

1.6   *Generic Programming*

In addition to constructs that are more or less similar to those in Java, C++ supports the generic programming technique, which is not available in Java. *Generic programming* means that you can parameterize data structures and algorithms with data types. This makes it possible to build generic data structures and algorithms capable of storing and operating on any data type. For example, the standard C++ library provides a generic class vector, which has a parameter defining the type of the vector's elements. To create a vector of employees, you use an *instantiation* of the form vector<Employee>. Using this vector, you can implement a collection of employees like this:

```
vector<Employee> staff(100);            // a vector of 100 employees
```

It is important to note the essential difference between this kind of vectors and those provided by Java: The use of the C++ vector does not require a run-time cast. The previous instantiation is performed at compile time, allowing you to simply use the available employee methods; for example:

```
staff[0].getName();                     // staff[0] is an employee
```

The next section presents the second example of a C++ program. Again, this example is not meant to show all the essential constructs of the language but rather to illustrate some constructs that are different from the corresponding ones in Java.

1.7   *Second Example: Arithmetic Expressions*

Some pocket calculators support evaluation of arithmetic expressions written in the so-called reverse Polish notation (RPN, named after its inventor, a Polish logician, J. £ukasiewicz). In this notation, an operator, such as +, is applied to two operands that immediately precede it; for example:

```
1 2 +            means     1+2
27 3 4 + *       means     27*(3+4)
```

Expressions in RPN can be evaluated using a stack. They are read from left to right. If an operand is read, it is pushed onto the stack. If an operator is read, two operands are popped from the stack, the operator that has just been read is applied to the pair of popped values, and the result is pushed back onto the stack.

In the rest of this chapter, I show two versions of a program that implements the evaluation of expressions in RPN. The first version uses a stack defined by the programmer, and the second version uses a stack provided by the C++ standard library. For simplicity, this example only deals with integer expressions that contain the following three operations: addition, subtraction, and multiplication. I also assume that the user enters the expression terminated with the $ character; for example:

```
1 2 + $
```

1.8   *Version I*

In the first version, the entire program consists of three files containing the interface for the stack, the main program, and the implementation of the stack:

```
// Version I
// File: intstack.h
// Interface for the bounded stack of integers
// There are three stack operations available:
//    push() to push an integer
//    pop() to pop and return the top of the stack
//    empty() to test whether or not the stack is empty
// logic_error exception is thrown if any operation fails
// Note: this implementation does not provide a top() operation
//        that returns the top of the stack without popping it.
#ifndef INTSTACK_H
#define INTSTACK_H

// include files
#include <stdexcept>                    // needed for standard exceptions
#include <iostream>
using namespace std;

class IntStack {
public:
  IntStack(int = 100);                              // default size
  ~IntStack();
  void push(int) throw(logic_error);
  int pop() throw(logic_error);
  bool empty() const;
```

```
private:
  IntStack(const IntStack&);
  IntStack& operator=(IntStack&);

  int top_;
  int* stack_;
  int size_;
};
#endif
// end of file: intstack.h
/////////////////////////

/////////////////////////
// File: example.cpp
#include <stdexcept>
#include <iostream>
#include <cctype>
using namespace std;
#include "intstack.h"

int main() {    // main program - here is where the execution starts
  int operand;
  char op;
  const char SENTINEL = '$';
  IntStack s;
  cout << "Enter integer expression in RPN, terminated with "
    << SENTINEL << endl;

  while(1) {
    try { // exceptions
      if(cin > op) {                          // get a single char
        if(isdigit(op)) {                     // check if it's a digit
            cin.putback(op);                  // put back on input
            cin >> operand;                   // read an entire integer
            s.push(operand);
      } else
          switch(op) {
          case '+': s.push(s.pop() + s.pop());
                  break;
          case '-': operand = s.pop();
                  s.push(s.pop() - operand);
                  break;
          case '*': s.push(s.pop() * s.pop());
                  break;
          case '$': // end of input
```

```
                   operand = s.pop();
                   if(!s.empty()) {
                     cerr << "incorrect expression" << endl;
                     return 1;
                   }
                   cout << "result is " << operand << endl;
                   return 0;

           default:  cerr << "incorrect op" << endl;
                     return 1;
             }
         }
      } catch(const logic_error& e) {
        cout << e.what() << endl;
        return 1;
      }
   }
}
// end of file: example.cpp
////////////////////////

////////////////////////
// File: intstack.cpp
// Implementation of stack operations
#include "intstack.h"
#include <stdexcept>
#include <iostream>
using namespace std;

IntStack::IntStack(int size) {
  top_ = -1;
  size_ = size;
  stack_ = new int[size];
}

IntStack::~IntStack() {
  delete [] stack_;
}

void IntStack::push(int i) throw (logic_error) {
  if(top_ == size_ - 1)                                // full
    throw logic_error("Stack full ");

  stack_[++top_] = i;
}
```

```
int IntStack::pop() throw (logic_error) {
  if(top_ == -1)                                    // empty
    throw logic_error("Stack empty ");

  return stack_[top_--];
}
bool IntStack::empty() const {
    return top_ == -1;
}
// end of file intstack.cpp
/////////////////////////
```

The following subsections describe the various constructs used by this program.

1.8.1   General Program Structure

The program just presented consists of three files:

- intstack.h, the header file containing the interface for the class IntStack
- intstack.cpp, the file containing the implementation of the IntStack class
- example.cpp, the file containing the main program

Include directives, starting with #include, are always needed in C++ programs to include special kinds of files, called header files. These files are used in C++ to store an interface to a class or a library, such as the class definition or the list of function declarations from a particular library (a function declaration provides only a signature of this function, which is made up of its list of parameters, and return type). The client's file, containing the main program, includes the header file and is linked with the implementation file. Header files that represent standard C++ libraries do not have any extension, while user-defined header files have the .h extension.

Comments in C++ are similar to those found in Java, except there is no standard tool such as javadoc to produce documentation in HTML format.

1.8.2   Class IntStack

The code in each header file is surrounded by so-called guards, used to ensure that the file is not included more than once by any other file:

```
#ifndef INTSTACK_H
#define INTSTACK_H

  ...
#endif
```

The namespace std is a standard predefined namespace, and the statement

```
using namespace std;
```

allows you to avoid having to qualify names of all of the attributes from this name-space; for example, you can use `cout` instead of `std::cout`. Rather than qualifying each class attribute with a *visibility specification,* a C++ class has two (or more) sections specified as `public` and `private`, as shown in the next example:

```
class IntStack {
public:
  IntStack(int = 100);            // constructor with the default size
  ~IntStack();                    // destructor

  void push(int) throw(logic_error);
  int pop() throw(logic_error);
  bool empty() const;
private:
  IntStack(const IntStack&);
  IntStack& operator=(IntStack&);

  int top_;
  int* stack_;
  int size_;
};
```

This interface provides only function *declarations,* which include function names, lists of their parameter types, and specifications of exceptions that may be thrown by each function. The complete function definitions appear in the implementation file, which for this class is `IntStack.cpp`.

The `logic_error` exception is a predefined C++ exception. The function `empty()` is specified as `const` because it is a query, which does not modify the state of the stack. The private section contains declarations of these two functions:

- `IntStack(const IntStack&)`, the copy constructor used to initialize the object by a copy of the existing object
- `IntStack& operator=(Instack&)`, defines an overloaded meaning of an assignment between two stacks

C++ provides *default* copy and assignment constructors, which are invoked if explicit ones are not provided. Most of the time this is convenient, but there are situations where you want to prevent *any* use of some operation. For example, you may not want the client to ever copy stacks using a simple assignment or to initialize a stack using an existing one. The implementation provided for the `IntStack` class accomplishes this goal. Both these operations are impossible because they are declared as private; in addition, they are merely *declared,* not actually defined. If another member of this class tries to call these operations, the linker will complain because of the missing definitions.

Of remaining private variables, only

```
int* stack_
```

requires an explanation: It is a pointer to an integer that is initialized in the constructor (see the following code) with a block of memory that allows it to be used as a dynamic array. (Note that in Java, all arrays are dynamic.)

   Now look at the implementation file, focusing on the constructor and the destructor:

```
IntStack::IntStack(int size) {
   top_ = -1;
   size_ = size;
   stack_ = new int[size];
}
```

The initialization of the variable stack_ allocates memory for size integers. This memory is deallocated in the destructor:

```
IntStack::~IntStack() {
   delete [] stack_;          // empty square brackets [] required here
}
```

1.8.3   The main() Function

Each C++ program must include a function called main, which is the entry point for program execution. Recall that the goal of the example is to evaluate arithmetic expressions written in RPN. The main program's job for this example is to read these expressions and use the stack to parse them. The main program reads an input expression using the following technique: First a single character is read, and if it is a digit, this character is pushed back on the input stream, so the entire integer can be read (for example, given the input 67, the 6 is read and pushed back, at which point the entire integer 67 is read). This method allows the program to differentiate operators (such as + or -) and integers. Three predefined C++ I/O streams are used:

- cin, which denotes a standard input stream; data are read using an extraction operator >>
- cout, which denotes a standard output stream, data are written using an output operator <<
- cerr, which is the output stream independent from cout (useful, for example, when the standard output stream is redirected), and is used to write error messages

Why is main() an integer function? Consider a program consisting of several components working in tandem, for example, in a pipe. A component may want to know if its predecessor successfully finished its task; this information may be represented by the return value of the main function. Typically, the convention is that the main function returns 0 if successful and a positive integer value otherwise.

1.9 *Version II*

In the first version of the program used to evaluate expressions in RPN, I defined my own stack. The second version of the program uses a stack predefined in the standard C++ library. This stack is a container parametrized by the element type, which in this example is `int`:

```
stack<int> s;
```

The interface for this stack consists of the following functions:

- `empty()`
- `size()`, the number of elements in the stack
- `pop()`, removes the top element from the stack, but does not return it
- `top()`, returns the top element from the stack
- `push(item)`

The stack is unbounded, so overflow is not a problem, but the implementation does not provide any error checking. For example, if you try to pop an element from an empty stack, the program will crash. This approach is typical for standard C++ libraries. Of course, I could easily add exception handling by extending the predefined stack, but for this example, I rely on the client of my code to perform any checking.

```cpp
// File: example2.cpp
#include <stack>                    // needed to use standard stacks
#include <iostream>
#include <cctype>                   // needed to use isdigit()
using namespace std;

int main() {
   int op1, op2;
   char op;
   const char SENTINEL = '$';
   stack<int> s;
   cout << "Enter integer expression in RPN, terminated with "
      << SENTINEL << endl;

while(1) {
   if(cin >> op) {                  // get a single char
      if(isdigit(op)) {             // check if it's a digit
          cin.putback(op);          // put back on input
          cin >> op1;               // read an entire integer
          s.push(op1);
      } else
```

```
        switch(op) {
        case '+': if(s.size() < 2)              // need 2 elements
                    return 1;
                  op1 = s.top();
                  s.pop();
                  op2 = s.top();
                  s.pop();
                  s.push(op1 + op2);
                  break;
        case '*': if(s.size() < 2)
                    return 1;
                  op1 = s.top();
                  s.pop();
                  op2 = s.top();
                  s.pop();
                  s.push(op1 * op2);
                  break;
        case '-': if(s.size() < 2)
                    return 1;
                  op1 = s.top();
                  s.pop();
                  op2 = s.top();
                  s.pop();
                  s.push(op2 - op1);
                  break;
        case '$': // end of input
                  operand = s.top();
                  if(s.size() < 1) {
                    cerr << "incorrect expression" << endl;
                    return 1;
                  }
                  cout << "result is " << operand << endl;
                  return 0;
        default:  cerr << "incorrect op" << endl;
                  return 1;
        }
      }
    }
  }
```

This ends a quick tour of C++. In the next chapter, I will present a description of how to use functions. Then, in the next four chapters, I will describe object-based and object-oriented programming. Finally, in Chapters 7 and 8, I will present the topic of generic programming.

Chapter 2

PROCEDURAL PROGRAMMING

2.1 *Preview*

This chapter discusses a number of essential concepts needed to write even the simplest programs. These concepts are limited to a paradigm called **procedural programming**, which uses only functions, not classes. Java programmers unacquainted with C++ are not used to this paradigm and should read this chapter carefully, even if they find it a bit mundane. Classes are discussed in the next two chapters.

First I describe a number of basic concepts that are similar in Java and C++, including standard data types, control structures, I/O, and functions. Next I start discussing dynamic memory management and, in particular, some basic pointer operations. This discussion leaves out many low-level details not needed for modern C++ programming (these details are briefly described in Section 9.4).

To help you get through this introductory chapter, I include many tables showing "at a glance" essential differences between Java and C++. In addition, several sections have "advanced" parts that you can omit from your first reading. Finally, I present various programming guidelines containing my recommendations for using naming conventions, comments, and other C++ design principles. The need for these conventions is explained in the following section.

2.2 *Introduction to Principles of Software Design and Implementation*

A programming language such as Java or C++ consists of syntax, which is a set of rules that define which sentences are grammatically correct, and semantics, which defines the meaning of correct sentences. What the language does not define are principles for design and implementation that specify how to use the language effectively and efficiently so that programs are correct, reusable, modifiable, and readable.

As I mentioned in the Preface, this book is not on object-oriented analysis and design; therefore, I don't provide detailed discussions as to what constitutes good or bad design. My hope is that the numerous examples of design patterns illustrated with UML diagrams will guide your future software projects and lead to good design decisions. In addition to design patterns, the book also provides design guidelines that include some widely used coding principles, such as naming conventions. These kinds of principles are typically described in books on software engineering (for example, Reiss 1998), and you have probably seen them while learning other languages.

As a specific example, consider **coding conventions**, which involve standards for commenting style, names of identifiers and files, lexical conventions for formatting files, and so on. For example, naming conventions can involve standards for names of variables, classes, methods, and files, as in "for a class name, use an identifier that starts with T." Although some of these conventions are truly useful, it may be difficult to enforce them. A typical programmer may not like to be told to use some conventions just because they make all programs adhere to a standard. While commercial organizations can enforce these rules among their employees, books written for academic use do not have this option; therefore, I restrict myself to conventions that are commonly accepted. All my conventions are formulated as *guidelines* rather than strict standards.

In the following chapters, I will continue this discussion in the context of object-based and object-oriented programming.

2.3 *Main Program*

Each program must contain exactly one `main()` function, where program execution starts (see Table 2.1).

There are two versions of `main()` that can be used: without any parameters (as shown in Table 2.1) and with parameters (see Section 2.6.4). `main()` returns an integer value that can be used by its calling environment. By convention, returning the value zero indicates success, returning a nonzero value indicates a failure, and the lack of any `return` statement indicates success.

Table 2.1 Main function

Java	C++	Comments About C++
```class C { public static void main(String args[]) { ... }```	```int main() { ... return 0; }```	The main function is not included in any class.

2.4 *Basics: Types, Control Structures, and Simple I/O*

Comments and identifiers are identical in both languages (see Table 2.2). A complete list of C++ keywords appears in Appendix C.

Programming Guidelines

(Remember that programming guidelines are only my guidelines and are not required by the language.)

Proper comments provide documentation and are essential for software *readability*. I suggest two lexical conventions for comments:

Short explanations are placed in comments at the *right end* of the line, using //; for example:

```
if(isdigit(i))                                    // cannot happen
```

Multiline explanations are formatted like this:

```
//
// Program to sort integer values
//
```

It is difficult to give a general guideline as to how much commenting is needed—over-commenting is as bad as under-commenting. You should provide enough comments that the user of your software does not have to read the actual code to understand *how* it works. These comments are usually separate from the code; for example, they precede a function. Provide additional comments inside the actual code to clarify any pieces of the implementation that require it. You will find that most code in this book is commented using these guidelines. This should help you understand the code's intended meaning and the way it should be used.

Table 2.2 Comments

Construct	Comments About C++
/* ...*/ //	C++ does not provide the Java comment /** ... */, used to create documentation.

Table 2.3   Primitive data types

Construct	Comments about C++
char	char is one byte long and does not use Unicode
short int long float double	The language does not define the size and range of numeric primitive data types, and consequently, they are implementation dependent. There are no predefined wrapper classes for primitive data types.

2.4.1   Primitive Data Types

Primitive data types are quite similar in Java and C++ (see Table 2.3). There are minor differences for some of the other built-in data types (see Table 2.4). Strictly speaking, in C++, a string is defined in the standard library and is not a primitive data type. I include it in Table 2.4 so that you can use some basic string operations in your first programs. For a complete listing of the available string operations, see Appendix E.

String constants are the same in both languages; for example, "C++".

String variables have values that are modifiable. They can be concatenated using +; for example:

```
string language = "C" + "++";
```

Strings can be lexicographically compared using standard relational operators (such as <); for example:

```
bool mark = language < "Java";
```

This is different from Java, where you cannot use the standard comparison operators and must instead use functions such as compareTo(). Substrings can be extracted using a string member function substr(int, int) and replaced using another string member function replace(int, int, string). Individual charac-

Table 2.4   More primitive data types

Java	C++	Comments About C++
byte	--	Similar to unsigned char; see Appendix D.
boolean	bool	Any nonzero numeric value can be treated as true; a zero value can be treated as false.
String	string	To use strings, you must include the <string> library; see Appendix E.

ters can be extracted using the `[]` operator and specifying indices from 0 to
`length( )`; for example:

```
string plus2 = language.substr(1, language.length());         // "++"
char first = language[0];
```

Advanced

You are not likely to need more data types than those listed in Table 2.3 when
writing a general-purpose, portable C++ program. However, C++ can also be used
for writing special-purpose applications; for example, ones for which it is essential
to map primitive data types to the specific requirements of the target machine,
such as the amount of memory, range, or precision available. For this reason, C++
supports a variety of specialized data types that you can use to optimize specific
applications. I briefly describe these types in this section (for more details, see Appendix D).

To specify an integer type, you can declare it as an `int` with either one or two
(in any order) *qualifiers* selected from the following list:

```
short or long
unsigned or signed
```

or as a plain integer:

```
int
```

(without any qualifiers).

If you do use qualifiers, you can drop the word `int`—it will be assumed by the
compiler (for example, you can write `short`). Also, a `signed int` is the same as an
`int`. In the majority of cases, you should just use a plain `int` (although `unsigned`
`int` may give you a larger range than `int`, the conversion rules will probably take
away this advantage).

There are three character data types in C++: `char, unsigned char,` and
`signed char`. A plain `char` may be stored as either a `signed char` or `unsigned`
`char`; this is implementation dependent. A `char` has 8 bits, so to represent Unicode
characters, C++ provides another type called `wchar_t`.

In addition to two floating-point types, `float` and `double`, that are similar to
those in Java, there is another type, `long double`. For most applications, you can
use `double`; the use of the other types requires that you understand floating-point
computations.

The major difference between how Java and C++ deal with primitive data
types is that Java defines the exact size of each type; for example, a `short` is a 16-
bit signed integer. On the other hand, C++ makes few assumptions about data size,
leaving the details up to the implementation. The main reason for this difference is

that Java attempts to be portable, while C++ strives to be efficient. In C++, you can always assume that long integers have at least as many bits as integers, which in turn have at least as many bits as short integers. Similarly, long doubles have at least as many bits as doubles, which in turn have at least as many bits as floats.

2.4.2 typedef and sizeof

C++ allows you to define a *synonym* for an existing type, using the following syntax:

```
typedef existingType NewType;
```

This syntax is useful for improving code readability. For example, if you want to use a `Boolean` type identifier, you can define it using

```
typedef bool Boolean;
```

The `sizeof` operator returns the size, in bytes, of a type or an object; for example:

```
int k = 5;
... sizeof(int) ... //size of int
double d = 3;
... sizeof d ...    // size of double, no brackets around d required
```

2.4.3 Variables, Constants, and Expressions

Variables and constants can be declared both within functions and classes and outside them (in which case they are global variables). Global variables are implicitly initialized to zero; the programmer must initialize all other variables. The C++ compiler does not detect uninitialized local variables.

Any data can be declared as constant (see Table 2.5); for example:

```
const int LINES = 25;
```

Notice that, as in Java, a C++ variable may be declared `volatile` to signify that it can be modified asynchronously. The compiler does not perform optimizations of volatile variables (for example, it does not rearrange variables) because it cannot

Table 2.5 Constants

Java	C++	Comments About C++
final	const	—

assume that the value of such variables will not be changed *asynchronously* at some point during program execution.

Programming Guidelines

1. Whenever possible, use class attributes instead of global variables. Global variables work against program modularization and make program maintenance more difficult.

2. To increase program readability, use the following naming conventions. Names of classes start with an uppercase character. Variable and function names start with a lowercase character. Both names use mixed case as appropriate to make the identifiers more readable; for example, `NewClass` and `longId`. When a new type is specified using `typedef`, the type identifier starts with an uppercase letter.

3. Constant declarations help make a program modifiable and readable. For example, you can use them to specify the screen width, maximum number of lines permitted, and other values. If constants are not used, and the actual numbers are used in the code, then they are referred to as "magic numbers"; these should be avoided. Constant names are in uppercase, and an underscore is used to separate words; for example, `MAX_LINES`.

4. A variable that is initialized in a definition is always defined in a *single definition*, rather than in a list separated by commas; for example:

    ```
    int i = 1;
    int j = 2;
    // not: int i = 1, j = 2;
    ```

    As you will see later, this conventions helps avoid various mistakes.

5. Variables are always declared at the point they are first needed. (Note that some programmers prefer to define all variables at the beginning of the current scope, such as a function.)

Expressions, including assignments, are similar in both languages. The only operator available in C++ and not present in Java is a **comma operator**, as in

```
e1, e2
```

The first operand of the comma expression is always evaluated first, and the result is discarded. The second operand is then evaluated, and the type and value of that operand become, respectively, the type and value of the comma expression. Comma expressions are often used to perform several updates at once, as in the following `for` statement:

```
for(i = 1, j = 2; i < N && j < M; ++i, ++j) ...
```

C++ provides the following operators to access individual bits in a memory word:

&	bitwise and
|	bitwise or
^	bitwise xor, also called exclusive or
<<	left shift
>>	right shift
~	one's complement

All these operators take integral parameters and have a similar functionality to the corresponding Java operators. However, the Java bitwise operators &, |, and ^ applied to *Boolean* values return the same values as the corresponding logical operators, while in C++, the bitwise operators always have "bitwise" semantics, even when applied to logical parameters (for example, when the & operator is evaluated with logical parameters, the corresponding bits of operands are "multiplied" on a bit-by-bit basis). In C++, there are no corresponding Java >>> and <<< operators.

2.4.4   Type Conversions

Like Java, C++ is a language with strong typing (which means it does not allow certain operations, such as assignment among variables of different types) and provides implicit and explicit type conversions. First, there is a conversion between bool and int, where true is converted to 1, and false to 0; for example:

```
int i = ... ;
if(i) ...              // same as if(i!=0); does not compile in Java
```

Implicit type conversions, or **casts**, are performed when the value is *promoted* to a more precise type; for example:

```
double d = 3;                         // 3 is promoted to 3.0
```

Implicit type conversions are also performed when the value is *demoted*, resulting in a loss of precision:

```
double d = 3.14159;
int i = d;             // 3.14159 is demoted and i gets the value 3
```

Although most compilers do warn you about the loss of precision, it best to avoid a demoting by using an **explicit cast**, of the form

```
static_cast<type>(value)
```

For example:

```
i = static_cast<int>(d);
```

Here is another example:

```
int i, j;
...                                         // initialization of i and j
double d = static_cast<double>(i) / j;   // avoids int division
```

Another kind of cast, called `const_cast`, is used to remove *constness,* which allows a `const` identifier to be modified; for example:

```
const int i = 3;
const_cast<int>(i) = 1;                              // not constant
```

Finally, there are two more casts:

> `reinterpret_cast`, used to perform a low-level reinterpretation of the bit pattern to force the type conversion and described in Section 9.4.1.

> `dynamic_cast`, used for derived classes and described in Section 5.5.

2.4.5   Control Structures

Control structures are almost identical in the two languages (see Table 2.6).

Table 2.6   Control structures

Construct	Comments About C++
Conditional and switch statements	—
Loops	`break` or `continue` cannot be labeled. A `goto` statement is available.

Advanced

Java and C++ control structures differ in only one respect: C++ does not support the *labeled* `break` and `continue` statements, which are useful for controlling program flow through *nested* loops (such as loop exit). Instead, C++ provides the infamous `goto` statement, which unconditionally transfers control to the statement with the given label. Note that the labeled `break` and `continue` statements are simply limited forms of the more general `goto` statement.

A *label* is any user-specified identifier followed by a colon; for example:

```
done:
```

The definition of the identifier occurs when it is used as a label. Its scope is limited to a single function. Consider the following Java statement that uses a labeled `break` to terminate the outer loop:

```
done:
for(i = 0; i < length; ++i)
  for(j = 0; i < length1; ++j)
    if(f(i, j) == 0)              // f() represents a condition
      break done;
```

In C++, this code would be written as follows:

```
for(i = 0; i < length; ++i)
  for(j = 0; i < length1; ++j)
    if(f(i, j) == 0)              // f() represents a condition
      goto done;

done:
```

I believe that *jumping out of nested loops* is the only justifiable reason to use a `goto` statement (that is, to emulate a labeled `break` or `continue`). Any other use leads to unreadable programs.

As a final comment regarding the programming style of the previous `for` statement: Notice that it is equivalent to use `++i` and `i++` when incrementing the variable `i`. I always use `++i` because for general iterators (covered in Section 7.5), this expression is more efficient than `i++`.

2.4.6 Basic I/O

Standard I/O is completely different in C++ and Java, so I introduce it in this section without even trying to compare the two languages. Here I provide only the basics of I/O, and give a more complete description in Section 9.2.

The `<<` (**put to**) binary operator is used for output, and the `>>` (**get from**) operator is used for input. The left side parameter specifies the stream. There are three predefined streams:

```
cout    the standard output stream
cin     the standard input stream
cerr    the standard error stream
```

The type of the right side parameter determines the specific I/O operation performed. This type can be any primitive data type; for example:

```
cout << "Enter value ";                    // prompt

int i;
cin >> i;                                  // input integer value
```

```
cout << "The value is:";
cout << i;                                    // output integer value
```

As you can see from these examples, both binary I/O operators use infix notation. In addition, they both are functions that return the respective streams, so they can be **chained**, as in this example:

```
cout << "The value is:" << i << endl;
              // same as: ((cout << "The value is:") << i) << endl;
```

(endl represents the *newline* character). You can use the same technique for input:

```
cin >> i >> j;                                // same as: (cin >> i) >> j;
```

To test whether or not the input operator was successful, you can take advantage of a built-in conversion to a bool type, which makes it possible to write:

```
if(cin >> i)                                  // success
    ...
```

● EXAMPLE 2.1

```
// File ex2.1.cpp
// Read integer values until a positive value is entered
// If a non-integer value is entered, abort the program
// Otherwise, output the integer value
#include <iostream>
int main() {
  int i = 0;
  bool correct = false;
  cout << "Enter a positive integer value" << endl;

  while(cin >> i) {
    if(i > 0) {
      correct = true;
      break;
    }
    cout << "You entered a non-positive value; re-enter" << endl;
  }

  if(!correct)
    cout << "You entered an incorrect integer value" << endl;
  else cout << "You entered " << i << endl;
}
```

Table 2.7   Arrays

Java	C++	Comments About C++
`int [] marks = new int [10]`	`int marks[10]`	As in Java, arrays in C++ have a lower bound equal to zero, but unlike Java arrays, their size must be known at compile time and they are not resizable.

2.4.7   Arrays

Java arrays are very flexible; they are object based, and their size is specified at runtime. C++ arrays are borrowed from C and do not have the same power (see Table 2.7).

The C++ standard library also provides **vectors**, which are similar to Java's arrays and should be used instead of the arrays described in Table 2.7 above. Vectors will be described in future chapters. Unfortunately, there are some situations in which you still need to use arrays, so I describe them here.

> **Advanced**
>
> The size of the array can also be defined using a compile-time constant:
>
> ```
> const int SIZE = 20;
> int id[SIZE];
> ```
>
> The runtime system of the language does not check if the value of the index expression (that is, the value used to access a particular element in the array) is less than the upper bound of this array. For example, the use of
>
> ```
> id[1000];
> ```
>
> is not guaranteed to generate a runtime error. In the Java language, an exception would be thrown, but this will not happen in C++; instead, the program's behavior will be undefined (and may result in an error at that point, later on, or not at all).
>
> Note that arrays cannot be copied and compared by simply using an assignment = and equality ==; you have to write code to perform any of these tasks.
>
> Arrays can be *initialized* using a list of constant values, enclosed in curly braces:
>
> ```
> {v1, v2, ..., vn}
> ```
>
> For example:
>
> ```
> int x[2] = {1, 2};
> ```

The array size in the code can be omitted:

```
int x[] = {1, 2};                                      // size 2
```

The size of an array can be larger than the number of initializers, and if this is so, the trailing elements are set to 0; for example:

```
int x[3] = {1, 2};                                     // x[2] = 0
```

Arrays can be defined as constant; for example:

```
const int y[] = {0, 1};
y[0] = 3;                            // constant, can't be changed
```

Finally, you can define multidimensional arrays; for example:

```
bool grid[10][20];                       // 10 rows, 20 columns
```

2.4.8   Reference Data Types

A **reference data type** (which differs from Java references) is of the form

```
type&
```

and is typically used for passing parameters and returning values. It can also be used in a variable definition, in the same way as any other type; for example, for providing an *alias* (an alternative name for an object). Therefore, a reference *must* be initialized in the definition; for example:

```
int i = 1;
int& pi = i;                             // pi is an alias for i
pi++;                                    // now i is 2
```

Once a reference variable is initialized, it cannot be changed; for example:

```
int j = 4;
pi = j;
```

The last assignment is correct but does *not* make pi an alias for j; instead, it assigns the value of j to the existing alias of pi, which is the variable i (therefore, the value of i becomes 4).

   Avoid possible errors like this one:

```
int i = 1;
int j = 2;
int& pi = i, pj = j;                     // pj is int, not int&
```

Declaring variables on separate lines helps avoid such errors:

```
int& pi = i;
int& pj = j;
```

In general, references must be initialized with expressions that are lvalues. An **lvalue** is an expression that can be used on the left side of an assignment; for example a variable is an lvalue but a constant is not.

If you want to make sure that an alias introduced by a reference cannot be changed through this reference, you can declare the reference as constant; for example:

```
const int& cpi = 8;
```

Constant references may be initialized with expressions that are not lvalues (like the constant 8 in the previous code).

As previously noted, references are typically used for passing parameters and returning values (described in a later section of this chapter). They can also be used as auxiliary variables. For example, to set all values equal to 0 in the array a to 1, you can use the following code:

```
for(int i = 0; i < SIZE; ++i) {
  int& p = a[i];                              // alias for a[i]
  if(p == 0)
    p = 1;
}
```

It is more efficient to use this auxiliary variable rather than using a[i] twice each time through the loop.

2.5 *Functions*

C++ functions do not have to appear in a class definition (see Table 2.8). In this book, I use the following terminology: An expression that appears in a function call, such as x in f(x), is called an **actual parameter** as opposed to the **formal parameter**

Table 2.8 Functions

Construct	Comments About C++

`int foo(pars) {`
 `  body`
 `}`
	C++ allows global functions; that is, functions that are defined outside of any class (also called **stand-alone** functions)

that appears in the function definition. (If it is clear from the context as to which kind of a parameter is discussed, I call a formal parameter a *parameter.*)

Programming Guidelines

1. Stand-alone functions other than `main()` should be avoided because they do not contribute to program *modularization.* Typically, you have several related functions that should be packaged together using one of the techniques introduced later in this book (namespaces, Section 2.8.2 or pure static classes, Section 3.6).

2. To improve program *readability*, always try to use meaningful function names, especially if a function modifies its actual parameters. This can done by using specific prefixes, suffixes, and even *infixes*. For example,

```
double getX();                         // prefix "get"
void checkForOverflow();               // infix "For"
void updateKey(int&);                  // suffix "Key"
```

3. Global variables should be used carefully and should always be well documented. In particular, avoid changing the value of a global variable as a result of calling a function; these side effects make testing, debugging, and generally maintaining the code very difficult. If the function must modify a global variable, then this should be clearly documented.

A function may be defined as `inline`; for example:

```
inline int sum(int i, int j {
   return i + j;
}
```

This keyword is a *request* to the compiler to generate code inline rather than compile it and store in a symbol table. Inline code generation means that each call to the function is replaced at compile time by its body, as in

```
int i = sum(1, k);              // replaced by:  int i = 1 + k
```

I called the inline specification a *request* because the compiler is free to ignore this specification, for example, because it cannot inline the code for some reason (such as the code of the function is too complicated to be inlined). Therefore, you have to check that the function specified as `inline` is really inlined, and if it is not, either modify it so that it can be inlined or drop the `inline` specification. The reason that inlining can create problems is related to the placement of inline functions in header files and is described in Section 3.2. The `inline` specification may dramatically increase the efficiency of a function. However, it does not affect the semantics of this function and requires experimenting with the specific implementation, so I rarely use this specification in this book.

2.5.1   Declarations and Definitions

A **function declaration** merely provides a *function signature* (sometimes called a function prototype), which consists of the list of formal parameters, and the return type. Parameters in function *declarations* do not have to be named. For example:

```
bool prime(int);                        // note the semicolon
```

declares `prime()` to be a function that returns `bool`, and its signature specifies one `int` parameter. However, the name of the formal parameter may be useful when writing the documentation:

```
bool prime(int p);     // return true if p is prime; false otherwise
```

On the other hand, the **function definition** includes the declaration and the implementation of the function. In the previous code, the definition of this function must have exactly the same signature and return type. A function can be called *only* if it has been declared or defined.

Note that the client of the function (who calls this function) typically has access only to the function declaration, which does not say anything about the implementation. To properly use the function, the client must have enough information about the semantics of the function. Therefore, it is essential that each function declaration come with the *documentation* to be used by the client. A different kind of information is needed by the implementor of the function, so the function definition comes with its own documentation.

● EXAMPLE 2.2

```
// File: ex2.2.cpp
#include <iostream>
using namespace std;

// Purpose: Test a prime() function
bool prime(int n);                        // returns true if n is prime

int main() {
  int i;
```

```
    cout << "Enter an integer value" << endl;
    cin >> i;
    cout << i << " is " << (prime(i) ? "" : " not")
        << " prime" << endl;
}


#include <cmath>                                // needed to use sqrt()
// Function prime(n); returns true if n is prime
bool prime(int n) {
    int divisor;
    double root;

    if(n < 4)
        return n >= 1;                          // 2 and 3 are prime

    if(n % 2 == 0)                              // even
        return false;

    root = sqrt(n) + 0.5;    // check all odd numbers less than sqrt(n)
    for(divisor = 3; divisor <= root && n % divisor != 0; divisor += 2)
        ;

    return divisor > root;
}
```

2.5.2   Pass by Value, Pass by Reference, and Constant Pass by Reference

Both Java and C++ support passing parameters **by value**, which means that the formal parameter is assigned the *value* of the actual parameter, and the actual parameter is not modified. In this section, I illustrate how this works with an example of a procedure used to swap the values of two integer variables. The following implementation

```
    void swap(int x, int y) {
    int temp = x;
    x = y;
    y = temp;
    }
```

is wrong, because its two parameters are passed by value, so the call

```
    swap(i, j);
```

does not change the values of i and j. To help you understand why this is so, I will trace this call, assuming that the initial values of the variables i and j are 3 and 4, respectively. The state of memory immediately after the call has been made is shown in Figure 2.1. You can see that the formal parameters have been assigned the values of the actual parameters and that modifications made to the parameters x and y will not affect the actual parameters i and j.

The state of memory after the body of swap() has been executed and immediately before this function terminates is shown in Figure 2.2. It is clear that after swap() terminates, the values of parameters i and j are not changed.

C++ provides another mode called **passing by reference**, which allows the function to modify the actual parameter. (The C++ reference is not the same as Java's reference; in Section 3.8.1, I will compare the two.) The type of the parameter passed by reference is a reference type with an & following the parameter type; for example:

```
void swap(int& x, int& y) {
    int temp = x;
    x = y;
    y = temp;
}

int i = 3;
int j = 4;
swap(i, j);                      // i and j passed by reference
```

Again, to help you understand how this works, I will trace this call. The state of memory immediately after the call has been made is shown in Figure 2.3. You can see that the formal parameters have been become aliases of the actual parameters, shown as arrows from the formal parameters to the actual parameters.

Figure 2.1   State of memory immediately after the call to swap() with parameters passed by value

Figure 2.2   State of memory just before swap(), with parameters passed by value, terminates

Figure 2.3 State of memory immediately after the call to swap() with parameters passed by reference

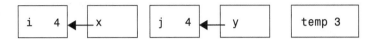

Figure 2.4 State of memory after the execution of x = y in the call to swap() with parameters passed by reference

Figure 2.5 State of memory just before swap(), with parameters passed by reference, terminates

After the execution of x = y, the state of memory is shown in Figure 2.4.

Finally, the state of memory after the body of swap() has been executed and immediately before this function terminates is shown in Figure 2.5. From this figure, it is clear that after swap() terminates, the values of the parameters i and j have been correctly changed.

In addition to allowing the value of the actual parameter to be modified, an additional advantage of passing parameters by reference is efficiency, because the value of the actual parameter is not copied. Therefore, you may want to use this technique whenever you are passing a large data set.

There is a danger associated with passing parameters by reference: The client may *inadvertently* modify the actual parameter. Therefore, the call to a function whose parameter is passed by reference should always be commented. Fortunately, there is another solution to this problem: the use of the const qualifier, which provides a **constant pass by reference**. For example, given

```
double product(const double& block, int size);
```

any attempt to change the value of block within the product() function would result in a compile-time error. This technique is clearly redundant for parameters of primitive data types, because it is equivalent to a pass by value, but it is very useful for parameters of structured data types, such as classes.

Idiom 2.1, Pass by Value and by Reference

1. If you do *not* want to modify the value of the actual parameter, use

   - Pass by value for parameters of primitive data types
   - Constant pass by reference for parameters of structured data types, such as classes

2. If you *do* want to modify the value of the actual parameter, then use pass by reference.

A function that has a parameter passed by constant reference promises not to modify this parameter, and its actual parameter does not have to be constant. On the other hand, if a function has a nonconstant parameter, it may *not* be called with a constant actual parameter; for example:

```
double productConst(const double& block, int size);
double productNonConst(double& block, int size);

double b;
const double bc;
double result;
...
result = productConst(b, size);
result = productConst(bc, size);
result = productNonConst(bc, size);   // can't call non-const function
result = productNonConst(b, size);
```

Idiom 2.1 is useful not only because of efficiency and correctness considerations but also because specifying function parameters as constant (when appropriate) makes them more versatile.

Advanced

There is one more important consideration associated with using parameters passed by reference and constant reference. Nonconstant reference parameters are not subject to implicit type conversions, while constant reference parameters are; for example:

```
void foo(const double&);
void goo(double&);

foo(2);
float f = 2.0;
double d = 1.33;
```

```
foo(f);
foo(d);

goo(2.0f);              // constant; 2.0f is a float constant 2.0
goo(f);
goo(d);                      // no type conversion
```

2.5.3 Default Values of Parameters

In C++, formal function parameters may be given default values. A **default value** of a formal function parameter is useful if the function is frequently called with the same actual parameter. The client of such a function then has the choice of calling it either without the actual parameter for this formal parameter (and so using the default value) or with an actual parameter to override the default value. For example, a function move() that typically moves to position 0 by a step of 1 may be given two default values:

```
void move(int from, int to = 0, int by = 1);
```

Only *trailing* parameters may be assigned default values. Once a parameter is assigned a default value, all parameters following it must be assigned default values:

```
void move(int from, int to = 0, int by);    // illegal: non-trailing
```

Then the function move() may be called with a single actual parameter:

```
move(2);                        // equivalent to calling move(2, 0, 1)
```

This function may also be called with two or three parameters, in which case the overriding values of the actual parameters are assigned from left to right:

```
move(2, 3);                                 // move(2, 3, 1)
move(2, 3, 4);                              // move(2, 3, 4)
```

In this example, it is not possible to override the second trailing default parameter without overriding the first default parameter.

Programming Guidelines

1. When designing a function that uses default values, arrange the parameters so that those more likely to be overridden occur first.

2. Specify default values of function parameters in the function declaration in the header file (for details, see Section 2.8.1).

Advanced

In all the examples with default values, the defaults were constants. In general, a default value does not have to be a constant expression but can be any expression. This expression is evaluated when a function is called.

A parameter may have its default value specified only once; either in the function declaration or in the definition. If this value is specified in the declaration, then subsequent declarations of this function can specify additional default parameters (as long as only values for trailing parameters are specified). For example, let's look at the declarations of a function shrink():

```
void shrink(int, int, int = 1);
void shrink(int, int, int = 1);        // illegal redeclaration
void shrink(int = 1, int, int);        // illegal; non-trailing
void shrink(int, int = 0, int);
              // OK, adds default to the first declaration of shrink()
```

Typically, the first and last declaration in this code would appear in different files. If a default value for a parameter is provided in a function definition stored in some file, the value is available for function calls only within this file.

2.5.4   Overloading Functions

The name of a function should identify the action performed by the function. In some situations, it is useful to be able to use the same function name for a *set* of functions that perform the action that may be assigned the same name. For example, the name max may be assigned to a function that finds the maximum of two integers, or two real numbers.

As in Java, **overloading** a function in C++ means that you can have more than one function with the same name in a single scope, provided that the functions have *different* signatures (that is, the number or specifications of formal parameters are different). For example:

```
double max(double, double);
int max(int, int);             // overloaded
bool max(int, int);            // identical signatures
```

If a single function name is overloaded by many functions, the code may become difficult to read. Also, overloading that involves more-complicated type conversions may be hard to understand and should be avoided (see the example in the Advanced section that follows). In some cases, overloading can be replaced by using default parameter values. For example, two overloaded functions

```
void move(int from, int to);
void move(int from, int to, int by);
```

can be replaced by a single function:

```
void move(int from, int to, int by = 0);
```

Programming Guidelines

Consider using default parameter values to minimize the number of overloaded function declarations.

Advanced

The constness of a parameter can be used to define an overloaded function but *only* if this parameter is passed by reference; for example:

```
double product(const double&, int);
double product(double&, int);              // OK different signature
double product(const double&, const int);  // int is passed by value
```

If two declarations differ in their default values but are otherwise identical, they are not overloaded:

```
int max(int, int);
int max(int, int = 0);                                 // not overloaded
```

These two lines declare the same function max() instead of two overloaded functions; the second line merely specifies a default parameter.

Overloaded functions should be used with caution; for example, the following code generates a compile-time error:

```
void show(int);
void show(int&);                          // OK different type of parameter
show(0);                                  // OK calls show(int)
```

```
int i = 2;
show(i);                                // ambiguous; compile-time error
```

The resolution of overloaded functions (that is, the process used to associate a function call with the function declaration) is rather complicated and will not be described here in detail (see Stroustrup, 1997). I will provide one more example that should help you understand the basics of this process. Let's consider three overloaded functions

```
void move();
void move(int);
void move(double, double = 0.0);
```

and the call

```
move(1.2);
```

This call can be associated with either of the last two declarations (the double value 1.2 can be demoted to the integer value 1). In this situation, the resolution process will select the *best* match, which for this example, is the last declaration, because the type of the actual parameter matches the type of the formal parameter.

2.5.5 Functions and Arrays

When an array is used as a function parameter, and this function needs to know the size of the array, the size of the array must be passed as another parameter, because unlike Java, you *cannot* ask C++ arrays for their size; for example:

```
int maxi(const double arr[], int size);
```

In the following example, the function maxMin() returns, through its parameters, the largest and the smallest value stored in a double array:

```
void maxMin(const double arr[], int size, double& max, double& min) {
  int i;
  for(max = min = arr[0], i = 1; i < size; ++i) {
    if(max < arr[i])
      max = arr[i];
    if(min > arr[i])
      min = arr[i];
  }

}
```

This function may be called as follows:

```
double arr[] = {1.3, 1.2, 1.1};
double maxi, mini;
maxMin(arr, 3, maxi, mini);
```

The function `maxMin()` defines its array parameter `arr` as constant for two reasons. First, to do otherwise would mean this function could not be called with constant arrays, so its generality would be limited:

```
const double x[] = {3, 1, 7.8};
void maxMin(double arr[],int size, double& max, double& min);

maxMin(x, 3, max, min);                            // error, x is const
```

Second, declaring the parameter as constant prevents the function from modifying the values in the array. Therefore, constant array parameters should be used for functions that do not intend to modify the parameters.

2.5.6 Functions Returning References

A function can return a reference type, and if it does, it can be called on either side of an assignment statement or in an I/O statement. In other words, a function call is an lvalue (see Section 2.4.8) if the function returns a reference. Although this technique is more useful for classes, I briefly describe it here. Consider the following function definition:

```
int& index(int x[], int i) {
              // gives read/write access to the i-th element of x
    return x[i];
}
```

This function can be used to access elements of an array; for example:

```
int a[5];
for(int i = 0; i < 5; ++i)
  cin >> index(a, i);

for(int i = 0; i < 5; ++i)
  cout << index(a, i);

index(a, 0) = 2;                                   // a[0] = 2
```

To understand the last assignment, in which `index()` was used as an lvalue, recall that a reference provides an alias; specifically, the `index(a, 0)` call returns an alias to `a[0]`.

Functions can also be designed to provide read-only access by returning a *constant* reference; for example:

```
const int& get(const int x[], int i) {
   return x[i];
}
```

get() can be used to read elements of an array, but it cannot be used to modify these elements; for example:

```
cout << get(a, 2);
get(a, 1) = 5;                    // error - can't change the value
```

This completes the discussion of functions. In the next section, I briefly describe pointers and dynamic memory management.

2.6 *Pointers and Dynamic Memory Management*

A program can get its memory from one of three separate memory areas: the heap, static memory, or the runtime stack (see Figure 2.6).

Static memory is used to store the values of global variables as well as function and class static variables (described in Sections 2.7 and 3.5.2). **Stack-based** memory is implicitly managed by function calls and function returns. **Heap-based** memory is used to dynamically manage memory as a result of a program's request, such as Java's new call. **Dynamic memory allocation** means that a block of memory requested by a program is removed from the heap and can be used by the program. **Dynamic mem-**

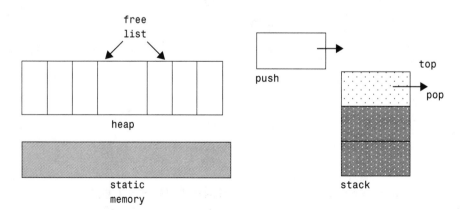

Figure 2.6 Heap, static memory, and runtime stack

ory deallocation means that a program returns a block of memory to the heap; the deallocated memory can be used the next time a memory request occurs.

A Java programmer decides when objects are created by calling constructors, and the **garbage collector** decides when these objects are deallocated. Java objects are *always* allocated on the heap and never on the runtime stack, so all memory deallocation is done automatically by the garbage collector. This decreases the likelihood of **memory leakage**, which occurs when memory that is no longer needed by the program has not been freed and made available for reuse.

In C++, the situation is quite different. Objects may be allocated both on the stack and in the heap. In addition, there is no garbage collector, and the programmer is fully responsible for explicitly deallocating memory. This may lead to various programming errors, such as the so-called *dangling reference problem*. This problem is the result of a variable referencing a memory block whose lifetime has expired; in other words, one that has been allocated on the stack and then deallocated. Another serious problem with improper memory management is the already mentioned memory leakage.

Java programmers are used to seeing statements like "A variable of a reference type can hold a reference to any object." What's a reference to an object? Technically, it is a memory address; specifically, it is the address of a block of memory allocated for the object on the heap.

Dynamic memory management in C++ is done with pointers. A *pointer* is a variable whose value is a memory address representing a memory location. Being based on C, C++ defines a full set of operations on pointers; there are pointer types, pointer assignments, etc. The main difference between C++ pointers and Java references is that pointers are much more versatile and can point to any memory location, while references can only point to objects. As a result, pointers are also more dangerous, and their use in C++ should be limited to cases where pointers are necessary. In the next section, I provide a basic description of pointers. I will describe other essential pointer operations in later sections and chapters.

2.6.1 Basic Pointer Operations

Pointer variables, or just pointers, have names, types, and values. The value of a pointer is the address of a memory block; the type of a pointer determines the size of that block (the size is essential to access data stored at the address).

For any C++ data type T—for example, `int`—you can define a variable of type "pointer to T," such as "pointer to `int`." For example

```
int* p;                         // pointer to int
char* s;                        // pointer to char
```

When you want to declare more than one pointer, be careful to avoid pitfalls like this:

```
int* pi, pj;                    // pi is a pointer, pj is an int
```

Once you have a pointer pointing to a memory block, you can access the contents of that block; this operation is called **dereferencing**. To deference a pointer, you use its name, prefixed with an asterisk *. For the previous example, *p is the contents of the memory block that p points to, and *p behaves as an int variable.

You can take a nonpointer variable and get a pointer by applying the **address operator** & to it; for example:

```
int i = 1;
...i...          // is an int variable
...&i...         // is like an int pointer, pointing to the variable i

int* p;
p = &i;          // p points to i; see Fig. 2.7
... *p ...       // dereferenced p is equal to i
```

Neither of these two operations (dereferencing and applying an address) are available in Java.

Figure 2.7 shows that p points to the variable i and changing *p modifies the value of i.

In Java, when two references point to the same object, changing some value in the object influences both references; this is also the case with C++. Specifically, given two pointers p and q that point to the same variable i, you can change the value of i using the pointer p, which also affects the value pointed to by the pointer q (see Fig 2.8). This is called a *reference semantics* of assignments.

A special 0 pointer value is similar in both languages (see Table 2.9).

NULL is not, strictly speaking, part of C++, and its definition is implementation dependant. Therefore, even though you may find it more readable to use NULL, you should use 0. This may seem to go against the "no magic numbers" guideline mentioned earlier. However, this case is different; you will never need to change this value, and if you do define a constant such as NULL, then your programs will no longer be portable (unless everybody else uses your definition of this constant), also see Stroustrup [1997].

Two common errors associated with C++ pointers is the use of either uninitialized pointers or pointers that point to 0. The language's runtime system does not provide the same safety as Java's exception-handling mechanism; instead, your

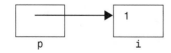

Figure 2.7   State of the memory after executing p = &i

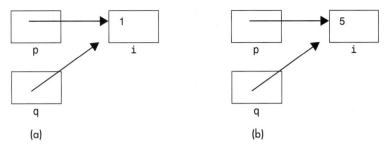

Figure 2.8 State of memory before (a) and after (b) the assignment
`*p = 5`

Table 2.9 Null pointer

Java	C++	Comments About C++
nil	0	C++ provides `NULL`, but rather than using it, use 0.

program may continue to execute following the use of an uninitialized pointer and crash unexpectedly at a later time.

A `const` qualifier applied to a pointer can mean one of three things (it may help if you read these pointer declarations from right to left):

```
const int* p;
```

- A pointer to an integer that is constant; the value of p may change, but the value of `*p` cannot

```
int* const cp;
```

- A constant pointer to integer; the value of `*cp` can change, but the value of `cp` cannot

```
const int* const cpc;
```

- A constant pointer to a constant integer

The `const`ness of a pointer serves as documentation and is used by the compiler to make sure that the program does not violate it. In some exceptional cases, you may want to remove `const`ness by using the cast operator, which avoids sacrificing readability (the cast operator was introduced in Section 2.4.4). The form of this cast operator is

```
const_cast<type>(value)
```

For example, to make pointer p declared in previous code point to the value 3 (that is, to assign 3 to *p), you can use

```
*(const_cast<int*>(p)) = 3;
```

C++ also provides generic pointers (pointers to void), but they are not necessary unless you need to write low-level routines that need to know more about the underlying platform (generic pointers are described in Section 9.4.1).

2.6.2   Pointers as Parameters

Array parameters are treated like pointers; that is,

```
void maxMin(double arr[], int size, double& max, double& min);
```

is equivalent to

```
void maxMin(double* arr, int size, double& max, double& min);
```

Constant pointer specifications are often useful. For example, consider a constant array and two functions that respectively have as one of their parameters an array and a constant array:

```
const double a[] = {1.5, 3.1};
void maxMin(double* arr, int size, double& max, double& min);
void maxMinConst(const double* arr, int size,
        double& max, double& min);
```

The first function is designed so that it can modify its array parameter, and the second function is designed for read-only access to its array parameter:

```
double max, min;
maxMin(a, 2, max, min);                             // a is const
maxMinConst(a, 2, max, min);
```

Is there a way to apply maxMin() to a constant parameter? The answer is yes, but to do so, you have to explicitly show that this is your intention by removing the constness of this parameter:

```
maxMin(const_cast<double*>(a), 2, max, min);
```

All parameters are passed by value, and so if you want to modify a pointer parameter, you have to use Idiom 2.1, Pass by Reference; for example:

```
void modify(int*& p, int j) {
  p = &j;
}
```

Idiom 2.2, Pointer Parameter

1. For functions that do not modify values pointed to by their pointer parameters, specify the parameters as `const`; for example, `const double*`. This allows you to call the function both with nonconstant and constant pointer parameters.

2. For functions that modify their pointer parameters, specify the parameters as passed by reference.

2.6.3 Functions Returning Pointers

A function may return a pointer; for example:

```
int* changeable(int arr[], int size, int i) {
                          // return a pointer to the i-th element
  if(i < 0 || i >= size)
    return 0;                                              // error

  return &arr[i];
}
```

If a function returns a pointer to some memory that should not be modified, then that pointer should be specified as `const`:

```
const int* nonChangeable(const int arr[], int size, int i) {
  // as above
  ...
}
```

Now, consider the following code:

```
int x[] = {1, 2, 3};
int* i = changeable(x, 3, 2);
*i = 3;                                    // OK, can modify through i

const int *j = nonChangeable(x, 3, 2);
cout << *j;
```

```
*j = 3;                              // can't assign to a const
i = nonChangeable(x, 3, 2);          // can't assign to a non-const
```

In rare cases, you might like to use a function to access a *constant pointer to a constant*. The following example shows such code:

```
const int* const constAccess(const int arr[], int size, int p);
const int* const p = constAccess(x, 3, 1);
```

I will describe how to allocate and deallocate memory for pointers in Section 3.4.

Common Errors

A **dangling reference** is created when a pointer or a reference points to memory that has been deallocated and no longer belongs to the program. Dangling references are dangerous because they corrupt memory and can cause a program crash at any point following their first appearance. To avoid dangling references, do not return pointers or references to local objects; for example:

```
int* foo() {
   int a[2] = {1, 2};
   return &a[0];                              // wrong
}
```

In the previous example, the memory storing the value returned by the function disappears as soon as this function terminates (because it is allocated on the stack). Therefore, the assignment

```
int* p = foo();
```

results in a dangling reference; p points to memory that has been popped from the stack.

2.6.4   C-Style Strings and `main ()` Function Parameters

C++ provides two kinds of strings:

string   briefly described in Table 2.4 and elaborated on in Appendix E
char*   pointer to char, used as strings in C so available in C++

There are very few places in which C-style strings need to be used; in general, using them is not considered good programming style. Unfortunately, they cannot be avoided in the main function and several file operations; therefore I provide a short description of them in this section.

    C-style strings may be assigned to string literals and used in output operations; for example:

```
char* str = "C++";
cout << str << endl;
```

A C-style string can be passed as a parameter of a function:

```
int foo(char* str);
```

Within the body of this function, str is treated as an array of characters (terminated by the zero character, that is the character with the ASCII code 0). The size of this array is the length of the string, which can be obtained by using the strlen() function.

    This description is short but should be sufficient to understand the basics. In general, you should use C-style strings *only* when they are really necessary (such as in the main function). For a comparison of the main function in Java and in C++, see Table 2.10.

    The first integer parameter of the main function is required in C++ because an array does not "know" its size. Unlike Java, C++ passes the name of the program, taken from the command line, as argv[0]; therefore, argc is always greater than zero. The successive command-line parameters are stored in argv[1], argv[2], and so on.

● EXAMPLE 2.3

In this example, I show a simple program that uses command-line parameters:

```
// File: ex2.3.cpp
// The program displays all command line parameters;
//    each on a separate line.
#include <iostream>
int main(int argc, char* argv[]) {
  for(int i = 0; i < argc; ++i)
    cout << argv[i] << endl;
}
```

Table 2.10 Main function (with parameters)

Java	C++	Comments About C++
void main(String[] args)	int main(int argc, char* argv[])	Integer function with two parameters: • The number of command line parameters • An array of C-style strings representing parameters

If the program in Example 2.3 is executed using

```
prog2.3 a1 b1
```

it prints:

```
prog2.3
a1
b1
```

Note that *redirection symbols*, such as

```
> filename
```

or

```
< filename
```

do not count as parameters; for example, executing the example program using

```
prog2.3 a1 b1 > c1.f
```

prints the same output as previously shown.

You also need to be aware of the existence of C-style strings when you want to use file I/O. To open an input or output file, you use, respectively, constructors for ifstream and ofstream, passing the filename as a parameter. Unfortunately, these constructors expect filenames of the char* type rather than the string type, which means that you may need a variable to store the filename. If you used C-style strings, and declared

```
char* fileName;
```

you would have to allocate memory for the pointer. It is easier (and better) to use strings and declare

```
string fileName;
```

because now you do not have to worry about memory allocation. However, with this declaration, you cannot write something like

```
ifstream inFile(fileName);          // can't take a string parameter
```

You first need to make a conversion from a string to a C-style string, using the built-in function c_str():

```
ifstream inFile(fileName.c_str());
```

The variable `inFile` is convertible to Boolean, which is useful to verify that the opening of a file was successful:

```
if(!inFile) ...                                        // failed
```

Once a file has been opened for input or output, you can use the familiar operators `>>` and `<<`, respectively, to read from and to write to the file. Note that when a variable of type `ifstream` or `ofstream` goes out of scope, its destructor is executed, and the corresponding file is closed.

● EXAMPLE 2.4

In this example, I show two versions of a program that copies words from an input file to an output file and counts the number of words. In the first version, the program prompts the user for the filenames; in the second version, the filenames are passed on the command line.

```
// File: ex2.4.cpp
// Copy words from the input file to the output file;
//   prompting the user for filenames
// In the output, each word is on a separate line
// Output the total number of words to the standard output
// Return 1 if can't open input file; 2 if can't open output file
#include <iostream>
#include <fstream>
#include <string>
int main() {

                                             // get both files
   string inFileName, outFileName;

   cout << "Enter input and output file names: ";
   cin >> inFileName >> outFileName;

   ifstream inFile(inFileName.c_str());
   if(!inFile) {
     cerr << "can't open " << inFileName << endl;
     return 1;
   }

   ofstream outFile(outFileName.c_str());
   if(!outFile) {
```

```
    cerr << "can't open " << outFileName << endl;
    return 2;
  }

                                                  // copy words

  string word;
  long wordCounter = 0;
  while(inFile >> word) {
    outFile << word << endl;
    wordCounter++;
  }

  cout << "Read " << wordCounter << " words" << endl;
  return 0;
}

// File: ex2.5.cpp
// Copy words from the input file to the output file;
//    passing filenames on the command line
// Output the total number of words to the standard output
// Return 1 if can't open input file; 2 if can't open output file
#include <iostream>
#include <fstream>
#include <string>
int main(int argc, char* argv[]) {

                                                  // check command line
  if(argc != 3) {
    cerr << "Usage: " << argv[0] << " file1 file2" << endl;
    return 1;
  }

                                                  // get both files

  ifstream inFile(argv[1]);
  if(!inFile) {
    cerr << "can't open " << argv[1] << endl;
    return 1;
  }

  ofstream outFile(argv[2]);
  if(!outFile) {
    cerr << "can't open " << argv[2] << endl;
    return 2;
  }
```

```
                                                      // copy words
   string word;
   long wordCounter = 0;
   while(inFile >> word) {
     outFile << word << endl;
     wordCounter++;
   }

   cout << "Read " << wordCounter << " words" << endl;
   return 0;

}
```

2.7 *Static Local Variables*

Local variables in a function have a lifetime associated with the function's invocation: They exist from the time this function is called until it terminates. In other words, local variables are allocated on the stack, in the so-called instance, or frame, for this function. It is sometimes useful to limit the *scope* but not the lifetime of a variable. For example, a login() function may have a counter to count how many times it was called. The scope of this counter should be limited to the login() function, but memory for the counter should not be deallocated each time login() terminates. Instead, the lifetime of the counter should be the same as the lifetime of the program using the login() function. **Static local variables** serve this purpose; they are defined with the static specification:

```
void login() {
   static int counter = 0;
   counter++;
   ...
}
```

When login() is called for the first time, the value of counter is set to 0 and then incremented. However, when the login() call terminates, the storage for counter is retained, so when login() is called for the second time, the initialization of counter is not performed again, and as a result of executing counter++, its value is changed from 1 to 2. Static variables such as counter are allocated using static memory and always implicitly initialized to 0 (for example, 0 for integers and pointers, 0.0 for float and double values, and so on.).

A static local variable may also be of a class type (see Section 3.5.1).

2.8   *File Organization and Standard Facilities*

I begin this section with a description of a typical UNIX-like command line use of a compiler. Although this description may vary from system to system, it should be useful for those readers who have used only integrated development environments. Assuming that the compiler name is g++, the command to compile the program stored in the file f.cpp is

```
g++ f.cpp
```

which stores the object code in f.o and the executable code in a.out, while

```
g++ f.cpp -o f
```

stores the executable code in f. If a program is stored in several files—for example, f1.cpp, f2.cpp and f3.cpp—you can either compile all of them at once

```
g++ f1.cpp f2.cpp f3.cpp -o f
```

or use the so-called **separate compilation**; that is, compile one file at a time and suppress the linking. For example,

```
g++ -c f1.cpp
```

stores the object code in f1.o. The compiler can also be used as a *linker;* for example, to link three files and store the executable code in a file called f:

```
g++ f1.o f2.o f3.o -o f
```

A Java program typically consists of multiple files, yet when you compile it, you usually use the name of a single file, which contains the main function to be invoked. The Java compiler checks what other files are needed and whether these files have been compiled recently. All files that have been modified since the last compilation are recompiled, and finally, all compiled files are linked. Therefore, the Java compiler takes care of tasks that in other environments are performed by specialized tools, such as a linker (which links all compiled files) and a utility program (which checks the dependencies and recompiles those files that need to be compiled), such as make in UNIX.

A C++ program also typically consists of multiple files, but the programmer is responsible for compiling all the necessary files, where each file is a unit of compilation. A program is a set of compilation units that must be linked together to form the executable code. In the case of a large program, you would typically use separate compilation and a tool such as make to update the executable code. *Separate compilation* means that you can compile parts of your program, where each part is a file considered to be a single unit of compilation. (In C++, each program may contain exactly one instance of the function `main()`. Note the difference between this approach and that used in Java, in which every class may have its own main function.)

The Java platform provides a number of standard packages (for example, the `java.lang` package defines classes such as `String`, and the `java.io` package defines I/O facilities). To use these standard packages, as well as other user-defined packages, the Java programmer must import them. C++ uses a different approach, which I describe in the following section.

2.8.1 Preprocessing and Header Files

In C++, related function *declarations* are typically stored in **header** files. A function cannot be called before it is defined, or at least declared. Therefore, to use an externally defined function in your program, you typically include the header file containing its declaration. In this section, I describe the syntax to do so.

Any line of C++ code that begins with # (the pound symbol) is referred to as a **preprocessor** command line and has its own syntax, which does not adhere to C++'s syntax rules. From a logical point of view, preprocessing is performed before compilation; consequently, these lines are removed and the source file is accordingly processed. The preprocessor has two important functions. First, it provides the so-called **include** command, which is used to include external files in the current file. Second, it provides a **conditional compilation** command, which tells the compiler that a *part* of the source file is included conditionally (that is, the compiler will ignore it if some condition is met). There are also other preprocessing commands that are rarely used in C++ (see Stroustrup 1997).

As I mentioned earlier, header files contain declarations of various entities (mostly functions) and are included in other files that will use these entities. Header files contain both standard (system-defined) functions and user-defined functions and classes. For each specific implementation, there are several standard header files, such as `iostream`, `string`, and so on. (Typically, there are 32 standard header files; for a complete list, see Appendix G.) In addition to predefined header files, user programs typically contain user-defined header files.

Lets look at some preprocessing commands in some detail. The `#include` command specifies that the text of a file is to be included in the current source file. There are two formats for the include command. For *standard* header files, the format is

```
#include <filename>
```

(Usually, for predefined header files, C++ does not use the extension `.h` used by C, although there are some rarely used header files borrowed from C that do.) For *user-defined* header files, the format is

```
#include "filename.h"
```

(User-defined header file typically have the h extension; for example, screen.h.)

These two formats differ in how the specified file is located by the compiler. If the first format is used, the compiler will typically look for the file in special *system* directories—which directories depends on both the system and the programmer's specifications. If the second format is used, the system will typically scan the *current* directory (the directory in which the source file being compiled is located), and if it does not find the file, it will continue to look for it in other directories. The exact search rules are implementation dependent and vary from system to system.

C++ also provides 18 standard header files from the C language, which are mostly needed for upward compatibility and are rarely used in this book. These headers come in two forms: names that start with the letter c and without the extension .h (for example <cassert>) and names without the letter c but with the extension .h (for example <assert.h>). However, the second form is available for upward compatibility only; formally, it is deprecated and will not be used in this book.

Now consider how you can create your own header files. Since header files may be nested, it is important to avoid multiple processing of the same file. Therefore, you should use the following approach: Each included file begins a **conditional compilation directive**, based on the definition of a name, called a **macro**, that specifies whether this file has already been included. By convention, the name of this macro is made up of the header filename, using uppercase characters, with the period (.) in the filename replaced by the underscore (_) character. For example, an include file screen.h has the macro name SCREEN_H. The header file might look like this:

```
#ifndef SCREEN_H            // conditional compilation
#define SCREEN_H
    ...                     // contents of the header file
#endif
```

This #ifndef SCREEN_H directive instructs the preprocessor to include the text that follows, up to the corresponding #endif, if the macro SCREEN_H has *not* been defined; otherwise, the preprocessor should exclude this text. Following Stroustrup 1997, I call these directives **include guards**. Consider a file called main.cpp that includes screen.h:

```
#include "screen.h"
#include "screen.h"                // a second #include by accident
```

This code will not include the header file twice, because only the first include statement actually includes the screen.h file. Once SCREEN_H is defined, the

```
#ifndef SCREEN_H
```

statement is false, and the file is not included for the second time. This technique is very useful for avoiding linking problems caused by including the same file multiple times.

Include Guards Idiom 2.3

The header file should use conditional compilation; for example:

```
#ifndef SCREEN_H                      // conditional compilation
#define SCREEN_H

    ...                               // contents of the header file
#endif
```

From this point on, the code in the examples provided in this book will not necessarily be complete; in particular, I will not show the conditional compilation guards defined in the previous code. Each example will include a reference to the complete code listing, available on the Addison Wesley Longman Web site.

Common Errors

1. Make sure that in a header file, you use

   ```
   #ifndef
   ```

   which means "if not defined," rather than

   ```
   #ifdef
   ```

   which means "if defined."

2. To specify path expressions, always use forward slashes (/) rather than backslashes (\) in your #include filenames (no matter whether you use Unix or Windows operating system); for example:

   ```
   #include "source/types/include.h"
   #include "source\types\include.h"
   ```

   In the second version, \t is treated a tab character. Note that this code will not work on MACOS-based computers, and in general path expressions are platform specific.

2.8.2   Namespaces, Part I

To avoid name collisions, C++ provides **namespaces**, which are similar to Java's packages; however, the number of small differences warrants a separate discussion rather than a direct comparison. Each namespace defines a new scope, so a single name used in one namespace does not conflict with the same name used in another namespace. In this section, I describe how standard namespaces are used; in Section 4.6, I will describe how you define your own namespaces.

The C++ standard library is defined in a namespace called `std`. Various facilities from this library are made available through header files, such as `iostream` for I/O operations and `string` for string operations. These header files must be included; for example:

```
#include <iostream>
```

To make every name from this namespace directly available, you specify the namespace with the `using` keyword:

```
using namespace std;
```

In this book, I will assume that every program includes these two commands and will not explicitly show them.

2.9 *Exercises*

EXERCISE 2-1

Write a program that outputs the sizes of all primitive data types. If you have access to several different computers, compare the results.

EXERCISE 2-2

Write a program that reads integer values from standard input and writes to standard output the smallest of the input values and the average input value. Reading should stop when either a value equal to –1 or greater than 100 is encountered; it should also stop when an incorrect integer value is entered. If there is no integer value in the input, the program should output the message "no integer values found."

EXERCISE 2-3

Write a program that reads double values from standard input and writes the smallest of the input values and the average input value to standard output. Reading should stop when ten values have been entered or an incorrect double value is encountered. If there is no double value in the input, the program should output the message "no double values found."

EXERCISE 2-4

Write a program that compares two text files one character at a time. The program using

```
compare f1 f2
```

should output a message stating whether two files are identical or not, while the program using

```
compare -d f1 f2
```

should output line numbers for all lines for which the two files differ and should not output any message if the two files are identical.

EXERCISE 2-5

This exercise has two parts:

a) Write a program, `encode`, that reads a file, encodes it, and stores the encoded version in an output file. The encryption algorithm is a simple one: A positive integer N ($0 < N < 128$) is added to the ordinal value of each character. The value of N and the names of both files are passed on the command line; for example:

```
encode 2 f1.txt f2.txt
```

b) Write a program, `decode`, that reads the encrypted file, decodes it, and stores the decoded version in an output file (the names of both files are passed on the command line). The decryption algorithm is a simple one: A positive integer N ($0 < N < 128$) is subtracted from the ordinal value of each character in the input. As in (a), the value of N and the names of both files are passed on the command line. The decryption code N must be the same as the one used for encryption, or the file will not be decoded properly.

To test your program, do these sample runs:

```
encode 2 encode encode.encoded
encode 12 decode decode.encoded
decode 2 encode.encoded encode.new
decode 12 decode.encoded decode.new
encode.new 24 f1.txt f1.encoded
decode.new 24 f1.encoded f2.txt
```

Here, `f1.txt` is an arbitrary text file. Then compare the contents of `f1.txt` and `f2.txt` (they should be identical).

EXERCISE 2-6

Write a program that reads a text file and counts the length of every line in the file. After reading the file, your program should output a message that states how many lines had more than 20 characters.

EXERCISE 2-7

Write a recursive function

```
double power(double x, int n)
```

that implements the following algorithm to compute x^n. For even values of n, compute

$$x^{n/2} * x^{n/2}$$

For odd values of n, compute

$$x * x^{n/2} * x^{n/2}$$

Test this function in the main program.

EXERCISE 2-8

Write a function, reverse(), that reverses an array (the first element becomes the last element, the second element becomes the second from the last, and so on) and returns the reversed array through the second parameter.

Then write a function, reverseMyself(), that modifies the array passed as a parameter by reversing it. Test these functions in the main program.

EXERCISE 2-9

Write a function that returns the average of all the values stored in an integer array arr of size n; the return type of this function should be double. Test this function in the main program.

EXERCISE 2-10

Write a procedure, alter(x,y), that changes the values of x to x-y and the value of y to 2 (x and y are of type double). Test this function in the main program.

EXERCISE 2-11

Write a procedure, error(), that has two string parameters, one of which is optional and by default represents the string "Wrong". This procedure writes to the standard output the first string followed by the second string. Then write an overloaded procedure that has one string and one integer parameter and which outputs to the standard output stream the integer value (by default equal to 0) followed by the string parameter. Test these functions in the main program.

EXERCISE 2-12

Write two functions that take as parameters an array and the size of this array. The first function returns a reference to the largest element of the array (if there are several such elements, a reference to the last occurrence should be returned). The second function is similar, except it returns a pointer to the largest element. Test these functions in the main program.

EXERCISE 2-13

Write a program, longest, so that

```
longest f1 f2 ... fn
```

reads each of the n input files f1, f2, ..., fn, and writes to the standard output the length of the longest file.

EXERCISE 2-14

Write a random function with the following signature:

```
int randomInt();
// Returns a pseudo-random integer value in the range 0..100
```

To generate random numbers, use the mathematical expression

```
r(i+1) = (a*r(i) + b) mod c
```

where c is 101, a is prime, and r(i) (i > 0) is the value the function returns the i-th time it is called. Choose your own values for the constants a and b (a must be prime), and for r(1) (this value must be between 0 and 100).

Chapter **3**

OBJECT-BASED
PROGRAMMING, PART I

3.1 *Preview*

In this chapter, I discuss object-*based* programming, which unlike object-*oriented* programming does not use extended (derived) classes. I delay the discussion of inheritance until chapter 5, which allows me to concentrate on discussing the similarities and differences between class-related concepts in Java and C++. In particular, I describe stack-based and heap-based memory management in C++ and compare it with heap-based memory management in Java. Then I describe various C++ techniques used to manage objects, such as destructors; initializing objects by copying existing objects; returning new objects; and redefining the meaning of the assignment operation. In the next chapter, I will continue the discussion of object-based programming.

This chapter includes only a few sections labeled "advanced," because most of the concepts presented here are essential ones you should understand before you move on to the next chapter. Also, there are fewer programming guidelines because there are not many universal standards for writing classes. Instead, you will find a number of programming idioms and the first design pattern.

3.2 *Basic Terminology and Class Definition*

The class is the most fundamental construct in both Java and C++, and it has a similar meaning in both languages (see Table 3.1). In this book, I use terminology consistent with that used by the standard Unified Modeling

Table 3.1   Class

Construct	Comments
class	A class definition contains the definitions of attributes, but it does not contain the definitions of operations; only their declarations. Sections consisting of one or more declarations rather than single methods are tagged with visibility specifications, such as public. Definitions of operations are provided outside the class definition.
	A class definition and the definitions of its operations are usually stored in separate files—respectively, in a header file and an implementation file.

Language (UML): class fields are called **attributes**, and class methods are called **operations** (sometimes called functions). Collectively, attributes and operations are called **features** (or members). The set of all public features is called a public interface, or simply **interface** (note that the meaning of the term *interface* is different from the Java definition). I recommend that you acquaint yourself with this terminology to make the transition to UML easier.

Features can be referred to using the following scope operator :

```
ClassName::featureName
```

This C++ scope operator : : is used to define operations outside the class definition. The following example should help to clarify these concepts.

● EXAMPLE 3.1

This example consists of the declaration and the definition of a simple class, Student, used to store student numbers. (Although they are not shown here, remember that each header file always uses the include guards described in Section 2.8.1.)

```
// File: ex3.1.student.h
// Header file with the class definition
class Student {
public:
  Student(long);        // declaration of a constructor operation
  void setNumber(long); // declaration of an operation
private:
  long number_;         // attribute
};                      // note the semicolon
```

This class has three features: two public features, which are operations, and one private feature, which is an attribute. The interface of this class consists of two operations: the constructor `Student()` and the function `setNumber()`. Here are the *definitions* of class operations:

```cpp
// File: ex3.1.student.cpp
// Definitions of operations from the class Student
// (placed outside of the class)
#include "ex3.1.student.h"

Student::Student(long number) {          //constructor definition
  number_ = number;
}

void Student::setNumber(long number) {   // operation definition
  number_ = number;
}
```

Common Errors

1. Remember to use a scope operator when defining a class operation outside the class definition. For example, consider the definition of `setNumber()` from the class `Student`. If you omit the scope operator and write

   ```cpp
   void setNumber(long number) { ... }
   ```

   you define `setNumber()` as a *stand-alone* function rather than a class operation. To define it as a class operation, you must use the scope operator:

   ```cpp
   void Student::setNumber(long number) { ... }
   ```

2. Attributes cannot be initialized in the class declaration:

   ```cpp
   class Student {
   private:
     long number_ = 2;                      // illegal initialization
   ...
   };
   ```

3. Terminate class definitions with a semicolon.

Within the definition of class operations, the scope rules are similar to those in Java. The visibility specification for class attributes and operations may be `public`, `private` or `protected`. In C++, the first two specifications mean the same as in Java; the meaning of `protected`, which is used in subclasses, will be explained in Section 5.7. There may be multiple sections, listed in any order; for example:

```
class Student {              // preferred format (used in this book)
public:
  Student(long);
  void setNumber(long);
private:
  long number_;
};
```

This example lists the *public interface* first, followed by the private features. I use this format in this book because it shows first the class interface and then the implementation of this class. The alternative format uses the fact that if the visibility specification is omitted, then by default, the first section of the class specifies private features:

```
class Student {          // alternative format (not used in this book)
// private: by default the first section is private
  long number_;
public:
  Student(long);
  void setNumber(long);
};
```

To define a class that has *only* a public interface, you can use the keyword `struct` instead of `class`; for example:

```
struct Info {                    // all features are public
  string address;
  string name;
  Info(string, string);
};

Info::Info(string a, string n) {
  address = a;
  name = n;
}
```

For anyone who already knows Java or any other object-oriented programming language, it is clear that making all features public goes against the encapsulation principles and in general is not a good idea. Therefore, structures are useful only in a few cases, most notably in the standard library.

Class operations may have parameters of the following kind: constant, reference, and pointer. In Section 3.8.2, I will explain how to use these kinds of parameters.

The function `modify()` defined in Example 3.1 is called a **modifier** (or a muta-tor) because it modifies the state of the object from which it is invoked. Any opera-tion that does not change the state of the object is called a **query** or accessor. C++ provides a special syntax, absent in Java, for queries. The signature is suffixed with the keyword `const`; for example:

```
class Student {
public:
  Student(long);
  void setNumber(long);                      // modifier
  long getNumber() const;                    // query
private:
  long number_;
};
```

Because the keyword `const` is part of the signature, you have to repeat it in the function definition:

```
long Student::getNumber() const {
  return number_;
};
```

An attempt to use a `const` function to change the object state generates a compile-time error; for example:

```
long Student::getNumber() const {
  number_ += 100;                     // can't change the object
  return number_;
};
```

There are three important reasons why you should use the keyword `const` for every query:

- As for all constant specification, it improves readability (the programmer does not have to read the actual function code to verify that the object state is un-changed, because this is guaranteed by the compiler).
- Constant operations can invoke other operations only if they are constant (therefore, if you decide to change your code and make an operation constant, this may have a ripple effect of having to make other operations constant).
- Only constant operations may be invoked for objects, which are declared as con-stant (therefore, a query not defined as constant will be unnecessarily limited in its applications).

Class operations can be *overloaded.* In the previous example, instead of using two function names, `getNumber()` and `setNumber()`, you could use a single overloaded function name:

```
class Student {
public:
  Student(long);
  void number(long);                           // modifier
  long number() const;                         // query
private:
  long number_;
};
```

This use of an overloaded function is problematic because a modifier and a query are overloaded; in general, it is better (more readable) to overload functions of the same kind, such as two accessors or constructors.

Advanced

A member function can refer to its class members directly (that is, by omitting the scope operator). Alternatively, you can refer to class members by using the scope operator

```
ClassName::memberName
```

or by using the `this` pointer (which has a similar meaning as in Java):

```
this->memberName                              // note the use of ->
```

For example:

```
void Student::setNumber(long number) {

  number_ = number;           // direct access
  Student::number_ = number;  // access using the scope operator
  this->number_ = number;     // access using "this"
}
```

Often these three formats are equally readable, and it is a matter of taste as to which one you use. In this book, I use the first format. The second or the third format is useful or even necessary if there is a name conflict between the formal parameter name and the class attribute; for example:

```
class Student {
public:
  Student(long);
  long getNumber() const;
private:
  long number;
};

void Student::getNumber(long number) {
  // number = number;          name conflict using direct access
  Student::number = number;    // access using the scope operator
}
```

This example justifies my programming guideline, described later in this section, which states that private class members have suffix _.

A class **declaration** is of the form

```
class className;
```

A class must be declared or defined *before* it can be used. For example, if the definition of a class List uses the class Item, then you first have to declare Item:

```
class Item;                                    // declaration
class List {
public:
  Item* first();
};

class Item {                                   // definition
  ...
};
```

In this example, Item is declared but not defined before it is used. This is only legal for types, which are either *pointers* or *references* to classes. A class must be defined before being used in a function definition; for example:

```
class Item;
class List {
public:
  Item boo();                    // OK, this is a declaration
};

Item List::boo() {               // error, needs a class definition
  ...
}
class Item {
```

```
  ...
};
```

Classes can be nested:

```
class List {
public:
  ...
private:

  class Item {
  public:
    Item();                                          //constructor
    ...
  };

};
```

The scope operator :: is used for defining functions in nested classes; for example:

```
List::Item::Item() {                          // constructor definition
  ...
}
```

The standard rules that govern public and private features apply to nested classes, so a nested class has no special access privileges to its outer class, or vice versa. More details about the subject of nested classes will be provided in Section 7.5.1.

Programming Guidelines

1. Name classes according to what they represent; using suffixes can help to convey meaning. For example, if your class makes use of FTP then use "Ftp" as a suffix and name the class UseFtp.

2. List the three sections defining the visibility specifications for a class in the following order: public, protected and private. This convention shows the class interface first and the class implementation last.

3. Use the suffix _ for private class variables (Note that this convention is not universally accepted, but it is used by many programmers.)

4. Define every query as a const function.

5. Header files should only include class declarations, stand-alone function declarations, and definitions of constants. A header file should provide all the documentation necessary to understand the semantics of this file by the client. Header files have the .h extension.

6. Place definitions of class operations in a separate file, with a standardized extension (for example, .C or .cpp; in this book, I use the .cpp extension). This file should always include (using #include) the header file containing the class *declaration*. Place the *documentation* for the implementor of the class in the implementation file. Note that the documentation for the client and for the implementor may be different because they may explain different things.

3.2.1   Inline Functions

As I indicated in Section 2.5, *inline functions* are candidates for in-place code generation; that is, instead of being compiled, their code can be replaced by the corresponding function body. Both stand-alone functions and class operations can be specified as inline; for example:

```
inline int min(int i, int j) {
    return i < j ? i : j;
}
```

Class members that are defined within the class definition are considered inline. (I do not recommend that you ever define class members within the class definition, because it makes it difficult to determine what's the interface of this class.)

Inlining functions will typically result in more efficient code. One place they are useful is in combination with member functions. Typically, the only way to access or modify class data is through these member functions, so they are frequently used. This frequent use may make their efficiency critical for some applications.

Because inline functions are expanded at compile time, definitions of these functions, unlike other definitions, cannot be separately compiled and must be placed in header files. This creates a problem if the compiler does not actually inline a function (you may end up having multiple definitions of the same function). Therefore, you have to check that the your inline functions will actually be inlined, and if they cannot be inlined, you must remove the inline specification. In most of the examples in this book, I do not use the inline specification because its use is only related to efficiency and does not contribute to the understanding of high-level programming techniques.

3.3   Exception Handling

C++ supports a model of exception handling similar to that in Java (see Table 3.2). I only describe the basics of exceptions handling here (I will continue this discussion in Section 5.13).

Table 3.2   Exception Handling

Java	C++	Comments About C++
`Throwable Exception`	`exception`	Both primitive and class types can be used for exceptions. To use predefined exceptions, include `stdexcept`.
`catch(Exception e)`	`catch(...)`	To catch all exceptions, use ellipsis.

`catch(Exception e){`
`   throw e;`
`}`
	`catch(exception e){`
	`   throw;`
	`}`
		To rethrow an exception, an exception identifier is not needed.

`finally { ... }`	`--`	There is no `finally` keyword.
`void f() throws Ex;`	`void f() throw (Ex);`	To declare exceptions, use `throw`, not `throws`. The exception type must be in brackets. Exceptions do not have to be included in the method's signature.

In Java, all exceptions are classes derived from `Throwable`. There are two kinds of exceptions: *unchecked exceptions,* derived from the classes `RunTimeException` and `Error`, and *checked exceptions,* derived from the class `Exception`. The difference between the two is that unchecked exceptions do not appear in the method's signature and therefore are not checked by the compiler, while checked exceptions must be declared (included in the signature) and therefore they are checked.

Although in C++, exception objects may be of any type, including primitive data types, it is more useful to follow the Java philosophy and use exceptions that are of class types. The header file `stdexcept` provides a hierarchy of exceptions (classes derived from the class `exception`), which may be thrown by the standard library operations. On the other hand, predefined language constructs do not throw any exceptions. For example, an array index that is out of bounds in an array will not generate an exception but will generate the `out_of_range` exception if used in a vector (that is part of the standard library). Another example is the `bad_alloc` exception thrown by `new` if there is not enough memory available.

Exception handling is similar in C++ and Java and is done within `try` blocks. However, checked exceptions are not mandatory. A function that throws an exception *may* declare it in its signature but does not have to; for example:

```
void foo() throw (range_error);          //note brackets
void goo() throw ();
void hoo();
```

The function `foo()` may only throw the exception `range_error`; this is consistent with the Java style (if this function throws another exception, the call to `std::unexpected()` will terminate the program; for a detailed description, see Section 9.6.5). The function `goo()` is not allowed to throw any exceptions. Unfortunately, you do not know anything about the function `hoo()`; it may or may not throw exceptions. Finally, if a declaration of a function specifies an exception, the exception has to be repeated in the function definition; for example:

```
void f(int) throw (range_error);          // declaration of f
void f(int) throw (range_error) {         // definition of f
   ...
}
```

I recommend using the first format shown in the previous example—a function that explicitly throws an exception should *document* this by listing the exception in its signature. Otherwise, calling such a function within another function might lead to unexpected problems. For example, consider functions `foo()` and `hoo()` previously described, and assume that the former function uses the latter function:

```
void foo() throw (range_error) {
   ...
   hoo();                                  // call to hoo()
   ...
}
```

Now if `hoo()` throws an exception different than `range_error`, the program will terminate. By now you may wonder why the language does not force you to specify exceptions the way Java does. The reason is that this would create problems linking current code with legacy code or with applications written in other languages.

3.4   *Managing Objects*

Recall from Section 2.6 that an executing program uses two separate memory areas: a *stack* for allocating data when a function is called and deallocating these data when the function terminates, and a *heap* for user-defined memory management.

The main difference between Java and C++ class variables is that in Java, these variables, called *references,* are actually pointers to objects, and their values are addresses of objects allocated on the heap. On the other hand, in C++, variables of the class type represent objects themselves rather than pointers to objects, and these objects are allocated on the stack. To use heap-based objects, the C++ programmer has to define variables that are of either pointer or reference types. The differences between Java references and C++ pointers are summarized in Table 3.3. (In this section, I discuss pointer types; for a description of C++ reference types, see Section 3.8.1.)

Table 3.3   Java references and C++ pointers

Java	C++	Comments About C++
`ClassType x;`	`ClassType* x;`	To declare a pointer, use an asterisk.
`x = new ClassType`	`x = new ClassType`	In both languages, the new operator allocates memory for a new object and calls a constructor to initialize this memory.
`x.attribute`	`x->attribute`	To access an attribute pointed to by the pointer, use the `->` operator.
garbage collector	`delete x;`	In C++, the programmer has to deallocate objects explicitly.

Section 2.6 introduced pointers. In the following sections, you will find more examples of code that use both pointers and references. Once again, the question of whether pointers should be used at all comes up. Although programming with pointers is tricky and can make it difficult to find bugs, there is no simple answer to this question. There are situations in which pointers can be avoided, but there are also others in which they are suitable. By the time you finish reading this book, you should have an idea of when to use pointers and how to use them when you need to do so.

The following section will show you how to create and initialize objects. Then, in Section 3.4.2, you will see how objects are deallocated.

3.4.1   Initialization: Constructors

Consider the class `Student` again:

```
class Student {
public:
  Student(long);                              // constructor
  void setNumber(long);
  long getNumber() const;
private:
  long number_;
};
```

You can now declare variables of type `Student`; for example:

```
Student s(10);     // class variable s; object is stack-allocated
Student* sp;       // pointer variable sp; undefined initial value
```

It may be helpful to compare the first declaration with the corresponding Java declaration:

```
// Java:        Student s = new Student(10);
```

The very first action of an object should set its initial state, regardless of whether it is allocated memory on the stack or on the heap. In other words, all data fields of the object should be assigned appropriate initial values. As in Java, C++ uses a special function, called a **constructor**. Constructors can be overloaded and can use default parameters.

Constructors that do not require any actual parameters are called **no-arg** (for "no arguments"), or **default**, constructors. Default constructors have either no parameters, or they provide default values for *all* existing parameters. If you do not define a constructor, C++ will implicitly generate one for you. The compiler-generated constructor does not initialize attributes that are of primitive data types, pointers, or references but does call the default constructors for all nonstatic attributes of the class type (Section 3.4.6 will amplify this topic).

In Java, a constructor may call another constructor in the same class by using the `this` keyword. In C++, this can only be accomplished by defining an auxiliary function, which is then called by your constructors.

In C++, when a variable of a class type is declared, memory for it is allocated *on the stack,* and the appropriate constructor is invoked; for example:

```
Student kasia(100);
```

You can also create an object by assigning an object initialized by a constructor to a class variable; for example:

```
Student kasia = Student(100);
```

Remember that the variable `kasia` is a class variable, not a pointer or a reference. Once the object has been created, its public features can be accessed in the same way as in Java, using the dot notation:

```
kasia.setNumber(10);
cout << kasia.getNumber() << endl;
```

Now look at the creation of objects using pointers. The operator `new` allocates memory *on the heap* and then calls the constructor; for example:

```
Student* michael = new Student(100);
```

`michael` is a pointer that points to an object of class `Student`.

If the runtime system cannot allocate memory for an object on the heap, a `bad_alloc` exception is thrown:

```
try {
  michael = new Student(100);
} catch (bad_alloc b) {
  ...
}
```

You can also use an error-handling function to deal with the failure of `new`; this more advanced topic will be described in Section 9.6.5.

Once an object has been created, you can access its attributes. Recall from Section 2.6.1 that pointers can be dereferenced using `*`; therefore, for the previous example

- `michael` is a pointer that points to the `Student` object
- `*michael` is the value of this pointer, that is, the object

To access an attribute of the object pointed to by a pointer, you use `->` (rather than Java's `.`); for example:

```
cout << michael->getNumber() << endl;
```

You should not use the dot access to a dereferenced pointer, such as

```
*michael.getNumber()
```

because the `*` operator has lower precedence than the `.` operator, resulting in the expression being parsed to

```
*(michael.getNumber())
```

Compare this code with the code that used the class variable `kasia`:

```
kasia.getNumber()                    // class variable
michael->getNumber()                 // pointer
```

3.4.2   Clean up: `delete` and Destructors

Compare the assignment

```
Student* michael = new Student(100);
```

with the following declaration:

```
Student kasia(100);
```

Memory for the object kasia has been allocated on the stack, so when this object goes out of scope, it will be automatically deallocated (popped from the stack). On the other hand, memory for the object pointed to by michael has been allocated on the heap, and because C++ does not provide garbage collection, you must remember to free this memory when it is no longer needed.

What happens if memory is not reclaimed and cannot be reused? If your program does not take long to execute, likely nothing wrong will happen. On the other hand, if your program takes a very long time to execute, the unfreed memory could cause a problem. Some programs run "forever"—such as ones used by operating systems or reservation systems—and sooner or later will run out of available heap memory. To convince yourself of this, consider a hypothetical program that does not free memory and allocates 10K of memory for every request (such as a reservation). Assume that the heap has 100MB. If on average a request is made every five minutes, after 36 days your program will run out of memory (and the rest of the system will become painfully slow before this happens).

To deallocate memory, you use the delete operator; for example:

```
Student* sp = new Student(100);
...
delete sp;
```

If sp has the value 0, then delete sp is correct but does not do anything. Note that

```
delete sp;
```

merely returns the memory allocated to sp to the heap but does not change the value of sp. After the call, the value of sp is ill-defined because it points to a heap-based object that has been deallocated. To avoid future errors, remember to clean up after a call to delete by setting its parameter to 0:

```
delete sp;
sp = 0;
```

The need for cleanup applies not only to memory but also to other types of resources. For example, assume that a class, such as Student, maintains a certain resource, such as a file or port. It is natural to have the constructor acquire this resource (open the file), but the question is, how should this resource be released (the file closed)? Providing a function member Student::release() is error prone because the user may forget to call this function, leaving the resource unfreed. Java provides a finalize() method, which is called when the garbage collector retrieves the object. This solution is not ideal because the garbage collector may not be called at all, may be called "too late" (when you run out of all available resources), or may be called at the wrong time (using up precious CPU time in real-time applications). Pros and cons of garbage collectors aside, C++ does not provide a standard garbage collector. Ideally, a cleanup action should be invoked *implicitly,* every time an object goes out of scope. C++ provides a function to do just this: the **destructor**. A destructor's name is the same as the name of the constructor, but with the prefix ~. We now add a destructor to the slightly modified Student class:

```
class Student {
public:
    Student(long);              // constructor; acquire resource
    ~Student();                 // destructor; release resource
    void setNumber(long);
    long getNumber() const;
private:
    long number_;
    Resource r_;
};
```

A destructor's task is to clean up any resources acquired by the object. The destructor is not allowed to have any parameters, cannot be overloaded, and cannot be specified as const. If you do not provide a destructor, the compiler generates a destructor with an empty body.

Consider the following function:

```
void foo(long number) {
    Student kasia(number);
    ...
}
```

When foo() is called, memory for the parameter number and the object kasia is allocated (pushed) on the stack, and the constructor for this object is executed. When the function terminates, the destructor for the object kasia is executed, and then memory for both data is deallocated (popped). For the above example, the destructor releases the resource allocated for the Student object. Therefore, in general, destructors are useful in automatically releasing resources whenever an object maintaining these resources goes out of scope and is popped from the stack.

Destructors are also used in conjunction with the delete operator. Simply deallocating a block of memory may leave behind inaccessible resources; this is why the delete operator implicitly calls the destructor of the corresponding class before deallocating memory. Note, however, that the destructor is not automatically called for the pointer going out of scope; it has to be invoked through delete.

Consider the following class, AccountForStudent, which manages an account for a single student:

```
class AccountForStudent {
public:
    AccountForStudent(long number, double balance);
```

```
  ~AccountForStudent();
  ...
private:
  Student* stud_;                                          // pointer
  double balance_;
};
```

The constructor and the destructor of this class look like this:

```
AccountForStudent::AccountForStudent(long number, double balance) {
  stud_ = new Student(number);
  balance_ = balance;
}

AccountForStudent::~AccountForStudent() {
  delete stud_;
}
```

To convince yourself that the destructor is needed, consider a declaration of a variable of type AccountForStudent in some scope, such as a function body:

```
void foo() {
  AccountForStudent as(100, 20.00);
  ...
}
```

At the end of the function's scope, the variable as goes out of scope, and its destructor is called. This destructor executes

```
delete stud_
```

which in turn calls the destructor for the class Student. The latter destructor deallocates the resource maintained by this class, and then delete frees memory allocated for the object pointed to by stud_. Finally, memory for the object as is freed. Without a destructor in the AccountForStudent class, memory for the object pointed to by stud_ would not be deallocated.

There is a very important difference between what happens when a *class variable* goes out of scope and when a *pointer* to a class does. In the former case, a destructor for the class is executed; in the latter case, no such action is performed. This is because the type "pointer to class type" is not a class type and does not have its own methods. When you use class variables, the language's runtime system implicitly helps you to manage resources (provided that you have correctly defined destructors). On the other hand, when you use pointers, you have to remember to explicitly manage resources and, when appropriate, release them by using delete. As I will show later, it is sometimes useful to design a wrapper class for a pointer (that is, a class in which the pointer is an attribute) and use the constructors and destructors of the class.

Common Errors

1. To declare variables of a class that has a no-arg constructor, do not use parentheses. For example, to declare a variable of the class `Student`, which has the no-arg constructor

   ```
   Student::Student(long number = 0) { ... }
   ```

   you write

   ```
   Student maryAnn;
   ```

   If instead you use brackets, as in

   ```
   Student maryJoe();
   ```

   you would be declaring a function `maryJoe()`.
      Note that

   ```
   Student maryJoe = Student();
   ```

   does call a constructor.
2. To access a member `x` of an object pointed to by the pointer `p`, use `p->x` rather than `p.x`.
3. Calling `delete p` twice, one call right after the other, is incorrect and leads to undefined behavior and possibly to runtime errors.
4. Do not throw exceptions from the destructor.

Note that you cannot assume that all resources are automatically released when the *entire program* terminates. While this is true for resources allocated exclusively for this program, such as internal memory, there are other resources obtained from the operating system, such as file locks or ports, that must be explicitly released when the program terminates.

   As yet another example of a destructor, this time whose use is not related to resources, consider an application that must perform some actions after the last use of an object of a certain class. For example, to time the performance of the methods of a class called `B`, you can use the `B` destructor to stop the clock and save or display the timer results.

   Destructors are also involved in the process of throwing an exception. An exception throw results in the **unwinding** of the runtime stack, which means that all objects created between the time the exception is thrown and caught are destroyed (that is, their destructors are called). This process is essential to the proper cleanup of resources. For example, suppose that an exception is thrown in the constructor, which has already created one or more objects. Then not only must these objects be popped from the stack, but also their destructors must be called to release any resources that could have been maintained by the objects on the stack. I will describe this process in more detail in Section 5.14.

Advanced

Both new and delete can be applied to variables of primitive data types. These types have built-in constructors that accept a single value (the initialization value), for example:

```
int* p = new int(10);    // allocate memory for one integer, store 10
cout << *p;              // prints 10
delete p;                // free memory

int* ap = new int[10];   // allocate block of memory for 10 integers
                         // this block works as if it was an array

for(int i = 0; i < 10; ++i)
  cin >> ap[i];                          // ap[i] refers to the i-th element

...
delete [] ap;                            // release the block; note [ ]
```

You need the brackets ([]) in the destructor call because this tells the compiler to release a block of memory rather than a single memory "cell." The size of the block is initialized by the call to new int[], stored internally within the block, and used to release the appropriate number of cells.

There is another version of the new operator that uses **placement syntax** to allocate new objects at a predetermined memory location rather than a block of memory obtained from the heap. This version can be used for passing parameters to the allocation routine rather than to the constructor, which is useful for various low-level routines (for example, the ones working with memory-mapped I/O). To explain this concept, I present a superficial example that avoids the use of specific memory addresses:

```
#include <new>
Student* p = new Student(100);
Student* q = new(p) Student(101);                          // placement
```

The execution of

```
new Student(100);
```

results in first allocating memory, followed by the execution the constructor `Student(100)`. However, for the call

```
new(p) Student(101);
```

no new memory is allocated; instead, the constructor `Student(101)` is called to reinitialize the memory allocated by the first `new`.

Objects created with the placement syntax should not be deallocated using `delete`, because the placement `new` does not allocate memory; it gets a block of memory from the memory pool allocated by other means. For the previous example, the memory pool is represented by the variable `p` and is allocated using the standard version of `new`; on the other hand, memory for `q` has been allocated using the placement `new`. You can only deallocate the entire memory pool, which is done by using `delete p` for the previous example.

The placement syntax can also be used to allocate a character buffer and store objects in the buffer; for example:

```
char* buffer = new char[2 * sizeof(Student)];
Student* p1 = new(buffer) Student(101);      //use the first half
char* second = &buffer[sizeof(Student)];     // place for the second
Student* p2 = new(second) Student(102);      // use the second half
```

If you want to hold onto the memory buffer but get rid of the object stored in the buffer, you have to explicitly call a destructor; for example:

```
p1->~Student();
```

3.4.3 Copying Class Objects

Pointers have reference-assignment semantics similar to those in Java. For example, after the assignment

```
Student* john = michael;
```

both `john` and `michael` *share* the same object. This type of an assignment is different than value-assignment semantics used by class variables, as in

```
Student kasia(10);
Student barbara(11);
...
kasia = barbara;
```

The result of the above assignment is a memberwise copy of all class attributes (described in detail later on in this section), which for this example is a copy of the attribute `number_`. The two types of assignments, reference and value, are also known as a shallow copy and a deep copy, respectively. In general, a **deep copy** operation involves copying the entire object recursively, in the same way that you would implement a clone operation in Java. A **shallow copy** means that some attribute may be shared by the original object and the copied one. For variables of a primitive data type, there is no difference between a shallow and a deep copy. For other variables, the two kinds of copy produce different results. As an example, consider again the class `Student`:

```
class Student {
public:
  Student(long);
  long getNumber() const;
  ...
private:
  long number_;
};
```

and the class `AccountForStudent`:

```
class AccountForStudent {
public:
  AccountForStudent(long number, double balance);
  ~AccountForStudent();
  long getNumber() const;
  ...
private:
  Student* stud_;
  double balance_;
};
```

Now consider an object of class `AccountForStudent`:

```
AccountForStudent as(100, 1000.25);
```

The result of assigning a shallow and a deep copy of as to another variable bs is shown in Figure 3.1. You can see that the result of a deep copy is that the new object is "independent" of the object that has been copied.

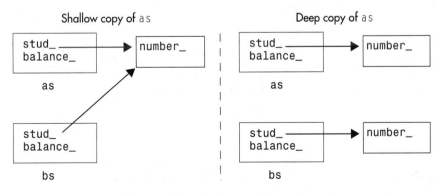

Figure 3.1 Shallow and deep copy

In general, every C++ class provides two *default* member functions used to define an assignment and a copy constructor, respectively. If C is some class, the following two functions will be implicitly defined by the language:

- The copying of objects (**assignment operator**), such as

```
x = y
```

  where x and y are existing objects of class C;

- An initialization of a new object using the existing object (**copy constructor**), such as

```
C x = y;
```

  where y is an existing object of class C.

Given this description, you can see that an assignment operator and a copy constructor are usually slightly different. Specifically, an assignment operator assigns to a constructed, initialized object, while a copy constructor assigns to a brand new, uninitialized object.

By default, both functions perform **memberwise copying** of nonstatic attributes, which results in a shallow copy of these values. This means that every member of a new object is assigned a value of the corresponding member of the existing object. In some cases, the default shallow copy is sufficient; for example, if a class contains only members of primitive types, or when no resources are managed by class objects. As an example, consider again the class Student:

```
Student kasia(100);
Student maryAnn = kasia; // copy constructor; maryAnn.number_ is 100

Student michael(200);
michael = maryAnn;       // assignment; michael.number_ is 100
```

In this example, the default assignment and copy operations are sufficient. In other situations, the *default meanings* of the assignment and the copy constructor are not satisfactory. To see why this is so, consider two objects, s1 and s2, of the class AccountForStudent previously shown. We do not want the assignment

```
s1 = s2;
```

to invoke a memberwise copy; this would make the Student object previously managed by s1 inaccessible and would make the Student object managed by s2 a shared object, managed by both s1 and s2 (see Figure 3.2).

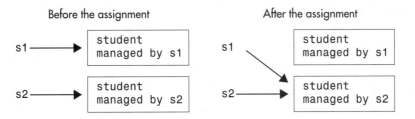

Figure 3.2 Default assignment

There are several reasons why the state of execution after this assignment may lead to problems, all of which are related to memory use. For example, if one of the variables goes out of scope and its destructor is called, then the destructor will deallocate the Student object, and any attempt to access this object through the other variable will result in an error. Using the default copy constructor may cause the same kind of a problem, because the result of such a copy is that the Student object is shared by two variables.

To solve this problem, the assignment should deallocate the student object managed by s1 and then copy the Student object managed by s2. In general, this may require *cloning* the resource managed by s2 by making a deep copy. Similarly, an initialization using an existing object such as

```
Student s1;                      // initialize s1
Student s2 = s1;                 // initialize s2 by copying s1
```

should copy the Student object managed by s1 instead of invoking a memberwise copy (it does not deallocate the Student object managed by s2 because there is none yet; the object s2 has just been created and is being initialized).

Next I describe how you can define your own copy constructor so it can be used to initialize a new object using the existing object; in Section 3.9.1, I will describe the implementation of the assignment operator. A **copy constructor** uses a constant pass by reference and has the following signature:

```
ClassName(const ClassName&);
```

The parameter of this constructor is a constant reference to the object that is being used to initialize the new object.

Now you can define your own copy constructor for the class AccountFor-Student:

```
//copy constructor definition
AccountForStudent::AccountForStudent(const AccountForStudent& from) {
   stud_ = new Student(from.stud_->number());
   balance_ = from.balance_;
}
```

With this in place, you can make the declarations

```
AccountForStudent kasia(100, 2000);
AccountForStudent maryAnn = kasia;
```

to generate two independent Student objects, managed by kasia and maryAnn, respectively. Note that the initialization of maryAnn is equivalent to

```
// pseudocode:  maryAnn.AccountForStudent(kasia);
```

There is an alternative syntax for initialization using the existing object, which also invokes the copy constructor:

```
AccountForStudent maryAnn(kasia);
```

You have seen that the copy constructor is invoked when an object is initialized by being *assigned* an existing object. The copy constructor is invoked in two other contexts:

- When a parameter of a class type is passed by value
- When a value of a class type is returned by a function

The concept behind its use in these contexts is quite clear: When a parameter is passed by value, the formal parameter is initialized using the value of the actual parameter, and this initialization is performed using the copy constructor. A similar argument applies when a function that returns a value is called; for example:

```
val = op();
```

The return value from op() is copied using the copy constructor and used to initialize val. Now look at two examples. First, consider a function that has a class parameter representing a student account passed by value and which returns true if the number of the student passed as the first parameter is equal to the number passed as the second parameter:

```
bool equal(AccountForStudent as, long number) {
   return as.number() == number;
}
AccountForStudent kasia(100, 2000);

if(equal(kasia, 200))
   ...
```

To initialize the formal parameter, the value of the actual parameter is used, and a copy constructor is called to initialize the parameter as. With the use of the default copy constructor, both as and kasia would share the same student, because only a shallow copy would be performed (see Figure 3.3). When the function

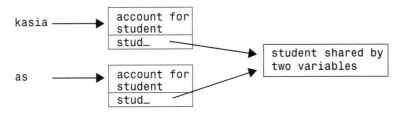

Figure 3.3 Sharing resulting from using the default copy constructor as a formal parameter

`equal()` terminates, the formal parameter `as` goes out of scope, its destructor is called, and the `Student` object is deallocated. As a result, a subsequent call to `kasia.number()` would fail because the `as` object no longer exists. On the other hand, if you use the modified copy constructor, which makes a deep copy, you do not have this problem.

Note that the copy constructor is not invoked if the actual parameter is a reference, as in

```
bool equal(AccountForStudent& as, long number);
```

As promised, here is a function that returns a value of a class type:

```
AccountForStudent create(long number) {
  AccountForStudent local(number, 0.0);
  return local;
}
```

When `create()` is called, its return value is typically assigned to another variable:

```
AccountForStudent global;
...
global = create(300);
```

This assignment represents the following sequence of actions:

1. Program execution enters the body of `create()`, and the variable `local` is initialized (by calling the constructor).
2. A temporary variable, `temp`, created by the compiler, is initialized by calling the copy constructor and using the value of the `local` variable: `temp.AccountForStudent(local)`.
3. An assignment operator is called, which assigns the value of the temporary variable `temp` to `global`.
4. The destructor for the temporary variable `temp` is called.
5. `create()` terminates.

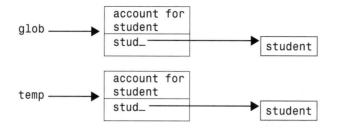

Figure 3.4   Copy constructor performing deep copy

Figure 3.4 shows the state of memory after the third action has been executed, assuming that the copy constructor has been defined to perform a deep copy.

What would happen if the class AccountForStudent did not have a user-defined copy constructor and instead used the default predefined one? When the copy constructor in

```
temp.AccountForStudent(local)
```

executes, temp and local share the same Student object. When the destructor for temp executes, the Student object is deallocated, and therefore you now cannot access the Student object through the variable global. On the other hand, if we use our definition of the copy constructor, everything is fine.

This looks like a long and complicated description that is hard to remember, but the actual idea is quite simple: If your class manages any resources, then it should have an appropriate constructor, copy constructor, assignment operator, and a destructor for those resources (I will summarize this discussion in Section 3.9). In addition, you should remember about the consequences of passing an object by value, which results in an invocation of the copy constructor. When using nonprimitive data types, it is often preferable to pass objects by reference, or constant reference, rather then by value.

Finally, note that a copy constructor may have a default value for its parameter, and if so, it becomes a no-arg constructor; for example:

```
class Student {
public:
  Student(long);
  Student(const Student& = Student(0));
  ...
private:
  long number_;
};

Student::Student(const Student& s) {
  number_ = s.number_;
}
```

Now, if you write

```
Student s;
```

then the no-arg copy constructor will be called. Note that if you define a no-arg copy constructor, you cannot define a no-arg constructor (otherwise, the compiler can't tell which no-arg constructor should be used).

3.4.4 Member Initialization List

Initialization of class attributes in the constructor does not have to be performed using assignment statements; instead, you can use the **member initialization list**, which is a comma-separated list of initializers of the form

```
member(value)
```

This syntax means that variables of primitive data types are initialized through assignments, while variables of class types are initialized by calling copy constructors (either default or user-defined). For example:

```
class Student {
public:
  Student(long, string);
  ...
private:
  long number_;
  string name_;
};
//constructor definition; note the colon ':' below
void Student::Student(long number, string name) :

     number_(number), name_(name)        // comma-separated list
{ }                                      // empty body
```

Since `number_` is of a primitive data type, the initialization

```
number_(number)
```

is equivalent to the *assignment*:

```
number_ = number;
```

On the other hand, the initialization

```
name_(name)
```

does not use an assignment operation; it makes use of a *copy constructor* from the predefined class string instead.

Consider a version in which the assignment to name_ is placed in the body of this function:

```
void Student::Student(long number, string name): number_(number) {
  name_ = name;
}
```

In this function, the constructor of the class string was called to initialize name_, and then the assignment operator reinitialized this object. Since the second action is not needed, it is inefficient and should be avoided.

Initialization of class attributes Idiom 3.1

Use the member initialization list to initialize the following class attributes: constant, reference and any attributes of class types.

Common Errors

The elements of the member initialization list are executed in the order in which they are declared in the class. Therefore, the initializers should be listed in declaration order. Avoid using attributes in the initializer expressions. For example:

```
class A {
public:
  A(int s);
private:
  int i_;
  int j_;
};

A::A(int s) : j_(s), i_(j_)      //wrong order
{}
```

This implementation of the constructor is misleading. When this constructor is executed, it does not perform the operations found in the member initialization list in the correct order; instead, it executes them in the order that the declarations appear inside the class

```
i_(j_), j_(s)
```

resulting in undefined values.

Some attributes have to be initialized using the member initialization list, such as constant features (see Section 3.5.1), reference attributes (see Section 3.8.5), and all class attributes (see Section 3.4.6).

3.4.5   Exception Handling in the Member Initialization List

Since the constructor does not return any value, the only way to handle errors that occur during its execution is to use exception handling. You can deal with errors that occur during the execution of the constructor's body by using the `try` block within this body. The constructor can also catch exceptions thrown by other constructors invoked from the member initialization list. The syntax to do so extends the `try` block as follows:

```
void Student::Student(long number, string name)
try
   : number_(number), name_(name) {
}
catch(exc& e) {
   ...
}
```

where `exc` is any exception that can be thrown by the class `string`. A more general discussion of this syntactic structure will be provided in Section 9.6.6.

3.4.6   Nested Objects

Consider a class with attributes that are of some *class type* (that is, not pointers or references to class types). An object of such a class contains **nested objects**, rather than references to objects (this is never the case in Java). For example, for the class `Student`, you can define a class describing an account for the student with a nested object representing a student (see Figure 3.5).

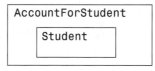

Figure 3.5   Nested object

```
class AccountForStudent {
public:
  AccountForStudent(Student, double balance);
  AccountForStudent(long number, string name, double balance);

  . . .
private:
  Student stud_;                                    // nested object
  double balance_;
};
```

You can define the first constructor for this class using a member initialization list:

```
AccountForStudent::AccountForStudent(Student s, double balance):
    stud_(s), balance_(balance)
{ }                                                 // empty body
```

The attribute stud_ is initialized by calling a copy constructor from the class Student; the attribute balance_ is of a primitive data type and is initialized with the value of balance. balance_ can also be initialized through an assignment inside the constructor body as follows:

```
AccountForStudent::AccountForStudent(Student s, double balance):
    stud_(s) {
  balance_ = balance;
}
```

Can stud_ be initialized through a similar assignment, as in the following?

```
AccountForStudent::AccountForStudent(Student s, double balance) {
  stud_ = s;
  balance_ = balance;
}
```

The answer is yes, provided there is a no-arg constructor for the class Student, otherwise, the initialization is not possible. Specifically, for class attributes that are not explicitly initialized using a member initialization list, there is *always* a compiler-generated initialization. For the above version of the constructor, this initialization looks like this:

```
AccountForStudent::AccountForStudent(Student s, double balance):
    stud_() {          // compiler-generated call to no-arg constructor
  stud_ = s;
  balance_ = balance;
}
```

Therefore, it is inefficient *not* to initialize a class attribute in the member initialization list, because not doing so results in two actions: first a no-arg constructor is called, and then an assignment is used to set the value of this attribute.

Now consider the second constructor, implemented using a member initialization list:

```
AccountForStudent::AccountForStudent(
  long number, string name, double balance) :
    stud_(number, name), balance_(balance)
{}
```

Recall from Section 3.4.1 that if you do not define a constructor for a class that contains a nested object, the default constructor generated by the compiler will call the default constructor for the nested object. When an object of this class goes out of scope, the destructors for its nested objects are called (in the *reverse* order of construction).

● EXAMPLE 3.2

In this example, we have a class Student made up of a student number and an associated file that stores notes. The student number is set in the constructor, which also opens the notes file. The number can be accessed by the function number(), and the file can be displayed on standard output using the operation show(). This operation is not a query (defined as const) because it does modify the state of the file variable (although it does not modify the contents of the file). The destructor closes the notes file.

In this implementation, I use a number of operations from the class ifstream, defined in the standard library fstream: the constructor, which takes a C-style string as a parameter (see Section 2.6.4); seekg() to rewind the file; getline() to read a line; and close() to close the file (details of file I/O are described in Sections 9.2.3 and 9.2.4).

```
// File: ex3.2.student.h
// Class Student, with two attributes: number and file
```

```
// Both attributes are set by the constructor and cannot be changed
// The file attribute is a nested object
class Student {
public:
  Student(long, const string&);  // constructor
  long number() const;           // shows the number
  void show();                   // shows the file
  ~Student();                    // destructor
private:
  long number_;                  // student number
  ifstream inFile_;              // file variable
  bool validFile_;               // has file been successfully opened
};

// File: ex3.2.student.cpp
#include "ex3.2.student.h"
#include <iostream>
#include <fstream>

Student::Student(long number, const string& filename) :
    number_(number), inFile_(filename.c_str()), validFile_(inFile_)
{ }

long Student::number() const {
  return number_;
}

void Student::show() {

                                                  // open a file
  if(!validFile_) {
    cout << "Can't open the input file" << endl;
    return;
  }
  inFile_.seekg(0);                               // rewind

                                  // read file, one line at a time
  string line;
  while(getline(inFile_, line))
    cout << line << endl;

                    // eof reached, need to clear the error state
  inFile_.clear();
}

Student::~Student() {
```

```
    inFile_.close();
}
```

After the function `show()` reads the file, it has to call `clear()` before the file can be read again (for details, see Section 9.2.3). Because `inFile_` is a nested object and a destructor for the `ifstream` class closes the file, it was not really necessary to define a destructor for the class `Student`.

In this example, I used a nested object (specifically, the `inFile_` variable). What changes would I have to make to the code if instead I used a pointer to a file? First, the constructor would look like this:

```
//constructor definition
Student::Student(long number, const string& filename) {
    inFile_ = new ifstream(filename.c_str());
    number_ = number;
    validFile_ = *inFile_;
}
```

`inFile_` would no longer be a nested object and would not be destructed (that is, the destructor would not be called for this object) if a `Student` object were destructed; therefore, I would need to define a destructor to do the cleanup:

```
Student::~Student() {
    inFile_->close();
}
```

3.4.7 Type Conversion and Constraining Constructors

A constructor of a class that has a single parameter of type T defines an **implicit type conversion** from type T to the class type. For example, in the following class

```
class Student {
public:
    Student(long);                              // constructor
    ...
private:
    long number_;
};
```

the constructor `Student::Student(long)` provides a type conversion from the type `long` to the type `Student`. This conversion will take place whenever the compiler expects to see an expression of type Student but instead gets an expression of type long; for example:

```
Student michael = 200;                      // michael = Student(200);
```

In some cases, this conversion is undesirable; for example, if you want to perform range checking rather than allowing Student to be initialized by an arbitrary long value. The conversion can be suppressed by specifying the constructor to be **explicit** (which means that the constructor must be called explicitly); for example:

```
class Student {
public:
    explicit Student(long);              // explicit constructor
    ...
private:
    long number_;
};
```

This statement is illegal:

```
Student michael = 200;                  // implicit: Student(200);
```

But this statement is correct:

```
Student michael(200);                   // explicit construction
```

Explicit Constructor Idiom 3.2

If a class has a constructor that takes a single parameter, under most circumstances, the constructor should be explicit; otherwise, the implicit type conversion invoked by the constructor might be confusing or, in the presence of other operations, might lead to ambiguous code.

A constructor's use can be restricted by making it private. In the following example, one constructor is available to the *clients* of the class and the other only to *class operations*:

```
class Student {
public:
    explicit Student(long);                     // public constructor
    ...
private:
```

```
  Student();                    // constructor only for members
  long number_;
};
```

3.4.8 this

As in Java, `this` is a pointer to "this" object. You cannot assign to this pointer because it is always a *constant* pointer. For example, for the class `Student`, its type is

```
Student* const this;
```

The `this` pointer is also used by the compiler to ensure that within a `const` function, attributes cannot be modified by giving it the following type:

```
const Student* const this;
```

Subsequent sections will show various applications of the `this` pointer (Section 3.8.3 describes how to design object modifiers and Section 3.9 shows how to avoid self-destruction in assignments).

3.5   Constant and Static Features; Enumerations

In the following two sections, I will describe constant and static features, which in C++ are somewhat different from Java. In the third, following section, I describe enumerations, which do not have anything to do with Java's enumerations; instead they are used to define ordered collections of named integer constants.

3.5.1 Constant Features

C++ data, including variables of class types, may be defined using the `const` qualification (similar to Java's `final` qualification). Recall that defining a member function as nonconstant makes it impossible for it to be invoked from a constant object. Therefore, queries should always be specified as `const` to avoid unnecessarily limiting their usage. The following code shows the consequence of not specifying a query as `const`:

```
class Student {
public:
  explicit Student(long);
  void setNumber(long);      // modifier
  long getNumber();          // compiles but a query should be const
private:
  long number_;
```

```
};

Student kasia(100);
kasia.setNumber(200);                // OK, kasia is not constant
cout << kasia.getNumber() << endl;   // as above

const Student barbara(101);
cout << barbara.getNumber() << endl;         // barbara is const
```

If `getNumber()` were specified as `const`, then this code would be correct. Of course, a modifier function cannot be applied to a constant object:

```
barbara.setNumber(300);                    // can't modify constant
```

Unlike Java, C++ does not allow you to initialize constant attributes in a class definition; they have to be initialized with a constructor using the *member initialization list*; for example:

```
class Student {
public:
  explicit Student(long, int);
  const int sin;                     // no initialization here
  ...
private:
  long number_;
};
Student::Student(long number, int s) : sin(s) {
  number_ = number;
}
```

Common Errors

Constant attributes cannot be initialized in a class definition; they can only be initialized through the member initialization list of the constructor.

Now consider a more detailed description of a constant function. In some cases, the specification of a function—such as one that uses a cache—appears to be different, considering the functionality required for the *implementation* and the *use* of the function. (Recall that a cache is a buffer used to hold a local copy of data that are likely to be needed by the program.) To see why the two specifications appear to be different in the cache example just given, recall that a client does not need to know about the existence of a cache, so cache modifications should be transparent to the client. On the other hand, the implementation may need to modify the cache as a result of a client request. To summarize this situation, as far as the client is concerned, an operation is constant (does not modify object attributes). From the implementation's point of view, however, it isn't: Data—specifically, the cache—is modified. We could deal with this situation by not specifying the function as `const`, but this would not be in the spirit of good object-oriented design. Luckily, C++ provides a `mutable` specification for data attributes that may be *changed by constant functions.*

● **EXAMPLE 3.3.**

Consider an example of a class `FileOps` that provides three file-processing functions: to find the number of words, characters, and lines in a file, respectively. For reasons of efficiency, values computed by these functions are cached. For each cached data, there are two variables: one to store the data and another to store the information about the validity of the cached data. Functions such as `lines()` are declared as `const`, although they may modify the cache.

```
// File: ex3.3.fileops.h
// Class with three file processing functions
class FileOps {
public:
  explicit FileOps(const string&);
  FileOps(const FileOps&);
  ~FileOps();

  long lines() const;
  long words() const;
  long chars() const;
private:
                  // mutable can be changed by constant functions
  mutable ifstream fileVar_;


                                            // cache
  mutable bool linesCached_;
  mutable long lines_;
  mutable bool wordsCached_;
  mutable long words_;
  mutable bool charsCached_;
  mutable long chars_;
};
```

The following code shows only the implementation of one member function:

```cpp
// File: ex3.3.fileops.cpp
long FileOps::lines() const {
  if(linesCached_)
    return lines_;
  lines_ = 0;
  linesCached_ = true;
  if(!charsCached_)                      // cache characters as well
    chars_ = 0;

  char c;
  while(fileVar_.get(c)) {
    if(c == '\n')
      ++lines_;
    if(!charsCached_)
      ++chars_;
  }
  charsCached_ = true;
  fileVar_.clear();
  fileVar_.seekg(0);
  return lines_;
}
```

The next section describes static features, including static constant data.

3.5.2   Static Features

As in Java, class members that are allocated on a *per class* basis rather than a *per object* basis—and therefore shared by all objects of this class—are called **static** (see Table 3.4).

Here's an example of a class with static features:

Table 3.4.   Static features

Construct	Comments About C++
static	Static features are merely *declared* in the class declaration; they have to be *defined* in a separate place. To refer to a static feature, use `ClassName::feature` rather than Java's `ClassName.feature` syntax.

The *definitions* of static members occur outside the class in the implementation file,

```
class Student {
public:
  explicit Student();
  long number() const;
private:
  long number_;
  static string university_;              // declaration
  static long currentNumber_;             // declaration
};
```

which means that they are hidden from the client of the class:

```
string Student::university_("Acadia");          //definition
long Student::currentNumber_ = 0;               //definition
```

The constructor can assign consecutive student numbers:

```
Student::Student() {
  number_ = currentNumber_++;
}
```

As in Java, member functions can be static. Such functions can refer *only* to static features of the class:

```
class Student {
public:
  ...
  static string getUniversity();
  static long getNumberedIssued();
private:
  static string university_;
  static long currentNumber_;
  ...
};

string Student::getUniversity() {
  return university_;
}
```

```
long Student::getNumberedIssued() {
  return currentNumber_;
}
Student kasia;
Student michael;

cout << "kasia's university = " << kasia.getUniversity() << endl;
cout << "kasia's number = " << kasia.number() << endl;
cout << "issued " << Student::getNumberedIssued() <<
          " numbers" << endl;
```

Sometimes, it is useful to have **constant static attributes** (similar to Java's `final static`). C++ constant static attributes can be initialized within the class definition only if they are of an integral type, and the initialization expression must be constant. Otherwise, these attributes have to be initialized outside the class definition. For example, assume that the class `Student` uses `-1` as an invalid student number:

```
class Student {
public:
  ...
  const static int invalidNumber = -1;     // OK to initialize here

  const static string university;
  // const static string university = "Acadia"; - not integral
private:
  ...
};
```

In this example, `invalidNumber` and `university` are only declared. Both still have to be defined:

```
const int Student::invalidNumber;  // initialization not needed here
const string Student::university("Acadia");
```

Common Errors

1. Static attributes can be initialized within a class definition only if they are constant and integral.
2. Static operations cannot use the `this` pointer and cannot be `const` or `volatile`.

Integral static constants can also be defined in a class by using enumerated data types, also called enumerations (not to be confused with Java's enumerations). I will introduce these in the next section.

3.5.3 Enumerations

Enumerations are ordered collections of named integer constants, called **enumerators**; for example:

```
enum opcodes {
   lvalue, rvalue, push, plus
};

enum opcodes e;
```

The definition of the type `opcodes` introduces four enumerators—`lvalue`, `rvalue`, `push`, and `plus`—all of type `int`. C++ assigns integer values to enumerated types; by default, the first enumerated type constant receives the value 0, and subsequent constants receive a value one greater than the value of the previous constant.

A declaration of an enumerated type can also explicitly define integer values associated with enumerated constants; for example:

```
enum opcodes {
   lvalue = 1, rvalue, push = 5, plus
};
```

`rvalue` equals 2, and `plus` is equal to 6.

Enumerated type variables can be assigned enumerated type values; for example:

```
e = lvalue;                          // the value of e is lvalue
```

They can also be compared for equality; for example:

```
if(e == push) ...
```

Enumerations do not have to be named if the name of the enumerator is sufficient:

```
class Student {
public:
   enum {invalidNumber = -1};      // no need for the enumeration name
   enum Gender {female, male};
   Student(string, long, Gender);
   long number() const;
private:
   string name_;
   Gender gen_;
   long number_;
};
```

Using these definitions, it is now possible to write:

```
Student::Student(string name, long number, Gender g) :
    name_(name), gen_(g) {
    number_ = number < 0 ? invalidNumber : number;
}


Student kasia("Kasia", 100, Student::female);
if(kasia.number() == Student::invalidNumber) ...
```

Note that the scope operator must be used to refer to the enumerators female and invalidNumber.

3.6 Pure Static Classes

One of the most important principles of software design is modularization. Therefore, as the programming guidelines in Sections 2.4.3 and 2.5 already pointed out,
you should avoid using stand-alone functions (that is, functions not belonging to
any class) and global variables whenever possible. There are two ways to package
related functions and variables together. The most general solution is to use namespaces, which are described in Section 4.6. If there is a *single* global resource, you
can define a **pure static** class with only static features. The following example uses
an integer variable to represent a resource:

```
class SharedResource {
public:
    static int value();
    static void value(int k);
private:
    SharedResource();
    static int value_;
};

int SharedResource::value() {
    return value_;
}

void SharedResource::value(int k) {
    value_ = k;
}

int SharedResource::value_ = 0;
```

You would never create objects of this class (which is why the constructor is private). Instead, you can operate on the resource by using the two functions defined in the interface; for example:

```
int i = SharedResource::value();
...
SharedResource::value(i+1);
```

Java uses many pure static classes, such as StrictMath and java.rmi.Naming.

Pure Static Class Idiom 3.3

To encapsulate global variables and the functions operating on these variables, use a pure static class in which all features are static.

3.7 *Initialization of Local and Global Variables*

Global variables are defined outside any function and, in particular, outside the main function. They include static class variables, which are declared in the class and defined outside the class, as Section 3.5.2 already pointed out.

Local variables are variables defined within a function. They have *undefined* initial values unless they are static (then they are implicitly initialized to a zero value), or they are explicitly initialized by the programmer. Java programmers are used to having to explicitly initialize local variables to avoid compiler warnings or errors. C++ compilers are not so stringent, but since uninitialized local variables can make finding errors difficult, I recommend that local variables be explicitly initialized in a declaration (unless they are initialized through an assignment or an input statement shortly after the declaration).

The constructors of global class variables are executed before the main function starts executing, and their destructors are executed after the main function terminates. If there are several global variables defined in a *single* file, they are initialized in the order of their definition. If there are several global variables defined in separate files, the order of initialization is not determined.

Therefore, whenever possible, you should try to avoid using global variables and, in particular, global static variables. As an alternative to such variables, you can define static variables within functions and take advantage of the fact that static local variables are initialized when the function containing their definitions is called for the first time. For example, here is a function containing a local static variable:

```
int& foo() {
  static int x = 0;
  return x;
}
```

Since this function returns a reference, it provides read/write access to its local variable; for example:

```
cout << foo() << endl;                        // writes 0
foo() += 3;
cout << foo() << endl;                        // writes 3
```

This design is preferable to having a global variable defined outside any function

```
static int x = 0;
```

because of the initialization problem previously described.

Static non-local Variables Idiom 3.4

Instead of declaring global static variables, define static variables within functions that return values of these variables.

3.8 *Reference Types and Their Applications*

In Section 2.4.8, I briefly introduced reference types and showed how you can use them with primitive data types. In this section, I describe some more applications of references used with user-defined class types.

3.8.1 Java References Versus C++ References and Pointers

In this section, I present a complete comparison of Java references and C++ pointers and references (see Table 3.5). First, a C++ reference is an alias to another object. Although references are typically implemented using pointers, they are *not* pointers. On the other hand, Java references are really pointers in disguise, but the permissible operations are different from those in C++.

3.8.2 Passing Parameters by Reference

Function actual parameters can be used in two ways: to pass a value to the function (pass by value) or to pass a value to the function and then return a new value from the function (or just return a new value). Recall Idiom 2.1, which states that to pass

Table 3.5 Java references and C++ pointers and references

Java	C++	Comments About C++
| ```
class Student {
 public Student()
 { ... }
 public long number()
 {  ... }
 ...
};
``` | ```
class Student {
 public:
   Student();
   long number() const;
   ...
};
``` | In C++, you can have a variable of type:<br>• Student<br>• **Reference** to Student<br>• **Pointer** to Student |
| ```
Student ref = new Student();
System.out.println(
   ref.number());
``` | ```
Student s = Student();
Student& ref = s;
Student* pp =
  new Student();
cout << s.number();
cout << ref.number();
cout << pp->number();
``` | A reference must be initialized in a declaration. Once it is initialized, it cannot be changed.<br><br>For objects and references, use the dot notation to access a member; for pointers, use the right-arrow notation. |
| -- | ```
pp = &s;
``` | You can apply the address operator to the existing object. |

class parameters by value, you use a constant pass by reference, and to modify the value of an actual parameter, you use a reference parameter. As always, it is essential that you use constant pass by reference whenever you do not intend to modify the value of the parameter.

To begin this section, I briefly discuss pointer parameters. Although you will probably be able to avoid using these types of parameters (using reference parameters instead), it is still useful to understand how they work.

Whenever you call a function in which you use a pointer parameter passed by value in a function, you may change the value of the object the pointer points to but not the value of the pointer. For example, the operation below modifies the *value to which the pointer points:*

```
// change number if less than 100
void modifySmall(Student* s) {
  long number = s->number();
  if(number < 100)
    s->setNumber(number + 100);
}
```
```

Since the use of pointers is often tricky, you may prefer to modify the parameter by passing it by reference:

```
void modifySmall(Student& s) {
  long number = s.number();          //note: "." rather than "->"
  if(number < 100)
    s.setNumber(number + 100);
}
```

The following operation incorrectly tries to modify the *value of the pointer* s:

```
// create a new student; wrong version
// does not change the actual parameter
void create(Student* s, long number) {
  s = new Student(number);
}
```

The reason that this code is incorrect is that s is passed by value. Recall that to change the value of a parameter, you must pass the parameter by reference:

```
void create(Student*& s, long number) {
  s = new Student(number);
}
```

A better alternative for this example is to use a *function* rather than a procedure:

```
Student* create(long number) {
  return new Student(number);
}
```

Finally, when a parameter of a class type is passed as a nonconstant reference, its value may be changed in the function body; for example:

```
void foo(Student& s) {
  s = global;                          // global variable
  ...
}
```

However, this assignment in the body of foo() is a copy assignment rather than a reference assignment. Therefore, by default, if the assignment operation is not defined, a memberwise copy is performed.

3.8.3   Function-Returning References and Designing Modifiers

In this section, I return to the topic discussed in Section 2.5.6, where I described functions returning references and constant references, except that here the context is class types rather than primitive types. A function may return a reference to a class type; for example:

```
Student& foo();
```

Because that return references do not invoke copy constructors, they may be more efficient than functions that return objects. Using functions that return references can be tricky—you have to have a good understanding of stack-based and heap-based memory allocation. The related issues will be discussed both in this section and the next section.

One of the important applications of functions returning references is writing modifier functions that change *the object from which they are called.* Such functions could be defined as procedures (that are returning void), but this would make the *chaining* of function calls impossible. For example, when you overload an assignment operator, you do not want to be limited to a single assignment:

```
x = y;
```

Instead, you want to be able to "chain" several assignments; for example:

```
x = y = z;
```

You can apply the same technique to other operators—for example, overloading the I/O operators << and>>. Even if it isn't appropriate to use infix notation for the operator you are modifying, the ability to chain calls can still be useful; for example:

```
modifier().modifier();
```

To allow for this operation, the modifier should return a reference type and terminate with a statement of the form

```
return *this;
```

To understand this technique, consider an example of a wrapper class for integers. A **wrapper class** for an item is the class that defines an interface to operate on this item; therefore, a wrapper class for integers would define a private int variable and one or more functions to operate on this variable.

● **EXAMPLE 3.4**

The class `Integer` defined in the following example provides an interface consisting of a constructor, a query, and two modifiers that respectively set the integer value and add another `Integer`. Both modifiers return `*this`:

```
// File: ex3.4.integer.h
// Wrapper for integer
class Integer {
public:
  Integer(int = 0);
  int get() const;
  Integer& set(int);
  Integer& add(const Integer&);
private:
  int value_;
};
```

```
// File: ex3.4.integer.cpp
Integer& Integer::set(int n) {
  value_ = n;
  return *this;
}
```

```
Integer& Integer::add(const Integer& i) {
  value_ += i.value_;
  return *this;
}
```

You can now use this class to chain function calls as follows:

```
Integer i(5);
Integer j(i);            // default copy constructor
i.add(j).add(j);         // chaining: (i.add(j)).add(j)
j = i.set(2).add(3);     // set i to 2 and then add 3, store in j
```

You can also use an `int` as a parameter of `add()`:

```
Integer j = i.add(3);
```

because the single parameter constructor provides a type conversion, which means that the right side of the previous assignment is executed as follows:

```
i.add(Integer(3));
```

Recall that if for some reason this conversion is not desirable, you can make the constructor explicit and add another overloaded operation to perform addition:

```
Integer& Integer::add(int);
```

The modifier function shown in Example 3.4 returns a reference to the *object* being modified. You may be tempted to design a function that returns a reference to an *attribute* of a class. For example, consider a modified version of the class `Integer`:

```
class Integer {
public:
  Integer(int = 0);
  int& value();

private:
  int value_;
};

int& Integer::value() {                                 // modifier
  return value_;
}
```

Recall that a function returning a reference type may appear on the left side of an assignment so it can modify the object from which it is called. For example, you can write

```
Integer i(5);
i.value() = 2;
```

I do *not* recommend this design, however, because the modifier function `value()` provides back-door access to the private variable. You may try to fix this problem by defining a query, declared as a constant member returning a constant reference:

```
const int& Integer::value() const {                     // query
  return value_;
}
```

Because this query function has been specified as `const`, it must return a constant reference. Unfortunately, in general, returning constant references can also be dangerous because the lifetime of the reference can exceed the lifetime of its alias, resulting in a dangling reference. The following example is based on an example from Cline et al. 1999.

```
Integer createZero() {          // a function returning a new object
   return Integer(0);
}

const Integer& yuk(const Integer& i) { // returns constant reference
   return i;
}

void foo() {
   const Integer& g = yuk(createZero());
   cout << g.value();
}
```

When the function yuk() is called, a temporary variable, say temp, is created, making the call equivalent to

```
temp = createZero();
g = yuk(temp);
```

When the function yuk() terminates, the temporary variable temp is deallocated, but g is still an alias to this variable (recall that references result in aliases; see Section 2.4.8). Therefore, the result of the output statement in the function foo() is ill defined.

   Here is a brief summary of this section. A function that is a member of a class and modifies the object from which it is called should be designed to return a reference to the modified object using return *this (this will allow chaining of such functions). For any other situations, functions that return references and constant references should be used with utmost caution. In the next section, I provide more examples to justify this statement.

3.8.4 Returning New Objects

Modifiers return values of a *reference type* because they only modify the existing object (that is, they do not return a new object). In some cases, you want to have the function return a *new object,* as in the following modification of the Integer class:

```
class Integer {
public:
   Integer(int = 0);
   Integer clone() const;
private:
   int value_;
};
```

```
Integer Integer::clone() const {
  Integer res(value_);
  return res;
}
```

This implementation creates a new object *on the stack* and returns it. You can use this function as follows:

```
Integer k(5);
Integer m = k.clone();
m.clone() = 7;
```

The second line clones the object k and then assigns the new object to the variable m (using a copy constructor—in this case, its default version). The third line is syntactically correct but not very useful; it creates a clone of the object m and initializes it with the value 7. Although this new object is not accessible anymore, this is not a memory leak. The object is allocated on the stack, so it will be popped off the stack when the temporary variable used to store the clone goes out of scope.

Returning New Object Idiom 3.5

An operation in a class C that returns a new object should have a return type C and should allocate this object on the stack.

Advanced

In many cases, it is sufficient to understand the description preceding Idiom 3.5, but to cover all your bases, you should also understand the following more detailed description of the order of constructor and destructor calls. To make the example more constructive, I add a destructor to the class Integer:

```
Integer::~Integer() {
  cout << "destructor = " << value_ << endl;
}
```

When the following three lines of code are executed:

```
Integer k(5);
Integer m = k.clone();
m.clone() = 7;
```

the output looks like this:

```
destructor = 5
destructor = 5
destructor = 7
destructor = 7
destructor = 5
destructor = 5
```

To understand this output, first take a close look at this line of code:

```
Integer m = k.clone();
```

When this line is executed, the function clone() is called, a local variable res is pushed onto the stack, and the value of res is returned. The latter action is performed by using a temporary variable, temp, and initializing this variable with the value of res using a compiler-generated copy constructor. Next, the function clone() terminates, and the variable res goes out of scope, resulting in the first call to the destructor. Finally, the variable temp is destructed, calling the destructor for the second time. Now consider this line of the code previously executed:

```
m.clone() = 7;
```

First, the constructor for the class Integer is called to convert the value 7 to Integer(7), and then the copy constructor is called. Next, the function clone() is called, and as before, this call results in two calls to the destructor. Finally, variables m and k and the clone of m go out of scope, resulting in three more calls to the destructor.

You may consider all these calls to be inefficient, but in C++ , *there is no better way* to implement operations that return new objects. Several examples help show why this is so. First, the following implementation of a function that returns a reference to a new object is incorrect:

```
Integer& Integer::clone() {          // can't return object on stack
  Integer copy(value_);
  return copy;
}
```

This code does not compile because copy is an object allocated on the stack and will be deallocated as soon as the function terminates. In general, the compiler tries not let you create an external reference to a stack object that might result in a *dangling reference.* However, you can create a new object on the heap using the new operator:

```
Integer& Integer::clone() {          // creates dangling reference
  Integer* copy = new Integer(value_);
```

```
    return *copy;
}
```

Note that in the `return` statement, I used `*copy` because `copy` is a pointer. The previous version is *incorrect* (although it does compile), because it creates a memory leak. For example, consider:

```
Integer i(5);
Integer j = i.clone();
```

The call to `clone()` allocates an object on the heap, and this object is used to initialize the variable `j`. Unfortunately, that object is not deallocated and becomes unusable (garbage). Therefore, as I explained previously, the only correct way to return a new object is to allocate this object on the stack and return it.

Common Errors

1. Never return a reference to a local stack-based object.
2. A function should not return a reference to a heap-based object that was allocated in the function.
3. A function should not return a constant reference to its parameter passed by constant reference.

3.8.5   Class Attributes of a Reference Type

A pointer class attribute provides a link with an external object, effectively supporting object composition (described in more detail in Section 4.3). You must take care to ensure that the external object pointed to by the pointer attribute is not deallocated before it is accessed through the pointer (deallocating such an object would lead to a *dangling pointer*). This link between the pointer attribute and the external object can be modified at runtime by changing the value of the pointer. A reference class attribute provides a slightly different type of link—an alias, which is a *permanent link* with the enclosing object established in the constructor. For example, in the `Student` class, you can add a reference class attribute to `string` that will represent a unique name:

```
class Student;
class NamedStudent {
public:
```

```
    NamedStudent(string&, const Student&);
    void setName(const string&);
    ...
private:
    string& name_;
    const Student& stud_;
};

NamedStudent::NamedStudent(string& name, const Student& s) :
    name(name_), stud_(s)
{}
```

Once a reference attribute has been assigned a value, it cannot be changed. In the previous code, the name can be modified but the student cannot; for example:

```
    string t("tom");
    Student s(100);
    NamedStudent ns(t, s);
    string t1("Tom");
    ns.setName(t1);                           // set name to "Tom"
```

As I stated at the beginning of this section, you have to be careful to avoid dangling references. For example

```
void foo() {
    string t("tom");
    Student s(100);
    NamedStudent ns(t, s);
    ...
}
```

is safe because the objects t, s, and ns have the same lifetime. On the other hand, the following code leads to a dangling reference:

```
string* p = new string("tom");
Student s(100);
NamedStudent ns(*p, s);
delete p;                                  // now, stud_ is dangling
```

The next example uses the class FileOps from Example 3.3, which provides three file-processing functions to find the number of words, characters, and lines in a file, respectively, using caching. An alternative implementation uses class attributes that are of a reference type instead of mutable members. But first the Cache must be defined:

```
struct Cache {
  bool linesCached;
  long lines;
  bool wordsCached;
  long words;
  bool charsCached;
  long chars;

  Cache();
};

Cache::Cache() {
  linesCached = wordsCached = charsCached = false;
  lines = words = chars = 0;
}
```

The structure Cache has all its attributes specified as public; this is not a design flaw because it is hidden from the client. Now consider the class FileOps, which contains a cache:

```
class FileOps {
public:
  FileOps(const string, Cache&);
  FileOps(const FileOps&);
  long lines() const;
  long words() const;
  long chars() const;
  ~FileOps();
  // should have assignment operator
private:
  string filename_;
  ifstream fileVar_;
  Cache& myCache_;
};
```

If the variable myCache_ were defined to be of type Cache, then the variable would represent a nested object, and it would have to be defined as mutable because its value is modified by constant functions, such as lines(). Reference and pointer attributes have the values referenced by them changed instead of their own values, and so they do not have to be specified as mutable. Note that reference variables, like constants, must be initialized by the constructor. Therefore, the constructor for FileOps is defined as follows:

```
FileOps::FileOps(const string filename, Cache& c) : myCache_(c) {
```

```
    . . .
  }
```

The weakness of this solution is that the client has to provide the value for the variable `myCache_`, which means that the cache structure is made visible to the client. The cache structure should only be visible to the implementation. The client can be released from the responsibility of providing the actual parameter by making use of a default parameter in the constructor:

```
FileOps::FileOps(const string filename, Cache& c = Cache())
  : myCache_(c) {
  . . .
}
```

But the visibility problem remains (that is, `Cache` still appears in the constructor's *declaration*). To solve this problem, the reference type of `myCache_` can be replaced by a pointer type:

```
class FileOps {
public:
  FileOps(const string);                      // new constructor
  FileOps(const FileOps&);
  long lines() const;
  long words() const;
  long chars() const;
  ~FileOps();
private:
  string filename_;
  ifstream fileVar_;
  Cache* myCache_;
};
```

With this technique, the `Cache` type can be hidden from the client. The initialization of the cache is done through a member-initialization list, which appears only in the constructor *definition,* in the implementation file:

```
FileOps::FileOps(const string filename) : myCache_(new Cache()) {
  . . .
}
```

Because of this change, a destructor is now needed:

```
FileOps::~FileOps(){
  delete myCache_;
}
```

A class with a constant member or a member of a reference type does not have a default constructor; you need to write one.

3.9 Resources Management, Part I: Using Constructors, Assignment Operators, and Destructors

Section 3.4.6 described how the C++ runtime system maintains nested objects. They are allocated and initialized when the surrounding object is created, and destroyed and deallocated when the surrounding object is destroyed. In some instances, you need more control over the maintenance of an object; for example, when an object needs to explicitly maintain resources, such as a memory block or a file. In this section, I provide a more general discussion of resource maintenance and describe circumstances under which you need to define your own versions of the following four operations: constructor, copy constructor, assignment operator, and destructor.

3.9.1 Correct Approach

Following Coplien (1992), I introduce a **canonical construction idiom** that describes the basic requirements for a class that manages resources.

Canonical Construction Idiom 3.6

1. When a class manages a resource, it should have its own constructor, copy constructor, assignment operator, and destructor.
2. The constructor should initialize class attributes and, in particular, allocate required resources.
3. The copy constructor should copy every element that needs to be copied (excluding static data).
4. The assignment operator should release resources that are assigned to the left side of the assignment and then copy elements from the right side to the corresponding elements of the left side.
5. The destructor should release all resources.

The exact meaning of the term *copy* used in the canonical construction idiom depends on the specific kind of resource and on your application. For example, copying an object that maintains a list of elements will likely require a deep copy of all these elements.

To explain these concepts, consider a class that maintains information about a single student:

```
class Student {
public:
  Student(long);
  void number(long);
  long number() const;
private:
  long number_;
};

class InfoStudent {
public:
  InfoStudent(long);                          // constructor
  InfoStudent(const InfoStudent&);            // copy constructor
  ~InfoStudent();                             // destructor
  InfoStudent& operator=(const InfoStudent&); // assignment
  long number() const;
private:
  Student* rep_;
};
```

An object of the class InfoStudent does not have a nested subobject of the class Student; instead, it has a pointer to that object. In the following discussion, the Student object represents a resource to be maintained by the code.

The signature of the **assignment operator** requires additional explanation. The name

```
operator=
```

is used in C++ to *overload* the default meaning of the operator =. (As you will see in Section 7.3, other operators may be overloaded as well.) Overloading standard operators allows you to use well-known operations, such as = or + for parameters of user-defined classes; it also allows you to use the more familiar infix notation rather than a function call notation. The assignment operator is a modifier that does not change the value of its parameter, which represents the right side of the assignment (this is why the parameter is passed as a constant reference). The definition of the assignment operator for the current example follows:

```
InfoStudent& InfoStudent::operator=(const InfoStudent& s) {

                            // (1) Check for self-assignments
  if(this == &s)
    return *this;

                    // (2) release resource maintained by the LHS
  delete rep_;

                    // (3) copy resource maintained by the RHS
  rep_ = new Student(s.number());
  return *this;

}
```

The first conditional statement is needed because without it, the assignment

```
x = x;
```

where x is a variable of type InfoStudent would release a resource associated with
the right side of the assignment (statement 2) and would then be unable to copy it
to the left side. Note that statement 1 in the previous code compares two memory
addresses, the value of this and the value of the address of the object s. Changing
this comparison into

```
*this == s
```

is likely wrong because you cannot compare two objects (unless you previously defined an overloaded equality operator).

The code for the constructor, copy constructor, and destructor follows:

```
InfoStudent::InfoStudent(long number) {
  rep_ = new Student(number);
}


InfoStudent::InfoStudent(const InfoStudent& s) {
                            // (3) copy resource maintained by s
  rep_ = new Student(s.number());
}


InfoStudent::~InfoStudent() {
                            // (2) release resource
```

```
    delete rep_;
}
```

1. When overloading an assignment operator, check for self-assignments.
2. If a class has an attribute of a reference type or a constant attribute, and if you want to be able to assign class objects, you cannot use a default assignment operator. To support the described functionality, you must define an overloaded assignment operator.

Recall that `delete` calls the destructor to release any resources that may have been acquired by its parameter. For example, if a class `Registrar` maintains an object of the class `InfoStudent`

```
class Registrar {
  ...
private:
  InfoStudent* is_;
  ...
};
```

then

```
    delete is_;
```

works as follows:

- call a destructor for the class `InfoStudent`.
- this destructor executes: `delete rep_`.
- the `delete` statement executes a destructor for the class `Student` (void in this example).
- memory for the object pointed to by `rep_` is deallocated.
- the destructor for the class `InfoStudent` terminates.
- memory for the object pointed to by `is_` is deallocated.

From this example, it should be evident that a properly designed destructor always releases all resources automatically.

3.9.2 Incorrect Approach

In this section, I provide several examples that show what can go wrong if you do *not* use the canonical construction idiom. To understand this discussion, you need to know a bit about heap organization. Think of a heap as a list of memory blocks, called a free list; initially it is just a one-element list, consisting of a large memory block. Whenever there is a request to allocate a block of memory, this block is extracted from the free list. Typically, this block has enough memory to satisfy a request and to store a variety of system information, such as the size of the block. Deallocation of a block uses any necessary system information to insert this block back into the free list (for example, information may be needed to decide whether this block could be merged with one of its neighbors). If the user follows the rules of dynamic memory management, everything will work as expected. However, erroneous operations, such as an accidental overwriting of system information in a free list, will destroy the data needed to maintain the free list—a symptom known as a **heap corruption**. This is a very serious problem because even if the heap does get corrupted, your program may continue running for a while and then crash for no obvious reason.

Consider again the class that manages a `Student` resource but without the copy constructor, destructor, and assignment operators:

```
class InfoStudent {                        // creates a memory leak
public:
  InfoStudent(long);
  long number() const;
  void number(long);
private:
  Student* rep_;
};
```

The first problem is that without the destructor, a memory leak can occur:

```
void foo() {
  InfoStudent kasia(100);
  ...
}
```

When `foo()` terminates, the object `kasia` is popped from the stack; however, the object pointed to by the pointer `rep_` is *not* deallocated from the heap, which means that it now uses memory that cannot be accessed or reclaimed. To solve this problem, you could add a destructor (as shown in the previous section). Unfortunately, with the destructor and without a copy constructor, the problem has become even worse: instead of just having a memory leak, you may be *corrupting* memory. To see why, consider two `InfoStudent` objects that share the same student:

```
void foo() {
  InfoStudent kasia(100);
  InfoStudent michael(kasia);
  ...
}
```

When the function `foo()` terminates, a destructor for the object `kasia` will deallocate memory for the student. Then the destructor for the object `michael` will attempt to deallocate the same student object, which will result in a corruption of the heap. (The second `delete` may corrupt the heap because it assumes that its parameter is pointing to a block of used memory, although after the first `delete`, the block is already back in the free list.)

The addition of both a copy constructor and an assignment operator fixes this problem—and is equivalent to the use of the canonical construction idiom. Remember that you should use this idiom whenever the class manages a resource, for example, through a pointer.

3.10 *Arrays*

The usefulness of C++ arrays is limited because *vectors,* which will be described in Section 8.9.1, are more powerful and convenient (for example, the size of a vector can be determined at runtime). However, various programs may make rudimentary use of arrays of objects, so I describe them here (you may wish to review Section 2.4.7, where I first introduced arrays).

An array of objects requires a no-arg constructor because there is no way to specify the actual parameter of a constructor, which is called for all of the array elements when the array is created; for example:

```
class Student {
public:
  Student(long = 0);            // no-arg constructor
  ...
};

Student course[100];           // call constructor for each object
```

The size of the array `course` is a *compile-time constant,* and this array is allocated on the *stack.* When it goes out of scope, the destructor is called for each object in the array. Clearly, using the magic number 100 is not appropriate; a symbolic constant to represent the size of the array should be used instead. To specify the size of the array, you can use an enumerator; for example:

```
class StudentInfo {
public:
  StudentInfo(long = 0);                    // no-arg constructor
  enum {SIZE = 100};
  ...
private:
  Student course[SIZE];
};
```

You can also use a static constant attribute

```
class StudentInfo {
public:
  StudentInfo(long = 0);
  const static int Size = 100;
  ...
private:
  Student course[Size];
};
```

and include

```
const int Student::Size;
```

in the implementation code.

I recommend the first technique—that is, the use of an enumerator—because constant integer static variables are the only variables that can be initialized within the class definition, and that type of code is not very common and may be confusing to some.

An alternative solution is to create an array of objects of a size that is known at *runtime,* and allocate it on the *heap*; for example:

```
Student* registrar = new Student[n];
```

Note that the value of n does not have to be known at compile time. The call will use the heap to allocate a sufficiently large block of memory to store n objects of type Student, and then the constructor for each object will be executed to initialize each object. This type of array works the same in C++ as in Java, except you have to remember to explicitly deallocate the C++ array. To deallocate an array of objects that has been allocated on the heap, use delete[]; for example:

```
delete [] registrar;
```

It is important to understand that both course and registrar are arrays of objects rather than arrays of pointers to objects. Compare these with Java arrays:

```
Student[] reg = new Student[n];        // hold references to objects
reg[0] = new Student(...);
```

Common Errors

1. To create a dynamic array p of size n consisting of elements of type T, use the following syntax:

   ```
   p = new T[n];                              // square brackets
   ```

   Remember that T needs a no-arg constructor. If instead you wrote:

   ```
   p = new T(n);                              // round brackets
   ```

   it would work only if the type T had a constructor requiring a single parameter (for example, if T was a primitive data type, such as int), and if so, this statement would allocate memory for a *single* value of type T and initialize it with the value of n.

2. To delete an array p of objects, use delete [] p rather than delete p.

3. Use delete [] only for arrays allocated using new.

● EXAMPLE 3.5

In this example, I use a *bounded* integer stack, implemented as an array. The size of the stack will be fixed in the constructor. You should examine all of the constructors, destructors, and operator definitions carefully and make certain that you understand the need for them. This example uses a rather primitive form of error handling that uses various values of an enumeration data type and relies on the user to use these values to test whether an operation is successful or not. (Example 5.3 shows a different error technique using exception handling.)

```
// File: ex3.5.intstack.h
// Bounded stack of integers
// There are three stack operations available:
//    push() to push an integer
//    pop() to pop and return the top of the stack
//    top() to return the top of the stack without popping it.
// If any operation fails then it sets the appropriate error
//    code, which can be obtained with getError()
//    and cleared using clearError().
// Note: this implementation does not provide an empty() operation
//    that checks whether the stack is empty
class IntStack {
public:
  explicit IntStack(int = 100);                 // default size
```

```cpp
  IntStack(const IntStack&);
  ~IntStack();
  IntStack& operator=(const IntStack&);
  void push(int);
  void pop();
  int top() const;

  enum ErrorState {STACK_OK, STACK_FULL, STACK_EMPTY};
  void clearError();
  ErrorState getError() const;
private:
  int top_;
  int* stack_;
  int size_;
  ErrorState errorState_;
};

// File: ex3.5.intstack.cpp
IntStack::IntStack(int size) {
  top_ = -1;
  size_ = size;
  stack_ = new int[size];
  errorState_ = STACK_OK;
}


IntStack::IntStack(const IntStack& s) {
  top_ = s.top_;
  size_ = s.size_;
  stack_ = new int[size_];
  for(int i = 0; i <= top_; ++i)
    stack_[i] = s.stack_[i];
  errorState_ = s.errorState_;
}


IntStack& IntStack::operator=(const IntStack& s) {
  if(this == &s)
    return *this;
  if(size_ != s.size_) {
    delete [] stack_;
    stack_ = new int[s.size_];
  }
  top_ = s.top_;
  size_ = s.size_;
  for(int i = 0; i <= top_; ++i)
```

```
    stack_[i] = s.stack_[i];
  errorState_ = s.errorState_;
  return *this;
}

IntStack::~IntStack() {
  delete [] stack_;
}

void IntStack::push(int i) {
  if(top_ == size_ - 1) {                           // full
    errorState_ = STACK_FULL;
    return;
  }
  stack_[++top_] = i;
  errorState_ = STACK_OK;
}

int IntStack::top() const {
  if(top_ == -1) {                                  // empty
    errorState_ = STACK_EMPTY;
    return 0;                    // must return something
  }

  errorState_ = STACK_OK;
  return[top_];
}

void IntStack::pop() {
  if(top_ == -1) {                                  // empty
    errorState_ = STACK_EMPTY;
    return;
  }

  errorState_ = STACK_OK;
  top_--;
}

void IntStack::clearError() {

  errorState_ = STACK_OK;
}

ErrorState IntStack::getError() const {
  return errorState_;
}
```

The client can use the class as follows:

```
IntStack s(20), t = s;                    // t is a deep copy of s
s.push(20);
if(s.getError() == IntStack::STACK_FULL) {
  cout << "can't happen";
  s.clearError();
}
```

Note that on detecting an error, such as an attempt to pop from an empty stack, the execution of the code in this example proceeds. It is up to the user to check if an error has occurred and if so, how to handle it. Although this technique separates the detection of an error and the handling of it, it is inferior to exception-handling techniques.

3.11 *Exercises*

EXERCISE 3-1

Implement a class, Encoding, that implements this interface:

```
char encode(char c);
    // For any ASCII character c, encode(c) is an ASCII
    // character different from c; for any non-ASCII
    // character c, encode(c) = c
    //
char decode(char c);
    // For any character c, decode( encode(c) ) = c
```

EXERCISE 3-2

Implement a class, Fractions, that represents fractions. This class should provide a constructor and four functions to add, subtract, multiply, and divide fractions. Fractions should always be reduced to lowest terms. Test this class in the main program.

EXERCISE 3-3

Write a class, Lines, that provides the following four operations on lines:

- Test if two lines are parallel.
- Test if two lines are perpendicular.
- Find the intersection of two lines (assume that this function is not called if the two lines are parallel).
- Find the shortest distance between a line and a point.

Handle all kinds of lines, including lines of the form y=b and x=c. Test this class in the main program.

EXERCISE 3-4

Implement a class, SetOper, that provides several simple set operations. The class only needs to deal with sets that are closed intervals, specified by two real numbers; for example, the pair (2.5, 4.5) represents the interval [2.5, 4.5]. The following operations should be supported:

- Check if the value x belongs to the given interval.
- Check if the value x belongs to the intersection of two intervals.
- Check if the value x belongs to the union of two intervals.

Test this class in the main program.

EXERCISE 3-5

Write a class, Lists, that represents a list of double values. You will need to create a nested class that represents a list element; it should look like this:

```
struct node {
   struct node *next;
   double value;
}
```

The Lists class should have the following interface:

- Constructor, copy constructor, and destructor.
- remove(double d, int deleteFlag) to remove the first element containing the value equal to d if deleteFlag is equal to 0, greater than d if deleteFlag is 1, and less than d if deleteFlag is -1. By default, deleteFlag is equal to 0 (do nothing if there is no element equal to d).
- insert(), to insert a new double value in front of the list
- print(), to output all values
- largest(), to output the largest element of the list

Three functions listed above may have some parameters: Finally, write a menu-driven program to test all these functions.

EXERCISE 3-6

Write a class Point that represents a point in a three-dimensional space. Carefully design the interface for this class and include functions that appear to be useful for operating on points. Then, implement a class, Cube, which represents a cube whose sides are parallel to x, y, and z axes. Write two constructors: one that uses the bottom-left corner and the length of a side, and the other that uses two corners to create a cube. The corner, or corners, should be represented as nested objects of class Point. The constructor should throw an exception if its parameters are incorrect. Carefully design the interface for this class and include functions that appear to be useful for operating on points. Finally, write a program to test both classes.

EXERCISE 3-7

Repeat Exercise 3-6, but this time use pointers to points rather than nested objects in the class Cube.

EXERCISE 3-8

Write a class, Employee, that represents an employee with three attributes: name, salary, and ID. ID numbers for new employees are assigned values 1000, 1001, and so on. Carefully design the interface for this class, and then write the following classes:

- Company1, which represents a company that can hire up to 10 employees. These employees are stored in an array.
- Company2, which represents a company that can hire up to n employees, where the value of n is determined in the constructor. These employees are stored in an array.

Finally, write a main program to both classes.

EXERCISE 3-9

Design and implement the following classes:

- Flower, with three attributes: name, price, and color (use enumeration type to represent color)
- Book, with two attributes: name and price
- Gift, with two attributes representing a flower and a book, accomplished by using nested objects

Carefully design the interfaces for these classes, and write a program to test them.

EXERCISE 3-10

Repeat Exercise 3-9, but this time use pointers to represent a flower and a book.

EXERCISE 3-11

Implement wrapper classes for float and double values, similar to the class in Example 3.4.

EXERCISE 3-12

Write a class, Student, with two attributes, a name and an ID. Redesign the class IntStack from Example 3.5 and implement a stack of students. Carefully design the interfaces for these classes, and write a program to test them.

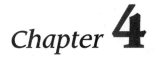

Chapter 4

OBJECT-BASED PROGRAMMING, PART II

4.1 Preview

In the previous chapter, I introduced object-based programming that uses objects but does not use inheritance. It is a complex topic, so in this chapter, I continue the discussion. The next chapter will cover inheritance and object-oriented programming.

In this chapter, I introduce the Unified Modeling Language (UML), which is a modeling language helpful for expressing software design. The remainder of the book uses UML, so you should read this section carefully. I also discuss object composition techniques, introduce several new idioms, and present the first design pattern, the singleton, which is used to constrain object instantiation. Next, I return to the topic of namespaces and provide a detailed discussion of how to use them. Then, I show how header files can be used to avoid unnecessary recompilations. Finally, I provide an example of an application that shows how to use namespaces.

4.2 UML Class Notations

In this section, I introduce UML and its notations used for classes; in the next chapter, I will introduce UML notations related to inheritance. As its name suggests, UML is a modeling language that provides graphical notations to express system design. UML reifies program structure and relationships between program entities; that is, it treats these abstract concepts as if they had a concrete existence. You get a better feel for a program's design by looking at UML's graphical presentation than by examining the source code. Although this book is *not* about object-oriented analysis and design, it is useful to show various idioms and patterns using UML, which is why I introduce a small subset of this language (for details of UML, see Fowler, 2000).

4.2.1   Terminology and Notations

UML supports graphical notations, called diagrams. In this book, I use the UML *class diagram,* which describes classes and their static relationships. UML defines other types of diagrams, such as use-case diagrams and interaction diagrams (which describe collaboration between objects), but because I do not use them in this book, I do not describe them here.

4.2.2   Class Diagrams

Class diagrams describe classes and two kinds of static relationships: associations and subtypes. In this section, I discuss classes and associations, postponing a discussion of derived classes until Chapter 5.

Figure 4.1 shows the UML representation of the following class:

```
class Student {
public:
  Student(long);
  static string university();
  void number(long);
  long number() const;
private:
  static string university_;
  long number_;
};
```

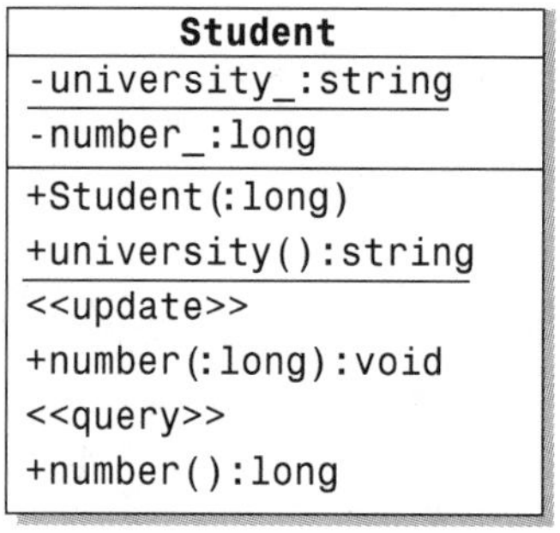

```
                    Student
          -university_:string
          -number_:long
          +Student(:long)
          +university():string
          <<update>>
          +number(:long):void
          <<query>>
          +number():long
```

Figure 4.1.   UML representation of class Student

Here is a summary of the notation used in the UML class diagram:

- A class is represented as a rectangle, with three compartments, showing the class name, attributes, and functions, respectively (see Figure 4.1).
- Static features are underlined.
- The visibility indicator is + for public features, – for private features, and # for protected features.
- Operations are represented using syntax different from C++, which is of the form

    visibility name(parameters, if any) : returnType

  for example

    +number(: long): void

  represents a public feature `number()`, which has one `long` parameter, and `void` return type.
- A **stereotype**, which is of the form <<text>>, is used to extend UML with your own notation. For example, you can use a <<constructor>> stereotype, or an <<interface>> stereotype (the former is used to describe classes that have only operations and no attributes). In Figure 4.1, two `number()` functions are defined: an <<update>> stereotype is in front of the first function `number(long)`, and a <<query>> stereotype is in front of the second function `number()`.
- **Constraints** may be included; for example, preconditions for operations may be specified, or the value of an attribute may be constrained to be *frozen*, or constant.
- Comments can be added to UML diagrams, using rectangles with their upper-right corners turned down. Each comment is attached by a dashed line to the appropriate element of the diagram (see Figure 4.2).
- Any information deemed irrelevant to the application at hand may be omitted from a UML diagram. A class may be represented by two compartments, if attributes are not important, or even one compartment, if just the name of the class is useful. Not all features have to be shown, if some are omitted, an ellipsis (...) is used.

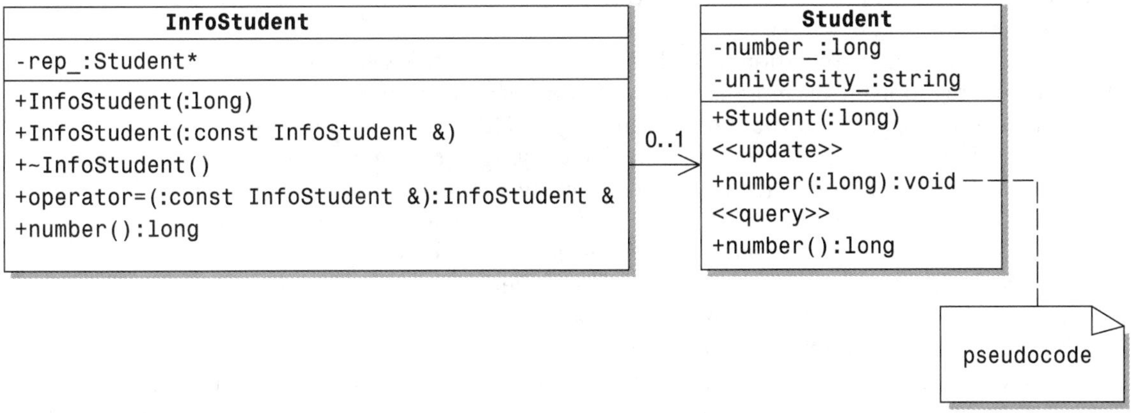

Figure 4.2 Association between two classes

In the following general description, I show two specific kinds of associations: aggregations and compositions. At this point, I do not provide implementation techniques for these kinds of associations; I will discuss some of these techniques later in Section 4.3.

Associations between classes represent relationships between objects of these classes (for example, a student information system stores various data about students). Associations represent **responsibilities** (for example, the information system is *responsible* for maintaining and providing information about students; or a factory is *responsible* for creating products). Gamma et al. (1995) use the term **acquaintance** rather than association because it implies that one object knows about another object.

There is an association between the `Student` and `InfoStudent` classes in the class diagram shown in Figure 4.2, depicted as a line between the two classes. Each association has two ends, sometimes called **roles**. An association, as well as its roles, may be labeled; association labels are capitalized, role labels appear in lowercase. In Figure 4.2, the association and roles are not labeled. When labels are missing, the roles are named after the target classes; (so the association in the figure has the roles `student` and `infostudent`).

Roles may have **multiplicity indicators**. In Figure 4.2, the multiplicity `0..1` of the role `student` indicates that there is at most one student object participating in this association. In general, you can use the following multiplicity indicators:

- A range of the form `i..j`, where `i<j`, and `i` and `j` are non-negative integers (to represent infinity, `j` is equal to `*`); for example, `1..*` represents at least one object
- A single number `i` to represent `i..i`
- A `*` to represent `0..*`
- A discrete range, such as `2,4`

Finally, note that associations may or may not have arrowheads, which indicate the direction of the association. The association in Figure 4.2 has an arrow to indicate that `InfoStudent` has a responsibility to specify which `Student` it corresponds to, but not the other way around. Lack of a navigation arrow indicates that the navigability is undecided (at this stage of modeling).

A special kind of association, called an **aggregation**, is the *whole/part-of* relationship. Aggregation means more than association, because in this type of relationship the aggregator is responsible for the aggregatee (therefore, this relationship defines a tighter coupling between objects). Typically, aggregation implies containment. In UML, aggregation is denoted by a *hollow diamond* at the end of an association that specifies the aggregator. To clarify this concept, consider a class `Student` (aggregator) that has a name (aggregatee) using an object of class `StudentName` (see Figure 4.3). Based on multiplicity indicators, each student has exactly one name, but the same name may be used to name many students (for example, there may be many students called John Smith or Jan Kowalski).

Aggregation does not imply lifetime dependencies between the classes; for example, in Figure 4.3, students can change their names. If both ownership and lifetime dependencies are required, then they can be expressed using a specific kind of aggregation, called a **composition** (or composite aggregation). A composition implies that

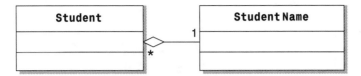

Figure 4.3 Aggregation between two classes

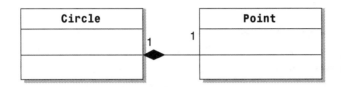

Figure 4.4 Composition between two classes

the part object may belong to only one whole object, and the composer and composee have identical lifetimes. In UML, a composition is denoted by a *filled diamond* at the end of an association that specifies the composer. Changing the aggregation in Figure 4.3 to composition would imply that the student's name cannot change. To clarify this concept, consider an example of a class `Circle` that uses the class `Point` to denote its origin (see Figure 4.4). Not only is a point part of a circle, but also a point and a circle have the same lifetime: a point is deallocated together with its corresponding circle.

4.3   *Reusability Through Object Composition*

To reuse existing functionality in object-oriented systems, you apply use two techniques: class inheritance and object composition. I will discuss the former technique in the next chapter and concentrate here on the latter technique, in Section 6.5.2 I will describe how you can use both techniques at the same time. **Object composition** provides new functionality by *composing* objects. This technique can be qualified as a **black-box reusability**, because objects appear as black boxes, with no internal details visible. For example, consider two classes: F, with the interface consisting of `foo1()` and `foo2()`, and G, with the interface consisting of `goo1()` and `goo2()`. You can combine these two interfaces if you let F have a pointer to G. Figure 4.5 shows the composition, in which F has 0 or 1 associated instances of G.

In general, you can implement object composition by using one of two techniques; the following terminology was first used by Lipmann (1998):

- **By value**, using nested objects
- **By reference**, using references or pointers

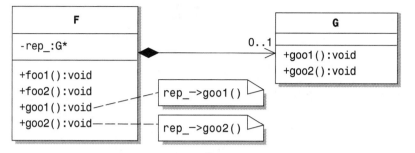

Figure 4.5 Combining interfaces

For example, consider two classes, called `Associator` and `Associatee`. By value object composition means that the `Associatee` object is *nested* in the `Associator` object, and by reference object composition means that the `Associator` object has a *pointer* or a *reference* to the `Associatee` object; see Figure 4.6.

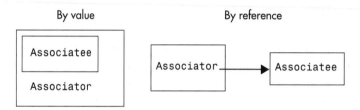

Figure 4.6 Two kinds of object composition

Which of these two techniques is better? By value object composition implies a static structure that cannot be updated to satisfy the changing requirements of the program. While access to objects is efficient (there is no need for indirect access through pointers or references), copying large objects may be inefficient. On the other hand, by reference object composition is defined dynamically, through pointers or references accessing other objects. The most important advantage of a by reference object composition is that it can be used for polymorphic programming, described in detail in Chapters 5 and 6.

As I mentioned in Section 3.8.5, using a reference to implement a by reference object composition requires that the reference attribute be initialized in the constructor. If you want to be able to switch between various `Associatee` objects at *runtime,* you have to use a pointer rather than a reference. For the same reason, you need to use a pointer to take advantage of lazy evaluation. Lazy evaluation means that you access the `Associatee` object through an operation that uses a pointer. This pointer is initialized to 0, and when the operation is executed for the first time, it sets the pointer to the `Associatee` object.

A specific application of object composition is **delegation**, in which an object that is receiving messages, a *delegator,* delegates these requests to a *delegatee* object. Often combined with inheritance, delegation is heavily used in design patterns. The reason for its popularity is that while inheritance nicely captures a "is a kind of" relationship, delegation is more suitable for capturing a "is a role played by" relationship. Pure inheritance is static, which means that to use it to represent an object whose role may change over time, you have to try to predict all possible roles. This leads to class proliferation and forces you to use multiple objects to play the different roles.

As an example of delegation, consider a general windowing system, which delegates all its requests to a base class containing various implementations of operations on windows. Due to the polymorphic nature of the language, objects of various classes, such as the object representing the X window implementation or IBM's PM window implementation, can be substituted for the object of the general base class.

Java programmers are quite familiar with delegation because the language classes include many examples of it (such as when an event model delegates events to the listeners). I will revisit delegation in Section 6.5.2.

4.4 *Managing the Creational Process, Part I*

Typically, the process of creating new objects involves the use of constructors, and the process of copying objects involves the use of copy constructors and overloaded assignment operations. However, sometimes you need to gain more control over these processes, for example, to forbid their use or to make them more flexible. In the next two sections, I describe how to accomplish both goals.

4.4.1 Forbidding Copying

Some classes do not support *copying* of their objects, for various reasons; for example:

- Each student should have a unique student number; therefore, it should not be possible to copy student object.
- A class represents a large collection that should not be copied.

For such classes, the copy constructor and assignment operator are made private (if a derived class needs these operators, they should be made protected):

```cpp
class Student {
public:
   explicit Student(long);
   ~Student();
   long number() const;
private:
   Student(const Student&);               // private copy constructor
   Student& operator=(const Student&);    // private assignment
   long number_;
};
```

This `Student` class does not allow you to copy its objects:

```
Student is(100);
Student js = is;                        // private copy constructor
```

Moreover, you cannot pass `Student` objects as value parameters or write functions that return objects of this class. Note that if I had not *declared* a copy constructor and an assignment operator in the preceding example, then I would have used implicitly generated, public versions of these operators.

You may wish to add an additional constraint to the class `Student` that would forbid even member functions (that always have access to private features) from calling the copy constructor and assignment operator. This technique is a bit strange in that it relies on the fact that it is possible to get a clean compilation of a program that declares but does not *define* a function, provided the function is never called. Therefore, to prevent the use of the two operations in the `Student` class, you declare them but don't define them; if they ever do get called, then the linker will complain.

Forbid Copying Idiom 4.1

To forbid the copying of objects, make the copy constructor and overloaded assignment operator private (or protected).

4.4.2   Forbidding Constructors: Instantiating Operations

In the previous section, I described how to forbid object copying by specifying the copy constructor and the assignment operator as private. In this section, I show how to take over the construction process by using regular class operations rather than constructors. Specifically, to construct an object, a class provides one or more public static functions, which in this book are called **instantiating operations**.

Instantiating Operations Idiom 4.2

To take over the creational process, make *all* constructors either private or protected and provide static functions, called instantiating operations, that create and return an object.

The next example is based on Cline et al. (1999).

● EXAMPLE 4.1

There are two commonly used coordinate systems in a two dimensional space: Cartesian (using x and y coordinates) and polar (using a radius and an angle). The class `Point` shown below incorrectly overloads its constructor in an attempt to support both kinds of coordinates:

```
class Point {
public:
  Point(double x, double y);    // Cartesian
  Point(double r, double a);    // Polar; error: duplicate declaration
  ...
};
```

Using the instantiating operations idiom, I hide the constructors and provide two static functions to construct the Cartesian and the polar systems, respectively. Both these functions return new objects, so they are designed following the returning new object idiom (Idiom 3.5):

```
// File ex4.1.point.h
class Point {
public:
  static Point cartesian(double, double); //instantiating operation
  static Point polar(double, double);     //instantiating operation
private:
  Point(double, double);
  double x_;
  double y_;
};

  // File: ex4.1.point.cpp
#include <cmath>
Point::Point(double x, double y): x_(x), y_(y) { }

Point Point::cartesian(double x, double y) {
  return Point(x, y);
}

Point Point::polar(double radius, double angle) {
  return Point(radius*cos(angle), radius*sin(angle));
}
```

The implementation of `polar()` uses `sin()` and `cos()` defined in `cmath`. Users of the class `Point` cannot define points using the constructor; for example, this is wrong:

```
Point p(1,2);                              // private constructor
```

but users can define points using the appropriate *instantiating operation*; for example:

```
Point p1 = Point::cartesian(5.7, 1.2);
Point p2 = Point::polar(5.7, 0.2);
```

The class `Point` from Example 4.1 does not know which coordinate system it is using. If this is essential, you can add an enumeration type constant to hold this information, modifying `Point` as follows (see also Figure 4.7):

```
// File: ex4.1a.point.h
class Point {
public:
  static Point cartesian(double, double);
  static Point polar(double, double);
  enum System {CARTESIAN, POLAR};
  const System kind;
private:
  Point(double, double, System);
  double x_;
  double y_;
};

// File ex4.1a.point.cpp
Point::Point(double x, double y, System k): kind(k), x_(x), y_(y) {
}

Point Point::cartesian(double x, double y) {
  return Point(x, y, CARTESIAN);
}
```

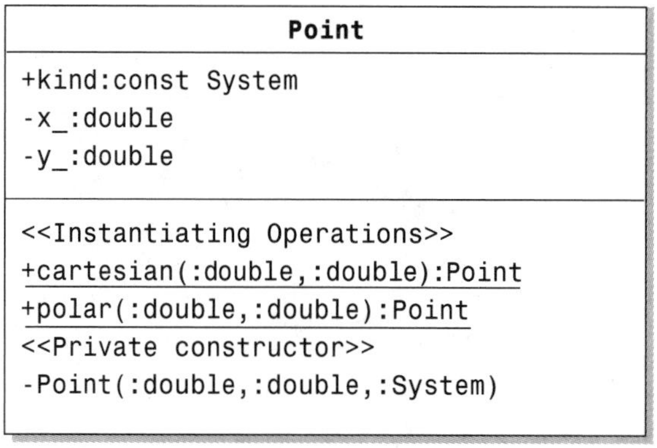

```
┌──────────────────────────────────────────────┐
│                     Point                      │
├──────────────────────────────────────────────┤
│ +kind:const System                             │
│ -x_:double                                     │
│ -y_:double                                     │
├──────────────────────────────────────────────┤
│ <<Instantiating Operations>>                   │
│ +cartesian(:double,:double):Point              │
│ +polar(:double,:double):Point                  │
│ <<Private constructor>>                        │
│ -Point(:double,:double,:System)                │
└──────────────────────────────────────────────┘
```

Figure 4.7   Instantiating operations

```
Point Point::polar(double radius, double angle) {
  return Point(radius*cos(angle), radius*sin(angle), POLAR);
}
```

Given this definition, the client can write:

```
Point p = Point::cartesian(1, 2);
if(p.kind == Point::CARTESIAN) ...
```

Note the use of `Point::CARTESIAN` as a scope operator to refer to a class member that is outside its class.

Java uses the instantiating operations idiom, for example, to implement the `InetAddress` class that has three static functions to create new objects. Two of these functions have identical signatures (but different names):

```
InetAddress getByName(String host);
InetAddress getAllByName(String host);
```

● EXAMPLE 4.2

In this example, I use the same class `Point` from the beginning of Example 4.1, except the instantiating operations return pointers to objects rather than objects:

```
// File: ex4.2.point.h
class Point {
public:
  static Point* cartesian(double, double);
  static Point* polar(double, double);
private:
  Point(double, double);
  Point(const Point&);
  double x_;
  double y_;
};

// File: ex4.2.point.cpp
Point::Point(double x, double y): x_(x), y_(y) { }

Point::Point(const Point& p): x_(p.x_), y_(p.y_) { }

Point* Point::cartesian(double x, double y) {
  return new Point(x, y);
}

Point* Point::polar(double radius, double angle) {
  return new Point(radius*cos(angle), radius*sin(angle));
}
```

Note that the client of this class has to take responsibility for deallocating objects; for example:

```
Point* p;

p = new Point(1,2);                          // private constructor

p = Point::cartesian(1,2);
...
delete p;
```

You can also use the instantiating operations idiom to ensure that objects are always allocated on the heap and never on the stack. Since this is useful in general, I have made a separate idiom out of it, calling it the heap idiom.

Heap Idiom 4.3

To allocate all objects on the heap, make all the constructors, including copy constructors, private or protected and provide static functions that allocate objects on the heap and return the objects.

4.5   *First Design Pattern: Singleton*

In this section, I introduce the first design pattern. First, however, I provide a general description of what design patterns are and why they are useful. Learning design patterns takes time. Most programmers find that when they start using patterns their productivity actually decreases. Only after several weeks of consistent use, do design patterns become beneficial.

4.5.1   General Philosophy of Design Patterns

Why should you use design patterns? To answer this question, consider a project for which you have to make several decisions such as: find the best way to create a complex object, decide how to encapsulate some actions, decide how to sequentially access the elements of an aggregate without knowledge of how the aggregate is implemented, find a way to provide for the undoing of some actions. All these decisions involve interactions between classes and objects, and you can address them using design patterns.

There are numerous books on design patterns, and there are various explanations of what design patterns really are. Apparently, the design pattern approach originated from the work of an architect, Christopher Alexander (1979), who proposed the use of patterns to design buildings. He described a design pattern as a three-part rule consisting of the description of a context, a problem, and a solution to this problem. This description has been modified for software applications, and the software **design pattern** consists of four parts: the name of the pattern, the problem, the solution, and the consequences of using the pattern. To provide a more intuitive description of a pattern, I paraphrase Coplien's (1998, 311–320) explanation: Suppose you want to make a dress. You can use a specification that gives you the route of the scissors by providing lengths and angles of cut. Using this specification does not ensure that you create the right dress, and you do not learn any technique that is useful for similar projects. If instead you use a pattern, then you have a rule that can be applied to this and other similar projects.

You use patterns to find solutions to complex problems, solutions that have been tried and approved by a large community of experts who have also cataloged the patterns. For example, chess players use many well-known strategies, such as the King's gambit. According to Alpert (1998), design patterns are recurring solutions to design problems that you see over and over. In particular, design patterns help you design how objects communicate. They provide a level of indirection that keeps classes from having to know about each other's internals, helping you write more reusable programs. Note that design patterns describe design techniques; there are also *analysis* patterns, not covered by this book (see Fowler, 2000). The most useful patterns are **generative**, which means that they tell you how to create something.

In addition to patterns, there are also idioms and frameworks. **Idioms**, which you often see in this book, are constructs that describe techniques for expressing low-level, *language-dependent* ideas. Ideas that go beyond a specific language represent patterns, which can also be thought of as medium-scale *language-independent* abstractions. **Software frameworks** are at an even higher level of abstraction, and typically their implementation makes use of several design patterns. They are not complete applications; instead, they consist of "sockets" into which the user can plug specific code to provide the required structure and behavior. For example, certain graphics applications, such as those available in Java, are frameworks. The user of these frameworks can create specific graphics applications by using derived classes, callbacks, and similar techniques. The framework provides a flow of control between its classes and the user, which is the *reverse* of what happens when using software libraries, in which the user provides the flow of control between the tools available in the library.

Books that provide catalogs of patterns are intended to be used by experienced programmers in their everyday work. In these books, patterns are described using a standard format that includes information such as the pattern name, description, and so on. In this book, I attempt to integrate design patterns into the course of learning C++, so I introduce design patterns along with other C++ constructs. Rather than using the catalog-like format that you find in most books on design patterns, I explain why patterns are important and often indispensable in the context of C++ constructs. Since the topic of design patterns is a large and developing area of computer science, as you gain experience with C++ you should consult other

design pattern books—in particular, Gamma et al. (1995) as well a more recent series of books on patterns, such as Martin (1997).

4.5.2   Singleton Design Pattern

You can use the singleton design pattern to constrain object instantiation; specifically, it can ensure that the client cannot create *more than one object* of a particular
class. Classes created using this pattern are referred to as the **singleton**. In Java, the
class java.lang.Runtime is a singleton class with a static method getRuntime(),
which is responsible for returning a single instance of this class. The singleton design
pattern is an example of a **creational object pattern** because it describes how to create an object so that no more than one instance of its class can exist. To implement
this pattern, you use a variant of the instantiating operations idiom: You hide all the
constructors and provide a static method responsible for creating a single object.

　　Using the singleton design pattern can ensure that there is *exactly one* window
manager or print spooler, a *single-point* entry to a database, a *single* telephone line
for an active modem, or a *single* keyboard for a PC, and so on.

　　The following is a general template for a class created using the singleton design pattern (Figure 4.8 shows the UML design):

```
class Singleton {
public:
  static Singleton* instance();
  void op1();           // anything that is useful for this singleton
protected:
  Singleton();
  Singleton(const Singleton&);
  Singleton& operator=(const Singleton&);
private:
  static Singleton* onlyInstance_;
};

Singleton* Singleton::onlyInstance_ = 0;

Singleton* Singleton::instance(){
  if(onlyInstance_ == 0)
      onlyInstance_ = new Singleton;
  return onlyInstance_;
}
```

Here are a few details of this design pattern:

- The static method instance() uses *lazy evaluation* (the instance is not created
  unless it is explicitly requested). If an object has already been created, then suc-

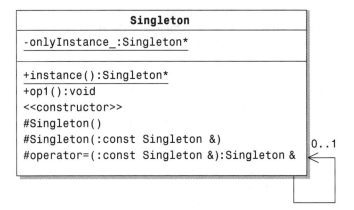

Figure 4.8   Singleton

cessive calls to `instance()` return a pointer to the existing object. For some applications, it may be useful to add an operation that specifies whether the object exists. Another alternative is to throw an exception if an attempt is made to create more than one instance.

- The constructors are private (or protected), so the client cannot create objects using code such as

```
Singleton* s = new Singleton();                // private constructor
```

For the same reason, the copy constructor is private (or protected).

- Private operations, such as a constructor, are not defined in the general template. They are defined for a specific application; for example, to define a singleton printer spooler, the constructor will perform the necessary initialization of the spooler.

- It is preferable that the client avoid using a variable of a singleton class, instead accessing operations through the instantiating operation:

```
Singleton::instance()->op1();
```

- Remember to avoid a memory leak; do not forget to deallocate the instance of a singleton. When you do not need it anymore, use the `delete` operator:

```
delete Singleton::instance();
```

The destructor of the class `Singleton` should always clean up after itself; in this case, it should set the value of `onlyInstance_` to 0.

- It is easy to extend the singleton design pattern to allow for at most *n* instances of a class rather than a single instance.

- An alternative implementation uses the static nonlocal variables idiom (Idiom 3.4). This implementation does not use pointers, which avoids any potential memory leaks or other memory management problems:

```
class Singleton {
public:
   static Singleton& instance();
   void op1();                              // whatever is useful
protected:
   Singleton();
   Singleton(const Singleton&);
   Singleton& operator=(const Singleton&);
};

Singleton& Singleton::instance() {
   static Singleton onlyInstance;
   return onlyInstance;
}
```

The client can call singleton functions as follows:

```
Singleton::instance().op1();
```

A local static object is initialized when the function containing its definition is called for the first time. Therefore, this solution also takes advantage of lazy evaluation, because the object is not constructed unless it is actually required. Static objects are destroyed (their destructors are executed) when the entire program terminates, relieving the client of the responsibility of deleting the singleton object.

At the end of this chapter, I present a longer example that shows an application of the singleton design pattern.

4.6 *Namespaces, Part II*

Modern programming languages provide tools to define a high level of encapsulation (i.e., to make constructs such as classes visible or invisible to the clients); this encapsulation is represented in C++ by a namespace. Namespaces also help avoid name conflicts. In Java, namespaces are called packages; to minimize the possibility of name conflicts, packages have hierarchical names. Entire packages or parts thereof may be imported.

4.6.1   Declaring Namespaces

The syntax used to define **namespaces** is similar to that used to define classes. However, there is no syntax to specify the accessibility of members—for example, to specify that some members are public and others are private (I will later describe how to achieve this by splitting a namespace into several parts). To discuss the various aspects of namespaces, I use the example of a company that hires various kinds of employees. I use two kinds of classes in this example: those related to the company, such as `Employee` or the exception class `NegativeSalaryException`, and those related to storing employees in a certain collection, such as a list. Therefore, there are two namespaces, one for each kind of class. First consider the namespace `Company`, which stores the classes `Employee` and `NegativeSalaryException`:

```
namespace Company {
  class Employee {
    ...
  };

  class NegativeSalaryException {
    ...
  };
}                                            // no semicolon here
```

C++ has a global anonymous namespace that is similar to Java's global anonymous package. All declarations not explicitly placed in named namespaces are placed in the **global namespace**. A single namespace defines a *scope,* so all names that occur in this namespace must be distinct. Anything that can be globally defined can also be defined in a namespace, including constants, variables (with initializations if desired), stand-alone functions (except main), classes, and (nested) namespaces.

Outside the namespace, you use the scope operator :: to refer to members of this namespace; for example:

```
Company::Employee e;              // Use "::" rather than Java's "."
```

Inside the namespace, in definitions of its members, you can refer to a name `Id` in the *global* namespace, using `::Id`. For example, if the namespace `Company` has a function `remove()`, to refer to a global `remove()`, you use

```
::remove()
```

A namespace can contain only the *declaration* of a member. The corresponding *definition* may be provided outside the namespace; for example:

```
namespace Company {
  class Employee;                            // class declaration
```

```
  ...
}

class Company::Employee {                          // class definition
  ...
};
```

You cannot define members that have not been previously declared.

UML uses a rectangle with a smaller rectangle above it to show namespaces (see Figure 4.9). Sometimes the contents of the namespace show more information than just the names of its attributes. In this example, there is a dependency between the two namespaces, because `Company` depends on `Collections` (see Figure 4.10).

A namespace definition is **open**, which means you can add members to the existing namespace by writing a second namespace with the same name. For example, assuming `Company` is defined as previously shown, you can add an additional member to the namespace by writing

```
namespace Company {                          // extend existing namespace
  class Volunteer {
    ...
  };
}
```

Classes are similar to namespaces, but classes are not open because they serve as a pattern for the creation of objects.

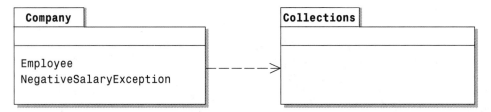

Figure 4.9 UML diagram for namespace

Figure 4.10 UML diagram for two dependent namespaces

4.6.2 Namespace Aliases and the `Using` Directive and Declaration

Unlike a Java package name, a name given to a C++ namespace has no structure, so it is useful to have long names. The longer and more informative the name, the smaller the chance of a name conflict. On the other hand, long names are cumbersome. To simplify the use of long names, you can introduce one or more local **aliases**. For example, to use a namespace called `Company_From_the_Middle_of_Nowhere`, you can create an alias, such as `Company`:

```
namespace Company = Company_From_the_Middle_of_Nowhere;      // alias
Company::Employee e;
```

Writing code using the fully qualified names of features of the namespace, such as

```
Company::Employee
```

can be considered a part of the documentation, because this line makes it clear that `Employee` is an attribute of `Company`. This option may not be practical when you use many features from the same namespace. In such a case, you may use a `using` **directive**, which is the same as Java's `import` statement:

```
using namespace Company;
Employee s;                           // means: Company::Employee s;
```

The `using` directive does not extend the scope in which it is used; instead, it makes names from the namespace available. Therefore, there is no conflict between locally declared names and names declared in the namespace. Names locally declared take precedence over names from the namespace (which are still accessible using full qualification); for example:

```
namespace ResourceNamespace {
  int value();
  void value(int);
  int value_;
}

void foo() {
  int value_;
  using namespace ResourceNamespace;
  value_ = 1;                           // local value_
  cout << value();                      // value() from namespace
  ResourceNamespace::value_ = 2;        // value_ from namespace
}
```

Rather than importing an entire namespace, you can also select specific names from the namespace and add them to the local scope, employing a using **declaration**:

```
using Company::print();          // add a declaration
print();                         // means: Company::print()
```

The using declaration adds a declaration to the scope, so it can cause conflicts, as here for the ResourceNamespace namespace:

```
void goo() {
  int value_;
  using ResourceNamespace::value_;     // duplicate declaration
  using Company::print();
  print();                             // Company::print();
  ::print();                           // global print():
}
```

4.6.3   Standard Namespaces

Virtually all programs use the standard library, which defines many useful facilities. These are included by the user as needed; for example:

```
#include <string>
```

The standard library is declared in the **standard namespace**, called std. Therefore, many programs start by importing this namespace:

```
using namespace std;                          // using directive
```

If you want to use some specific members of this namespace, you can specify only the required ones; for example:

```
using std::string;                            // using declaration
```

4.6.4   Namespaces and Information Hiding

As I previously mentioned, unlike Java, C++ does not allow you to specify the visibility of namespace members. However, since you can define members outside namespaces, and namespaces are *open*, you can split a single namespace into several pieces, some visible to the clients and some not. You do this by placing the interface sections of the namespace in the header file that is accessible to the client and placing the implementation details in files that are available only in a binary form to be linked with the rest of the program.

Consider the example of maintaining a single resource, here represented by an integer variable. The following interface goes in the header file:

```
//File: resource.h
#ifndef RESOURCE_H
#define RESOURCE_H
namespace ResourceNamespace {
  int value();
  void value(int);
}
#endif
```

The client can now use this interface as follows:

```
#include "resource.h"
ResourceNamespace::value(4);
cout << ResourceNamespace::value();
```

The implementation of the resource is not accessible to the client; it is placed in another file:

```
// File: resource.cpp
#include "resource.h"
namespace ResourceNamespace {      // extends ResourceNamespace
  int value_ = 0;                  // private variable
}

// implementation of value()
int ResourceNamespace::value() {
  return value_;
}

// implementation of value(int)
void ResourceNamespace::value(int k) {
  value_ = k;
}
```

The definition of `value_` is not accessible outside the implementation file `re-source.cpp`.

This example shows how to expose the class declaration (by placing it in a header file) and hide the implementation (by placing it in the implementation file). You can have additional **helper** functions that are not members of a class but are associated with the class. For example, you can have a class `Matrix` and a function to add two matrices:

```
Matrix plus(const Matrix&, const Matrix&);
```

(I will discuss helper functions further in Section 7.3.2). In this situation, the header file should include the *declarations* of such functions:

```
// File: mymatrix.h
namespace MyMatrix {

  class Matrix {                              // class definition
    ...
  };

  Matrix plus(const Matrix&, const Matrix&);  // helper declaration

}
```

The implementation file contains definitions of all member functions as well as the helper functions:

```
// File: mymatrix.cpp
namespace MyMatrix {

  ... definitions of Matrix member functions

  Matrix plus(const Matrix& m, const Matrix& n) {
    ... definition of plus

  }
}
```

Namespace Idiom 4.4

Place a class declaration and all related helper functions in a single namespace.

Namespaces are also useful if you want to *limit the scope* of a declaration to the file containing this declaration; you can accomplish this by using an **unnamed namespace**. For example, if you want to limit the scope of two functions and one variable to a single file, you can place them in an unnamed namespace:

```
namespace {                                   // unnamed

  int value() {
    return value_;
  }
```

```
void value(int k) {
    value_ = k;
}

int value_ = 0;
}
```

The definitions of the members of an unnamed namespace must appear within this namespace. An unnamed namespace has an implied `using`, which allows its members to be accessed outside of the namespace without using a qualification:

```
value(4);
cout << value();
```

As you can see from this example, standard overloading rules are valid within namespaces. Note that an unnamed namespace is *not* the same as a global anonymous namespace; in particular, you cannot refer to members of an unnamed namespace by using the scope operator.

Single File Scope Idiom 4.5

To limit the scope of a variable, function, or class to a single file, place it in an unnamed namespace.

4.7 *Need for Recompiling and Header Files, Part I*

As I mentioned in Section 3.2, class definitions are placed in header files. In this section, I discuss the dependencies between classes and the corresponding header and implementation files.

Consider the following class `Student`:

```
// File: ch4.student.h
class Student {
public:
    Student(long);
    long getNumber() const;
private:
    long number_;
};
```

The class definition is placed in the header file ch4.student.h, which must be included in the implementation file ch4.student.cpp because the compiler needs to know the class definition to compile the code for the features of this class.

The situation for the clients of the class Student is different. First look at one version of a definition of the class AccountForStudent:

```
// File: ch4.accountforstudent.h
#include "ch4.student.h"                    // compiles, but unnecessary
class AccountForStudent {
public:
  AccountForStudent(long number, double balance);
  ~AccountForStudent();
  long getNumber() const;
  double getBalance() const;
private:
  Student* stud_;
  double balance_;
};
```

To understand why it is not necessary to include the header file ch4.student.h, think about what information is required from the class Student to compile the operations of AccountForStudent. If the compiler sees the definition of a variable of type Student

```
Student s;
```

it does need to know the size of the class; therefore, it needs *complete information* about this class. However, this information is not required for

- Pointers or references to the class; for example: Student* or Student&
- Operations with class parameters passed by value or returning objects of this class; for example:

```
Student getStudent() or print(Student)
```

Only a pointer to a class in AccountForStudent is used, so, to compile this file, it is sufficient to provide a class *declaration,* rather than the entire class definition. For the example here, the header file should look like this:

```
// File: ch4.accountforstudent.h
class Student;                                          // declaration

class AccountForStudent { ... as above . . .};
```

This arrangement breaks the dependency between the two files: `ch3.account-forstudent.h` and `ch3.student.h`. Note that the client of `AccountForStudent` must include both these header files; for example:

```
#include "ch3.student.h"
#include "ch3.accountforstudent.h"
  ...
  AccountForStudent afs(10, 10.25);
  ...
```

Unfortunately, C++ does not cleanly separate the interface and the implementation. As a result, any changes in the implementation require recompilation of the client's code. In Section 6.6.1, I will show how to use a bridge design pattern to separate the interface from the implementation.

A lesson from this section is that you should include a class definition in a header file only when it is really needed and consider using just a class *declaration* as an alternative.

The next section will show a skeleton of a larger example using namespaces.

4.8   *Application: List of Students*

In this section, I provide a slightly longer example of a program that uses the various techniques introduced in this chapter, focusing on the singleton design pattern and the use of namespaces. Although this example uses its own `List` class, the C++ standard library provides a default implementation of lists, so you do not really need to write your own.

● **EXAMPLE 4.3**

Consider a registrar application that maintains information about students using the following classes:

- `Student`, which maintains student records consisting of two attributes, the student number and the name
- `Registrar`, which maintains a list of students (at any point in time, there is always exactly one registrar; this makes it an ideal candidate for the singleton design pattern)
- `List`, which implements a linked list of students
- `DuplicateNumberException`, `NoStudentException`, and `NoNumberException`, which are exception classes used when registrar operations fail

These classes are stored in a single namespace, split over two files to hide the implementation details. The header file is accessible to the client:

```
// File: ch4-registrarnamespace.h
namespace Registrar_Namespace {
class Student {
public:
  Student(const string&);                // constructor
  long number() const;                   // shows the number
  string name() const;                   // shows the name
private:
  long number_;                          // student number
  string name_;                          // student name
  static long number_();                 // used by the constructor
};

class List;                              // declaration

class Registrar {
public:
  static Registrar& instance();
  void insert(const Student&) throw (DuplicateNumberException);
  void insert(const string&);
  void remove(const Student&) throw (NoStudentException);
  void remove(long) throw (NoNumberException);
  bool member(const Student&);
  bool member(const string&, long&);
  bool member(long, string&);
private:
  Registrar(int = 100);                  // default size of registrar
  Registrar(const Registrar&);
  Registrar& operator=(const Registrar&);
  List* rep_;
};

class NoNumberException {
public:
  NoNumberException(const string&);
  void show();
private:
  string reason_;
};

class NoStudentException {
public:
  NoStudentException(const string&);
  void show();
```

```
private:
  string reason_;
};

class DuplicateNumberException {
public:
  DuplicateNumberException(const string&);
  void show();
private:
  string reason_;
};
}
```

The declaration of the class `Registrar_Namespace::List` in this namespace is
needed to declare `List* rep_` in the class `Registrar`. The namespace contains two
basic client classes and three related exception classes. The interfaces of some
classes in this namespace are shown in Figure 4.11.

```
┌─────────────────────────────────────────────────────┐
│         Registrar Namespace::Registrar              │
├─────────────────────────────────────────────────────┤
│ -rep_:List*                                         │
├─────────────────────────────────────────────────────┤
│ -instance():Registrar &                             │
│ -insert(:const Student &):void                      │
│ -insert(:const string &):void                       │
│ -remove(:const Student &):void                      │
│ -remove(:long):void                                 │
│ -member(:const Student &):bool                      │
│ -member(:const string &,:long &):bool               │
│ -member(:long,: string &):bool                      │
│ -Registrar(:inf):                                   │
│ -Registrar(:const Registrar &):                     │
│ -operator=(:const Registrar &):Registrar &          │
└─────────────────────────────────────────────────────┘
```

```
┌─────────────────────────────────────────────────────┐
│       Registrar Namespace::NoStudentException        │
├─────────────────────────────────────────────────────┤
│ -reason_:string                                      │
├─────────────────────────────────────────────────────┤
│ +NoStudentException(:const string &):                │
│ +show():void                                         │
└─────────────────────────────────────────────────────┘
```

```
┌─────────────────────────────────────────┐
│    Registrar Namespace::Student          │
├─────────────────────────────────────────┤
│ -number_:long                            │
│ -name_:string                            │
├─────────────────────────────────────────┤
│ +Student(string&:const):                 │
│ +number():long                           │
│ +name():string                           │
│ -number_():long                          │
└─────────────────────────────────────────┘
```

Figure 4.11 Some classes for the part of the namespace accessible to
the client

Students are assigned consecutive numbers using a private static attribute, which is initialized in the static function found in the implementation file:

```
long Student::number_() {
  static long number = 1000;              // initial student number
  return number++;
}
```

This implementation uses the static nonlocal variables idiom (Idiom 3.4). The following function defines `Registrar` as a singleton:

```
// File ch4-registrar.cpp
using namespace Registrar_Namespace;
Registrar& Registrar::instance() {
  static Registrar onlyInstance;
  return onlyInstance;
}
```

The other part of the namespace is hidden in the implementation file (see also Figure 4.12):

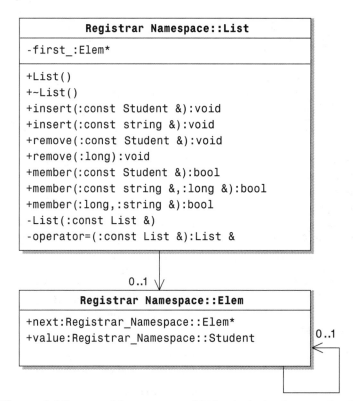

Figure 4.12 Part of the namespace hidden in the implementation file

```
// File: ch4-list.h
#include "ch4-registrarnamespace.h"
namespace Registrar_Namespace {
  struct Elem {
    Elem* next;
    Student value;
  };
  class List {
  public:
    List();
    ~List();
    void insert(const Student&);
    void insert(const string&);
    void remove(const Student&);
    void remove(long);
    bool member(const Student&);
    bool member(const string&, long&);
    bool member(long, string&);
  private:
    List(const List&);
    List& operator=(const List&);
    Elem* first_;
  };
}
```

The client can use this code as follows:

```
#include "ch4-registrarnamespace.h"
int main() {
  using Registrar_Namespace;

  Registrar::instance().insert("Mary");

  long number;
  if(Registrar::instance().member("Mary", number))
    cout << "Mary's student number is " << number;

  Student s("John");
  try {
    Registrar::instance().insert(s);

  } catch (DuplicateNumberException& e) {
    // can't happen
  }

}
```

4.9 *Exercises*

EXERCISE 4-1

Draw UML diagrams for Exercises 3-6 and 3-7.

EXERCISE 4-2

Implement the code for Exercise 3-5 so that copying of lists is forbidden (hint: use Idiom 4.1).

EXERCISE 4-3

Implement a wrapper class for integer values, similar to the class in Example 3.4, so it provides instantiating operations to create objects (hint: use Idiom 4.2)

EXERCISE 4-4

Implement the code for Exercise 3-9 so it provides instantiating operations to create objects (hint: use Idiom 4.2)

EXERCISE 4-5

Implement the code for Exercise 3-10 so it provides instantiating operations to create objects (hint: use Idiom 4.2)

EXERCISE 4-6

Use a singleton design pattern and implement the code for Exercise 3-8 to allow at most one instance of `Company1` and at most two instances of `Company2`.

EXERCISE 4-7

Implement a wrapper class for integer values, similar to the class in Example 3.4, in which there may be at most n instances of this class, where n is a static class variable.

EXERCISE 4-8

Implement the code for Exercise 3-6 using a single namespace. Carefully decide which part of this namespace should be visible to the client and which part should be visible to the implementation.

EXERCISE 4-9

Implement the code for Exercise 3-12 using a single namespace. Carefully decide which part of this namespace should be visible to the client and which part should be visible to the implementation.

OBJECT-ORIENTED PROGRAMMING, PART I

5.1 *Preview*

The last two chapters dealt with issues related to object-based programming. Now you should be ready to look at inheritance and object-oriented programming. In this chapter, I discuss one of the most important features of object-oriented programming—extending a class. I start with the basic terminology. I then compare the Java and C++ approaches to polymorphic programming and discuss the techniques introduced in the previous chapter in the context of inheritance: destructing objects, overloading assignment operators, overloading operations, and exception handling. I also cover the topic of abstract classes and introduce another design pattern, called the template method. Finally, I discuss the concept of a friend operation and class. The next chapter will provide a more advanced description of object-oriented programming and discuss three kinds of inheritance—public, protected, and private—and introduce five more design patterns.

5.2 *Basic Terminology and a Derived Class Definition*

If a class, D, extends another class, B, then D is called a **derived class** of B, and B is called a **base class** of D (B is also called a **superclass** for the **subclass** D). The base class provides a **generalization** of the derived class. Figure 5.1 shows a UML diagram for a general BankAccount class that has two derived classes: CheckingAccount and SavingsAccount. As you can see, to show generalization, UML uses an arrow with a hollow end to point from

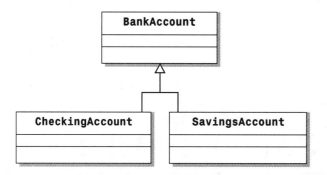

Figure 5.1 UML diagram for derived classes

the derived class to the base class. However, it is often useful to think about this hierarchy as a tree, with BankAccount as the parent and CheckingAccount and SavingsAccount as the children.

Recall from the previous chapter that the set of all public features of a class is called a public interface, or simply *interface*. When the inheritance hierarchy is properly designed, the derived class' interface conforms to the base class' interface. This leads to the **substitutability principle**: Whenever the base class object is expected, you can use an object of a derived class. For example, if an object of class BankAccount is expected, you can instead use an object of the class Checking-Account or of the class SavingsAccount. You may violate the substitutability principle if you override a nonpolymorphic operation.

An operation is defined to be polymorphic if the runtime *value,* rather than a declared type, of a variable used to invoke the operation determines which implementation of the operation is invoked. There are some differences between Java and C++ in this area. Unless specified as final, Java operations are always polymorphic; in C++, they are polymorphic only if explicitly specified as **virtual**. Also, in C++ the class hierarchy does not have a single root (called Object in Java). Finally, as you will see in Section 6.5.3, C++ supports both single inheritance and multiple inheritance of classes (there may be two or more base classes of a given class). Table 5.1 compares Java and C++ inheritance.

There are two Java constructs not available in C++. First, Java uses the super keyword to refer to methods in a base class. C++ does not support super, but you

Table 5.1 Inheritance

Java	C++	Comments About C++
class D extends B {	class D : public B {	This is called a **public inheritance**.
class D extends B {	class D : private B {	This is called a **private inheritance**.
class D extends B {	class D : protected B {	This is called a **protected inheritance**.
super	--	C++ does not support super.
final	--	C++ does not support final.

can use the scope operator : : to refer to a feature found in a base class that has the same name as a feature found in a derived class (for an example, see the description of class scope rules in Section 5.7). Java also uses this keyword in a constructor to invoke a constructor from the base class. Section 5.4 will show how this is done in C++. Second, Java uses the `final` keyword to disallow the creation of derived classes. In C++, this keyword does not exist; to finalize the design of a class and make it impossible to extend a class, you can use the instantiating operations idiom (Idiom 4.2). In the following section, I will discuss the details related to public inheritance, which happens to be the most frequently used kind of inheritance (other kinds of inheritance will be discussed in the next chapter).

5.3 *Public Inheritance*

Public inheritance is used when a derived class wants to inherit the *entire* public interface of its base class, and it works the same in C++ as it does in Java. All features that are public in the base class can be used by the derived class; in other words, the interface of the derived class is the union of the public features of the derived class and the base class. Typically, the interface of the derived class defines a constructor and one or more functions.

Consider a class, `Student`, that has an interface consisting of a constructor and three queries: to get a student name, to get a student number, and to print information about the student, respectively. The class `StudentWithAccount` shown here extends the functionality provided by the class `Student` and maintains an account balance associated with each student. The corresponding UML diagram is shown in Figure 5.2.

```
// File: ch5.student.h
class Student {
public:
  Student(long = 0, string = "");
  long getNumber() const;
  string getName() const;
  void printInfo() const;
private:
  long number_;
  string name_;
};

// File: ch5.student.cpp
void Student::printInfo() const {
  cout << "Student number:" << number_ << "; name:"
    << name_ << endl;
}
```

```
// File: ch5.studentwithaccount.h
class StudentWithAccount : public Student {          // no "extends"
public:
  StudentWithAccount(long, string, double = 0.0);
  double getBalance() const;
  void setBalance(double);
  void printInfo() const;
private:
  double balance_;
};
```

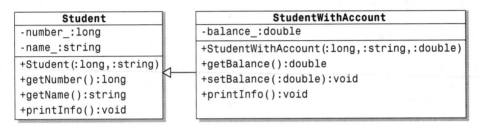

Figure 5.2   UML diagram for a class derived from `Student`

The class hierarchy in this example uses public inheritance to extend classes. To specify this type of inheritance, you cannot omit the word `public` found in the first line of the definition of the class `StudentWithAccount`. The following sections explain the implementation of the various operations found in a derived class.

5.4   *Creating Objects*

The **constructor of a derived class** must first take care of the initialization of the attributes of its base class. Unlike Java, C++ does not provide the keyword `super`; instead, the constructor invokes the base class constructor by using syntax similar to the *member initialization list* but this time with the base class' name:

```
// File: ch5.studentwithaccount.cpp
StudentWithAccount::StudentWithAccount(long number,
  string name, double balance) :
    Student(number, name)               // base class' constructor

{
  balance_ = balance;
}
```

Attributes of the derived class may also be initialized in the member initialization list:

```
StudentWithAccount::StudentWithAccount(long number,
  string name, double balance) :
    Student(number, name), balance_(balance)
{ }
```

This is the only context in which a constructor can be called in the definition of another constructor. If the base class has a no-arg constructor, this constructor does not have to be called explicitly in a derived class (it is called implicitly):

```
StudentWithAccount::StudentWithAccount(double balance)
                        //  : Student() no-arg base class' constructor
{
  balance_ = balance;
}
```

Derived Class Constructor Idiom 5.1

The constructor of the derived class D calls the constructor of the base class B using syntax similar to the member initialization list:

```
B(parameters)
```

5.5 *RTTI and Type Conversions*

Java provides a class called Class and a powerful reflection mechanism that retrieves information about any aspect of a class, such as its methods. On the other hand, C++ provides a very modest set of operations, called **runtime type identification (RTTI) constructs**, that allow you to find the current *type* of the value of a pointer or a reference whose declared type is of some base class.

There are two basic RTTI constructs:

- A dynamic cast
- typeid (rarely needed and described in Section 9.7)

Both constructs are designed to retrieve derived class information. They work only if used for classes that have *at least one virtual function*.

Pointers and references to a base class can be assigned objects of a derived class without using any *explicit cast* (**downcasting**, or moving down the inheritance tree). For example, consider the base class Student, its derived class StudentWithAccount (introduced in Section 5.3), and the following definitions of variables:

```
Student* ps = new StudentWithAccount(40, "john", 2000); //downcast
Student& s = StudentWithAccount(30, "barbara", 1000);   // downcast
```

Such variables can only be used to access features in the base class:

```
cout << s.getName();
cout << s.getBalance();              // can't access derived class
cout << ps->printInfo();             // calls Student::printInfo()
```

`Student::printInfo()` is invoked in the last line because, by default, functions in C++ are not polymorphic. This means that the function used is determined based on the *type* of the variable (and `ps` has the type `Student`).

A typical object-oriented program frequently uses downcasting like this one

```
Student* ps = new StudentWithAccount(40, "john", 2000);
```

because it is using a variable of the base class initialized to the object of the derived class, which is designed to perform a specialized task.

To access features found in derived classes, you can use an *explicit downcast* of a pointer to a derived class, called a **dynamic cast** (`instanceOf` in Java). This construct allows you to find the type of the variable value at runtime rather than at compile time. The syntax of a dynamic cast is as follows:

```
dynamic_cast<T>(p)
```

If `p` points to some object of type `T`, the previous expression returns `p` converted to `T`; otherwise, it returns 0. A dynamic cast is often used like this:

```
if(T* q = dynamic_cast<T>(p))
    ... here, q is of type T ..
```

This downcast can be applied only to pointers:

```
Student* ps;
... // initialize ps to point to the object of StudentWithAccount
if(StudentWithAccount* pswa = dynamic_cast<StudentWithAccount*>(ps)) {
  cout << pswa->getBalance();
  pswa->printInfo();                     // calls StudentWithAccount::printInfo();
}
```

Dynamic Cast Idiom 5.2

A dynamic cast should be used to safely cast a pointer of some base class type to a derived class type:

```
BaseClass* p = ...;
if(DerivedClass* q = dynamic_cast<DerivedClass>(p))
    ...              // here, q points to the object of the derived class
```

Dynamic casts can be used with *reference data types*, provided you use exception handling instead of testing for the 0 value; for example:

```
Student& s = ...                                    // initialize s

try {
  Student& rs = dynamic_cast<StudentWithAccount&>(s);
  cout << rs.getBalance();
} catch(std::bad_cast&) {
  ... dynamic cast failed

}
```

There are several reasons for avoiding dynamic cast:

- It is a runtime operation, which is more expensive than a compile-time operation, and it may be difficult to come up with good error handling if the cast fails.
- Downcasting using dynamic cast makes program extendibility and maintenance more difficult, because you have to make assumptions about the inheritance hierarchy, and the hierarchy cannot be changed without your code breaking.

When designing object-oriented programs, you will find that polymorphic functions defined in the base class often make it unnecessary to use dynamic cast (for an example, see the discussion at the end of Section 5.11 and Example 6.1).

There is another conversion, called **upcast** (moving up the inheritance tree), that is a cast from a derived class to a base class (allowed only for a public inheritance); for example:

```
void print(Student s) {
  s.printInfo();
}

StudentWithAccount swa(30, "barbara", 1000);
Student s;
s = swa;                // swa is upcast'ed; same as s = (Student)swa
print(swa);
```

In this assignment, only a part, or a **slice**, of the object swa is copied to the object s; all features from the derived class are sliced off (see Figure 5.3). Similarly, in the call to print(), parts of the object swa get sliced off.

swa   swa **sliced to** Student

```
Student(long = 0, string = "");      Student(long = 0, string = "");
long getNumber() const;              long getNumber() const;
string getName() const;              string getName() const;
void printInfo() const;              void printInfo() const;
long number_;                        long number_;
string name_;                        string name_;


StudentWithAccount(long,
   string, double = 0.0);
double getBalance() const;
void setBalance(double);
void printInfo() const;
double balance_;
```

Figure 5.3 Slicing

Slicing may be dangerous because it makes access to the derived features impossible; for example, the previous call to print(swa) invokes

```
Student::printInfo()
```

rather than

```
StudentWithAccount::printInfo()
```

Java avoids the slicing problem by using references to objects rather than values of objects. In C++, slicing is not dangerous if a function that uses a sliced object does not attempt to access features from the derived class, such as in the copy constructor code described in the next section. In other cases, however, slicing is best avoided.

5.6 Copy Constructors

The syntax used to define a constructor in a derived class is also used to define a copy constructor; for example:

```
Student::Student(const Student&) { ... }

StudentWithAccount(const StudentWithAccount& swa) : Student(swa) {
   balance_ = swa.balance_;
}
```

`Student(swa)` makes a call to the copy constructor of the base class, with the parameter `swa` sliced to the class `Student`. (The copy constructor of the base class operates on the memory allocated for the object of the derived class, but it "can see" only a slice of the object.) This does not cause any problems, because the copy constructor from the base class accesses only its own class' features.

5.7   *Scope and Visibility Modifiers*

Using public inheritance, a derived class inherits all the public features of the base class; however, all *private* features of the base class are not accessible in the derived class. Any future changes to the private part of the base class do not affect a derived class, and that's why this type of inheritance is also referred to as **inheriting the interface** (but not the implementation). For example, since `number_` and `name_` are private attributes of the class `Student` previously shown, they cannot be used in a derived class:

```
void StudentWithAccount::printInfo() const {     // can't use private
   cout << "Student number:" << number_ << "; name:"
       << name_ << "; balance:" << balance_ << endl;


}
```

These attributes can be printed using `Student::printInfo()`, but this function happens to have the same name as a function in a derived class. As I mentioned earlier, you can use the scope operator `::` to refer to a feature found in a base class that has the same name as a feature in a derived class; for example:

```
void StudentWithAccount::printInfo() const {
   Student::printInfo();               // access feature from base class

   cout << "balance:" << balance_ << endl;
}
```

As in Java, a C++ class has a public interface as well as a **protected interface** that its derived classes can use. A class feature may be qualified as `protected`, which means that it is private for the instantiating clients, but be accessible to its derived classes. The semantics of this construct in C++ is a bit different from the Java semantics and requires a more careful description. Specifically, a protected feature `f` may be accessed in *member operations* of a derived class only in the following two contexts:

- *Direct* access of the form `f` or `this->f`
- *Indirect* access of the form `ref.f` or `ref->f`, where `ref` is (or points to) an instance of a derived class

For example, if both `number_` and `name_` in the class `Student` are protected, you could define `printInfo()` using direct access as follows:

```
void StudentWithAccount::printInfo() const {
  cout << "Student number:" << number_ << "; name:"
      << name_ << "; balance:" << balance_ << endl;
}
```

To understand indirect access, assume that the class `StudentWithAccount` has the following operation to print student information:

```
void info(const Student&, const StudentWithAccount&);
```

Access to the attributes of the two classes is different:

```
void StudentWithAccount::info(const Student& s,
    const StudentWithAccount& swa) {
  cout << s.number_;        // can't access through Student
  cout << swa.number_;      // can access through StudentWithAccount
}
```

5.8 *Polymorphism and Virtual Functions*

In Java, all operations that are not `final` employ **late binding**. For example, given a variable `var` and the call

```
var.foo()
```

it is the *value* of `var` and not its *type* that determines which operation should be invoked. If the value of the variable is an object of a derived class that redefines an operation defined in a base class, this redefined operation will be invoked. For final operations, Java uses **early binding**: the type of the class variable and not its value determines which operation will be invoked.

C++ uses a different philosophy, which can be seen as a reversal of the Java philosophy. By default, early binding is used. Late binding is used only for pointers or references, and only if the operation is explicitly specified as `virtual` (see Table 5.2). The rationale behind the C++ approach is that there is a cost involved in using virtual functions. To implement late binding, the compiler has to create a so-called virtual table and use it to associate operation invocations with their bodies (implementations). Therefore, there is one step of indirection involved in using virtual operations. In many applications, this cost is negligible, but for some, it is considerable.

To clarify all this, here is an example consisting of the now familiar two classes `Student` and `StudentWithAccount` (which were defined in the previous sections) and the following declarations:

Table 5.2   Polymorphism

Java	C++	Comments About C++
Every non-final operation uses late binding.	Operations with late binding have to be specified as `virtual`.	Operations with late binding must be invoked through a pointer or a reference.
Final operations use early binding.	Operations that are not specified as `virtual` use early binding.	Early binding is used by default.
An operation may be defined as `final` and then cannot be redefined in a derived class.	Once an operation is specified as `virtual`, it cannot be made "nonvirtual."	There is no syntax to finalize operations or classes.

```
Student s(10, "kasia");
Student* ps = new Student(20, "michael");

StudentWithAccount sw(30, "barbara", 1000);
StudentWithAccount* psw = new StudentWithAccount(30, "mary", 0);

Student* pstud = new StudentWithAccount(40, "john", 2000);
// downcast; different declared type and the current value's type

s.printInfo();                    // Student::printInfo
ps->printInfo();                  // Student::printInfo

sw.printInfo();                   // StudentWithAccount::printInfo
psw->printInfo();                 // StudentWithAccount::printInfo

pstud->printInfo();               // Student::printInfo
```

The first four calls are clear, but the last one may need an explanation. Since early binding is used by default, `printInfo()` is selected based on the type of `pstud`, which is `Student`. To use late binding, `printInfo()` must be made virtual:

```
class Student {
public:
   ...
   virtual void printInfo() const;
   ...
};

void Student::printInfo() const {        // don't repeat virtual here
```

```
    cout << "Student number:" << number_ << "; name:"
        << name_ << endl;
}
```

Once an operation has been qualified as virtual, it remains virtual in any derived class, and this specification cannot be changed (recall that Java's final keyword does not exist in C++); in other words, you do not have to continue to explicitly qualify it as virtual. However, for the sake of readability, I always repeat the virtual specification in a derived class:

```
class StudentWithAccount : public Student {
public:
    ...
    virtual void printInfo() const;
    ...
};

void StudentWithAccount::printInfo() const {
    cout << "Student number:" << number_ << "; name:"
        << name_ << "; balance:" << balance_ << endl;
}
```

This version of printInfo() works if number_ and name_ are protected features. Otherwise, if these features are private, you can display them using the base class' printInfo() operation, provided that you use the scope operator, which turns off late binding:

```
void StudentWithAccount::printInfo() const {
    Student::printInfo();
    cout << "balance:" << balance_ << endl;
}
```

A class should use the virtual qualification as soon as polymorphism is potentially useful so the derived classes can take advantage of late binding. A class in the inheritance chain can introduce virtual, but this affects only its descendants and not its predecessors. In short, if you want to use the Java style, then qualify all nonfinal operations as virtual, and do not use the virtual qualification for final operations.

Polymorphism can be implemented by using two techniques: inheritance and object composition. In this section, I explained how to write programs that use the inheritance technique. In Section 6.5, I elaborate on the topic by discussing the implementation of polymorphism through object composition.

1. A virtual operation invoked from the base class' constructor is not really virtual (early binding is used).
2. A virtual operation in a derived class must have an operation signature *identical* to the corresponding operation signature in a base class (with the exception of covariant return types, described in Section 5.11).

5.9 *Destructing Objects*

Destructors are not inherited, and you cannot explicitly call a destructor of a base class in the definition of a destructor of the derived class. Therefore, it is easy to end up writing a destructor that will only be called for the base class—a grave mistake if the derived class has any resources that need to be released.

Consider the class `AccountForStudent`, which maintains an account for a single `Student`:

```
class AccountForStudent {
public:
  AccountForStudent(long number, const string& name,
    double balance);
  ~AccountForStudent();
  ...
protected:
  Student* stud_;
  double balance_;
};

AccountForStudent::AccountForStudent(long number,
    const string& name, double balance) {
  stud_ = new Student(number, name);
  balance_ = balance;
}

AccountForStudent::~AccountForStudent() {
  delete stud_;
}
```

The following derived class is designed to additionally maintain information about the bank:

```
class Bank;                                  // not shown here
class BankAccount : public AccountForStudent {
```

```
public:
  BankAccount(long, const string&, double, Bank*);
  ~BankAccount();
  ...
protected:
  Bank* bank_;
};

BankAccount::BankAccount(const string& name,
      long number, double balance, Bank* b) :
    AccountForStudent(number, name, balance), bank_(b)
{ }

BankAccount::~BankAccount(){
  delete bank_;
}
```

If you define

```
AccountForStudent* ba = new BankAccount("John", 100, 1200.50,
  new Bank("Royal Bank"));
```

then `ba` maintains two resources: a bank and a student. When an object pointed to by `ba` is deallocated, it is important that both these resources be released. Unfortunately, that does not happen with this design. In the call

```
delete ba;
```

the type of `ba` is used (by early binding) to determine which destructor to call; therefore, `delete` calls the destructor of the class `AccountForStudent`, and the bank is not released. To correct this, the destructor in the base class must be made `virtual`. The actual code for both destructors remains the same:

```
class AccountForStudent {
public:
  ...
  virtual ~AccountForStudent();
  ...
};

class BankAccount : public AccountForStudent {
public:
  ...
  virtual ~BankAccount();
  ...
};
```

Given the declarations just shown, in the call

```
delete ba;
```

the value of ba is used (by late binding), so the destructor of the derived class gets called. When the destructor of a derived class completes, the destructor of the base class gets called. This completes the cleanup process of the derived class, which always starts with the destructor of the derived class and ends with the destructor of the base class.

The destructor should never be private, because you want to be able to call it outside the class.

Virtual Destructor Idiom 5.3

When you design a class, make the destructor virtual; otherwise, it may be difficult or even impossible to design derived classes that clean up all memory. If this base class has no resources, then make the destructor's body empty.

5.10 *Overloaded Assignments*

An overloaded assignment operator defined in a derived class does not automatically invoke the assignment operator for its base class, so the base class part of the object may be left uncopied.

● EXAMPLE 5.1

Consider the classes AccountForStudent and BankAccount from the previous section, extended with an overloaded assignment. The complete UML diagram is shown in Figure 5.4 (recall that # signifies protected features).

```
class AccountForStudent {
public:
  AccountForStudent(long number, const string& name,
    double balance);
  virtual ~AccountForStudent();
  AccountForStudent& operator=(const AccountForStudent&);
protected:
  Student* stud_;
  double balance_;
};

AccountForStudent& AccountForStudent::operator=(
  const AccountForStudent& as) {
```

```
  if(this == &as)
    return *this;
  delete stud_;
  stud_ = new Student(as.stud_->getNumber(), as.stud_->getName());
  balance_ = as.balance_;
  return *this;
}

class BankAccount : public AccountForStudent {
public:
  BankAccount(long number, const string& name,
    double balance, Bank*);
  virtual ~BankAccount();
  BankAccount& operator=(const BankAccount&);
protected:
  Bank* bank_;
};

BankAccount::operator=(const BankAccount& b) {
  if(this == &b)
    return *this;
  AccountForStudent::operator=(b);            // assign base part
  // copy bank
  delete bank_;
  bank_ = new Bank(b.bank_->getName());
  return *this;
}
```

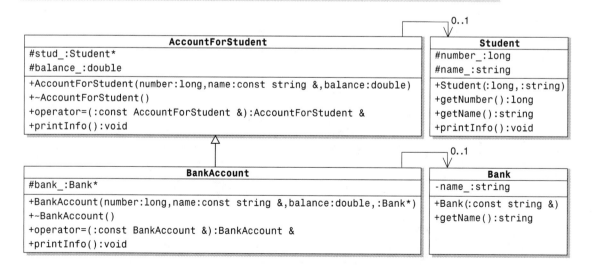

Figure 5.4   UML diagram for the overloaded assignment operator

In this example, `BankAccount::operator=()` makes a call to its base class operator `AccountForStudent::operator=()`; without this call, the base part of the Bank-Account object would not be copied.

If the base class defines a private overloaded assignment operator, the derived class must define this operator also.

Overloaded Assignment in Derived Class Idiom 5.4

An overloaded assignment operator in a derived class makes an explicit call to the overloaded assignment operator in the base class.

5.11   *Overloading and Overriding*

Recall from Section 2.5.4 that *overloading* a function means that in a single scope, several functions can have the same name (provided they have different signatures). This rule also applies to the scope defined by a class but does not apply to derived classes. Overloading an operation in a derived class means that the operation from the base class becomes *inaccessible*.

Consider a wrapper class, `Integer`, that provides read-only access to an integer value:

```
class IntegerReadOnly {
public:
  explicit IntegerReadOnly(int);
  int value() const;                          // query
protected:
  int value_;
};
```

The following is an attempt to define a derived class that overloads `value()` to provide a modifier function:

```
class Integer : public IntegerReadOnly {
public:
  explicit Integer(int);
  int value(int);                    // modifier, returns new value
};

Integer i(10);
cout << i.value(5);                  // modifier: sets the value to 5
cout << i.value();                   // wrong; accessor is hidden
```

If you wish to provide access to the hidden operation from the base class, you can add a function that calls the operation:

```
int IntegerReadOnly::value() {
  return Integer::value();
}
```

Another way to bring the hidden operation into the current scope is to employ the using directive, introduced for namespaces in Section 4.6.2:

```
using BaseClass::featureName;                            // no brackets
```

For example, you can modify the Integer class as follows:

```
class Integer : public IntegerReadOnly {
public:
  explicit Integer(int);
  int value(int);                      // modifier, returns new value
  using IntegerReadOnly::value;        // makes int value() accessible
};
```

Now the class Integer has two overloaded value() operations, and it is correct to write:

```
cout << i.value(5);                    // modifier: sets the value to 5
cout << i.value();                     // accessor
```

Overriding a function is different from overloading a function: An operation defined in a base class can be overridden in a derived class, which means it will have an identical signature but a different implementation. Overriding virtual functions is the main technique used to achieve polymorphism. With overloaded functions, the decision as to which function to call is made at compile time, while with overridden virtual functions, this decision is made at runtime.

A virtual operation must have exactly the same signature in a derived class as it does in the base class. As a warning about the pitfalls of changing the signature of a virtual operation, consider the following class, which represents a mutable integer:

```
class IntegerMutable {
public:
  explicit IntegerMutable(int);
  virtual int value(int = 0);                 // modifier, returns new value
protected:
  int value_;
};
```

Now consider a derived class with an accessor:

```
class Integer : public IntegerMutable {
public:
  explicit Integer(int);
  virtual int value() const;                            // query
};

IntegerMutable* i = new Integer(10);
cout << i->value();                    // modifier: sets the value to 0
```

The query operation `value()` is invoked from the *base* class instead of from the derived class. This is because `value()` is overloaded instead of being overridden (it is not overridden because its signature is different in the base and derived classes).

There is one important exception to the rule that governs the management of the signatures of virtual operations: the **covariant return types** rule. If a virtual operation in the base class returns a class type, a reference to a class type, or a pointer to a class type, then the same virtual operation defined in a derived class can return a class (or a reference or a pointer) that is publicly derived from the base class (that is, the return types in the base class and in the derived class do not have to be strictly identical). This is a useful exception because it helps avoid unnecessary casting. For example, consider two functions: `foo()`, whose return type is the same in the base and derived classes, and `goo()`, whose return type takes advantage of the exception just described:

```
class Base {
public:
  virtual Base* foo();
  virtual Base* goo();
  ...
};

class Derived : public Base {
public:
  virtual Base* foo();        // same return type as in Base
  virtual Derived* goo();     // different return type than in Base
  void doo();
  ...
};
```

Now consider the following code:

```
Base* p = new Derived;
```

The reason the return type of goo() is better than the return type of foo() is that you can access attributes of Derived, such as doo() through goo() but not through foo():

```
p->goo()->doo();           // OK, goo()'s return type is Derived*
p->foo()->doo();           // wrong, foo()'s return type is Base*
```

The latter call requires casting:

```
if(Derived* d = dynamic_cast<Derived*>(p->foo()))
   d->doo();
```

Notice that using allows you to selectively choose which operations are overloaded in a derived class. For example, consider a Visitor class that has a number of overloaded visit() operations:

```
class Visitor {
public:
   virtual void visit(A*);
   virtual void visit(B*);
   virtual void visit(C*);
   ...
};
```

To update this class by overriding a specific operation in a derived class—for example, by overriding the first visit() operation but leaving the others unchanged—you can do the following:

```
class NewVisitor : public Visitor {
public:
   using Visitor::visit;         // all visits are in the scope
   virtual void visit(A*);       // override this visit
   ...
};
```

Overloading and Overriding Idiom 5.5

1. Overriding works as follows:
   a. A nonvirtual operation in a derived class hides an operation with the same signature in an ancestor class.
   b. The hidden operation can be made available through the using keyword.
   c. The implementation of a virtual operation can be replaced in a derived class, provided the signature is not changed.
2. Overloading works only within the scope of a single class.

5.12   *Passing Parameters by Value and by Reference*

When a parameter of an operation is passed by value, and the type of the formal parameter is a base class of the type of the actual parameter, then the resulting *slicing* that occurs can create a problem: The actual parameter will be upcasted to the type of the formal parameter. This can be a problem because polymorphism will not work as you might expect it to in this situation. For example, consider the classes Shape and SpecificShape:

```
class Shape {
public:
  virtual void display() const;
  ...
};

class SpecificShape : public Shape {
public:
  virtual void display() const;
  ...
};
```

Now, consider a function, display(), that performs some computations and displays a shape:

```
void display(Shape s) {
  ...
  s.display();
}
```

If this function is called with an object of type SpecificShape

```
SpecificShape ss;
display(ss);
```

the parameter s is sliced, and therefore the call

```
s.display()
```

invokes Shape::display() rather than SpecificShape::display(). Passing parameters by reference avoids these problems because objects are not sliced off and polymorphic operations work as expected. Consider

```
void display(const Shape& s) {
  ...
  s.display();
}
```

and the same call as before, `display(ss)`. Since the parameter is passed by reference, the parameter is not sliced, and the operation `Shape::display()` is invoked.

5.13 *Standard Exceptions*

The C++ standard library defines a hierarchy of exceptions, which is used by operations in this library and can also be used in any user-defined program (provided the program includes `<stdexcept>`). The class hierarchy of standard exceptions in UML format is shown in Figure 5.5.

   The standard exceptions are organized as a class hierarchy with `exception` as the root. This class has the operation

```
virtual const char* what() const throw();
```

which is a query that returns a constant C-style string and does not throw any exceptions. This function can be used to retrieve the reason for throwing an exception and is defined in a derived class.

   Exceptions are divided into logic errors and runtime errors. Logic errors represent *static* errors that can be prevented and detected at compile time. Runtime errors represent *dynamic* errors that can be detected only at runtime. Derived classes of logic errors use self-explanatory names; for example, the `invalid_argument` exception should be used if an operation receives a parameter with an invalid value, such as 0. Each of these classes has an explicit constructor used to specify the value returned by `what()`:

```
logic_error::logic_error(const string& argumentForWhat);
```

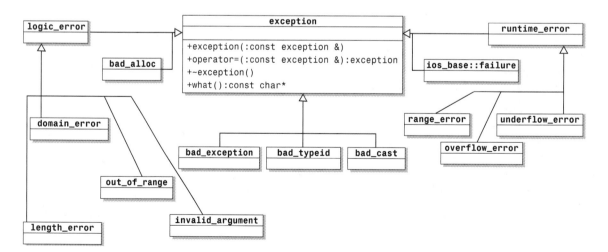

Figure 5.5 Hierarchy of standard exceptions

There is a similar arrangement for runtime errors.

● EXAMPLE 5.2

In this example, I define a function that computes the sum of its integer parameters and throws exceptions if an overflow or an underflow occurs. First, I define two classes that represent an overflow and an underflow error, respectively; both these classes are derived from the standard exception classes:

```
//File: ex5.2.myoverflow.h
#include <stdexcept>
class My_overflow_error : public overflow_error {
public:
  explicit My_overflow_error(const string&, int, int);
  int getArg1() const;
  int getArg2() const;
private:
  int x_;
  int y_;
};

//File: ex5.2.myunderflow.h
class My_underflow_error : public underflow_error {
public:
  explicit My_underflow_error(const string&, int, int);
  int getArg1() const;
  int getArg2() const;
private:
  int x_;
  int y_;
};
```

The standard header file `<limits>` defines the template class `numeric_limits`; to find the largest available integer value, I use `numeric_limits<int>::max()`. The function `add()` and its application are shown here:

```
#include <limits>
#include "ex5.2.myoverflow.h"
#include "ex5.2.myunderflow.h"
int add(int x, int y) throw(My_overflow_error, My_underflow_error) {
  if(x > 0 && y > 0 && x > numeric_limits<int>::max() - y)
    throw My_overflow_error("can't add ", x, y);
  if(x < 0 && y < 0 && x < numeric_limits<int>::min() - y)
    throw My_underflow_error("can't add", x, y);
```

```
    return x + y;
  }

int main() {
  try {
    int x, y;
    cout << "enter two integers ";
    cin >> x;
    cin >> y;

    int result = add(x, y);
    cout << endl << result << endl;
  }
  catch(const My_overflow_error& exc) {
    cerr << exc.what() << exc.getArg1()
      << " " << exc.getArg2() << endl;
  }
  catch(const My_underflow_error& exc) {
    cerr << exc.what() << exc.getArg1()
      << " " << exc.getArg2() << endl;
  }
}
```

Note that the handler must pass its parameter by reference; otherwise, the call to what() will not be virtual, and its implementation from the base class will be used.

● **EXAMPLE 5.3**

In this example, I use the integer stack example from Example 3.5, but this time I include exception handling. The UML diagram for this example is shown in Figure 5.6.

```
┌─────────────────────────────────────────────┐
│                  IntStack                     │
├─────────────────────────────────────────────┤
│ -top_:int                                     │
│ -stack_:int*                                  │
│ -size_:int                                    │
├─────────────────────────────────────────────┤
│ +IntStack(:int)                               │
│ +IntStack(:const IntStack &)                  │
│ +~IntStack()                                  │
│ +operator=(:const IntStack &):IntStack &      │
│ +push(:int):void                              │
│ +pop():int                                    │
└─────────────────────────────────────────────┘
```

Figure 5.6   UML diagram for IntStack

```cpp
// File: ex5.3.intstack.h
#include <stdexcept>
class IntStack {
public:
  IntStack(int = 100);                                  // default size
  IntStack(const IntStack&);
  ~IntStack();
  IntStack& operator=(const IntStack&);
  void push(int) throw(logic_error);
  int pop() throw(logic_error);
private:
  int top_;
  int* stack_;
  int size_;
};

// File: ex5.3.intstack.cpp
IntStack::IntStack(int size) {
  top_ = -1;
  size_ = size;
  stack_ = new int[size];
}

IntStack::IntStack(const IntStack& s) {
  top_ = s.top_;
  size_ = s.size_;
  stack_ = new int[size_];
  for(int i = 0; i <= top_; ++i)
    stack_[i] = s.stack_[i];
}

IntStack& IntStack::operator=(const IntStack& s) {
  if(this == &s)
    return *this;

  if(size_ != s.size_) {
    delete [] stack_;
    stack_ = new int[s.size_];
  }
  top_ = s.top_;
  size_ = s.size_;
  for(int i = 0; i <= top_; ++i)
    stack_[i] = s.stack_[i];
  return *this;
}
```

```
IntStack::~IntStack() {
  delete [] stack_;
}

void IntStack::push(int i) throw(logic_error) {
  if(top_ == size_ - 1)                                    // full
    throw logic_error("Stack full ");

  stack_[++top_] = i;
}

int IntStack::pop() throw(logic_error) {
  if(top_ == -1)                                           // empty
    throw logic_error("Stack empty ");

  return stack_[top_--];
}
```

The client of this IntStack can copy stacks; if this is not desirable, then the copy constructor and the overloaded assignment operator can be made *private*.

The client can now take advantage of the exceptions that IntStack provides, as well as bad_alloc, which is thrown by new if no memory can be allocated:

```
try {
  IntStack s(20);
  IntStack t = s;
  s.push(20);
}
catch(const bad_alloc&) {
  cout << "run out of memory" << endl;
}
catch(const logic_error& e) {
  cout << e.what() << endl;
}
```

Exceptions Passing Idiom 5.6

Pass exceptions by reference; otherwise, they may be sliced off.

Issues related to the maintenance of resources while handling exceptions are more complicated and warrant a detailed discussion, which I provide in the next section.

5.14 *Resource Management, Part II*

Recall that throwing an exception results in an **unwinding** of the runtime stack, which means that all objects created between the time the exception is thrown and the time it is caught are destroyed through a call to their destructors.

Unfortunately, as is often the case with pointers (which some claim to be the source of all evil), you can run into trouble if you use a pointer to an object. Consider the following example that uses the IntStack described in the previous section:

```
try {
  IntStack* s = new IntStack(20;
  s->push(20);
}
catch(const bad_alloc&) {
  cout << "run out of memory" << endl;
}
catch(const logic_error& e) {
  cout << e.what() << endl;
}
```

It appears that the programmer played by the rules and placed the code within the try block. Unfortunately, if the logic_error exception is thrown, the destructor for IntStack is never executed, making the code a source of a memory leak. One solution to this problem involves catching the exception, invoking the destructor, and then rethrowing the exception:

```
IntStack* s;

try {
  s = new IntStack(20;
  s->push(20);
}
catch(const logic_error& e) {
  delete s;
  throw;                          // rethrow
}
...
delete s;                         // no exception thrown, clean up
```

The last statement is needed because C++ does not provide the `finally` keyword. This solution is rather cumbersome and, because this kind of problem appears quite often—in particular, any time you deal with resources such as files and windows—it is best avoided. Another possible solution is creating a *wrapper* class `Resource` for a pointer to a resource:

```
typedef Resource* ResourcePointer;

class ResourceHandle {
public:
  ResourceHandle(const ResourcePointer&);
  virtual ~ResourceHandle();
  operator ResourcePointer() const;
private:
  ResourcePointer handle_;
  ResourceHandle(const ResourceHandle&);
  ResourceHandle& operator=(const ResourceHandle&);
};
```

The copy constructor and the assignment operator are private to disallow copying of `ResourcePointer` handles (see Idiom 4.1). The constructor associates the handle with the pointer to `Resource`, and the destructor deletes this pointer:

```
ResourceHandle::ResourceHandle(const ResourcePointer r) : handle_(r) {}

ResourceHandle::~ResourceHandle() {
  delete handle_;
}
```

This code introduces one new construct: a *type conversion* from `Resource-Handle` to `ResourcePointer`:

```
ResourceHandle::operator ResourcePointer() const {
  return handle_;
}
```

I will describe this construct in more detail in Section 7.3.4; for now, it is sufficient to understand that it makes *implicit type conversions* possible. Therefore, you can use `ResourceHandle` anywhere you can use `ResourcePointer`; for example, for a wrapper

```
ResourceHandle r(new Resource());
```

and an operation

```
void op(Resource*);
```

you can use

```
op(r);                      // gets implicitly converted to op(r.handle_)
```

The resource operations can now be used through a handle:

```
void foo() {
  ResourceHandle r(new Resource);
  op(r);
  ...
}
```

If an exception is thrown in `foo()`, then the execution of this function will terminate and the destructors for all local objects will be executed. In particular, the destructor for the object `r` will be executed, and this destructor will release the `handle_` resource.

   The code works for this example but is not a general solution that works for all cases. In Section 7.7, I will show more general techniques that maintain general resources rather than pointers to resources.

5.15 *Abstract Operations and Classes*

An **abstract operation** only defines a signature and does not define an implementation. An **abstract class** has at least one abstract operation. Both these concepts are very useful, allowing derived classes to decide on the implementation of some or all operations. A **concrete operation** is an operation that has its implementation provided. Java's syntax provides the means for the programmer to specify both abstract operations and classes as well as interfaces—that is, classes with all operations abstract. C++ provides no syntactic tools to express these concepts, which are summarized in Table 5.3. To specify abstract operations, in C++ often called **pure virtual operations**, you specify the body as empty by using this syntax:

```
= 0
```

To avoid confusion with Java's terminology, in this book a class that has an interface consisting *entirely* of abstract operations is said to have an **abstract interface**.

   Using the conventions I present in this section, the first line of the class specifies whether a class is *abstract* or whether a class *implements* an abstract base class.

Table 5.3   Abstract operations and classes

Java	C++	Comments About C++
`class A {` `  abstract void f();`	`class A {` `  virtual void f() = 0;`	A pure virtual operation with an empty body is abstract.
`abstract class A`	`class A { // abstract` `  virtual void f() = 0;`	A class with *at least one* pure virtual operation.
`interface Ifc`	`class Ifc { // interface` `  virtual void f() = 0;`	A class with *all* operations that are pure virtual.
`class Imp` `  implements Ifc {`	`class Imp : public Ifc {` `  // implements`	A derived class of the abstract class that implements all abstract operations.

● EXAMPLE 5.4

This example is based on a Java program from the book by Arnold and Gosling (1998). It shows a benchmark class used to measure the time some operations take to execute. (In general, a **benchmark** is a task or series of tasks used to test speed or performance.) To allow reuse of this class to perform various kinds of benchmarks, the `benchmark()` operation is abstract and is implemented in the derived classes that know what is required in the benchmark. The class provides a concrete operation to perform a benchmark a specified number of times and to measure the elapsed time.

```
// File: ex5.4.benchmarkclass.h
class BenchmarkClass { // abstract
public:
  virtual void benchmark() const = 0;
  double repeat(long count) const;
};

// File: ex5.4.benchmarkclass.cpp
#include <ctime>
#include "ex5.4.benchmarkclass.h"
double BenchmarkClass::repeat(long count) const {
  time_t start, finish;
  time(&start);
  for(long loop = 0; loop < count; ++loop)
    benchmark();
  time(&finish);

  return difftime(finish, start);
}
```

I use the standard time library `<ctime>` to find the elapsed time. A class derived from the class `BenchmarkClass` knows the details of the specific benchmarking required and so defines the `benchmark()` operation. For example, to find out how much time it takes to multiply two numbers, the derived class looks like this (this example is rather trivial, but it shows the actual code used for benchmarking):

```
// File ex5.4.mybenchmarkclass.h
class MyBenchmarkClass : public BenchmarkClass { // implements
public:
    virtual void benchmark() const;
};

// File ex5.4.mybenchmarkclass.cpp
#include "ex5.4.mybenchmarkclass.h"
void MyBenchmarkClass::benchmark() const {
    double res = 1.23 * 4.56;
}
```

The client can benchmark multiplication 10 million times:

```
BenchmarkClass* b = new MyBenchmarkClass;
cout << b->repeat(10000000);
```

As I mentioned in Section 5.8, virtual operations called in a constructor use early binding. Therefore, you must avoid calling pure virtual operations in constructors. For example, consider the class `BenchmarkClass` modified to include a constructor:

```
BenchmarkClass::BenchmarkClass() {
    benchmark();
}
```

The following code fails

```
BenchmarkClass* b = new MyBenchmarkClass;
```

because it tries to invoke a pure virtual operation in the constructor of the base class.

The example of the `BenchmarkClass` class is simple, but it follows a particular approach to design:

- An abstract class has a complete interface and only provides the implementation of operations that can be specified at this general level. These

implementations can use other operations defined in the class, both concrete and abstract.
- The derived classes are responsible for implementing the abstract operations.

It turns out that the above approach is sufficiently useful to be formulated as a design pattern, as I describe in the next section.

5.15.1   Template Method Design Pattern

One way to reuse the existing code is to have an *abstract class*, which implements most of the required functionality and does not implement some specific operations, leaving them as abstract. This approach has the additional advantage of eliminating redundant code. If you have two similar operations in a class, you can define a single common operation in the base class. Operations that are not similar are expressed as abstract, to be defined in derived classes. The **template method design pattern** describes how to use the **template method**, which defines the algorithm in terms of abstract operations called **primitive operations**. Unfortunately, the word *template* is ambiguous because C++ also has a syntactic concept of a template that defines parameterized operations and classes. From this point on, the term *template* used in the context of a design pattern or method refers to the template method design pattern; outside of this context, the term *template* refers to the other kind of template (which is a C++ construct and is covered in Section 7.6).

A nonsoftware example of this design pattern (based on Duell, 1998) a is plan for a house. A typical home design, a *template,* consists of a number of floor plans, with variations, or *primitives,* available for each floor plan. Some parts of a floor plan, such as the foundation, framing and wiring, are identical for every house. A different model is designed by specifying variations to the floor plan—for example, by adding a particular type of fireplace.

In Java, the class `java.io.Reader` is an example of the application of the template method design pattern. This abstract class has three overloaded `read()` operations:

- `int read()`, which is a template method to read a single character
- `int read(char[] cbuf)`, which is a template method to read characters into an array
- `int read(char[] cbuf, int off, int len)`, which is an abstract operation to read characters into a portion of an array

The first two operations are implemented in terms of the third operation, which itself is implemented in a derived class—for example, in `java.io.InputStreamReader`.

The first design pattern discussed in this book was the singleton—a *creational pattern*, concerned with the creation of objects. The template design pattern is an example of a **behavioral pattern** because it describes class behavior. In general, behavioral design patterns describe patterns of objects, classes, and the communication between them. There are two kinds of behavioral patterns: **class patterns** that use inheritance and **object patterns** that use object composition.

The template method design pattern is a class behavioral pattern that describes how to define an algorithm so that the specification of some of its steps is deferred

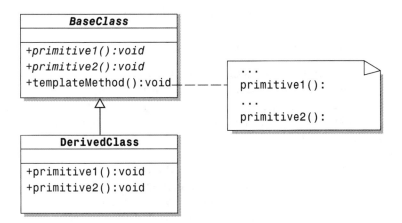

Figure 5.7 Template method design pattern

to the derived classes. Therefore, this pattern manages alternative behaviors of the same algorithm, without a need to recode the common portions.

The template method design pattern is useful if a class has only partial information about its implementation. Such a class may have one or more abstract (primitive) operations that represent the missing information; remaining template methods use these abstract operations. The derived classes are responsible for implementing these abstract operations. The next piece of code shows the skeleton of the template method (see also Figure 5.7; in UML, abstract classes and operations appear in italics):

```
returnType BaseClass::templateMethod() {

    ...                         // constant part
    primitive1();               // derived class responsibility
    ...                         // another constant part
    primitive2();               // derived class responsibility
    ...

}
```

You should use the template method design pattern to implement certain algorithms, such as sorting algorithms. These algorithms can be defined in terms of a primitive `compare()` operation to compare two elements. The abstract base class has a template method, `sort()`, that uses `compare()`. Various derived classes of this class then define different ways of comparing elements.

Another example is a class responsible for logging users into an application (for details, see Grand, 1998). The algorithm used for this task consists of four steps:

- Prompting for the user ID and password (concrete)
- Authenticating the user (primitive)

- Displaying appropriate information while the authentication is in progress (concrete)
- Notification that the login is complete (primitive).

The login operation is a template method that uses these four operations.

For a final example of the template method design pattern, consider the task of printing text using various methods, for example, ASCII and HTML. The printing task can be implemented as a template method that uses an abstract print operation. This operation will be implemented in the derived classes, which know about the details of printing specific styles, such as ASCII and HTML.

All these examples show that the derived classes provide the concrete implementation for the base class' abstract operations. In addition, a derived class can also redefine (override) other concrete operations. Concrete operations that are overridden in derived classes are called **hook operations**. Notice that the abstract operations *must* be overridden, but the primitive operations *may* be overridden. For example, in Java's `java.io.Reader` class, `read()` is a hook operation, and it is overridden in `java.io.InputStreamReader`.

The template method should not be overridden, so it is not defined as `virtual`. On the other hand, all operations that are used by the template method are defined as `virtual`, as well as `private` or `protected`, so the client cannot directly call them.

● EXAMPLE 5.5

Consider the task of computing the billable amount for a store, which is the number of units times the price of each unit, plus the tax, which is different for various kinds of stores (for details, see Fowler, 1999). To represent this information, we need the following three classes: a store, which is designed according to the template method design pattern; and two specific stores, a downtown store or a neighborhood store. The UML diagram for this example is shown in Figure 5.8.

```
// File ex5.5.store.h
class Store { // abstract
// A class to maintain general information about a store
// Provides four functions with self-explanatory names
// One of these functions is abstract and defined in a
//  derived class
public:
  double getBillableAmount(int) const;          // template method
  Store(double pricePerUnit = 1);
  double getPricePerUnit() const;
  void setPricePerUnit(double);
protected:
  virtual double getTaxAmount(int) const = 0;    //primitive operation
  double pricePerUnit_;
};
```

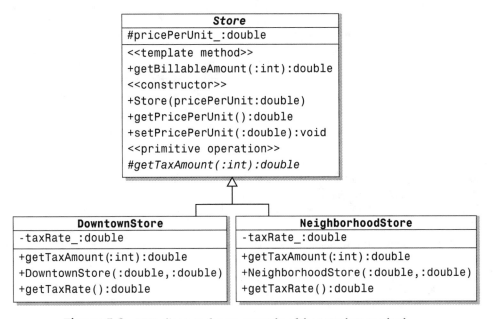

Figure 5.8   UML diagram for an example of the template method design pattern

```
// File ex5.5.store.cpp
// implementation of the template method
double Store::getBillableAmount (int units) const {
  return units*pricePerUnit_ + getTaxAmount(units);
  }

// File ex5.5.downtownstore.h
class DowntownStore : public Store { // implements
public:
  virtual double getTaxAmount(int) const;
  DowntownStore(double, double = 0.07);          // default tax rate
  double getTaxRate() const;
private:
  double taxRate_;
};

// File ex5.5.downtownstore.cpp
// implementation of the abstract operation
double DowntownStore::getTaxAmount(int units) const {
  return units*pricePerUnit_*taxRate_;
  }

// File ex5.5.neighborhoodstore.h
class NeighborhoodStore : public Store {
```

```
public:
  virtual double getTaxAmount(int) const;
  NeighborhoodStore(double, double = 0.01);
  double getTaxRate() const;
private:
  double taxRate_;
};

// File ex5.5.neighborhoodstore.cpp
// implementation of the abstract operation
double NeighborhoodStore::getTaxAmount(int units) const {
  return units*pricePerUnit_*taxRate_;
}
```

The client can use the store classes like this:

```
#include "ex5.5.store.h"
#include "ex5.5.downtownstore.h"
#include "ex5.5.neighborhoodstore.h"
int main() {
  const int UNITS = 25;
  const double PERUNIT = 10;
  Store* s1 = new DowntownStore(PERUNIT);
  // default tax rate, 25 units
  Store* s2 = new NeighborhoodStore(PERUNIT);
  cout << "for " << UNITS << " units, pay " << endl;
  cout << "downtown: " << s1->getBillableAmount(UNITS) << endl;
  cout << "neighborhood: " << s2->getBillableAmount(UNITS) << endl;
}
```

The template method design pattern is an example of a design strategy for which the derived classes cannot alter the behavior of the template method; they can only define or redefine the meaning of the primitive operations. Therefore, the derived classes cannot alter the flow of control of the template operation—a technique often referred to as the Hollywood principle ("Don't call us; we'll call you"). This principle is always used to design software frameworks.

5.15.2   Postponing Creation of Objects

There are three ways to disallow the creation of objects:

- Specifying at least one operation as abstract (i.e. pure virtual)
- Specifying constructors as private or protected
- Defining a pure virtual destructor:

```
class B {
public:
  virtual ~B() = 0;
  ...
};
```

Such a destructor must also be *defined*; otherwise, your program will likely crash:

```
B::~B() { }
```

This may sound strange: The operation is abstract and has no body, but at the same time, its body is defined. C++ allows this for technical reasons, such as those associated with defining a pure virtual destructor or to provide default implementations (discussed in detail in Section 6.5.1).

5.16 *Friends*

In Java, protected features are accessible to any code within the package. C++ does not support Java's packages, and namespaces have limited power; therefore, it must provide another technique to allow two classes to access each other's private attributes, while at the same time preventing other clients from accessing the attributes.

Consider two classes that cooperate to perform a certain task; for example, the classes List and ListElem. The class List needs access to the private attributes of the class ListElem, and it would be inefficient to use queries and modifiers for this purpose. C++ provides a **friend declaration**, which ListElem can use to declare that one of the following constructs is a friend and therefore has access to the class, private features:

- Another class
- A single operation from another class
- A global operation

For example, the ListElem class gives access to its private features to the *entire* List class as follows:

```
class ListElem {
  friend class List;     // gives access to features from List
  ...
};
```

Friend declarations can be placed in any section of the class; I will always put them at the beginning of the class.

If the class ListElem does not want to provide List with unlimited access but only give access to a *specific operation* in say, show(), it can do so as follows:

```
class ListElem {
   friend void List::show();      // gives access to one operation
   ...
};
```

Finally, consider a *global function,* print(), that is given access to the private features of ListElem:

```
class ListElem {
   friend void ::print();              // gives access to global function
   ...
};
```

The friend declaration can appear in either the private or public section. Note that external operations specified as friends are not a part of a class' interface, but they have the same access rights as regular class operations that are in this interface.

Consider yet another example of an implementation of the singleton pattern, this time using a separate class to handle the deallocation of a singleton (this example is based on the example from Vlissides, 1998):

```
class Singleton {      // This version is not quite correct; see below
public:
   static Singleton* instance();
   void op1();
private:
   Singleton();
   Singleton(const Singleton&);
   Singleton& operator=(const Singleton&);
   virtual ~Singleton();
   static Singleton* onlyInstance_;
   static SingletonDeallocator deallocator_;
};

Singleton* Singleton::onlyInstance_ = 0;
SingletonDeallocator::deallocator_;
```

When the program terminates, deallocator_ goes out of scope, the destructor for the SingletonDeallocator is executed, and this destructor deletes the instance of the singleton. The variable is initialized when the user calls instance():

```
Singleton* Singleton::instance() {
  if(onlyInstance_ == 0) {
      onlyInstance_ = new Singleton;
      deallocator_.setSingleton(onlyInstance_);
  }
  return onlyInstance_;
}
```

The class `SingletonDeallocator` is essentially a wrapper class for the `only-Instance_` **pointer:**

```
class SingletonDeallocator {
public:
  SingletonDeallocator(Singleton* = 0);
  virtual ~SingletonDeallocator();
  void setSingleton(Singleton*);
private:
  Singleton* singleton_;
};

SingletonDeallocator::SingletonDeallocator(Singleton* s) {
  singleton_ = s;
}

SingletonDeallocator::~SingletonDeallocator() {
  delete singleton_;
}

void SingletonDeallocator::setSingleton(Singleton* s) {
  singleton_ = s;
}
```

The class `SingletonDeallocator` *seems* to obey the standard encapsulation rules because it does not access the private features of the class `Singleton`. However, this turns out to be false because the destructor of the class `Singleton` is private. Therefore, the class `Singleton` has to give the class `SingletonDeallocator` access to its private features:

```
class Singleton {
  friend class SingletonDeallocator;
public:
  ...
};
```

Friendship is limited to the class specified as a friend. When you declare that X is a friend, you do not give special privileges to X's friends. Friendship is not transitive (nor is it symmetric: If Y is a friend of X then X is not automatically a friend of Y). Also, a derived class of X is not considered to be a friend. Finally, friendship cannot be declared for an existing class, because only the class can specify it.

Since a derived class does not have unlimited access to the features of its base class, you may be tempted to specify in the base class that one or more of its derived classes are friends. While technically speaking this solves the problem (that is, gives a derived class access to the base class), it is also a bad idea because it hard-codes the design.

Note that friends do not completely break encapsulation; the class that declares friends allows *only* these friends to access this class' private features. However, you should avoid declaring friend unless absolutely necessary; an alternative may be to use namespaces.

5.17 *Exercises*

For all the exercises in this chapter, you should carefully design the interface of each class; in particular, decide if you need to implement functions such as the copy constructor, destructor, and assignment operator. When an exercise requires you to create a namespace, you should design it carefully, and split it into files available to the client and to the implementation. For each exercise, include a program that tests your code.

EXERCISE 5-1

State and explain the output produced by the following program:

```
#include <iostream>
#include <string>
using namespace std;

class X {
public:
  virtual void show(string = "") const;
  X(int);
  virtual ~X();
private:
  int i_;
};
void X::show(string s) const {
  if(s != "")
    cout << s << i_;
}
X::X(int j): i_(j) {
  show();
```

```
}
X::~X() {
  cout << "X" << endl;
}

class Y : public X {
public:
  virtual void show(string s = "") const;
  Y(int, double);
  ~Y();
private:
  double d_;
};
void Y::show(string s)  const {
  cout << d_ << ' ' << s << endl;
}
Y::Y(int j, double s) : X(j), d_(s) {
  show();
}
Y::~Y() {
  cout << "Y" << endl;
}

class Z : public Y {
public:
  void show(string = "");
  Z(string, int, double);
  ~Z();
private:
  string c_;
};
void Z::show() const {
  cout << c_ << endl;
}
Z::Z(string s, int j, double d) : Y(j, d), c_(s) {
  show(s);
}
Z::~Z(){
  cout << "Z" << endl;
}

int main() {
  X* m = new Y(3, 3.5);
  m->show("2");
  delete m;
```

```
m = new Z("Z", 4, 4.5);
m->show("3");
delete m;
}
```

EXERCISE 5-2

You want to create a simple database of books. Assume that there are two types of books: reference books and text books. For every book, you must know its name (you can make assumptions about the maximum size of the name). For a reference book, you also need to know the subject of the book (for example, math, computer science, or physics). You can use a single character (*m*, *c*, or *p*) to represent the required information. For a textbook, you also need to know the course associated with this book (represented as an integer). The database will be stored in an array of pointers to books.

Implement a class hierarchy (with the class Book as a root) to represent this scenario. Create a database with two books: the textbook *OOPS* for the 3773 course and the reference book *Relativity Theory* for physics. Write a method to print information about all books.

Assume that the class ReferenceBook has a member, getSubject(), that returns the subject of the book. Also, assume that you don't have access to the code in the class Book. Use RTTI to write a function to print the subject of all reference books.

EXERCISE 5-3

Implement a function, safeDivision(), that tries to divide two real numbers and throws an exception if the division cannot be performed because the second number equals zero. Show how you can call this function.

EXERCISE 5-4

Implement a class, Address, that has two members: a string name and a string address. Then implement a class, ExtendedAddress, that is derived from Address and has an additional member representing a zip code. Both classes should be stored in a namespace.

EXERCISE 5-5

Implement a class, Address, that has the two members: a string name and a string address. Then implement a class, ExtendedAddress, that has a nested Address and has a member representing a zip code. Finally, implement a class, PostAddress, derived from ExtendedAddress, which has an additional member representing a post-box number. All three classes should be stored in a namespace.

EXERCISE 5-6

Implement a class, Address, that has two members: a string name and a string address. Then implement a class, ExtendedAddress, that has a pointer to an object of type `Address` and has a member representing a zip code. Finally, implement a class, `PostAddress`, derived from `ExtendedAddress`, which has an additional member representing a post-box number. All three classes should be stored in a namespace.

EXERCISE 5-7

Implement the class `Book` with a single attribute name. Then implement a class, `Shelf`, that has two nested objects of type `Book`. Finally, implement a class, `Library`, that has a stack of shelves. (Hint: base your design on the class `IntStack` from Example 5.3.) All three classes should be stored in a namespace.

EXERCISE 5-8

Implement the class `Book` with a single attribute name. Then implement a class, `Shelf`, that has two pointers to objects of type `Book`. Finally, implement a class, `Library`, that has a stack of shelves. (Hint: base your design on the class `IntStack` from Example 5.3.) All three classes should be stored in a namespace.

EXERCISE 5-9

Write the class `IntStackNew`, similar to the class `IntStack` from Example 5.3 but with two additional functions in its interface : `empty()` and `full()`. In addition, the copying of objects of type `IntStackNew` should not be allowed. This class should be stored in a namespace.

EXERCISE 5-10

Add a namespace to Example 5.3. Then write the class `IntStackExtended`, derived from the class `IntStack` from Example 5.3, with the interface that has the additional functions `empty()` and `full()`. This class should be stored in the same namespace as the class `IntStack`.

EXERCISE 5-11

Write the class `Queue`, similar to the class `IntStack` from Example 5.3, in which the elements of the queue are stored in an array. This class should be stored in a namespace. Use exception handling.

EXERCISE 5-12

Write the abstract class `IntStackIfc` whose interface is the same as the one in Example 5.3. Then provide two implementations of this class; one using an array and one using a linked list.

EXERCISE 5-13

Write a class derived from the class `BenchmarkClass` from Example 5.4 to benchmark two sorting algorithms for double values stored in the array: bubble sort and quick sort (you can find the description of these algorithms in Aho, 1983).

EXERCISE 5-14

Use the template method design pattern to implement classes that deal with drawing and moving two-dimensional figures; this will involve two classes: `Figure` and `Point`. The class `Figure` has an abstract function `draw()` and a template function `moveTo(int, int)`, which moves a figure. The class `Point` is derived from `Figure` and implements drawing by printing the coordinates of the point.

OBJECT-ORIENTED PROGRAMMING, PART II

6.1 Preview

In this chapter, I continue the discussion of object-oriented programming I started in the previous chapter. First I present various issues surrounding the object creational process and introduce the abstract factory design pattern. Then I discuss private, protected, and multiple inheritance, and I compare delegation and inheritance. Finally, I describe a very important programming technique called programming to an interface and show several related design patterns, including the bridge, the prototype, the adapter and the state.

6.2 Managing the Creational Process, Part II: Abstract Factory Design Pattern

Recall the instantiating operations idiom (Idiom 4.2), which specifies how to design classes so you can control the creation of their objects. This was accomplished by making all the constructors either private or protected and creating user-defined functions responsible for object creation, copying, and so on. This idiom is useful if your programs do not use inheritance. We saw a second technique for controlling the creational process when we looked at the singleton design pattern, which permits creation of at most one instance of a class. You can also use design patterns to manage the general creational process in the context of classes and inheritance by using the **abstract factory design pattern** and its associated **factory method**. Both the singleton and the abstract factory design patterns are creational patterns because they provide techniques that control the creation of objects.

Why are creational design patterns useful? In all object-oriented programs, sooner or later an object is asked to create new objects. An object is created in response to a need for a "thing" that has a certain behavior; for example, the program may have a "function thing" that represents either a polynomial or a rational function (quotient of two polynomials), and it may be asked to perform function-related operations such as printing. As another example, the program may have a "room thing" that represents a particular type of room in a maze and may be asked to find an exit (if one exists). To satisfy the requirements made in these examples, you need to create an object (or objects) so you can use the functionality it provides—you need the object's behavior, which is specified by its public interface. When a class constructor is used to create an object, it creates two dependencies: It makes your code dependent on the objects of this particular class, and it makes it dependent on the *name* of the specific class used to create it. The second dependency is the reason the class name is said to be hard-coded.

This gives rise to two questions: Is there anything wrong with hard-coding class names? If so, is it possible to avoid it? The answer to the first question is generally yes, because hard-coding class names makes it difficult to modify your program should you want to replace some class in the program with a different class—say, because the new class has a better implementation but has the same behavior. In addition, you want to minimize the dependencies between the various elements of your program; the more dependencies you have, the more difficult it is to maintain the code. These two examples should convince you that hard-coding class names makes program maintenance and modification difficult. To avoid the problem, you can use creational design patterns. Justifying this statement demands a closer look at the two examples.

Consider a polynomial function represented by a string. To operate on the polynomial—for example, to display it—you need to read in the string, use it to create an object of type `Polynomial`, and then use its interface to perform the display operation. Suppose you decide that you also need to deal with other kinds of functions, for example, rational functions. You now have to change your code: After the string is read, you have to parse it to decide what type of function it represents and create an object of either type `Polynomial` or type `Rational`. In this scenario, you are hard-coding the class used to create new objects in your program; whenever new function types are added, each part of the code that creates objects representing these functions has to be modified. This problem can be remedied by encapsulating the creation of objects in another class and using the interface of this class to get new objects whenever they are required. Any future changes to the creational process will be isolated to the class that produces objects. The situation can be roughly compared to using literal constants, such as 20, rather than using symbolic constants, such as `const int SIZE = 20`; symbolic constants make it much easier and safer to modify the value of the constant.

At this point, it is useful to borrow from standard "production" terminology and call the object being created a **product** and the object that creates other objects a **factory**. The factory is responsible for producing a specific product; this is done using the **factory method**. The example begun in the previous paragraph has two products: a polynomial function and a rational function. The factory method has a string parameter used to decide which product it should produce. Your code would use two classes: an abstract product class (which is the base class for all products) and the factory class (which may or may not be abstract). You would create a factory object and use its factory method to create a specific product. By doing this, you would avoid hard-coding concrete product names. Then you would use the abstract product interface to invoke the required operation for a product—for example, to display the rational function. Thus, the product dependency is now encapsulated in the factory class, which means that the remainder of your code is not dependent on a specific product.

Here's another example (for the complete description of this example, see Gamma et. al., 1995). Consider a maze consisting of a number of rooms, represented by objects of class `Room`, and `RoomWithSpell`; each room has an interface consisting of operations such as enter, exit, and so on. If you create a specific maze and hard-code class names by using class constructors, then dependencies exist between the class names and every piece of code using the constructors. A change made to the behavior of the room with the spell or the addition of a new type of room, such as an enchanted room, requires many modifications in your code. To minimize these dependencies and encapsulate them in a single class, you can use a factory. In the factory, a room is the abstract product, and a specific kind of a room, such as a room with a spell, is a class derived from the room. A factory class has a factory method that creates a room; your code creates an object of a factory class and then asks the object's factory method to create various kinds of rooms. Using this design, dependency on object creation is limited to a single class.

Both these examples describe a creational design process. Note that creational design patterns do more than just hide how objects are created; they also hide how objects are combined to exhibit the desired behavior. This is accomplished by having the client of the factory *program to the abstract interface* provided by the products of the factory.

Recall that constructing an object requires knowing the type of the object. However, the constructor cannot be virtual; in particular, it cannot be abstract, which would allow the derived class to decide what type of object is created. On the other hand, a factory method may be (and is) virtual and is declared as follows:

```
AbstractProduct* Factory::factoryMethod(...);
```

This factory method returns a product derived from the class `AbstractProduct`. This type of factory method is also known as a **virtual constructor** because it lets various classes derived from `Factory`, such as `AnotherFactory`, decide on the specific type of product to create:

```
AbstractProduct* AnotherFactory::factoryMethod(...);
```

The factory method is often useful in combination with the template method design pattern. Recall that the *template method design pattern* specifies that a template method define an algorithm in terms of abstract operations, called primitive operations. If the template method needs to create an object, it can use a factory method rather than hard-coding class names. For example, consider the abstract class Factory, which has a factory method to create products derived from the abstract class Product. Concrete factories (that is, classes derived from Factory) create concrete products (see Figure 6.1). The template method templateOP() uses the factory method to return objects of classes derived from the class Product (see the note attached to the template operation in Figure 6.1).

Now, to invoke the template method that uses a specific product, a client has to follow this procedure:

1. Create a concrete factory.
2. Call the template method, which will use a factory method to create a product and then use the product.

Therefore, changing the product does not require any changes in the template method; it merely requires a change to the factory class.

The abstract factory design pattern is a *class creational pattern* based on the concept of a factory method (see Figure 6.2). The abstract factory is typically implemented as an abstract class that provides a method to return specific factories (this method is often static). The abstract factory class also has abstract factory methods to return instances of concrete derived classes of the abstract product. The user of this pattern never creates objects directly but instead gets a factory and asks it to create a concrete product.

A nonsoftware example of this design pattern (based on Duell, 1998) is the sheet metal stamping equipment used in the manufacture of Japanese automobiles.

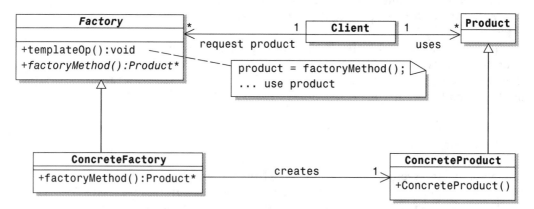

Figure 6.1   Factory method

Based in part, by permission, on Gamma, E., et al., *Design Patterns: Elements of Reusable Object-Oriented Software* (Reading, Mass: Addison-Wesley, 1995) p. 88.

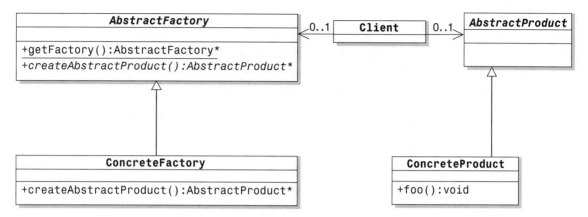

Figure 6.2 Abstract factory design pattern

The stamping equipment, analogous to an abstract factory, stamps various body parts of different models of cars, such as left and right doors, fenders, and so on. The stamping dies can be changed using rollers, thereby producing *concrete factories*.

Now consider two software examples of the abstract factory design pattern. The first example is a system where various kinds of objects are created from interactive file input on a local machine, or from a remote machine on the network. The user should be able to code to the same interface—that is, use the same function to open a file for reading or writing, regardless of where the file is located. To support this functionality, you will design an abstract product class (see Figure 6.2) with two abstract functions: on that opens a file for reading and one that opens a file for writing. There will be two concrete product classes derived from this abstract class: one to implement a local file access and one to implement a remote file access. In this example, there is no need for an abstract factory like that shown in Figure 6.2; there will be only a concrete factory that implements a `createAbstractProduct(string filename)` function. This function will examine `filename` and, depending on whether it represents a local filename or a remote filename, it will return the appropriate concrete product.

The second example involves the indexing of Web pages using the page titles (for more details of this example, see Cooper, 1998). There are several ways in which the titles can be organized—for example, inside an `<h1>` HTML or `<meta>` tag. A title is represented by a product; there is also an abstract product class with an abstract function that returns a title. For each kind of title, there is a concrete product class that implements the specific function to retrieve the title—for example, a function that returns a title between `<h1>` and `</h1>` tags. Finally, there is a concrete factory, that implements a `createAbstractProduct(string filename)` function, which reads the Web page determined by the filename, parses the beginning of the page, and returns the appropriate concrete product.

Java uses factory methods; for example, the `URLConnection` class has an association with the factory `ContentHandlerFactory`, which is set through a method in

URLConnection **called** getContent(). The URLConnection getContent() **method** delegates the task of getting the contents of a page to the getContent() method from the ContentHandlerFactory. This method is a template method; it uses a factory method to get an instance of ContentHandler and then get the actual page contents from this instance. Other applications of abstract factories include the creation of sockets and URL objects.

I now provide two examples of programs that use the abstract factory design pattern.

● EXAMPLE 6.1

This example implements some simple file operations, such as computing the number of lines in a file. These operations can be implemented without caching; each time an operation is invoked, it reads the file and returns the required result. Alternatively, these operations can be implemented with caching; the file contents can could be stored in a cache that is read when you want to compute the number of lines. This is a good candidate for the factory method, because you need to create two different products (instances that either do or do not cache). The responsibility of creating products will be assigned to an abstract factory method; the derived class will implement this abstract method as a function returning an instance of the class. The function lines() is a template method that uses the factory method to create the product (which is a cached or noncached application) and then invokes the operation lines() from this product (the name of this operation happens to be the same as the name of the template operation). The complete design of this example using UML is shown in Figure 6.3.

Note that dashed links represent **dependencies** between two classes; for example, a dependency may indicate that a modification of an interface of one class

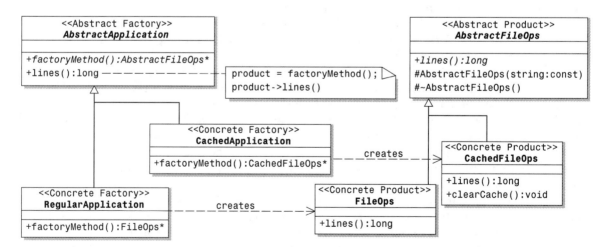

Figure 6.3 Example of the factory method

implies the need for the modification of the interface of another class (Gamma et. al., 1995, use a dashed link to indicate a special kind of dependency that occurs when a class instantiates objects of another class).

   First, consider the product classes. There are two kinds of products: objects with and without caching. Consequently, the class hierarchy consists of one abstract base class and two concrete derived classes:

```
// File ex6.1.abstractfile.h
class AbstractFileOps {  //abstract product
public:
  virtual long lines() const = 0;
protected:
  virtual ~AbstractFileOps();
};


// File ex6.1.fileops.h
// concrete product
class FileOps : public AbstractFileOps { // implements
public:
  virtual long lines() const;   // computes number of lines every time it is called
  FileOps(const string&);
  ~FileOps();
private:
  mutable ifstream fileVar_;
};

// File: ex6.1.cachedfileops.h
// concrete product
class CachedFileOps : public AbstractFileOps {   // implements
public:
  virtual long lines() const;                              //uses cache
  virtual void clearCache();
  CachedFileOps(const string&);
  ~CachedFileOps();
private:
  mutable long lines_;
  mutable bool linesCached_;
  mutable ifstream fileVar_;
};
```

   The application is designed as a set of *factory classes*, with one abstract class that has an abstract factory method and two concrete implementations:

```
// File: ex6.1.abstractapplication.h
class AbstractFileOps;
class AbstractApplication { // abstract factory
```

```cpp
public:
  virtual AbstractFileOps* factoryMethod() const = 0;
  long lines() const;                               // template method
  virtual ~AbstractApplication();
};

// File: ex6.1.abstractapplication.cpp
long AbstractApplication::lines() const {
  AbstractFileOps* afo = factoryMethod();
  return afo->lines();
}
AbstractApplication::~AbstractApplication() {}

// File: ex6.1.regularapplication.h
// concrete factory
class RegularApplication : public AbstractApplication {  // implements

public:
  RegularApplication(const string&);
  ~RegularApplication();
  virtual FileOps* factoryMethod() const;
private:
  string filename_;
};

// File: ex6.1.cachedapplication.h
// concrete factory
class CachedApplication : public AbstractApplication {  // implements

public:
  CachedApplication(const string&);
  ~CachedApplication();
  virtual CachedFileOps* factoryMethod() const;
  void clearCache();
private:
  string filename_;
};

// File: ex6.1.regularapplication.cpp
FileOps* RegularApplication::factoryMethod() const {
  return new FileOps(filename_);
}
RegularApplication::RegularApplication(const string& filename)
  : filename_(filename)
{}
```

```
RegularApplication::~RegularApplication()
{}

// File: ex6.1.cachedapplication.cpp
CachedFileOps* CachedApplication::factoryMethod() const {
  return new CachedFileOps(filename_);
}

CachedApplication::CachedApplication(const string& filename):
  filename_(filename) {}
CachedApplication::~CachedApplication()
{}

void CachedApplication::clearCache() {
  AbstractFileOps* afo = factoryMethod();

  if(CashedFileOps* cs = dynamic_cast<CachedFileOps*>(afo))
    cs->clearCache();
  else
    cerr << "non caching application tried to cache " << endl;
}
```

The implementation of `clearCache()` uses `factoryMethod()` to get a *product*. This method is virtual and called from the object of `CachedApplication`, therefore it will return an object of type `CachedFileOps`. However, in this case, you cannot avoid using a dynamic cast, because the factory method is declared to be of type `AbstractFileOps`. The error message in `clearCache()` will never be displayed.

To use a cached application, the client creates a concrete factory and then uses a template method:

```
// File: ex6.1.driver.cpp
int main(int argc, char* argv[]) {
if(argc != 3) {
  cerr << "usage " << argv[0] << " file1 file2" << endl;
  return 1;
}

CachedApplication* cached = new CachedApplication(argv[1]);
cout << "lines in " << argv[1] << " " << cached->lines() << endl;
cached->clearCache();
cout << "lines in " << argv[1] << " " << cached->lines() << endl;

AbstractApplication* regular = new RegularApplication(argv[2]);
cout << "lines in " << argv[2] << " " << regular->lines() << endl;
```

● EXAMPLE 6.2

This example uses two kinds of functions: polynomials and rational functions (quotients of two polynomials). Functions are passed into the application as strings of the following form:

- Sequence of integers separated by commas to specify coefficients of polynomials
- Two sequences of integers separated by a slash (/) to specify rational functions

While this application is not particularly interesting, it does show the advantages of using the abstract factory pattern. The UML diagram for this example is shown in Figure 6.4. The client of the program uses an abstract factory, FunctionFactory, and an abstract product, Function. There are two concrete factories, RationalFactory and PolynomialFactory, which create the concrete products Rational and Polynomial, respectively.

```
// File: ex6.2.function.h
class Function {   // abstract product
public:
   virtual void display() const = 0;
   Function(const string&);
   virtual ~Function();
```

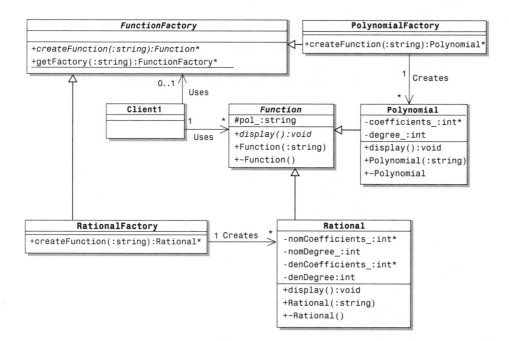

Figure 6.4   Example of the abstract factory design pattern

```cpp
protected:
  string pol_;
};

// File: ex6.2.polynomial.h
// concrete product
class Polynomial: public Function { // implements
public:
  virtual void display() const;
  Polynomial(const string&);
  virtual ~Polynomial();
private:
  int* coefficients_;
  int degree_;
};

// File: ex6.2.rational.h
// concrete product
class Rational : public Function { // implements
public:
  virtual void display() const;
  Rational(const string&);
  virtual ~Rational();
private:
  int* nomCoefficients_;
  int nomDegree_;
  int* denCoefficients_;
  int denDegree_;
};

// File: ex6.2.polynomial.cpp
void Polynomial::display() const {

  cout << "Polynomial" << endl;
  for(int i = 0; i < degree_-1; ++i)
    cout << coefficients_[i] << "*x^" << i << " + ";
  cout << coefficients_[degree_] << "*x^" << degree_ << endl;
}

Polynomial::Polynomial(const string& pol) : Function(pol) {
  degree_ = 0;
                                    // retrieve degree
  istringstream is(pol_);
  while(is >> double d)
    ++degree_;
```

```
    coefficients_ = new int[degree_];
                                                    // fill in
    istringstream is1(pol_);
    for(int i = 0; i < degree_; ++i)
      is1 >> coefficients_[i];
}
Polynomial::~Polynomial() {
    delete [] coefficients_;
}
```

To retrieve double values from the string, this example uses string stream operations (which I describe in detail in Section 9.2.5). Here is the code for the abstract factory, which has a method to return a specific factory:

```
// File: ex6.2.functionfactory.h
class FunctionFactory { // abstract
public:
    virtual Function* createFunction(const string&) const = 0;
    static FunctionFactory* getFactory(const string&);  //note: static
    virtual ~FunctionFactory();
};
```

```
// File: ex6.2.functionfactory.cpp
FunctionFactory* FunctionFactory::getFactory(const string& s) {
    string::size_type pos = s.find_first_of('/');

                                    // if s represents a polynomial
    if(pos == string::npos)
      return new PolynomialFactory();
    return new RationalFactory();

}
FunctionFactory::~FunctionFactory() {}
```

The interface for the two concrete factories follows:

```
// File: ex6.2.polynomialfactory.h
// concrete factory
class PolynomialFactory : public FunctionFactory {
public:
    virtual Polynomial* createFunction(const string&) const;
    virtual ~PolynomialFactory();
};
```

```
// File: ex6.2.rationalfactory.h
// concrete factory
```

```
class RationalFactory : public FunctionFactory {
public:
    virtual Rational* createFunction(const string&) const;
    virtual ~RationalFactory();
};
```

The implementation of the latter factory follows:

```
// File: ex6.2.rationalfactory.cpp
Rational* RationalFactory::createFunction(const string& s) const {
    return new Rational(s);
}
RationalFactory::~RationalFactory() {}
```

The client's code follows the general procedure described earlier: The client gets a concrete factory, asks the factory for a product, and finally uses the product:

```
string s;
cin >> s;
FunctionFactory* factory = FunctionFactory::getFactory(s);
Function* foo = factory->createFunction(s);
foo->display();
```

The client's code does not use any concrete classes, which means that it is possible to modify the factory's behavior (by deriving a new factory class from factory and redefining its behavior) without modifying the client's code.

Unfortunately, this design allows the client to construct polynomial or rational functions using the corresponding constructors rather than factory methods. If I moved these constructors to the protected sections of the class, these actions would become impossible, but then the factory would not work either because it needs to use the constructors. One way to solve this problem is to make the factory class a friend of each of the three classes: Function, Polynomial, and Rational (it is not enough to make it a friend of Functions because friendship is not inherited).

───▶

Typically, you need at most one concrete factory object in your application, so concrete factories are often implemented as singletons.

6.3 *Private Inheritance*

Recall that with *public inheritance*, all public features of the base class are inherited; that is, they are available to the clients of any derived class. This kind of inheritance, similar to the one used by Java, allows you to substitute properly implemented objects of derived classes for objects of the base class.

In some cases, you do not want to inherit the entire interface, or even a part of it; instead, you want to inherit just the *implementation* of the various operations. For example, to operate on data with more stringent requirements, you may need to restrict the original interface. To understand these concepts, consider a class, Dequeue, that contains operations to insert and delete elements at either end of the queue:

```
// File: ch6.dequeue.h;  circular queue of integers
class Dequeue {
public:
  Dequeue(int size = 10);
  virtual ~Dequeue();
  void insertL(int);
  void insertR(int);
  int removeL();
  int removeR();
protected:
  int size_;
  int* elem_;
  int left_
  int right_;
};
```

Suppose you want to use queues in which you can only insert at the front of the queue and remove at the end of the queue; the two remaining operations are to be disallowed. Using public inheritance to derive a class from Dequeue would give the client access to operations that are not allowed. To support these kinds of requirements, C++ provides **private derivation**, in which the interface is not inherited. More specifically, with private derivation, all public and protected features of the base class are available as private features of the derived class.

The following code shows how to inherit part of an interface (later in this section I show how to inherit only the implementation). You can select features from the base class and make them available in a derived class with the using keyword, which effectively restores the inherited feature:

```
// File: ch6.queue.h
class Queue: private Dequeue {              // note: private
public:
  using Dequeue::insertL;                   // restore insertL();
  using Dequeue::removeR;                   // restore removeR();
  Queue(int size = 10);
  virtual ~Queue();
};
```

This code is equivalent to the following *pseudo-code:*

```
class Queue {
public:
  void insertL(int);
  int removeR();
  Queue(int size = 10);
  virtual ~Queue();
private:
  Dequeue(int size = 10);
  virtual ~Dequeue();
  int removeL();
  void insertR(int);
  int size_;
  int* elem_;
  int left_;
  int right_;
};
```

Two operations inherited from the base class have been made public with the
using keyword. The remaining features in the base class are private in the derived
class. You can define a derived class without using any derivation qualification; for
example:

```
class Queue : Dequeue {... }
```

This is equivalent to a private derivation. However, this convention is less readable,
and I will not use it in this book.

Private inheritance also allows you to inherit only the *implementation*, without
inheriting any part of the interface. For example, consider an implementation of the
class Stack, except this time using operation names such as push() or pop(). Private inheritance allows you to implement the interface of the derived class using
operations from the base class:

```
// File: ch6.stack.h
class Stack : private Dequeue {      // doesn't inherit the interface
public:
  Stack(int size = 10);
  ~Stack();
  void push(int);
  int pop();
  bool full() const;
};
```

To implement the interface of Stack, you can use operations from its base class; for example:

```
void Stack::push(int i) {
   insertL(i);
}

bool Stack::full() const {
   return left_ == right_;
}
```

Note that using can be applied to restore features not only in the public section but also in the protected section. However, the access level cannot be changed; it has to be the same as in the base class. For example, the protected attributes of Dequeue can be restored to the protected level in Stack. This is useful if a class derived with private inheritance has additional derived classes of its own:

```
class Stack : private Dequeue {
public:
   Stack(int size = 10);
   ~Stack();
   void push(int);
   int pop();
protected:
   using Dequeue::size_;
   using Dequeue::elem_;
   using Dequeue::left_;
   using Dequeue::right_;
};
```

Here is a summary of the description of private inheritance: Since the interface is not inherited, private inheritance does not support *is-a* relationships; for example, a Queue is not a Stack, and Queue objects cannot be used where Stack objects are expected. Probably the most concise way to describe private inheritance is to say that it represents an *is-implemented-in-terms-of* relationship; for the previous example, Stack *is-implemented-in-terms-of* Dequeue. In other words, private inheritance allows the derived class to reuse the code of the base class.

6.4 *Protected Inheritance*

Protected inheritance means that all public features of the base class become *protected* features of the derived class (protected features of the base class continue to be protected in the derived class). Therefore, protected inheritance is useful if you do not want to finalize the derivations; that is, you want to make it possible to have additional derived classes. For example, the following declaration

```
class Stack : protected Dequeue {
public:
  Stack(int size = 10);
  ~Stack();
  void push(int);
  int pop();
  bool full() const;
};
```

is equivalent to the following pseudo-code:

```
class Stack {
public:
  Stack(int size = 10);
  ~Stack();
  void push(int);
  int pop();
  bool full() const;

protected:
  Dequeue(int size = 10);
  virtual ~Dequeue();
  void insertL(int);
  void insertR(int);
  int removeL();
  int removeR();

  int size_;
  int* elem_;
  int left_;
  int right_;
};
```

In this example, all public and protected features of Dequeue are protected in Stack.

6.5 *Revisiting Inheritance*

Here's a summary of what you have learned inheritance so far:

- *public inheritance* means inheriting the interface.
- *private inheritance* means inheriting the implementation.

Also, recall that *virtual operations* come in two flavors: abstract and concrete (the latter provide the implementation), each with unique inheritance properties:

- For an *abstract operation*, a publicly derived classes inherits only the interface, not the implementation.
- For a *concrete operation*, a publicly derived class inherits both the interface and the implementation (the latter means that the derived class can make use of the implementation available in the base class).

In the next section, I describe the concept of a default implementation; in subsequent sections, I will compare inheritance and delegation and briefly introduce multiple inheritance.

6.5.1   Default Implementations

Typically, virtual functions are designed to be abstract, and their implementations are provided in derived classes. In some cases, it may be useful to provide a default implementation of a virtual function that will be used in a derived class. However, a default implementation may turn out to be dangerous because the designer of the derived class may forget to add her or his own implementation. For example, consider the following class Shape (this example is based on the example from Meyers, 1998):

```
class Shape {
public:
  virtual void draw() const;
  ...
};

void Shape::draw() {
  // default implementation; for example draws a logo shape
  ...
}

class Rectangle : public Shape {
public:
  ...                         // no draw() here
};

Shape* s = new Rectangle;
s->draw();                    // draws the logo, not the rectangle
```

It would be useful to force the inheriting clients to provide their own implementations but, at the same time, have a default implementation in the base class. C++ supports this option by allowing you to specify a pure virtual operation *and* its default implementation:

```
class Shape { // abstract
public:
   virtual void draw() const = 0;
   ...
};

void Shape::draw() {
   // default implementation; for example draws a logo shape
   ...
}

class Rectangle : public Shape { // still abstract
public:
                                    // no implementation of draw()
   ...
};
```

This attempt to create and use Shape objects

```
Shape* s = new Rectangle;
s->draw();                  // draws the logo, not the rectangle
```

results in a compile-time error because Rectangle is still an abstract class; the client of Rectangle will be told that the implementation of draw() is missing. Similarly, you cannot create Shape objects:

```
Shape* s = new Shape;  // can't create objects of an abstract class
```

However, the base class default implementation of draw() can be used to implement the derived implementation:

```
void Rectangle::draw() {
   Shape::draw();                    // default implementation
                                     // specific for Rectangle
   ...
}
```

Default Implementation Idiom 6.1

To provide a default implementation that must be redefined in a derived class, use pure virtual operations *and* provide their implementation.

6.5.2 Inheritance Versus Delegation

In this section, I discuss various techniques that help support the *reuse* of the interface and the implementation. Clearly, inheritance is one such technique. This kind of reusability is called **white-box reusability** because the internals of the parent classes are visible to the derived classes. However, as we discussed earlier, using only inheritance implies that a tight binding exists between the interface and the implementation. There are several reasons for this: One is that inheritance is a compile-time operation, which means that you cannot make modifications at run-time. In addition, the derived class needs to have access to the features of its base class; therefore, the base class cannot be fully encapsulated. Clearly, what you want to avoid is being forced to modify the implementation of the base class when implementing the derived class.

Another reusability technique is *delegation* (introduced in Section 4.3). Recall that delegation makes it possible to combine various objects; specifically, requests sent to one object can be delegated to another object. This kind of reusability is called **black-box reusability** because the internal details of the objects are not visible.

Delegation and inheritance can be compared as follows (see Figure 6.5):

- White-box reusability through inheritance uses a *compile-time* relationship between two classes (a base class and a derived class).
- Black-box reusability through delegation uses a *runtime* relationship between two objects; these objects appear to the client as a single object.

I used object composition by reference in Figure 6.5 to describe black-box reusability. Recall from Section 4.3 that with this kind of object composition, an Associator has either a pointer or a reference, here called a *delegate*, to an Associatee. Following standard C++ terminology, I call the class Associator a Handle class and the class Associatee a Body class in this figure. The handle represents an abstraction and is visible to the client, while the invisible body provides the implementation.

Object composition combined with inheritance is often a better alternative to inheritance because it allows the client to program to an interface provided by a class (the handle) whose objects delegate requests to the objects providing the implementation (the body). The use of inheritance alone means that the client's code has to be recompiled whenever a concrete class that is used by him or her is modi-

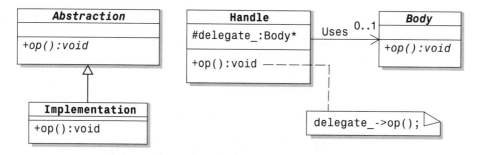

Figure 6.5 White-box (left) and black-box (right) reusability

fied. On the other hand, the combination of *object composition* with *inheritance* means that the client's code only has to be relinked with the modified code. In addition, object composition (represented by the handle-body pair) decomposes an abstraction into smaller, more manageable parts. It also helps the programmer define additional functionality for the implementation without affecting the client (this additional functionality could be, for example, support for the sharing of objects by using reference counting or the implementation of specific memory management techniques).

As we discussed in an earlier section, if you want to reuse only the implementation but not the interface, you should use *private inheritance*. In this scenario, operations in the derived class have access to both the public and protected features of the base class. In the next section, I briefly discuss multiple inheritance (this topic is continued in Section 9.8).

6.5.3   Multiple Inheritance, Part I

Java supports abstract interfaces and classes, and it allows *interfaces* to be both implemented and extended but allows *classes* only to be extended. Therefore, Java allows for multiple inheritance of interfaces and single inheritance of their implementations. C++ is more flexible, allowing multiple inheritance of arbitrary classes. This flexibility has an associated cost: the complexity associated with general, multiple inheritance. In this section, I describe basic concepts related to multiple inheritance (see Table 6.1) and leave more advanced details, such as a diamond inheritance, for Section 9.8.

Table 6.1   Multiple inheritance

Java	C++	Comments About C++
```class CE implements Ifc {```	```class CE : public Ifc {```	To implement an abstract interface, use public derivation.
```interface Ifc extends Ifc1, Ifc2 {```	```class Ifc : public Ifc1, public Ifc2{```	To extend the abstract interfaces of several classes, use public derivation from these classes.
```class CE extends C {```	```class CE : public C {```	To inherit an interface, use public derivation.
```class CE extends C implements Ifc {```	```class CE : public C, public Ifc {```	To implement the abstract interface and inherit another interface, use public derivation from these classes.
```class CE extends C implements Ifc {```	```class CE : private C, public Ifc {```	To implement an abstract interface and inherit only the implementation of a class, use public derivation from the interface and private derivation from the class (this is called a **mixin** class).

● EXAMPLE 6.3

This example is based on a Java program from Arnold and Gosling (1998). Consider the task of assigning attributes—that is, name-value pairs—to objects. In Java, every class inherits from the `Object` class. In C++, there is no single root of the inheritance tree; therefore, in this example, I assume that attribute values are objects of a class derived from the `AttributedObject` class:

```
//File: ex6.3.attributedobject.h
class AttributedObject {  // abstract
protected:
  virtual ~AttributedObject();
};

//File: ex6.3.attributedobject.cpp
AttributedObject::~AttributedObject() {
                        // do nothing, just define virtual destructor
}
```

To represent attributes, I use the class `Attr`:

```
//File: ex6.3.attr.h
class Attr {                              // name-value pairs
public:
  Attr(string);
  Attr(string, const AttributedObject*);
  Attr(const Attr&);
  virtual ~Attr();
  Attr& operator=(const Attr&);

  virtual string getName() const;
  virtual AttributedObject& getValue() const;

  virtual AttributedObject* setValue(AttributedObject&);
                                          // return old value
private:
  string name_;                           // attribute name
  AttributedObject* value_;               // attribute value
};
```

The class `Attr` can be extended to create specialized attributes. Attributes can be represented in various ways; here I use the abstract interface class `AttributedIfc` to show the general design:

```
//File: ex6.3.attributedifc.h
class Attr;
```

```
class AttributedIfc { // abstract
public:
  virtual void add(const Attr&) = 0;
  virtual bool find(const string& name, Attr&) const = 0;
  virtual bool remove(const string& name, Attr&) = 0;
};
```

The last two operations, remove() and find(), return false if the attribute with the specified name does not exist; otherwise, they return true and return through the second parameter the value of the attribute.

This interface may have various implementations—for example, one using a hash table or a linked list. These data structures are available in the standard C++ library, so I postpone the discussion of AttributedIfc's implementation until Section 8.10, Example 8.6 and for now assume that the class AttributedImp implements AttributedIfc:

```
class AttributedImp : public AttributedIfc { // implements
  ...
};
```

Also, note that the previous interface is missing a method to iterate over the collection of attributes (an iteration over a collection provides a means of accessing elements of this collection one at a time). Once again, I postpone the explanation of how this can be done to Example 8.6.

Now consider the class Student:

```
//File: ex6.3.student.h
class Student {
public:
  explicit Student(long);
  long getId() const;
private:
  long id_;
};
```

Suppose you want to assign attributes whose values represent students. Unfortunately, the class Student does not inherit from AttributedObject, which is necessary to be able to assign attributes. To solve this problem, you can use **multiple inheritance** and inherit from two classes. Specifically, you need to create an intermediate class that inherits from both AttributedObject and Student:

```
// File: ex6.3.attributedstudent.h
class AttributedStudent : public AttributedObject, public Student {
public:
  AttributedStudent(long);
  virtual ~AttributedStudent();
```

```
    . . .
};
```

Suppose you have a class called Registrar that maintains information about students, and you want to design the class RegistrarWithAttributes to maintain attributes of Registrar. In this example, the values of these attributes are objects of AttributedStudent. The complete design is shown in Figure 6.6.

The interface of RegistrarWithAttributes requires operations on attributes, so this class either inherits the AttributedIfc interface and implements it, or it simply defines its own interface. The latter is shown here:

```
// File: ex6.3.registrarwithattributes.h
class RegistrarWithAttributes : public Registrar {
public:
  RegistrarWithAttributes();
  virtual ~RegistrarWithAttributes();

  virtual void add(const Attr&);
  virtual bool find(const string&, Attr&) const;
  virtual bool remove(const string&, Attr&);
```

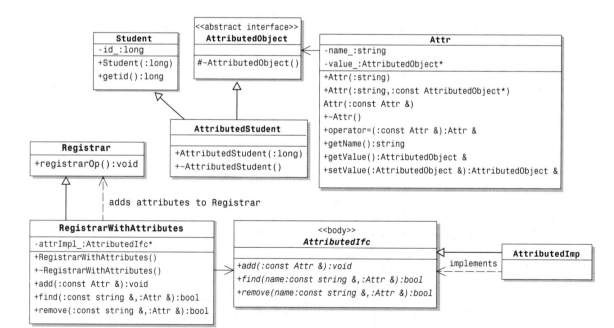

Figure 6.6 Design of a system that uses multiple inheritance

```
private:
  AttributedIfc* attrImpl_;
};
```

The `RegistrarWithAttributes` class essentially provides the handle for `AttributedIfc`'s body; all operations are implemented through the `attrImpl_` delegate; for example:

```
RegistrarWithAttributes() {
  attrImpl_ = new AttributedImp;
}

bool RegistrarWithAttributes::find(const string name&, Attr& a)
  const {
  return attrImpl_->find(name, a);
}
```

You can use these classes as follows:

```
RegistrarWithAttributes reg;
AttributedStudent s1(10);
AttributedStudent s2(20);
Attr attr1("Brilliant", s1);
Attr attr2("Outstanding", s2);

reg.add(attr1);
reg.add(attr2);

Attr attr;
if(reg.find("Brilliant", attr)) {
  if(AttributedStudent* as =
      dynamic_cast<AttributedStudent*>(attr.getValue())) {
    cout << as.getId() << endl;
    reg.remove("Brilliant", attr);
  }
}
```

Note that `AttributedStudent` has access to `Student`'s operations; if this is not appropriate, you can use a *mixin*: a private inheritance for one class, and a public inheritance for the other:

```
class AttributedStudent: public AttributedObject,
       private AttributedStudent
```

6.6 *Programming to an Interface*

One important goal of writing good code is reusability. To achieve this, you have to try to minimize the dependencies between subsystems, because such dependencies mean that a single modification may have a major ripple effect on the entire system. In this section, I describe various techniques to achieve this essential goal. Quoting from Gamma et al. (1995), the following principle stands out: *Program to an interface, not an implementation.* More specifically, there are benefits to accessing objects in terms of their abstract interfaces—that is, interfaces consisting entirely of abstract operations—rather than accessing them in terms of concrete operations, which binds to a specific implementation.

6.6.1 Decoupling Interfaces and Implementations: Bridge Design Pattern

Recall the handle-body technique from Section 6.5.2, in which the *handle* represents an abstraction and is visible to the client, while the invisible *body* provides the implementation. As an example of this technique, consider various kinds of bank accounts with operations such as open, deposit, and withdraw. The Bank class can be designed as the handle and the Account class as the body. This design is shown in Figure 6.7, which uses class stereotypes to help identify the handle and the body classes.

The Account class is abstract; there may be various derived classes, such as SavingsAccount, that implement Account. The handle class Bank does not need to be changed when new derived classes are used.

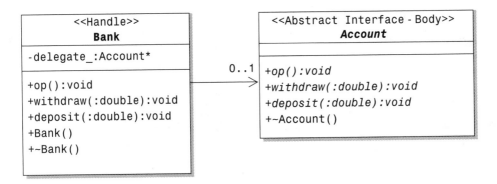

Figure 6.7   Example of a handle and a body

```
class Bank {                                    // handle to Account
public:
  void open();
  void withdraw(double);
  void deposit(double);
  Bank();
  ~Bank();
  ...
private:
  Account* delegate_;
};

class Account { // abstract body
public:
  virtual void open() = 0;
  virtual void withdraw(double) = 0;
  virtual void deposit(double) = 0;
  virtual ~Account();
};
```

Operations of the handle class are usually not virtual, while all the operations of the body class are abstract (pure virtual).

The handle-body technique leads to another design pattern, called the **bridge design pattern**. This is the first example of a **structural design pattern**, which deals with the composition of objects rather than the creation of objects. Specifically, the bridge design pattern provides a design for the composition of objects, which helps to promote a *loose coupling* between classes, between a class' interface and its implementation, and between classes and the hardware platform.

A nonsoftware example of this design pattern (based on Duell, 1998) is a household switch—an abstraction that controls devices such as lights and can turn a device on or off. The abstraction is separated from the implementation; the actual switch can be implemented in a variety of ways—for example, a simple two-position switch or a variety of dimmer switches.

Java uses the bridge design pattern to achieve platform independence. The client writes Java code using the Abstract Windows Toolbit (AWT), and this code runs on a virtual machine that can be implemented across multiple platforms. The AWT forms the abstraction level, and the clients interact through this abstraction. Client requests get handled by peer objects from the AWT components, which are associated through the peer interface. The peer interface forms the concrete implementation, which is native to the platform running the application.

The use of inheritance to provide various implementations of a single abstraction tightly binds these implementations to the abstraction. Therefore, it is difficult to update the client's code and reuse the abstraction. In C++, the complete class definition, including the private and protected sections, is needed to compile the client's code; this leads to a tight coupling between the abstraction and its implementations, which makes modifications more difficult. The bridge design pattern separates and decouples the abstraction and the implementation into two independent class hierarchies; it completely hides the implementation details from the clients, who access only the abstraction (see Figure 6.8). Both the abstraction and the implementation classes can be extended independently. These two hierarchies are *bridged* through a delegate. A client's code that uses the abstract interface is independent of its implementation and does not have to be recompiled when the implementation changes (I will discuss the need for recompiling and relinking further in Section 6.6.3). It is even possible to change the implementation at runtime.

I will provide a number of examples of the application of this pattern in the following sections.

6.6.2   Reference Counting

A garbage collector, such as the one used in Java, maintains a record of whether or not an object is currently being used. An unused object is tagged as *garbage*, which means that it can be collected and returned to the pool of available memory. One simple technique used to implement a garbage collector is called **reference counting**: Multiple objects share a single representation that keeps track of the number of objects currently in use. Reference counting is useful in everyday programming; for example, you can use a `String` class, in which multiple objects can share the same representation. Another example is borrowed from a project I was involved in several years ago. In this project, I represented an electronic book as a tree; nodes of the tree represented pages of the book. Nonleaf nodes represented chapters, sections, and so on, and leaves pointed to multimedia objects. A single multimedia object could have been pointed to by more than one leaf, representing the fact that for the sake of efficiency, several

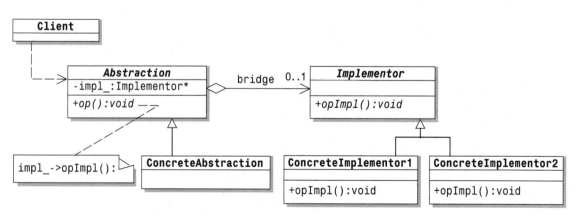

Figure 6.8 Bridge design pattern

Based in part, by permission, on Gamma, E., et al., *Design Patterns: Elements of Reusable Object-Oriented Software*, (Reading, Mass.: Addison-Wesley, 1995) p. 153.

pages shared these large objects. If any page did not use an object, it had to be deallocated, which was accomplished using reference counters associated with every object.

You can use the bridge design pattern to *share* objects and use reference counting to deallocate them when they are no longer used. The idea is to have the counters in the body and have the copying operations in the handle. These copying operations could deal with things like object assignments, for which they would be
responsible for incrementing the reference counter of the right side and decrementing the reference counter of the left side

This design is shown in the following pseudo-code:

```
class Body {
public:
   ...
private:
  int counter_;
};

class Handle {
public:
  Handle& operator=(const Handle&);
private:
  Body* bridge_;
};

Handle& Handle::operator=(const Handle& rhs)  {
   if(this == &rhs)
     return *this;
   ++rhs._body->counter;                         // right-hand side
   -bridge_->counter;                            // left-hand side
   if(bridge_->counter == 0) {                   // unused
      delete bridge_;
   }
   ...
   return *this;
}
```

In general, reference counters can be added to either an existing class or a new
class that is being designed; the addition results in improved efficiency. For simplicity, I describe only the former here (the existing class is not modified). The next example is based on the discussion provided by Koenig & Moo (1997). Consider the
simple class Point with the following form:

```
// File: ch6.point.h
class Point {
```

```
public:
  Point(double = 0, double = 0);
  virtual ~Point();
  double getX() const;
  double getY() const;
private:
  double x_;
  double y_;
};
```

To add reference counters to Point objects requires creating a new class, here called PointCounted, which is used by the clients. Therefore, this PointCounted class is the handle, while the class Point is the body:

```
// file: ch6.pointcounted.h
class PointCounted {
public:
  PointCounted(double = 0, double = 0);              // creates a point
  PointCounted(const PointCounted&);
  PointCounted(const Point&);
  PointCounted& operator=(const PointCounted&);
  ~PointCounted();
  double getX() const;
  double getY() const;
private:
  Point* p_;                        // bridge to the implementation
  int* count_;                      // reference counter
};
```

It is important to understand why pointers to integers are used, rather than plain integers, to represent reference counters. The reason is that the same reference counter may be used by more than one object of PointCounted (see Figure 6.9), and integer counters are shared.

```
// File: ch6.pointcounted.cpp
PointCounted::PointCounted(double x, double y) {
  p_ = new Point(x, y);
  count_ = new int(1);
}

PointCounted::PointCounted(const PointCounted& pc) {
  count_ = pc.count_;
  p_ = pc.p_;
  ++(*count_);                                      // one more reference
}
```

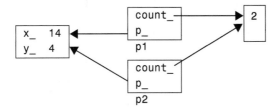

Figure 6.9 Sharing integer counters

```
PointCounted::PointCounted(const Point& pp) {
  p_ = new Point(pp);
  count_ = new int(1);
}

PointCounted& PointCounted::operator=(const PointCounted& pc) {
  if(this == &pc)
    return *this;
  ++(*pc.count_);                    // RHS has one more reference
  --(*count_);                       // LHS has one less reference
  if(*count_ == 0) {                 // garbage
    delete p_;
    delete count_;
  }
  count_ = pc.count_;                // initialize counter for LHS
  p_ = pc.p_;
  return *this;
}

PointCounted::~PointCounted() {
  --(*count_);                       // one less reference
  if(*count_ == 0) {                 // garbage
    delete p_;
    delete count_;
  }
}

double PointCounted::getX() const {
  return p_->getX();
}

double PointCounted::getY() const {
  return p_->getY();
}
```

Now the client can use these classes as follows:

```
PointCounted p1(1, 3);
if(...) {
  PointCounted p2(p1);
                    // share the same point; see Figure 6.10 (a)
  cout << p1.getX() << " " << p2.getY() << endl;
} // now there is only one copy

PointCounted p2(11, 4);    // see Figure 6.10 (b)
p1 = p2;                   // one copy is collected; see Figure 6.9
```

The use of reference counters brings up the question of whether the assignment statement should be shallow or deep; in other words, should you copy *references* or *values*? Given the interface in the previous example, it does not matter, because the state of Point cannot be modified. However, consider adding a modifier to Point:

```
void Point::setX(double x) {
  x_ = x;
}
```

You can add modifiers to PointCounted to provide a modification in one copy or all copies:

```
void PointCounted::setAllX(double x) {        // change in all copies
  p_->setX(x);
}
```

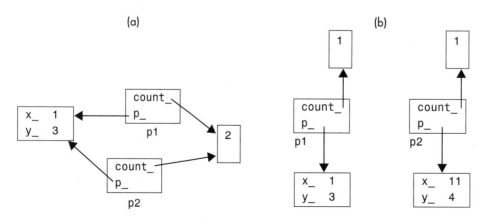

Figure 6.10 The state of the execution (a) after calling a copy constructor and (b) after creating another point

```
void PointCounted::setOneX(double x) {         // change in one copy
  if(*count_ != 1) {                            // shared
    --(*count_);
    p_ = new Point(p_);                          // new representation
    count_ = new int(1);
  }
  p_->setX(x);
}
```

Now, consider this code:

```
PointCounted pp(1, 3);
PointCounted qq = pp;                  // share
qq.setAllX(4);                         // change for both points
PointCounted rr = pp;                  // share
rr.setOneX(4);                         // change x for rr; not others
```

This technique is called **copy on write**: The object being written to is copied and does not share the representation with other objects. The weakness of this technique is that you have to duplicate almost the entire interface of the class for which you create reference counting (here, Point's interface was duplicated), and this is not good software engineering. In Section 7.8.2, I will show a design that avoids this problem.

6.6.3   Need for Recompiling and Header Files, Part II

In Section 4.7, I mentioned that to avoid unnecessary recompilation, whenever possible, the header file for a class should contain only the declarations of the classes used by the class. In this section, I continue this discussion and provide recommendations for designing header files.

   A typical class definition includes the private and the protected sections of the class; therefore, the interface and the implementation are not cleanly separated. As a result, any changes in the implementation require recompilation of the client's code. You have learned how to use the bridge design pattern to avoid recompiling the interface when you change the implementation. In addition to separating the interface and the implementation, you should also carefully consider the header files that are included; including unnecessary files creates a tight coupling between the interface and the implementation, which makes it difficult to modify your programs.

Avoiding Recompilation Idiom 6.2

To avoid the need for unnecessary recompilation of the client's code, separate the interface and the implementation using the bridge design pattern, and include only those header files that are absolutely necessary.

In some applications, you can use another technique that also helps avoid unnecessary recompilations and involves using an abstract interface. Clients program to the interface, and their code does not have to be recompiled when the implementation changes. I talk about this in the next section.

6.6.4 Creating and Copying Abstract Interfaces: Prototype Design Pattern

Java programmers are familiar with the cloning operation found in the `Object` class used to clone objects. This operation has its roots in yet another creational design pattern, called the **prototype**, which gives a flexible alternative to inheritance. The client class creates a *prototype* object; when this client again needs to create a new object, it asks the prototype object to clone itself. Therefore, objects that are used as prototypes must support the `clone()` operation in addition to their own operations (see Figure 6.11).

A nonsoftware example of this design pattern (based on Duell, 1998) is the mitotic division of a cell, resulting in two identical cells. When a cell splits, two cells of identical genotype result.

The prototype design pattern is used when the objects being created are instances of classes that differ only in the type of processing represented by an abstract operation. Once a prototype is cloned, it may be additionally modified by filling in the details. For example, if you query a database and receive an answer in the form of a table, you can operate on this table without issuing additional queries.

Another application of the prototype design pattern is creating and copying an abstract interface. Strictly speaking, it is not possible to create objects of an abstract interface, but it is possible and useful to create and copy objects of classes that implement such an interface. Since the type of these objects is not known at compile time, you have to use polymorphism (that is, virtual functions) to be able to clone.

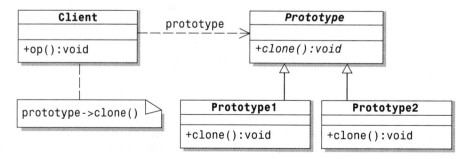

Figure 6.11 Prototype design pattern

Based in part, by permission, on Gamma, E., et al., *Design Patterns: Elements of Reusable Object-Oriented Software* (Reading, Mass.: Addison-Wesley, 1995) p. 119.

As a specific example of a prototype, consider the following abstract interface representing a bank account, which among other functions, provides two functions to, respectively, copy and create objects of derived classes:

```
class Account { // abstract prototype
public:
   virtual void open() = 0;
   virtual void withdraw(double) = 0;
   virtual void deposit(double) = 0;
   virtual ~Account();

   virtual Account* clone() const = 0;
   virtual Account* create() const = 0;
};
```

The clone() operation *clones* the object of any derived class that implements Account; the create() operation *creates* a new object of such a class. Both operations are implemented using a constructor in the derived class. For example, consider a concrete class, SavingsAccount, that implements Account:

```
class SavingsAccount : public Account { // implements
public:
   virtual void open();
   virtual void withdraw(double);
   virtual void deposit(double);
   virtual ~SavingsAccount();
   SavingsAccount();
   SavingsAccount(const SavingsAccount&);
   virtual SavingsAccount* clone() const;        // covariant type
   virtual SavingsAccount* create() const;       // covariant type
protected:
   ...
};

SavingsAccount* SavingsAccount::clone() const {
   return new SavingsAccount(*this);
};

SavingsAccount* SavingsAccount::create() const {
   return new SavingsAccount();
};
```

Before I explain how a prototype is created, consider its applications for the following declarations:

```
Account* prot = ...;
Account* a = prot->clone();
```

Since `clone()` is a polymorphic operation, the type of account created by this operation depends on the *value* of the prot. For example, if the value of the prot is an object of the class `SavingsAccount`, then `clone()` returns an object of the same class and `a` is assigned a clone of the savings account.

The *covariant type* is essential if the user wants to write the following type of code

```
SavingsAccount* sa = prot->clone();
```

because this statement does not compile if the return type of `Savings-Account::clone()` is `Account`. In addition, this technique enforces type checking for derived classes. For example, if `RegisteredSavingsAccount` were a class derived from `SavingsAccount` (designed to handle specialized savings accounts), then

```
SavingsAccount* sa;
... initialization of sa

RegisteredSavingsAccount* rsa = sa->clone();          // wrong type
```

To understand how the initial prototype can be created, consider the following code, which uses a bank factory that uses a constructor to build a prototype:

```
class BankFactory {
public:
  BankFactory(const Account*);
  virtual Account* makeAccount() const;
private:
  Account* accPrototype_;
};

BankFactory::BankFactory(const Account* a) {
  accPrototype_ = a;
}
```

To configure a factory to a particular type of account—for example, to build a prototype for a savings account—you can use the following declaration:

```
BankFactory saving(new SavingsAccount());
```

The client of `BankFactory` can use its operation `makeAccount()` to clone the prototype:

```
Account* BankFactory::makeAccount() const {
  return accPrototype_->clone();
}
```

Now look at the client code:

```
Account* sa = saving.makeAccount();

Account* sa1 = sa->clone();        // clone existing saving account
Account* sa2 = sa->create();       // create new saving account
```

When you need more than one prototype, it is useful to maintain a registry of prototypes. Each prototype can be registered under a certain name and associated with a factory method responsible for creating that prototype. Appropriate representations for this problem include a map to store the registry (described in Section 8.10) and pointers to member functions used to link factory methods that create the prototypes (described in Section 9.9.2).

The process of cloning abstract interfaces just described is also useful when creating wrapper classes. Consider a *collection* of accounts (for example, class Account shown earlier in this section). Such collections can be implemented in a variety of ways. Given what you have learned so far, I will use a rather primitive tool—an array. The question is, an array of what? Using pointers to Account allows you to work with objects of classes derived from Account but involves all the complexities of using pointers, which are best well hidden in the implementation code. An array of objects, such as

```
Account bank[MAX];
```

is not appropriate because an attempt to store an object of the derived class in the collection, such as a savings account object

```
SavingsAccount sa;
bank[0] = sa;
```

would result in a *slicing* of the object, leaving only its base part assigned to bank[0]. The solution is to use the bridge design pattern—specifically, to introduce a handle and store it in the collection (see Figure 6.12):

```
class AccountHandle {
public:
  AccountHandle();
  AccountHandle(const Account&);
  ~AccountHandle();
  AccountHandle(const AccountHandle&);
  AccountHandle& operator=(const AccountHandle&);

  void open();
  void withdraw(double);
  void deposit(double);
```

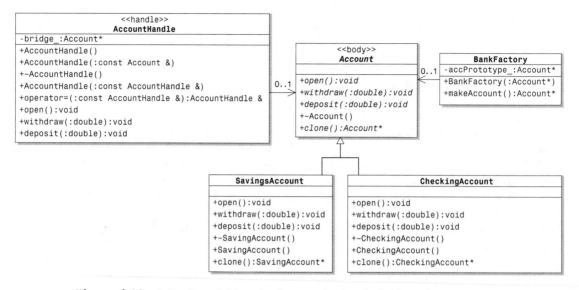

Figure 6.12   Collection of objects implemented using the bridge design pattern

```
private:
  Account* delegate_;                    // Account is an abstract body
};

AccountHandle bank[MAX];
```

The design of the class `AccountHandle` should be carefully examined; in particular, you should understand the first five operations. The default constructor creates an "empty delegate":

```
AccountHandle::AccountHandle() {
  delegate_ = 0;
}
```

You need a no-arg constructor for the handle class because you want to create an array of objects of this class. Now look at the second constructor:

```
AccountHandle::AccountHandle(const Account& a) {
  delegate_ = a.clone();
}
```

This constructor allows accounts to be assigned to handles. The destructor is "standard," but notice that `Account`'s destructor is virtual, so the resources used by the derived classes are properly destroyed:

```
AccountHandle::~AccountHandle() {
  delete delegate_;
}
```

The copy constructor and the overloaded assignment operator clone the abstract interface:

```
AccountHandle::AccountHandle(const AccountHandle& a) {
  if(a.delegate_ == 0)
    delegate_ = 0;
  else delegate_ = a.clone();
}

AccountHandle& AccountHandle::operator=(const AccountHandle& a) {
  if(this != &a) {
    delete delegate_;
    if(a.delegate_ == 0)
      delegate_ = 0;
    else delegate_ = a.clone();
  }
  return *this;
}
```

The "real work" on the account is delegated to the body class. For example, here is the withdraw operation, that delegates the work:

```
void AccountHandle::withdraw(double amount) {
  if(delegate_ != 0)
    delegate_->withdraw(amount);
}
```

In the implementation of this operation, I do not deal with the case of a null body class (it could be taken care of using exception handling).

Consider what happens when the following assignment is performed:

```
SavingsAccount a;
AccountHandle b;
b = a;
```

First, there is a type conversion of the right side to the type of the left side using the constructor

```
b = AccountHandle(a);
```

which in turn invokes the overloaded assignment operator

```
b.operator=(AccountHandle(a));
```

The parameter a of the constructor `AccountHandle()` is passed by reference; therefore, in its body, a.`clone()` is an invocation of the virtual `clone()` function—that is, an invocation of

```
SavingsAccount::clone()
```

which returns a copy of the `SavingsAccount` object. In a similar fashion, when the assignment operator is invoked, it calls a virtual destructor for `Account` and then invokes `clone()` from `SavingsAccount`. When the handle b goes out of scope, its destructor invokes the virtual destructor for `Account` through `delegate_`.

This concludes the discussion of the prototype design pattern, used to create and copy abstract interfaces. The next section deals with modifying existing interfaces.

6.6.5   Modifying Existing Interfaces: Adapter Design Pattern

The **adapter design pattern** is used to create a new class interface by converting an existing interface. The adapter lets two classes work together, even though they have *incompatible* interfaces.

Consider a class, `Adaptee` that has a given interface, and consider an application that needs *almost* the same kind of interface but with some minor differences. Modifying the class interface is not necessarily a feasible solution: first because you may not have access to the source code of this class, and second because this class is actually fine the way it is (it is useful for other applications, just not for this particular one). What would really be useful is the ability to *adapt* the existing `Adaptee` to the needs at hand. The adapter design pattern can help us accomplish precisely this. The pattern is an example of a structural pattern; this type of pattern describes how to compose existing objects and classes to form new structures.

A nonsoftware example of this design pattern (based on Duell, 1998) is a socket wrench. A socket attaches to a ratchet, which must have the same size as the drive. A 1/2-inch drive ratchet does not fit into a 1/4-inch drive socket unless a 1/2-inch to 1/4-inch *adapter* is used.

Java uses adapters for a variety of applications; for example, to simplify various event interfaces, such as the `WindowAdapter` class.

As a more specific example, consider a client application that programs to an abstract interface, `TargetIfc`, with two abstract operations, `foo()` and `goo()` (see Figure 6.13). The existing class `Adaptee` provides `foo()` but not `goo()`; instead, it has its own operation, `fool()`, that happens to be the appropriate way to implement `goo()`. It is not possible to implement `TargetIfc` using `Adaptee` because these

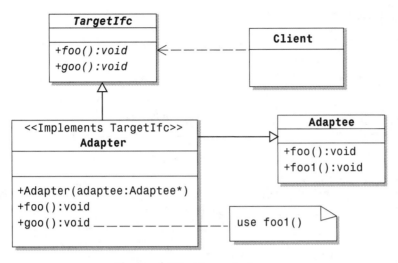

Figure 6.13 Class adapter

Based in part, by permission, on Gamma, E., et al., *Design Patterns: Elements of Reusable Object-Oriented Software.* (Reading, Mass.: Addison-Wesley, 1995) p. 141.

classes have incompatible interfaces. Instead, `TargetIfc` is implemented using a new class, called `Adapter`, which uses the implementation of `Adaptee`.

There are two kinds of adapters:

- **Class adapters** use *mixins* to inherit and implement the interface of `TargetIfc` and to inherit only the implementation of `Adaptee` (see Figure 6.13)
- **Object adapters** use object composition to delegate requests to `Adaptee` (see Figure 6.14)

Class adapters do not work when you want to adapt both a class and all its subclasses. Object adapters are better than class adapters if you need to adapt several existing classes. As an example, consider an application with an interface, `DictionaryIfc`, that represents dictionaries:

```
class DictionaryNamespace::DictionaryIfc {   // abstract
public:
  virtual void insert(const string&) = 0;
  virtual void remove(const string&) = 0;
  virtual bool member(const string&) const = 0;
};
```

I assume that this interface is in the `DictionaryNamespace` namespace. For simplicity, I also assume that there is no exception handling; `insert()` and `remove()` do nothing if they fail. Suppose that you have an existing class that has a

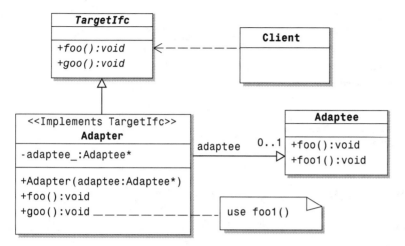

Figure 6.14   Object adapter

Based in part, by permission, on Gamma, E., et al., *Design Patterns: Elements of Reusable Object-Oriented Software*. (Reading, Mass.: Addison-Wesley, 1995) p. 141.

similar interface, except it uses C-style strings, and that this class is in the `Old-StuffNamespace` namespace:

```
class OldStuffNamespace::Dictionary {
public:
  void insert(const char* const);
  void remove(const char* const);
  bool member(const char* const) const;
private:
  ...  // not shown here
};
```

   To implement `DictionaryNamespace::DictionaryIfc` using the implementation provided by my existing class `Dictionary`, I need to write an *adapter mixin class*, which I will call `ClassDictionaryAdapter` (I only show the implementation of one function here):

```
class DictionaryNamespace::ClassDictionaryAdapter :
  public DictionaryNamespace::DictionaryIfc,   // implements
  private OldStuffNamespace::Dictionary {      // inherit implementation
public:
  virtual void insert(const string&);
  virtual void remove(const string&);
  virtual bool member(const string&) const;
};
```

```
void DictionaryNamespace::ClassDictionaryAdapter::
```

```
    insert(const string& s) {
      OldStuffNamespace::Dictionary::insert(s.c_str());
  }
```

As I mentioned before, in some cases object adapters are better than class adapters. For the application just shown, the class adapter and the *object adapter* are equally good. I will now show the code for the latter version:

```
class DictionaryNamespace::ObjectDictionaryAdapter :
  public DictionaryNamespace::DictionaryIfc { // implements
public:
  ObjectDictionaryAdapter(OldStuffNamespace::Dictionary*);
  virtual void insert(const string&);
  virtual void remove(const string&);
  virtual bool member(const string&) const;
private:
  OldStuffNamespace::Dictionary* adaptee_;
};

void DictionaryNamespace::ObjectDictionaryAdapter::
  insert(const string& s) {
    adaptee_->insert(s.c_str());
  }
```

This example shows how easy it is to adapt the existing class. Adapters are also used in the standard library, see Sections 8.8.3 and 8.9.4. Adapters are classes designed to modify existing interfaces, but in some cases, it is useful to have classes modify their interfaces themselves.

6.6.6   Self-modifying Interfaces: State Design Pattern

The first behavioral design pattern introduced in the previous chapter was the template design pattern, which was a *class* behavioral pattern. In this section, I introduce an *object* behavioral design pattern called **state**. The difference between a class behavioral pattern and an object behavioral pattern is that the former uses inheritance and the latter uses object composition. The state design pattern is useful for an object that can be in a large number of states and whose behavior changes at runtime whenever its state changes. Rather than coding the behavior using a large switch statement, the behavior is implemented by the subclasses of the state.

A nonsoftware example of this design pattern (based on Duell, 1998) is a vending machine that has several states based on factors such as the inventory, the amount of currency deposited, and the item selected. When currency is deposited and a selection is made, a vending machine consults the current state, performs an action and moves to another state. For example, the vending machine delivers a product with or without change, or it does not deliver a product either because there was not enough currency deposited or because in the current state there was no selected item available.

Traditionally, the client of the state design pattern communicates with a class called `Context`. This design pattern also includes an abstract class called the `State`; concrete states implement this class's behavior (see Figure 6.15).

There are several variants of the implementation of the state design pattern. First, a state may be set in the `Context` class through `setState()`. However, it is better to decentralize the code and let the subclasses of `State` perform this action. To be able to do this, each concrete derived class of `State` needs access to the `Context` object (it needs a pointer back to the `Context` object). A second important design decision is whether all `State` objects should be created on a demand basis or ahead of time and *never* destroyed. Finally, if there are only a few states, it may be more efficient to use the prototype design pattern, create objects representing states, and then clone them as needed. The state and bridge design patterns are similar; however, the state is designed to allow an object's behavior to change along with its state, while the bridge is designed to decouple the abstraction from its implementation so the two can vary independently.

An example of an application of the state design pattern involves Transmission Control Protocol (TCP) connections (for details, see Gamma et al., 1995), where a TCP object may be in several states, such as established or listening. When a TCP connection object receives a request, its response depends on its state; for example, the action taken for an open request depends on whether the current state is established or closed.

As another example of this pattern, consider a game in which a character called Zork is created and equipped with a vital food supply, candy. Zork may be in one of several states:

- Fresh: this is the initial state (after creation it has 10 candies)
- Hungry: the supply is 5 candies
- Starving: no candies
- Full: more than 20 candies
- Dead

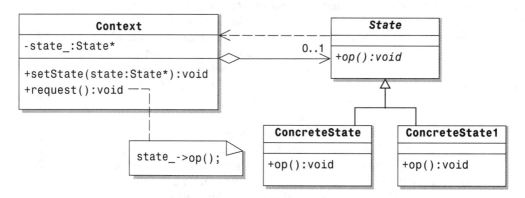

Figure 6.15 The state design pattern

Zork travels and picks up candies, which come in packages containing 5 or 10 candies each. Every now and then, Zork has to eat using the supply of candies. The transitions between states depend on the Zork's states and can be described as follows:

State/event	Fresh	Hungry	Starving	Full
Pick up 5	Does not pick up	Still hungry	Hungry	Full
Pick up 10	Gets full	Gets fresh again	Hungry	Full
Eat	Gets hungry	Gets starving	Dead	Fresh

As you can see, Zork's rules are a bit strange; for example, initially he does not pick up the supply of 5 candies but does pick up 10 candies. Zork can be in only one state at any given time; therefore, all states are *singletons* (introduced in Section 4.5). This means that states are created as needed and then destroyed when the program terminates (since they are static objects). For the states to have access to their context, each operation has a parameter, which is a pointer to the context.

The client communicates with the Context class for the Zork game. All operations of this class are virtual so derived classes can modify them:

```
class Context {
public:
  Context();
  ~Context();
  virtual void pick5();
  virtual void pick10();
  virtual void eat();
protected:
  friend class State;
  void changeState(State*);
private:
  State* state_;
};
```

Initially, Zork is in a *fresh* state; therefore, the constructor of the class Context initializes the state to an instance of Fresh state:

```
Context::Context() {
  state_ = Fresh::instance();                        // singleton
};

void Context::changeState(State* s) {
  state_ = s;
};
```

The class `State` has three abstract operations related to picking up objects and eating:

```
class State { // abstract
public:
  virtual void pick5(Context*) = 0;
  virtual void pick10(Context*) = 0;
  virtual void eat(Context*) = 0;
  void changeState(Context*, State*);
};


void State::changeState(Context* c, State* s) {
  c->changeState(s);
}
```

Here is the code for the singleton class `Fresh`:

```
class Fresh : public State {
public:
  static State* instance();
};


State* Fresh::instance() {
  static State* onlyInstance = new Fresh;
  return onlyInstance;
}


void Fresh::pick5(Context*) {
  // do nothing
}


void Fresh::pick10(Context* c) {
  changeState(c, Full::instance());
}


void Fresh::eat(Context* c) {
  changeState(c, Hungry::instance());
}
```

The UML diagram for the Zork game is shown in Figure 6.16.

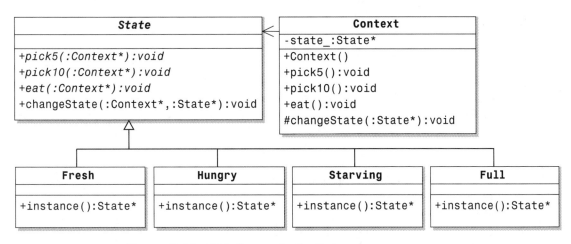

Figure 6.16   UML diagram for the Zork game

6.7 *Application of Design Patterns: Arithmetic Expressions*

This section, I provide an evaluation of arithmetic operations that uses several design patterns, including the bridge, the state, and the prototype. I show two versions: The first version is partly based on the example given by Koenig (1997) and unpublished notes by Doug Schmidt. The second version is new and is an improvement over the first in that its design is more easily modifiable.

● EXAMPLE 6.4

Consider arithmetic expressions with four binary operators—multiplication, addition, division, and subtraction—and with double operands. All operators have standard precedence levels. You want to evaluate and print these expressions.

The principle of *design for change* is stressed in this example. As I already pointed out, there are two versions. You should study both versions carefully to understand why the second is an improvement over the first in terms of modifiability.

To consider possible future modifications that you may want to make to the code, recall that currently four standard binary operators are specified. In the future, you may want to add more binary operators, as well as operators with other arities; for example, unary minus or ternary conditional expressions. These additions should not force you to change the existing code, perhaps with the exception of adding new derived classes.

In view of these considerations, it should be obvious that a specific representation of expressions should be decoupled from the client's code. In addition, any such

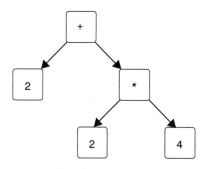

Figure 6.17   Expression for 2+2*4

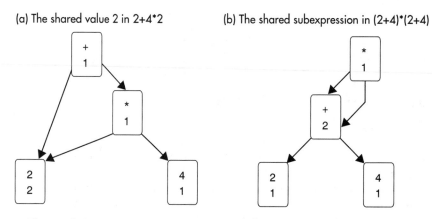

Figure 6.18   Expressions with shared subexpressions (the second value in each node represents the reference counter)

representation should allow for incremental updates; for example, the addition of new kinds of operators. You can accomplish these goals in both versions by having the client operate on expressions using the class Expression, and by using the bridge design pattern to bridge their code with a specific implementation.

This example uses a tree to represent expressions, which makes it possible to evaluate expressions, perform semantic analysis, or even generate intermediate code (see Figure 6.17).

To avoid creating objects that hold duplicate values, such as 2 in the example in Figure 6.17, you can use reference counting (see Figure 6.18).

The design of this example consists of two basic classes:

- Node, a base abstract class for representing all kinds of nodes, including values and operators
- Expression, a representation of expressions

The Expression class works as a *handle* and the Node class as a *body* to achieve the following goals:

- Decouple the interface and the implementation
- Provide reference counters for nodes of the expression

In the first version, operators are represented as strings. After I show the implementation of this version, I will discuss its suitability and present an alternative representation. First consider the *handle* class:

```
// File: ex6.4.expression.h
class Expression {
  friend class Node;
public:
  // constructors for values and sub-expressions
  Expression(double);                              // single value
  Expression(const string&, const Expression&);    // unary
  Expression(const string&, const Expression&,
      const Expression&);                          //binary

  // copy constructor, assignment and destructor
  Expression(const Expression&);
  Expression& operator=(const Expression&);
  virtual ~Expression();

  // output and evaluation functions
  virtual void print(ostream&) const;
  virtual double eval() const;
private:
  Node* rep_;                                      // delegate to Node
};
```

Note that there are two constructors for creating unary and binary expressions.

Although the Expression class has virtual functions, this example does not use it as a base class for any other classes. Now look at the *body* class, which, as I already mentioned, is represented by an abstract class Node:

```
// File: ex6.4.node.h
class Node {   // abstract
  friend class Expression;
protected:
  Node();
  virtual ~Node();
  virtual void print(ostream&) const = 0;
  virtual double eval() const = 0;
private:
  int use_;                                        // reference counter
};
```

Figure 6.19 shows a UML diagram with all the classes used in this version.

Now consider the remaining classes that appear in Figure 6.19. The `Expression` class serves as a *factory*; its constructors build various expressions:

```
// File: ex6.4.expression.cpp
Expression::Expression(double num) {
  rep_ = new ValueNode(num);
}


Expression::Expression(const string& op, const Expression& t) {
  rep_ = new UnaryNode(op, t);
}


Expression::Expression(const string& op,
    const Expression& t1, const Expression& t2) {
  rep_ = new BinaryNode(op, t1, t2);
}
```

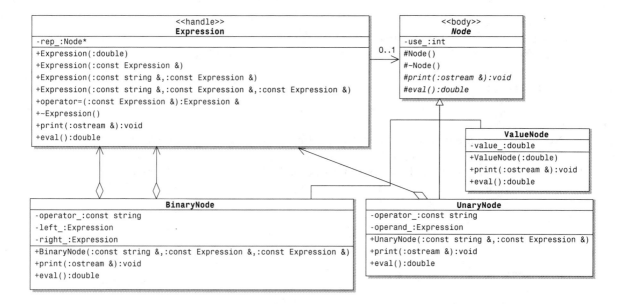

Figure 6.19 Design of the application to evaluate arithmetic expressions

```
Expression::Expression(const Expression& t) {
  rep_ = t.rep_;
  ++rep_->use_;
}

Expression::~Expression() {
  if(--rep_->use_ == 0)
    delete rep_;
}

Expression& Expression::operator=(const Expression& rhs) {
  if(this == &rhs)
    return *this;
  ++rhs.rep_->use_;
  if(--rep_->use_ == 0)
    delete rep_;
  rep_= rhs.rep_;
  return *this;
}

void Expression::print(ostream& os) const {
  rep_->print(os);
}

double Expression::eval() const {
  return rep_->eval();
}

Expression::Expression(const string& op, const Expression& a,
    const Expression& b, const Expression& c)
      : rep_(new TernaryNode(op, a, b, c)) { }
```

The Expression copy constructor, the assignment operator, and the destructor are all involved in reference counting, using techniques introduced in Section 6.6.2. Later you will see when reference counting is actually used.

Now look at the three derived classes that represent, respectively, a node that stores a double value, a node that represents a unary expression and a node that represents a binary expression:

```
// File: ex6.4.valuenode.h
// represents a double value
class ValueNode : public Node { // implements
  friend class Expression;
public:
  ValueNode(double);
```

```
  virtual void print(ostream&) const;
  virtual double eval() const;
private:
  double value_;
};

// File: ex6.4.unarynode.h
// represents a unary node
class UnaryNode : public Node { // implements
  friend class Expression;
public:
  UnaryNode(const string&, const Expression&);
  virtual void print(ostream&) const;
  virtual double eval() const;
private:
  const string operator_;
  Expression operand_;
};

// File: ex6.4.binarynode.h
// represents a binary expression
class BinaryNode : public Node {  // implements
  friend class Expression;
public:
  BinaryNode(const string&, const Expression&, const Expression&);
  virtual void print(ostream&) const;
  virtual double eval() const;
private:
  const string operator_;
  Expression left_;
  Expression right_;
};
```

Here are the implementations of the three classes just presented. Each of these classes implements eval() and print():

```
// File: ex6.4.valuenode.cpp
ValueNode::ValueNode(double v): value_(v) {}

void ValueNode::print(ostream& st) const {
  st << value_;
}

double ValueNode::eval() const {
    return value_;
}
```

```cpp
// File: ex6.4.unarynode.cpp
UnaryNode::UnaryNode(const string& op, const Expression& t):
  operator_(op), operand_(t) { }

void UnaryNode::print(ostream& st) const {
  st << "(" << operator_ << " ";
  operand_.print(st);
  st << ")";
}


double UnaryNode::eval() const {
  if(operator_ == "-")                                    // unary minus
    return -operand_.eval();
  throw invalid_argument("invalid unary operator");
}


// File: ex6.4.binarynode.cpp
BinaryNode::BinaryNode(const string& op,
  const Expression& t1, const Expression& t2):
    operator_(op), left_(t1), right_(t2) { }

void BinaryNode::print(ostream& st) const {
  st << "(";
  left_.print(st);
  st << " " << operator_ << " ";
  right_.print(st);
  st << ")";
}

double BinaryNode::eval() const {
    // *,-,+,/
  if(operator_ == "+") return left_.eval() + right_.eval();
  if(operator_ == "-") return left_.eval() - right_.eval();
  if(operator_ == "*") return left_.eval() * right_.eval();
  if(operator_ == "/") {
    double v = right_.eval();
    if(v == 0)
      throw invalid_argument("dividing by zero");
    return left_.eval() / v;
  }
  throw invalid_argument("invalid binary operator");
}
```

Take a close look at the constructors in the last two classes. Both of them call copy constructors in the class `Expression` and therefore invoke reference counting (to understand why reference counting is invoked, study the code carefully).

The main program uses only the handle class `Expression`. First, you need to create an expression shown in Figure 6.17:

```
Expression exp1 = Expression("+", 2, Expression("*", 2, 4));
```

It is possible to pass values, such as 2 and 4, as parameters of `Expression()` because the class `Expression` has a single-parameter constructor that performs the type conversion. However, careful examination of the previous line of code reveals that reference counting is not involved in reusing the value 2. This is because when `Expression(2)` is executed for the second time, it has no knowledge of the first execution. Only a compiler has access to the source code and can perform this kind of code optimization. Here, *you* are performing "by-hand" code optimization and therefore you have to first create an expression representing the value 2 and then use it:

```
Expression two(2);
Expression exp1("+", two, Expression("*", two, 4));
```

This solution works but relies on the client of the class to correctly create objects; this is not a very safe alternative, but stick with it for now. Figure 6.20 shows the

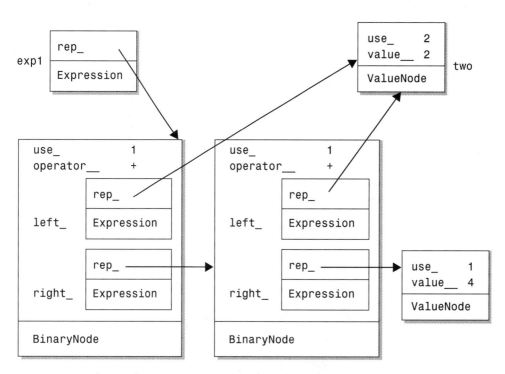

Figure 6.20   Use of reference counting for the shared value 2

state of the memory after the previous code has been executed. Note that the node `two` is shared, and its reference counter is 2.

You can create an expression with a shared subexpression in a similar way, with the help of temporary variables:

```
// File: ex6.4.driver.cpp
int main() {
  Expression two(2);
  Expression four(4);

  Expression exp1("+",two, four);              // Figure 6.17

  Expression common("+", two, four);
  Expression exp2("*", common, common);        // Figure 6.18

  exp1.print(cout);
  cout << endl << exp1.eval() << endl;

  exp2.print(cout);
  cout << endl << exp2.eval() << endl;
}
```

Now consider modifying this program by adding a nonbinary operator; specifically, a ternary conditional expression operator. This will require a number of changes:

- Deriving a new class, `TernaryNode`, **from** `Node`
- Adding additional constructor for the class `Expression`
- Modifying the code for two operations of the class `Expression`; specifically, `print()` and `eval()`

```
// File: ex6.4.ternarynode.h
class TernaryNode : public Node {
  friend class Expression;
public:
  TernaryNode(const string&, const Expression&,
    const Expression&, const Expression&);
  virtual void print(ostream&) const;
  virtual double eval() const;
private:
  const string operator_;
  Expression left_;
  Expression middle_;
  Expression right_;
};
```

```cpp
// File: ex6.4.ternarynode.cpp
TernaryNode::TernaryNode(const string& op, const Expression& a,
    const Expression& b, const Expression& c): operator_(op),
    left_(a), middle_(b), right_(c)   {}

void TernaryNode::print(ostream& st) const {
  st << operator_ << "(";
  left_.print(st);
  st << ", ";
  middle_.print(st);
  st  << ", ";
  right_.print(st);
  st << ")";
}

void TernaryNode::eval() const {
  if(operator_ == "?:") {
    if(left_.eval() return middle_.eval();
    return right_.eval();
  }
  throw invalid_argument("invalid binary operator");
}
```

The additional constructor for Expression looks like this:

```cpp
Expression::Expression(const string& op, const Expression& a,
  const Expression& b, const Expression& c)
  : rep_(new TernaryNode(op, a, b, c)) { }
```

As you can see, adding a new operator of a different arity requires several changes. Even adding new binary operators requires that we make modifications to the existing code because it hard-codes the representation of the operators. As another example of the lack of modifiability of the present version, notice that to add an exponentiation, you have to add another case to the switch statement.

The first version of the example represented arithmetic operators with strings, which made it necessary to use conditional statements to evaluate expressions. The second version attempts to avoid these problems but at the expense of using indirection.

Implementing the second version, requires using the state design pattern and splitting the single class representing all the operators into separate classes, derived from the abstract class AbstractOperator. When a new operator is added, the existing code will not have to be modified; instead, new derived classes will have to be added. The class AbstractOperator is an abstract class that represents all operators. Its name_ attribute is used only for printing. The prototype design pattern is used to create prototypes for all operators and then clone them.

```
// File: ex6.4a.AbstractOperator.h
class AbstractOperator {  // abstract
public:
  virtual double eval() const = 0;
  AbstractOperator(const string&);
  virtual AbstractOperator* clone() const = 0;
  string name() const;
  virtual ~AbstractOperator();
  void setOwner(Node*);
protected:
  string name_;
  Node* owner_;
};
```

The *owner* of an operator is an object of a class derived from Node; for example, for addition, a binary node will have its operator_ attribute set to the instance of Addition, whose owner will be this binary node.

Specific operators are produced by a factory; for example, the four basic arithmetic operators are produced by the following factory:

```
// File: ex6.4a.operatorfactory.h
class OperatorFactory {
public:
  static Addition* makeAddition();
  static Multiplication* makeTimes();
  ... and more
};
```

```
// File: ex6.4.operatorfactory.cpp
Operator* OperatorFactory::makePlus() {
  return new Addition;
}
```

Class Addition is an example of a concrete class that implements Abstract-Operator (for other classes that implement other operators, see the code available on the Addison Wesley Longman Website):

```
// File: ex6.4a.addition.h
class Addition : public AbstractOperator { // implements
public:
  virtual double eval() const;
  virtual Addition* clone() const;
  Addition(const string&);
  virtual ~Addition();
};
```

```
// File: ex6.4a.addition.cpp
double Addition::eval() const {
  BinaryNode* p;
  p = dynamic_cast<BinaryNode*>(owner_);
  if(p == 0) {
    cerr << "this cannot happen" << endl;
    exit(1);
  }
  return p->getLeft() + p->getRight();
}

Addition* Addition::clone() const {
  return new Addition(*this);
}
```

A dynamic cast is needed because, in general, owner_ may point to various kinds of nodes. However, for binary operations like addition, it will always point to an instance of BinaryNode. The operations getLeft() and getRight() return, respectively, the value of the left and the right parameter of addition. Class Node is similar to the class Node from the previous version of this example. It is still a *body* class for the *handle* class Expression, but it does not use a string representation of an operator:

```
// File: ex6.4a.node.h
class Node {    // abstract
public:
  friend class Expression;
protected:
  Node();
  virtual ~Node();
  virtual void print(ostream&) const = 0;
  virtual double eval() const = 0;
private:
  int use_;                                  // reference counter
};
```

The complete design for the second version is presented in Figure 6.21. As you can see from the figure, the class ValueNode does not use the class AbstractOperator. On the other hand, classes UnaryNode and BinaryNode do not know which operator is used, and they delegate the task of evaluating the expression to the class AbstractOperator (for example, see the definition of the class Addition). Now look at the class BinaryNode:

```
// File: ex6.4a.binarynode.h
// represents a binary expression
class BinaryNode : public Node {  // implements
```

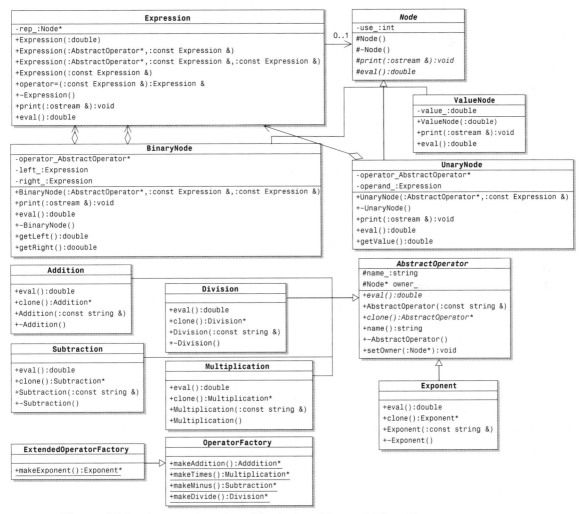

Figure 6.21 The second version of the design of the model for arithmetic expressions

```
   friend class Expression;
public:
   BinaryNode(AbstractOperator*, const Expression&, const Expression&);
   virtual void print(ostream&) const;
   virtual double eval() const;
   ~BinaryNode();
   double getLeft();
   double getRight();
private:
```

```
    AbstractOperator* operator_;
    Expression left_;
    Expression right_;
};

// File: ex6.4a.binarynode.cpp
BinaryNode::BinaryNode(AbstractOperator* op,
    const Expression& t1, const Expression& t2):
        left_(t1), right_(t2) {
    operator_ = op->clone();
    operator_->setOwner(this);
}

double BinaryNode::eval() const {
    return operator_->eval();
}

double BinaryNode::getLeft() const {
    return left_.eval();
}
double BinaryNode::getRight() const {
    return right_.eval();
}
```

The code of the remaining classes is not shown here.

The interface of the Expression class is the same as in the first version. Here is the modified main program:

```
// File: ex6.4a.driver.cpp
int main() {
    Expression two(2);

    Expression exp1 = Expression(OperatorFactory::makePlus(),
        two, Expression(OperatorFactory::makeTimes(), 4, two));

    expr2 = Expression(OperatorFactory::makeTimes(), exp1, exp1);

    exp1.print(cout);
    cout << exp1.eval() << endl;
    exp2.print(cout);
    cout << exp2.eval()<< endl;
}
```

As you can see, the user specifies the required operators by invoking factory methods.

To evaluate this new design, consider adding exponents to the original specification. First, a new class derived from `AbstractOperator` is needed:

```
// File: ex6.4a.exponent.h
class Exponent : public AbstractOperator { // implements
public:
  virtual double eval() const;
  virtual Exponent* clone() const;
  Exponent(const string&);
  virtual ~Exponent();
};
```

Next, you need to extend the factory:

```
// File: ex6.4a.extandedoperatorfactory.h
class ExtendedOperatorFactory : public OperatorFactory {
public:
  static Exponent* makeExponent();
};
```

With all this in place, the client can now use exponents that look like this:

```
Expression e = Expression(OperatorFactory::makeExponent(), 2, 5);
```

This version requires very few code additions compared to the previous one; *no changes* are required to define a new operator. The price for this flexibility is the extra level of indirection, caused by using delegation rather than inheritance. Unfortunately, the user still has to make sure that expressions are created in such a way that reference counting works.

To conclude this chapter, I want to review all the essential points from the previous example. In the first version, operators are represented as strings. To decouple the interface and the implementation and to provide reference counters for nodes of the expression, I used the bridge design pattern; specifically, a handle class `Expression` that represents expressions and an abstract body class that represents all kinds of nodes. The `Expression` class serves as a *factory*; its constructors build various expressions. In this first version, adding new binary operators or an operator of a different arity requires *several* changes.

In the second version, I used the state design pattern to split the single class representing all the operators into separate classes. I used the prototype design pattern to create prototypes for all operators and then clone them. In this version, when a new operator is added, the existing code does not have to be modified.

6.8 *Exercises*

For all the exercises in this chapter, you should carefully design the interface of each class; in particular, decide if there is a need to implement functions such as the copy constructor, destructor, and overloaded assignment operator. When an exercise calls for the creation of a namespace, you should design it carefully and split it into files available to the client and the implementation. For each exercise, include a program that tests your code.

EXERCISE 6-1

Use private inheritance to extend the class `IntStack` from Example 5.3 so that its interface consists of the following functions:

```
int pop() throw(logic_error);              // returns the value popped
int push(int) throw(logic_error);
                                // returns the previous top of the stack
int top() throw(logic_error);        // returns the top of the stack
```

EXERCISE 6-2

Redesign the class `IntStack` from Example 5.3 so that it uses protected attributes rather than private attributes. Then use protected inheritance to write a derived class interface that has the additional functions `empty()` and `full()`.

EXERCISE 6-3

Use the abstract factory design pattern to implement a program working with file encryption. The program is similar to the one from Example 6.1, but this time there are two products representing files encrypted using two different algorithms. Here is the first encryption algorithm: a positive integer N ($0 < N < 128$) is added to the ordinal value of each character. The user supplies the encryption code N at run-time. For the other algorithm, the user provides a keyword; an input file is divided into blocks equal to the size of the word, and then the ith character in that block is encrypted by adding the ASCII code of the ith character in the keyword. Provide the corresponding decryption algorithms.

EXERCISE 6-4

Use the abstract factory design pattern to implement a program that processes two kinds of text files based on the information stored in the first line of a file. This first line specifies the type of string used to denote a comment in the file and is one of the following:

- Double minus
- Double slash

The `display()` function displays input files and does not show comment lines or parts of lines; for example, if the comment is of the form `//`, then for the file

```
Hello // how
are -- you
```

the output is:

```
Hello
are -- you
```

EXERCISE 6-5

Consider a class, `Polynomial`, that represents polynomials with double coefficients. Its interface includes a pure virtual function `print()`, which prints the polynomial. Then consider a class `List` that represents a list of double values; its interface includes a `print()` that prints a list. Write a mixin class `ShowablePolynomial` that is publicly derived from the class `Polynomial` and privately derived from the class `List`. The mixin class implements `print()` using the implementation of `print()` from the class `List`.

EXERCISE 6-6

Using the bridge design pattern, design an abstract interface for a stack of integers and two implementations: one using an array and the other using a list. Then write the class `Stack`, which uses this design and maintains a stack. Changing the implementation at runtime should be possible, and can be accomplished by following this procedure: Initially, the array implementation is used. Whenever the number of elements in the stack exceeds the limit specified in the constructor of the class `Stack`, the implementation is switched to using the list. If the number of elements drops below this limit, the implementation is switched back to using the array.

EXERCISE 6-7

Use a reference counting technique from Section 6.6.2 to implement a program that maintains integer variables. Integer values are stored in a wrapper class. Use copy on writing when modifying the value of a constant. Add debugging messages that show the value of the reference counter for each constant; for example, when executing the following code:

Create a variable equal to 2
Copy the variable using a copy constructor
Create a variable equal to 4
Copy the variable using an assignment
Change the value of the first variable to 3

EXERCISE 6-8

Using the prototype design pattern, implement an abstract class `Polynomial` with two concrete derived classes that implement a polynomial using an array and a list, respectively. Then write a factory class to build these two prototypes. Finally, create several polynomials by cloning the prototypes, and perform various operations on these polynomials, such as addition and multiplication.

EXERCISE 6-9

Using the class adapter design pattern, implement a class `MyString` that adapts the interface provided by the library string class to the following interface (use a namespace):

- Basic constructors, etc.
- Two helper functions (not members) to insert and delete substrings
- The following members:

    `strpos(char c)`, which returns a position of `c`, or `-1` if the `c` has not been found

    `strlen()`, which returns the size of a string

    `at(int i)`, which returns a character at position `i`, or throws an exception if `i` is invalid

EXERCISE 6-10

Use the object adapter design pattern to implement Exercise 6-9.

EXERCISE 6-11

Implement a simple lexical analyzer that which reads integers, doubles, and punctuation symbols. Use the state design pattern to avoid having to use a switch statement.

EXERCISE 6-12

Consider a king on an 8 × 8 chessboard. Implement a class that provides a function to move the king. Use the state design pattern to avoid having to use a switch statement.

INTRODUCTION TO GENERIC PROGRAMMING: PARAMETERIZED TYPES

7.1 *Preview*

In this chapter, I introduce the generic programming paradigm. The topic is new to most Java programmers and will be further described in the next chapter. This chapter starts with a general description of three kinds of types—concrete, abstract, and parameterized—and continues with descriptions of generic programming and various overloaded operations. (You have seen three overloaded operators thus far; here I introduce the remaining ones, all of which are very important for implementing parameterized types.) I then describe template classes and functions in some detail. I also introduce the proxy and iterator design patterns. Finally, I compare the techniques described in previous chapters, such as inheritance and delegation, with parameterized types.

This chapter is an introduction to programming with the C++ standard library, which is further described in the next chapter.

7.2 *Introduction*

There are three ways to implement user-defined types: as concrete types, as abstract types, and as parameterized types.

A **concrete type** is a user-defined class whose interface is bound to its implementation. Therefore, a concrete type resembles a primitive data type, such as int. A concrete type is designed to meet a specific goal in an efficient way, which makes it difficult to adapt it to a new goal (either by extending the concrete type or modifying it). Examples of concrete types are a wrapper class for `int` and the class `Student`, used to maintain information about a student (this class was developed in previous chapters).

An **abstract type** is a user-defined class that is not tied to a particular implementation; it is an interface with many possible implementations. For example, a set represented by a class with a pure abstract interface is an abstract type. A change in the implementation of an abstract type does not necessarily force the user of the class to recompile the code. A concrete type often provides the implementation for an abstract type; for example, a bit-vector concrete type can be used to implement sets. Although abstract types can be extended using inheritance, typically their implementations, not their types, are extended. For example, consider the handle-body pair introduced in Section 6.5.2; we can use classes derived from the body to provide different implementations of the abstract body interface.

A **parameterized type** is a user-defined class that can have three kinds of parameters: types, constants, and functions (described in detail in the next paragraph). For example, a class `Stack<ElementType>` is a parameterized type, with one type parameter that represents the type of a stack element. A parameterized type is used to instantiate particular class types; for example, `Stack<int>` is a class type representing a stack of integers.

A **parameterized function** is a user-defined function that may have type parameters. For example, a function `swap<ElementType>(const ElementType&, const ElementType&)` is parameterized by the type of the elements swapped.

Parameterization of types and functions contributes to reusability and adaptability of software components; for example, instead of creating two types to represent, respectively, a stack of integers and a stack of strings, you can use a single parameterized type and instantiate it with `int` and `string`.

Implementation of parameterized types is inherently tied to generic programming techniques. The main goal of generic programming is to design and implement reusable, adaptable, and efficient software building blocks that consist of three components: **containers**, which store block elements; **algorithms**, which operate on the elements; and **iterators**, which the algorithms use to traverse the containers. All three components are fully described in the next chapter; here I describe them briefly as an introduction.

A container is a parameterized type. For example, a list container is parameterized by the type of the list elements. The container does not make any assumptions about the type of elements it holds. Since the user specifies the type, a container is both reusable and readily adaptable. For example, to create a list of integers, you need only specify that `int` is the actual type.

An algorithm is a parameterized function. This function does not know the actual type of the containers it operates on. To access the elements in the containers, the function uses iterators, which are passed as parameters.

An iterator is an abstraction (similar to a pointer) that provides access to elements; it can also be moved to get to the successive value. This allows the algorithm to be decoupled from the container, which means that the same algorithm can work for different types of containers. For example, you can implement a find algorithm by using two parameters: one that provides an iterator to traverse the container and a second that represents the value to be found. This algorithm uses the iterator to access each element in the container and compare it with the given value. Notice that this algorithm is independent of the container type; it works without any modifications for lists, queues, and so on; all you have to do is supply the actual iterator.

Version 1.4 of Java introduced generic type declarations and methods; earlier versions of Java did not provide any support for generic programming. To implement containers or algorithms not bound to specific data types using older versions of Java, you had to use references to the class `Object` (the root of all Java classes). To use such code with a primitive data type, you had to use a wrapper class. For example, you could implement a set using a bit-vector, which stores references to `Object` in an array. To invoke a method for a specific element type, you had to first cast the reference to `Object` to the particular type. All containers implemented with this technique were potentially heterogeneous and so could store elements of different types; enforcing homogeneous containers required additional checks. These runtime techniques, in particular the use of casting and polymorphic operations that use late binding, carried a cost, which could be prohibitive for some applications.

C++ provides support for generic programming through compile-time techniques. One of the most important features of generic programming is the ability to specialize containers and algorithms at compile time, making them more efficient than polymorphic programming, which relies on runtime techniques. Support for generic programming in C++ comes in the form of **template** classes and functions, which are parameterized by type (that is, they have type parameters). For example, a vector template may have a type parameter T that specifies the type of each element stored in the vector. Type parameters are enclosed in angle brackets:

```
vector<T>
```

You can use this template to create a vector of integers

```
vector<int>
```

or a vector of objects of your own class, such as Student:

```
vector<Student>
```

The operations performed using the template class can constrain the parameter types. For example, assume that one of the vector operations required involves the addition of two elements of its underlying parameter type:

```
T t1, t2;
... t1 + t2 ...
```

This implies that + should be supported by the type T, which is obviously true for all primitive data types but does not appear to be the case for user-defined types (classes). Disallowing natural operators such as + and instead relying on functions such as add(T, T) is one option. However, this not only makes the code harder to read and understand but also makes it necessary to define add() for primitive data types. A better option is to overload + with additional functionality that allows it to be used with both primitive and user-specified types; this option is supported by C++.

In general, C++ containers are template classes, and generic algorithms are template functions. To make the programmer's life easier, the language provides a built-in standard template library, which comes with a number of containers, such as Vector, and algorithms, such as find(). However, before getting into how you can use the library for generic programming, I want to clarify operator overloading and the concept of templates.

This section has summarized three kinds of types: concrete, abstract, and parameterized. You should not assume that one type is better than another; rather, each has its own place, and often a mix is used. For example, heterogeneous containers use both abstract and parameterized types.

7.3   *Overloaded Operators*

Providing a complete definition of a concrete data type often requires overloading the names of the standard operators. It is also useful to support the familiar *infix* notation; for example, adding two vectors x and y using

```
x + y
```

rather than implementing a function such as addVector(), and invoking it:

```
x.addVector(y);
```

You have already seen several examples of operator overloading in the previous chapters: specifically, the copy constructor, the assignment operator, and the type conversion operator. C++ allows you to overload most of the unary and binary operators (with several exceptions as described later in this section).

Just because it is possible to overload an operator does not mean that you should; only operators that have a meaning associated with their predefined use should be overloaded. For example, it is possible to overload the ! operator, which usually means logical negation, to mean the length of a string:

```
string s = ... ;
int len = !s;                    // correct, but not a good idea
```

This notation would be confusing to the user. On the other hand, it is perfectly natural to use an overloaded + for matrix addition or == for string comparison.

Several basic rules govern operator overloading:

- All operators can be overloaded except the scope operator ::, the member selection operator ., and the member selection through pointer to function operator .* (pointers to members will be described in Section 9.9.1).
- When an operator is overloaded, its precedence and associativity do not change (however, overloaded operators are not assumed to be commutative).
- The expressions +=, -=, ++, and -- are not translated into their standard forms (for example x += y is not translated into x = x + y) unless their arguments are of primitive data types; for example:

```
int x;
...
x++;                         // equivalent to:   x = x + 1

vector v, w;                 // assume vector overloads +
...
v += w;                      // error, unless vector supports +=
```

- If not overloaded, the constructor, copy constructor, assignment, address, and comma operators are always defined for all types. Recall that the default implementation of the copy constructor and assignment operator is memberwise copy.
- To overload an operator, such as +, declare a function whose name is operator+ (this function is called an **operator function**).

I start my description of operator overloading by showing how to overload arithmetic operators. I then show how to overload other operators.

7.3.1   Overloading Arithmetic Operators

A simple concrete type is used for all of the examples in this section: a class Integer, which is a wrapper class for int. The first example shows how to overload unary and binary addition. Both versions of operator+() return a new Integer object, instead of modifying the object from which they are called (see Idiom 3.5). Here is the Integer class:

```
class Integer {
public:
   explicit Integer(int = 0);
   Integer operator+(const Integer&) const;      //binary operator function
   Integer operator+() const;                     // unary operator function
   ...
private:
   int value_;
};
```

```
Integer Integer::operator+(const Integer& i) const {
  Integer local(value_ + i.value_);
  return local;
}

Integer Integer::operator+() const {
  Integer local(+value_);
  return local;
}
```

The client can use the `Integer` class like this:

```
Integer i(5);
Integer j(6);
Integer k = i + j;                          // binary +
k = +k;                                     // unary +
```

From this example, you can see that operators defined for class members have one less argument than is required for the operation: a *binary* operator has a single argument, and a *unary* operator has no arguments (with the exception of postfix operators, as shown later). This is because the object itself (or more precisely, the `this` pointer) also serves as an argument. Therefore, the two calls made to the overloaded + are translated, respectively, to

```
k = i.operator+(j);                         // binary +
k = k.operator+();                          // unary +
```

You can use this "functional" syntax in your programs, for example, to resolve ambiguity, although typically, there is rarely any other reason for doing so.

The class `Integer` may also have the following operator function to overload +=:

```
class Integer {
public:
  ...
  Integer& operator+=(const Integer&);
  ...
};
```

This operator function *modifies* the object from which it is called. It is implemented using the technique for designing modifiers described in Section 3.8.3:

```
Integer& Integer::operator+=(const Integer& i) {
  value_ += i.value_;
```

```
    return *this;
}
```

It is possible to overload both prefix and postfix versions of the ++ and --
operators:

```
class Integer {
public:
    ...
    Integer& operator++();                          // prefix
    Integer operator++(int);                        // postfix
    ...
};
```

There are two differences between the prefix and postfix increments: their return type and their arguments. The prefix version returns the modified object.
It may seem odd that the postfix version of ++ returns a new object rather than a
modified object. Since this operator function needs to return the object *before* it is
modified, the operator makes a copy of the object, modifies it, and then returns the
copy. Thus, the prefix and postfix versions of ++ and -- have different return types.
The prefix version is more efficient than the postfix version because it does not
create any new objects and returns a reference type:

```
++i;            // for overloaded operations, more efficient than i++
```

The postfix operator must have an additional integer argument so the compiler
can tell the difference between the prefix and postfix versions:

```
Integer& Integer::operator++() {        // prefix: modifier
    ++value_;
    return *this;
}

Integer Integer::operator++(int) {      //postfix: returns new object
    Integer local(value_);
    value_++;
    return local;
}
```

You do not provide the name of the int parameter, nor is it ever used. The
client uses the overloaded operators like this:

```
Integer i(5);
Integer j(6);
i = j++;                    // postfix, i.value_ is 6, j.value_ is 7
i = ++j;                    // prefix, i.value_ and j.value_ is 8
```

7.3.2 Members and Helpers

In general, operator functions can be defined either as *members* of a class or as global *stand-alone functions*, called **helper functions** (helpers were first introduced in Section 4.6.4). Operator functions implemented as helpers must have at least one argument of a class type. If these functions need to operate on private members, they have to be granted friendship status.

You can define the `Integer` class to support *mixed-mode* arithmetic:

```
Integer + Integer
int + Integer
Integer + int
```

In the following code, the first operation is a member function, the second is a helper that uses friendship status to access private attributes, and the third is a helper that uses the public interface of `Integer`:

```
class Integer {
public:
  explicit Integer(int = 0);
  int get() const;                                    // query

  Integer operator+(const Integer&) const;            // member
  friend Integer operator+(int, const Integer&);      // helper
  ...
};

Integer Integer::operator+(const Integer& i) const {
  Integer local(value_ + i.value_);
  return local;
}

// friend helper for adding: int+Integer
Integer operator+(int v, const Integer& i) {
  Integer local(v + i.value_);                        // friends can
  return local;                                       // access data
}

// helper for adding: Integer+int
Integer operator+(const Integer& i, int v) {          // not a friend
  Integer local(v + i.get());                         // needs accessor
  return local;
}
```

Only the first helper is a friend; therefore, its declaration appears in the class `Integer`. The client can use code like this:

```
Integer i(5);
Integer k = 5 + i;
```

The expression `5 + i` is translated to

```
operator+(5, i)
```

using the first helper. The expression

```
i + 5;
```

is translated to

```
operator+(i, 5)
```

using the second helper. If `Integer`'s constructor were not declared as `explicit`, the previous expression would have one more possible translation

```
operator+(i, Integer(5))
```

for which the constructor would first convert the value `5` to the `Integer` type, and then two objects of type `Integer` would be added. Therefore, the code would have an *ambiguous* translation, and the compiler would refuse to compile it. With the `explicit` specification, the latter possibility does not apply, and the code compiles.

Which operator functions should you implement as *members* and which as *helpers*? Often this is a matter of personal preference, but there are three rules that can guide you in making this decision:

- An operator function that accepts the first argument of a primitive data type must be a helper (by "the first argument," I mean the explicit first argument for nonmembers and `this` for members).
- An operator function that is a modifier should be defined as a member.
- An operator function that returns a new object should be defined as a helper (it can often be implemented using other members; if not, it needs to be a friend).

The first rule means that you cannot define

```
int + Integer
```

as a member operator function; for this task, you need a helper.

To understand the last two rules, consider the following example, in which I redefine the `Integer` class to support both + and +=. Since the += operator function is a modifier, I implement it as a member; I implement other operator functions as helpers.

First, I define two member operator functions that are modifiers:

```
class Integer {
public:
  explicit Integer(int = 0);
  int get() const;                        // query

  Integer& operator+=(const Integer&);    // Integer += Integer
  Integer& operator+=(int);               // Integer += int
  ...
};

Integer& Integer::operator+=(const Integer& i) {
  value_ += i.value_;
  return *this;
}

Integer& Integer::operator+=(int v) {
 value_ += v;
 return *this;
}
```

Next I define three helpers to represent various forms of addition, all of which are implemented in terms of the members. The first helper implements int + Integer:

```
Integer operator+(int v, const Integer& i) {
  Integer j = i;
  j += v;                     // call: Integer::operator+=(int)
  return j;
}
```

The second helper implements Integer + int, and has the same body as the first helper:

```
Integer operator+(const Integer& i, int v) {
  Integer j = i;
  j += v;                     // call: Integer::operator+=(int)
  return j;
}
```

The third helper implements Integer + Integer:

```
Integer operator+(const Integer& i1, const Integer& i2) {
  Integer j = i1;
  j += i2;            // call: Integer::operator+=(const Integer&)
```

```
    return j;
}
```

You can use the rules describing which operator functions should be members and which should be helpers to implement the prefix and the postfix operator functions. The prefix operator is a modifier and therefore is a member, while the postfix operator returns a new object and therefore is a helper. Start by looking at the definition of the prefix operator:

```
Integer& Integer::operator++() {          // prefix; member of Integer
    ++value_;
    return *this;
}
```

To define the postfix operator, its first argument must be of a class type:

```
Integer operator++(Integer& i, int) {     // postfix helper
    Integer local(i);                     // save i
    ++i;                                  // update i using member
    return local;
}
```

Recall that you need the dummy `int` parameter to specify the postfix version.

None of the helpers defined so far are friends of `Integer`; they all use the public interface of this class. Accessing the class members through the public interface may be considered inefficient because of the extra overhead of the calls made by the operators to the members. You can solve this problem by *inlining* members (see Section 3.2.1); for example:

```
inline Integer& Integer::operator+=(int k);
```

Looking back at the class `Integer` from the beginning of this section, you can see that the class definition shows only those helpers that are friends. For the sake of readability and to provide encapsulation, it is essential to use a *namespace* to encapsulate a class and its related helpers; for example:

```
// File: ch7.integernamespace.h
namespace IntegerNamespace {                        // declarations only
    class Integer {
        ...
    };
    Integer operator+(const Integer&, const Integer&);    // helper
}
```

The *definitions* of both the members and the helpers are placed in the same namespace but in separate files, which allows them to be hidden from the client:

```
// File: ch7.integernamespace.cpp
namespace IntegerNamespace {                                  // definitions
  Integer& Integer::operator+=(int k) {                       // member
    ...
  }
  Integer operator+(const Integer& i1, const Integer& i2) {   // helper
    ...
  }
  ...
}
```

This design hides the implementation and accommodates the future addition of helpers.

You can also overload various Boolean operators like == or <=. This is particularly useful for generic programming, specifically, for the template classes introduced later in this chapter. For example, if you need to add a helper to compare two objects of type `Integer`, you can do so by extending `IntegerNamespace` with the following two helpers:

```
// File ch7.integernamespace.ext.h
#include "ch7.integernamespace.h"
// extends namespace
namespace IntegerNamespace {
  bool operator==(const Integer&, const Integer&);
  bool operator!=(const Integer&, const Integer&);
}


// File ch7.integernamespace.ext.cpp
#include "ch7.integernamespace.ext.h"
namespace IntegerNamespace {
  bool operator==(const Integer& i1, const Integer& i2) {
    return i1.get() == i2.get();
  }
  bool operator!=(const Integer& i1, const Integer& i2) {
    return !(i1 == i2);
  }
}
```

Overloaded Members and Helpers Idiom 7.1

1. Define operator functions that are modifiers as members. Define operator functions that return new objects as helpers.

2. Specify helper functions as friends only if the class interface does not provide the necessary access to class data or if the accessors are not sufficiently efficient.

3. If you use helper functions, store them together with the underlying class in a namespace.

7.3.3   Overloading I/O Operators

A class that supports input or output of its objects must define overloaded I/O operator functions. These operator functions are defined as helpers with the following signatures and return types:

```
ostream& operator<<(ostream&, const classType&)          // output
istream& operator>>(istream&, classType&)                // input
```

The second parameter and the return type allow you to chain calls of I/O operators together; for example:

```
cin >> i >> j;
cout << i << j;
```

You can define two helpers for the `Integer` class that support the input and output of objects of this class. The first helper is a friend of `Integer`, and the second helper is not because it uses the public interface of `Integer`:

```
class Integer {
friend istream& operator>>(istream&, Integer&);
public:
  int get() const;
  ...
};

istream& operator>>(istream& is, Integer& i) {            // input
  is >> i.value_;                          //friends can access
  return is;
}
```

```
ostream& operator<<(ostream& os, const Integer& i) { // output
                                                       // not a friend
   os << i.get();
   return os;
}
```

This input operator function is defined as a friend. If the interface of `Integer` supports `operator+=()`, you can also implement the input operator using only existing members:

```
istream& operator>>(istream& is, Integer& i) {         // not a friend
   int v;
   is >> v;
   i += (v - i.get());
   return is;
}
```

As you can see, both overloaded operators return the stream from which they are performing input or output. You can use them as follows:

```
cout << "Enter an integer ";
Integer i;
cin >> i;
cout << "You entered " << i;                            // chained call
```

The last two statements are translated into

```
cin.operator>>(i);
(cout.operator<<("You entered")).operator<<(i)
```

In the last line of this code, the first call (in brackets) is a call to the overloaded

```
operator<<(ostream&, char*)
```

defined in the standard library, while the second call is a call to the overloaded operator

```
operator<<(ostream&, const Integer&)
```

that was previously defined.

7.3.4 Type Conversions

In Section 3.4.7, I described how given a class C, a class constructor with a single argument of type T can be used to *implicitly* convert T to C. For example, if a class

Integer has a nonexplicit constructor of type int, the constructor provides an implicit conversion from int to Integer, as in

```
void foo(Integer);
int n;
...
foo(n);                             // calls foo(Integer(n));
```

This implicit type conversion may lead to confusion. As I mentioned in Section 3.4.7, to disable this conversion, you use an explicit constructor.

Other user-defined type conversions may be required; for example, for converting from

- A class type to a primitive type (such as int)
- One class to another existing class
- One primitive type to another primitive type

While it is impossible to implement the last conversion in C++, you can implement the first two using a **type conversion operator** that has a rather unusual syntax (introduced in Section 5.14). For example, to define a conversion from the class Integer to another (primitive type or a class) type OldType, you would use the following signature:

```
operator OldType() const;
```

The conversion from the class Integer to int is shown here:

```
class Integer {
public:
  explicit Integer(int = 0);
  operator int() const;                         // conversion
  ...
private:
  int value_;
};

Integer::operator int() const {
  return value_;
}
```

This operator function resembles Java's Integer.intValue(), except C++'s type conversions are *implicit* rather than explicit:

```
Integer i(5);
int v = i;                 // convert i to int, then assign
v = i + 7;                 // convert i to int, add 7, then assign
```

Standard type conversions make it possible to use other primitive data types that are convertible to `int`:

```
Integer i(4);
Integer j;
j = i + 3.5;                              // i + 3
```

In a similar way, you can provide conversions that resemble Java's `toString()`:

```
Integer::operator string();              // convert int to a string
```

The use of the type conversion operator is a bit risky because it can lead to ambiguous translations. For example, if `Integer` has an additional operator function defined

```
Integer Integer::operator+(int);                    // Integer + int
```

then, given the declaration

```
Integer i;
```

the expression

```
i + 5
```

will not compile, because it has two possible translations:

```
i.operator+(5)                // using the above + operator
int(i) + 5                    // using type conversion operator
```

Similarly, the code will not compile if the constructor is not implicit.

You can incorporate range checking into the class `Integer`; for example, you may want the class to accept only integers within a certain range:

```
// File: ch7.integer.h
class Integer {
public:
  explicit Integer(int initValue = 0, int low = 0, int high = 100)
    throw(std::range_error);
  friend Integer operator+(const Integer&, const Integer&)
    throw(std::range_error);                          // friend helper
  operator int() const;
  ...
private:
  int value_;
```

```
    int low_;                          // low bound of the range
    int high_;                         // high bound
};
```

The default range is [0, 100], but it can also be set in the constructor. To define the adding of two Integers, assume that the two Integers must have *the same range,* and if the result of the addition is beyond this range, the std::range_error is thrown:

```
Integer operator+(const Integer& i, const Integer& j)
    throw(std::range_error) {

  if(i.low_ != j.low_ || i.high_ != j.high_)
    throw std::range_error("incompatible ranges");

  int value = i.value_ + j.value_;
  if(value < i.low_ || value > i.high_)
    throw std::range_error("beyond range");

  return Integer(value);
}
```

You can use this class as follows:

```
try {
  Integer i(2, 0, 5);                // initial value 2; range [0,5]
  Integer j(4, 0, 5);
  i = i + j;                         // will throw exception
} catch(std::range_error& e) {
  cout << e.what() << endl;
}
```

If you want to define a conversion operator function for a pointer type, you use typedef; for example, consider the Student and AccountForStudent classes:

```
class Student {
public:
  Student(long);                     // constructor
  void setNumber(long);              // set the student number
  long getNumber() const;
private:
  long number_;
};

class AccountForStudent {
```

```
public:
  AccountForStudent(long number, double balance);
  ~AccountForStudent();
  AccountForStudent& operator=(const AccountForStudent&);
  void show() const;
private:
  Student* stud_;
  double balance_;
};
```

To add a conversion from `Student*` to `AccountForStudent`, you need the following definition:

```
typedef const Student* StudentPointer;
```

Now you can define the conversion operator function:

```
class AccountForStudent {
public:
  ...
  operator StudentPointer() const;
};

AccountForStudent::operator StudentPointer() const {
  return stud_;
}
```

This allows you to use `AccountForStudent` whenever `Student*` is expected. The pointer to `Student` was defined as `const` because the class should provide read-only access to the private attribute `stud_`. For example, assume that that there is a function that modifies the student number:

```
void modify(Student* s) {
  s->setNumber(0);
}
```

If `StudentPointer` was defined without `const`

```
typedef Student* StudentPointer;
```

the client could use `modify()` on an object of class `AccountForStudent`, although this class' interface does not support modifications:

```
AccountForStudent afs(10, 12.8);
modify(afs);                        // converted to: modify(afs.stud_)
```

1. If you overload one element from one of the following four sets of operations, you should also overload the other elements of the set:

   ```
   ==  !=
   <   >  <=  >=
   + (unary),  + (binary),  +=,  ++
   - (unary),  - (binary),  -=,  --
   ```

2. For a class C:

   - A constructor with a single argument of type T provides an implicit type conversion from T to C (to disable this conversion, use an `explicit` constructor)
   - The type conversion function operator

     ```
     operator T() const;
     ```

   provides an implicit type conversion from C to T.

7.3.5 Overloading Subscripting and Function Call Operators

The previous sections described how to design operator functions for arithmetic operations, I/O, and type conversion. In this section, I describe overloading subscripting and function call operators. Both these operator functions must be members (that is, they cannot be defined as helpers).

The subscripting operator `[ ]` is typically used to refer to the *i*th element of an array. Since the argument of this operator is of an arbitrary type, you can use it to define associative arrays or to refer to an element of a collection implemented with some data structure. For example, you can implement the subscripting operator for a collection of Student objects, allowing the client to access students using both a string and a long index:

```
class Student;  // handle
class StudentImp; // body

class StudentNotFoundException;          // related exception class

class StudentCollection {
public:
   ...
   const Student& operator[](long) const    // query for
      throw(StudentNotFoundException);      // Student with this ID
```

```
    Student& operator[](long) throw(StudentNotFoundException); // modifier


    const Student& operator[](string) const                    // query for
        throw(StudentNotFoundException);        // Student with this name

    Student& operator[](string) throw(StudentNotFoundException); // modifier


    ...
private:
    StudentImp delegate_;
};
```

Note that two operator functions are overloading operator[](): one with a long
argument and one with a string argument. Each function has two versions: a constant function that returns a constant reference (a *query*) and a function that returns a reference (a *modifier*). You need both versions because the modifier does
not allow you to use it with constant objects; you need the query to do so.

The client can use these operator functions like this:

```
StudentCollection sc;
...
try {
    Student s = sc["John"];              // s = sc.operator[]("John")
    Student t = sc[123456];              // s = sc.operator[](123456)
    const Student e = sc[0000];
} catch(StudentNotFoundException& se) {

    ...
}
```

It is possible to create objects that behave like functions by overloading the
function call operator()(). For example, you can add a Boolean "function" that
checks whether there is a student with a specific ID:

```
class StudentCollection {
public:
    ...
    bool operator()(long) const;
    ...
};
StudentCollection sc;
```

```
...
if(sc(123456))                  // sc is an object, not a function
    ... exists
```

Note that the *functional* notation

```
sc(123456)
```

is translated into

```
sc.operator()(123456)
```

Objects that overload a function call `operator()()` are called **functors**. They are often used in the STL, which is covered in the next chapter.

It is important that you define these operators, as well as other operators, only when it is appropriate and avoid using unnecessarily confusing applications, such as defining

```
long Student::operator()() const;                    // return ID
```

because this makes the following code confusing:

```
Student s;
...
long i = s();
```

In general, you have to make a decision as to whether overloading an operator is justified and does not confuse the client of the code. For the previous example, I find

```
sc(123456)
```

to be clear but

```
s()
```

to be confusing.

Overloading Subscripting and Function Idiom 7.3

For the operator functions `operator[]()` and `operator()()` that return objects, define two versions: a constant query and a modifier.

7.3.6   Overloading Memory Management

By default, memory allocated using `new` comes from the system-defined heap, and memory deallocated using `delete` is returned to that heap (see Section 2.6). A general-purpose memory management system has to deal with memory blocks that may be of varying sizes and therefore cannot take advantage of special cases in which all blocks are of the same size. (Maintaining blocks of varying sizes is more difficult because you have to remember the size of each block, choose a policy for finding the best free block large enough to satisfy the request, split the block into the part that is needed for the allocation and the free "leftover" part, and finally possibly merge neighboring free blocks.) In addition, a specialized application may wish to allocate memory from specific memory regions rather than from a general memory pool. To make it possible to specialize memory management, C++ provides four functions declared in `<new>`—two for managing memory for a single object and two for managing memory for arrays of objects:

```
void* operator new(size_t) throw (std::bad_alloc);
void operator delete(void*) throw();

void* operator new[](size_t) throw(std::bad_alloc);
void operator delete[](void*) throw();
```

`void*` is a generic pointer type compatible with any other pointer type (see Section 9.4.1).

You can define your own operator functions `new` and `delete` to implement per-class memory management. For example, consider a simple wrapper class `Integer` for integer values; each object of this class is of the same size. You can preallocate one large block to be used as a user-defined heap (rather than the system-defined heap). Assuming that the functions `Integer::new` and `Integer::delete` have been defined, whenever the user creates a new object

```
Integer* i = new Integer(5);
```

`Integer::new` is called, and it allocates memory from the user-defined heap. Similarly, when the `Integer` object is deallocated

```
delete i;
```

the function `Integer::delete` is called, and it returns memory to the user-defined heap.

This kind of application is rarely needed, so I will postpone its description until Section 9.5, where I will describe one more application of overloading memory functions. Recall Idiom 4.3, which describes how to make sure that all objects are allocated on the *heap*. When overloaded memory management functions are defined as private, all objects are allocated on the *stack*.

Stack Allocation Idiom 7.4

To allocate all objects of a specific class on the stack and prohibit heap allocation, make overloaded `new` and `delete` private (you do not have to define their
implementations).

This idiom is useful if you want to prevent the user from dynamically allocating
memory:

```
SomeClass* p = new SomeClass;
```

(See the discussion of the iterator wrapper at the end of Section 7.5.2.)

7.3.7   Overloading Pointer Operations

There are two inherent problems with using pointers: They are not initialized using
constructors, and they are not disposed of using destructors. Specifically, if you have
a resource accessed through a pointer, you might either accidentally use uninitialized pointers or forget to deallocate the resource:

```
Resource *p = 0;
p->resourceOp();              // zero pointer; missing initialization

void foo() {
  Resource* p = new Resource();            // missing destruction
}
```

To deal with these problems, you can create **smart pointers**, which are wrappers
for pointers. Smart pointers are objects that behave as if they were pointers. Since
they are objects, they are initialized using constructors, and their destructors are automatically called when they go out of scope.

For smart pointers to behave like pointers, you have to overload two operators:

- `operator->`, for indirect member access
- `operator*`, for dereferencing

Both these operator functions must be members, and their return type must be either a pointer or an object to which this operator function can be applied. The following example of a pointer wrapper assumes that a resource is represented by a
pointer to class `Resource`:

```
class ResourceWrapper {
public:
  ResourceWrapper(const Resource*);
```

```
    virtual ~ResourceWrapper();

  Resource* operator->() const throw (std::runtime_error);
  Resource* operator*() const throw (std::runtime_error);

private:
  Resource* res_;                         // pointer being wrapped

  // copy disallowed
  ResourceWrapper(const ResourceWrapper&);
  ResourceWrapper& operator=(const ResourceWrapper&);
};

// construction and initialization
ResourceWrapper::ResourceWrapper(const Resource* r) : res_(r) {}

// destruction
ResourceWrapper::~ResourceWrapper() {
  delete res_;
}

ResourceWrapper::Resource* operator->() const
      throw (std::runtime_error){
  if(res_ == 0)
    throw std::runtime_error();
  return res_;
}

ResourceWrapper::Resource* operator*() const {
  if(res_ == 0)
    throw std::runtime_error();
  return *res_;
}
```

The smart pointer p behaves like a pointer; for example

```
p->resourceOp();
```

is translated to

```
p.operation->()->resourceOp();
```

How *smart* are these pointers? Consider the following code:

```
void foo() {
  ResourceWrapper p(new Resource);  // p initialized by constructor
  try {
    p->resourceOp();                // calls overloaded ->
                                    // assuming Resource overloads <<
    cout << *p;                     // cout.operator<<(p.operation*())
  } catch(const std::runtime_error&) {
    cerr << "using 0 pointer" << endl;
  }
}
```

As you can see, the initialization of a smart pointer is taken care of by the constructor; the access operator has an additional check to avoid using *zero pointers*; and finally, when foo() terminates, the object p goes out of scope, its destructor is called, and the resource is deallocated. The previous code includes extra error checking to make sure that both -> and * are applied only to nonzero pointers. Of course, smart pointers will not help if you accidentally use *uninitialized* smart pointers.

In Section 7.8.2, I will discuss smart pointers that use reference counting, thus allowing the values of pointers to be shared, and deleting objects no longer pointed to by *any* pointer.

Smart Pointer Idiom 7.5

To create a pointer wrapper class, overload pointer access operations operator->() and operator*(). Define a constructor that associates a pointer with its wrapper class and a destructor that deletes the pointer.

This completes the discussion of the most important operator functions. In the next section, I will show a design pattern called proxy and an example of a proxy that uses smart pointers.

7.4   *Proxy Design Pattern*

For applications that have two communicating layers of software, it is useful to introduce an intermediate layer, called a proxy. For example, consider the client/server layers of software in Java, which communicate using remote method invocation (RMI). RMI uses a proxy, which is a local representative for a remote object. Remote method invocations communicate with this proxy, which forwards them to the remote object; this kind of a proxy is called a **remote proxy**. A proxy is also useful when you need to use an existing interface of an object.

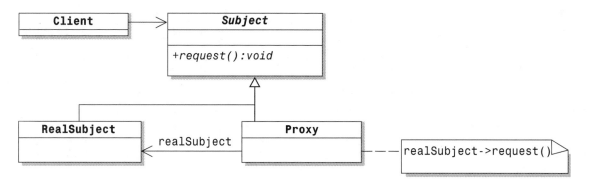

Figure 7.1 Proxy design pattern

Based in part, by permission, on Gamma, E. et al., *Design Patterns: Elements of Reusable Object-Oriented Software* (Reading, Mass.: Addison-Wesley, 1995) p. 209.

Your code can use the proxy to communicate with this interface rather than directly with the object. The proxy can filter the communication and decide how to pass the information to the object; this kind of a proxy is called a **protection proxy**.

In general, the **proxy design pattern** changes the communication between the client and the target object by introducing the proxy layer with which the client communicates; the proxy forwards the client requests to the target object. Figure 7.1 shows a general design for the proxy, where the abstract class Subject defines a common interface for two derived classes: the RealSubject, which is the implementation of the Subject, and the Proxy. The client programs to the abstract common interface (that is, the Subject). The Proxy does more than simply delegate requests to the Subject; for example, it filters these requests (protection proxy) or processes them for remote communication (remote proxy).

Another kind of proxy object, called a **virtual proxy**, creates other objects on demand. For example, consider an editor that allows you to embed graphical objects. When you open an existing document, the editor should only create objects that are initially visible; creating all the objects (both visible and invisible) would slow down the opening of your document and place memory demands on the system. The basic idea is to create objects on demand, as they are needed. This can be done by using proxies as *virtual* images. The editor's code communicates with the proxy whenever it needs to perform an operation on an image (such as displaying it). To do this, it uses the abstract image interface (which corresponds to Subject in Figure 7.1); both the concrete image and the virtual proxy are derived from this abstract class (in Figure 7.1, these correspond to RealSubject and Proxy, respectively).

To make this example more concrete, consider a very simple example of a virtual proxy used to implement an *on-demand* operation: the class FileOps, which

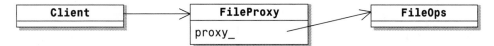

Figure 7.2 Client of the file virtual proxy

provides an operation to count the number of lines in a file (see Figure 7.2). This file will be opened only when the number of lines is actually requested. Start with an abstract class AbstractFileOps:

```
class AbstractFileOps {              // abstract; Subject in Figure 7.1
public:
  virtual ~AbstractFileOps();
  virtual long lines() const = 0;
};
```

The following code is for the two derived classes. Note the different implementations of lines();FileOps::lines() actually calculates the number of lines, while FileProxy::lines() merely delegates the work:

```
class FileOps : public AbstractFileOps { // RealSubject
public:
  explicit FileOps(const string&);
  virtual ~FileOps();
  virtual long lines() const;
private:
  string filename_;
  ifstream fileVar_;
};

class FileProxy : public AbstractFileOps { // Proxy
public:
  explicit FileProxy(const string&);
  virtual ~FileProxy();
  virtual long lines() const;
private:
  string filename_;
  ifstream fileVar_;
  FileOps* proxy
};

FileProxy::FileProxy(const string& filename) {
  filename_ = filename;
```

```
    proxy_ = 0;
}

long FileProxy::lines() const {                    // delegate to FileOps
    if(proxy_ == 0)
        proxy_ = new FileOps(filename_);
    return proxy_->lines();
}

long FileOps::lines() const {
    long lines_ = 0;

    char c;
    while(fileVar_.get(c))
        if(c == '\n')
            ++lines_;
    fileVar_.clear();
    fileVar_.seekg(0);
    return lines_;
}
```

The client operates on a file using its proxy (see Figure 7.2):

```
AbstractFileOps* f = new FileProxy("a.dat");    // doesn't open file yet
cout << f->lines();
```

Another possible implementation of a proxy does not follow the general pattern but has enough interesting properties to be included here. As previously pointed out, the proxy design pattern has an abstract base class Subject, and both the actual subject and the proxy classes are derived from this class. This design cannot be used for an existing subject class that cannot be modified; even if this class can be modified, you have to make sure that both the subject class and the proxy class have the same interface. In an alternative implementation, the client uses the proxy class as if it were a pointer by overloading operator->() and operator*(). A request made to the proxy class is then delegated to the subject through the overloaded functions (see Figure 7.3):

```
class Proxy {
public:
    Proxy(const string&);
    FileOps* operator->();
    FileOps& operator*();
private:
    FileOps* proxy_;
    string filename_;
```

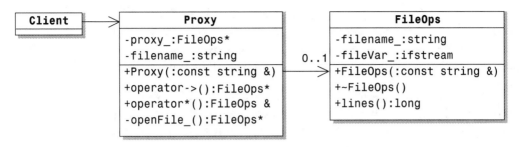

Figure 7.3   A proxy for caching file operations

```
   FileOps* openFile_();
};

Proxy::Proxy(const string& filename) {
   filename_ = filename;
   proxy_ = 0;                              // uses lazy evaluation
}

FileOps* Proxy::openfile_() {
   if(proxy_ == 0)
     proxy_ = new FileOps(filename_);
   return proxy_;
}

FileOps* Proxy::operator->() {
   return openfile_();
}
```

The client can use this class as follows:

```
Proxy p("a.dat");                    // doesn't open a file yet
cout << p->lines();                  // open now
```

The last line is translated into

```
p.openfile_()->lines();
```

which returns

```
p.proxy_->lines()
```

It should be noted that iterators, and in particular various arithmetic operations on iterators, generalize pointers. However, as I mentioned earlier, the various C++

pointer operations that were inherited from C are now deprecated, so I will not describe them here. (There is a very important difference between a bare pointer, and an abstraction of a pointer which is represented by a class that may have a constructor, a destructor, and other operations; unlike the abstraction of a pointer C-style pointers should typically be avoided.)

It may appear that a proxy introduces an extra overhead because all requests go through this proxy, thereby creating a level of indirection. While this is true, as I previously stated, there are much more important benefits of using this pattern, such as access to a remote object and protection of an object.

7.5 *Designing Iterators*

Now that you know how to overload various operators, I want to show how overloading is used by a very common operation: iteration over aggregate objects, such as collections of data. There are several essential requirements for iterators:

- Provide a sequential access to an object.

- Avoid exposing the underlying representation of the object to the client.

- Support various kinds of traversals—for example, forward and backward.

- Support simultaneous traversals.

- Exhibit reasonable behavior in case of modifications, such as additions or deletions while an iteration is in progress.

- Provide a uniform interface so the client's code does not need to be changed when the representation of the collection does.

- Avoid runtime overhead, such as late binding and dynamic casts.

This is a fairly long list of requirements, but since iterators are used in many applications, flexible and good design is very important.

Java provides a standard interface for iterations: Through version 1.2 it was the Enumeration interface, implemented with collections, such as Vector; from version 1.3 on, it is the Iterator interface with the additional remove() method.

To help you understand iterators, I start with an example of a list iterator. Then, I describe an iterator design pattern, which is another example of a behavioral object pattern. Finally, I compare the Java and C++ approaches to providing support for iterators.

7.5.1 Example: List Iterator

Java programmers often use enumerations over collections, such as lists. Specifically, the list provides a method called elements() that implements the abstract Enumeration interface and returns a new enumeration. The C++ approach to enumerations is different: The iterator is not the implementation of an abstract interface. In this section, I show an example of an iterator so you can get an idea of the basic functionality that is required. In Section 7.8, I will provide more details on iterators and explain the reasons for the design differences between C++ and Java.

Before I show the iterator example, I need to discuss several details related to *nested classes*. As I mentioned in Section 3.2, the nested class and the outer enclosing class are independent; neither class has special access privileges to the other class. In other words, it is as if the two classes were defined separately, although this does not appear to be so to the client of the enclosed class. To define members of the enclosing class that are pointers or references to the nested class, you must at least *declare* the nested class; for example

```
class List {
    ...
    class Link;                    // declaration
    Link* head_;
    Link elem;                     // can't declare variables of Link
    ...
};
```

You can first declare a nested class and later define it in the enclosing class:

```
class List {
    ...
    class Link;                                    // declaration
    Link* head_;
    ...
    class Link {                                   // definition
        ...
    };
    ...
};
```

You can also define it in a separate file. A nested class cannot directly access even the public members of the enclosing class; to access members, it must use pointers, references, or objects of the enclosing class; for example:

```
class List {
public:
    ...
    void foo();
private:
    class Link;
    Link* head_;
```

```
    ...
    class Link {
      void goo(List&);
    };
    ...
  };

  void List::Link::goo(List& li) {
    li.foo();

    foo();                 // can't directly access outer class attributes
  }
```

Finally, you can also define a class inside the body of a function. Typically, such a class is a structure that allows the enclosing function to access all of its members.

● EXAMPLE 7.1

In this example, I show a list iterator for a singly linked list of integers (this version does not use exception handling). However, this implementation can be easily generalized to work with a list containing elements of any data type T, as a result of the following definition:

```
  typedef int T;
```

This definition allows me to avoid referring to int in my implementation, making future type changes easy. Unfortunately, this technique has limitations. First, to make a list of floats, you have to modify the typedef definition. Second, you cannot have two lists containing different types of elements at the same time. You can solve both these problems by using the template construct introduced later in this chapter, which uses the type as a parameter for the class. For now, I use the previous type definition.

The classes for this example are stored in the namespace LIST_ITERATION_ NAMESPACE, which is split into two files (following Idiom 4.4): the file that stores the client's interface and the file that stores the implementation.

The class List has a nested public class ListIterator. It also uses a private class, Link_, that stores information about a single list element. Instead of nesting this class in the List class, I store only its *declaration* in the interface (that is, in the header file) and store its definition in the implementation of the namespace. The following is the public part of the namespace:

```
  // File: ex7.1.list.h
  namespace LIST_ITERATION_NAMESPACE {
    typedef int T;
    struct Link_;                                      // declaration
```

```
class List {
public:
  List();
  virtual ~List();

  void insert(const T&);    // insert in front
  bool remove(T&);          // delete first; return true if successful
  int size() const;         // size of the list

  class ListIterator {
  friend bool operator==(const ListIterator&, const ListIterator&);
  public:
    ListIterator(Link_* = 0);
    T& operator*();
    const T& operator*() const;
    ListIterator& operator++();                        // prefix
  private:
    Link_* current_;
  };

  ListIterator begin() const;
  ListIterator end() const;

private:
  List(const List&);
  List& operator=(const List&);
  Link_* head_;
  int size_;
};                                                     // end of List

// declarations of helpers

List::ListIterator operator++(List::ListIterator&, int);   // postfix

bool operator==(const List::ListIterator&,
        const List::ListIterator&);

bool operator!=(const List::ListIterator&,
        const List::ListIterator&);
}
```

The class List has an interface standard for lists; in addition, list copying is disallowed by moving the copy constructor and the assignment operator to the private section.

Now consider the part of the interface related to the iterator. Although this example uses a list, the following discussion applies to any containers, such as queues, trees, and so on. An iterator points to the value stored in the container, or just beyond the container. More precisely, an iteration is performed over a range, which typically is a half-closed interval [a, b); b can only be used for comparison purposes and cannot be accessed. List provides two functions, begin() and end(), that return the value of the iterator type and, respectively, indicate the beginning and *beyond* the end of the iteration range (see Figure 7.4). To access the objects in the collection, the iterator uses the dereferencing operation *; to advance the iteration, it uses ++.

The following code shows the standard way to iterate over lists:

```
using namespace ITERATION_NAMESPACE;
List myList;
... // set up a list

for(List::ListIterator it = myList.begin(); it != myList.end(); ++it)
    ... // here, use *it, which gives access to the i-th element
```

For technical reasons explained in Section 7.3.1, it is more efficient to use the prefix operator ++i rather than the postfix operator i++.

As a specific example of the general iteration, the following code reads ten values from standard input and then searches for an element among the values using the ListIterator:

```
List myList;
int j;
for(int n = 0; n < 10; ++n) {
  cin >> j;
  myList.insert(j);
}
cout << "Enter a value to search for:";
cin >> j;
```

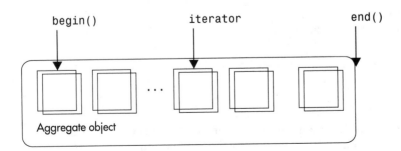

Figure 7.4 C++-style iterators

```
for(List::ListIterator it = myList.begin(); it != myList.end(); ++it)
  if(*it == j) {
    cout << "found" << endl;
    break;
  }
```

Here is the implementation of some of the List operations just defined (note that the private Link_ is a structure because there is no need to encapsulate its data):

```
// File: ex7.1.list.cpp
typedef  int T;
namespace LIST_ITERATION_NAMESPACE {

  struct Link_ {
    T value_;
    Link_* next_;
    Link_(const T&, Link_*);            // link with the next element
  };

  Link_::Link_(const T& t, Link_* h) : value_(t), next_(h) {}

  List::List() : head_(0), size_(0) {}

  List::~List() {
    T aux;
    while(remove(aux))                              // empty the list
      ;
    head_ = 0;
    size_ = 0;
  }

  int List::size() const {
    return size_;
  }

  void List::insert(const T& t) {
    Link_* temp = new Link_(t, head_);
    head_ = temp;
    ++size_;
  }

  bool List::remove(T& t) {               // remove the first element
    if(size_ == 0)
      return false;
    --size_;
```

```
  Link_* temp = head_;
  t = head_->value_;
  head_ = temp->next_;
  delete temp;
  return true;
}

List::ListIterator::ListIterator(Link_* t) : current_(t) {}

T& List::ListIterator::operator*() {
  return current_->value_;
}

List::ListIterator List::begin()  const {
  return List::ListIterator(head_);
}

List::ListIterator List::end() const {
  return ListIterator();
}

List::ListIterator& List::ListIterator::operator++() {
                                            // prefix member
  current_ = current_->next_;
  return *this;
}

List::ListIterator operator++(List::ListIterator& i, int) {
                                            // postfix helper
  List::ListIterator temp(i);
  ++i;
  return temp;
}

bool operator==(const List::ListIterator& i,
    const List::ListIterator& j) {
  return i.current_ == j.current_;
 }

bool operator!=(const List::ListIterator& i,
    const List::ListIterator& j) {
  return !(i == j);
}

}
```

The code in Example 7.1 is not safe because it does not use exception handling. It is possible for the client to use the List operations incorrectly—for example, to use the ++ operator for an iterator equal to end(),which would result in the iterator "falling off" the end of the list. The C++ standard library provides constructs similar to the ones previously described, which do not use exception handling and rely on clients to do their own checking. (The last statement should *not* be construed as a suggestion that exception handling is not useful.)

7.5.2 Iterator Design Pattern

Section 7.5 began with a look at the list of requirements for iterators and then gave a specific example of an iterator for lists. This section shows how you can use the iterator design pattern to design general iterators that satisfy some of the requirements.

The most general form of an iterator supported by the **iterator design pattern** involves two abstract classes, Aggregate and Iterator, which are the only classes used by the client (the Aggregate represents a collection of objects). These two classes represent the decoupling needed to allow the client to iterate over the aggregate without referring to its internal structure. A concrete implementation of an aggregate represents a specific collection, for example, a list or a tree. This concrete aggregate can be iterated over using the corresponding concrete iterator. The two class hierarchies are connected by a makeIterator() factory method (see Figure 7.5).

The Iterator shown in Figure 7.5 is called a **polymorphic iterator** because the client can use it without committing to a specific aggregate structure; the next example shows this kind of iterator. Iterators over aggregates can also be designed

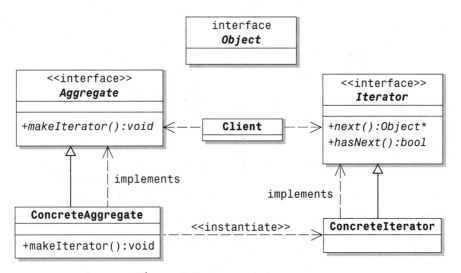

Figure 7.5 Iterator design pattern

Based in part, by permission, on Gamma, E., et al., *Design Patterns: Elements of Reusable Object-Oriented Software* (Reading, Mass.: Addison-Wesley, 1995) pp. 259.

using another technique that employs concrete iterators rather than polymorphic ones; this design will be discussed in Section 7.8.1.

● EXAMPLE 7.2

In this example, I implement a polymorphic list iterator according to the general design previously described. This iterator is different from the one in Example 7.1 because it follows Java's philosophy, using an abstract Iterator class (see Figure 7.6).

In this example, I use exception handling. First, look at the definitions of the AbstractList and AbstractIterator classes:

```
// File: ex7.2.abstractlist.h
namespace LIST_POLYMORPHIC_ITERATION {
  typedef int T;

  class AbstractList {  // abstract
  public:
    AbstractList();
    virtual ~AbstractList();
    virtual void insert(const T&) = 0;          // insert in front

    virtual bool remove(T&) = 0;
                                         // delete first; return
                                         // true if successful
```

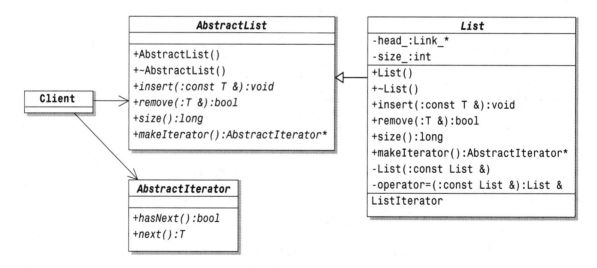

Figure 7.6 Polymorhpic list iterator

```
    virtual long size() const = 0;
    virtual AbstractIterator* makeIterator() const = 0;
                                        // in Java: elements()
  };
}


// File ex7.2.iterator.h
namespace LIST_POLYMORPHIC_ITERATION {
  typedef int T;

  class AbstractIterator { // abstract
  public:
    virtual bool hasNext() const = 0;
    virtual T next() throw(std::range_error) = 0 ;
  };
}
```

Now look at the implementation of a list (only the code relevant to this example is shown here). The class List represents a concrete aggregate.:

```
    // File ex7.2.list.h
  namespace LIST_POLYMORPHIC_ITERATION {

    struct Link_;    // declaration

    class List : public AbstractList {  // implements
    public:
      List();
      virtual ~List();

      virtual void insert(const T&);
      virtual bool remove(T&);
      virtual long size() const;

      virtual AbstractIterator* makeIterator() const;

    private:

      class ListIterator : public AbstractIterator { // implements
      public:
        virtual bool hasNext() const;
        virtual T next() throw(std::range_error);
        ListIterator(Link_* = 0);
      private:
        List* head_;
```

```cpp
        Link_* current_;
        long size_;
    };

    List(const List&);
    List& operator=(const List&);
    Link_* head_;
    int size_;
    };
}

    // File: ex7.2.list.cpp
namespace LIST_POLYMORPHIC_ITERATION {
    List::ListIterator::ListIterator(Link_* t) : current_(t) {}

    AbstractIterator* List::makeIterator() const {
        return new List::ListIterator(head_);
    }

    bool List::ListIterator::hasNext() const {
        return current_ != 0;
    }

    T List::ListIterator::next() throw(std::range_error) {
        if(current_ == 0)
            throw std::range_error("no current");
        int v =  current_->value_;
        current_ = current_->next_;
        return v;
    }
}
```

In general, there are two kinds of iterators: **External iterators** can be used by
the client to explicitly advance the current position—for example, by using ++ or
next(). **Internal iterators** are not under the client's control and implicitly advance
the current position. At each step, the operation specified in the iterator is applied
to the current object in the aggregate. For example, you can have an internal iterator that converts all strings in the aggregate (the collection) to lowercase. External
iterators are more general, so I concentrate on them.

A **null iterator** returns no objects; it is used for handling boundary cases. For example, the function end() in Example 7.1 returns a null iterator that can be used to
determine that the end of a list has been reached. Another example is the traversal
of a tree, where each node provides an iterator for its children; a leaf node provides
a null iterator.

What happens if a modification is made while the collection is being iterated over? One possibility is that the iteration could be invalidated. Alternatively, you could make a copy of the aggregate before the iteration starts and then iterate over this copy; however, this is hardly practical for larger aggregates. Both solutions are rather extreme and not considered robust. An iterator is **robust** if modifications such as insertions or removals do not interfere with the iteration and the iterator does not copy the aggregate. To implement a robust iterator, the aggregate must have a link to the iterator. If the aggregate is modified, it notifies the iterator and updates the internal information needed to iterate.

Specific concrete iterators, called **filtered iterators**, may select certain objects in the aggregate. For example, you can choose to iterate over a list of integers, filtering out all elements that are equal to zero. To print a list, you can use the following Java-style code:

```
List myList;
... // insert elements into myList
Iterator* j = myList.makeIterator();
try {
  while(j->hasNext())
    cout << j->next() << endl;
} catch(std::range_error& e) {
    cerr << e.what() << endl;
}
delete j;
```

There is a problem with this code: You can easily forget to delete the iterator, causing a memory leak. To solve this problem, you can use Idioms 7.4 and 7.5, and wrap a pointer around the `Iterator`:

```
class IteratorWrapper {
public:
  IteratorWrapper(const Iterator*);
  ~IteratorWrapper();
  Iterator* operator->() throw (std::runtime_error);
  Iterator* operator*() throw (std::runtime_error);
private:
  Iterator* res_;

  // copy disallowed
  IteratorWrapper(const IteratorWrapper&);
  IteratorWrapper& operator=(const IteratorWrapper&);

  // heap allocation disallowed
  void* operator new(size_t) throw (std::bad_alloc);
```

```
    void operator delete(void*) throw();
};
```

This wrapper allows you to write the following iteration code:

```
IteratorWrapper iw(myList.makeIterator());          // construction

while(iw->hasNext())
  cout << iw->next();
...
// automatic deallocation
```

Now you are ready to acquaint yourself with the most important concept of this chapter: templates.

7.6   *Templates*

C++ classes can be parameterized, which means they can have parameters that represent types. A parameterized class, also called a **generic class**, is not fully defined and cannot be used to create objects. Once the type parameters in a parameterized class are replaced by the actual parameters and the class is **instantiated**, objects of this instantiation can be created (an instantiation is also called *specialization*).

C++ functions can also be parameterized. In particular, all function members of a generic class are parameterized functions.

Type parameterization makes it possible to combine two representations. For example, the class Stack<T> and the class List<T> can be combined in one step to create a stack of lists of type T:

```
Stack<List<T> >                    // note the space between two >'s
```

The runtime and space efficiency of the resulting code is close to, and sometimes even better than, a client-written class for a stack of lists (for more on this topic, see Section 7.6.2).

7.6.1   Defining Template Classes

A generic class is defined using a **template definition**, which starts with the template keyword:

```
template <typename T>
```

The syntax

```
typename T
```

indicates that `T` is a type parameter (there may be more than one template parameter). The alternative, older syntax uses the keyword `class` rather than `typename`. Template parameters do not have to be types, they can also be compile-time constants or functions (that is, constants that can be evaluated at compile time or functions that can be expanded at compile time); for example:

```
template <typename T, size_t SIZE>
```

The syntax for defining templates can be confusing at first. You may find it helpful to first define a class using a `typedef` and then make a few simple changes that convert this class into a template. In the following example, I show how to use this technique.

● EXAMPLE 7.3

In this example, I show a template stack class. Following the above description, I first define a stack of `ints` using a `typedef`:

```
typedef int T;
const int SIZE = 100;

class Stack {
public:
  Stack();
  virtual ~Stack();
  void push(const T&);
  void pop();
  void top(T&) const;
  bool isEmpty() const;
  bool isFull() const;
private:
  int top_;
  T stack_[SIZE];
};
```

To convert this class definition to a template, I just need to add the template header line:

```
// File: ex7.3.stack.h
template <typename T>
class Stack {
```

```
public:
  Stack();
  ~Stack();
  void push(const T&);
  void pop();
  void top(T&) const;
  bool isEmpty() const;
  bool isFull() const;
private:
  int top_;
  T stack_[SIZE];
};
```

The constant `SIZE` can also be included as a parameter of the template:

```
template <typename T, size_t SIZE>
class Stack {
...
};
```

Note that within the template, a nontype template parameter is treated as a compile-time constant. Therefore, the definition of the array `stack_` is correct.

Now consider how to define *template member operations*. (For the sake of simplicity, I do not include exception handling here; Example 5.3 shows an example of a template with exception handling.) Each template member definition starts with a template header that is the same as the one used for the class definition except it is qualified by the class name and includes all of the template parameters; for example:

```
Stack<T, SIZE>::Stack()                              // constructor
```

Definitions of member operations follow (all these members are parameterized functions):

```
// File: ex7.3.stack.cpp
template <typename T, size_t SIZE>
Stack<T, SIZE>::Stack() : top_(0) { }

template <typename T, size_t SIZE>
Stack<T, SIZE>::~Stack() { }

template <typename T, size_t SIZE>
void Stack<T,SIZE >::push(const T& new_item) {
```

```
    stack_[top_++] = new_item;
}

template <typename T, size_t SIZE>
void Stack<T, SIZE>::pop() {
  --top_;
}

template <typename T, size_t SIZE>
void Stack<T, SIZE>::top(T& item) const {
  item = stack_[top_ - 1];
}

template <typename T, size_t SIZE>
bool Stack<T, SIZE>::isEmpty() const {
  return top_ == 0;
}

template <typename T, size_t SIZE>
bool Stack<T, SIZE>::isFull() const {
  return top_ == SIZE;
}
```

A UML class diagram of a generic class shows its type parameters in the upper-right corner, just below the class name (see Figure 7.7).

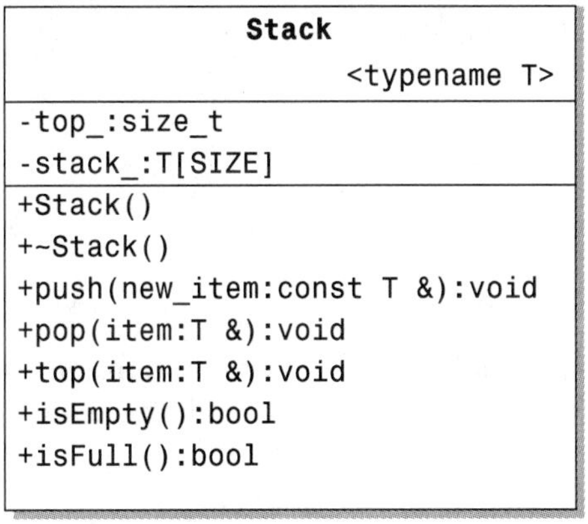

Figure 7.7 UML diagram for the Stack template

Functions can also be passed as template parameters; for example, you can add an error handler to the list of parameters. This requires a type definition that represents a pointer to a function, which gets a bit more complicated:

```
typedef void (*HTYPE)();   // HTYPE is a void function, no parameters

template <typename T, size_t SIZE, HTYPE handler>
class Stack { ... };
```

7.6.2   Instantiating Template Classes

As I mentioned earlier, a template definition cannot be used to define objects; it can only be used to create classes through the instantiation process performed at compile time. A template is also called a type generator because its instantiations generate various types.

Typically, when you **instantiate** a template, you create objects of the instantiated class. To do this, you use the template name and provide all the arguments for the template's parameters. For example, given the template

```
template <typename T, size_t SIZE>
class Stack {
   ...
};
```

you can instantiate it and create two objects as follows:

```
Stack<int, 100> si;            // for a stack of 100 integers
Stack<double, 50> sd;          // for a stack of 20 doubles
```

The instantiated class names, such as

```
Stack<int, 100>
Stack<double, 50>
```

use template names and actual parameters and are called **instantiations**, or **specializations**, of templates. These instantiated class names can be used wherever regular class names can, as in

```
typedef Stack<double, 50> StackOfDouble;
```

or

```
void foo(const Stack<int, 100>&);
```

A class template is instantiated only when necessary, that is when a complete class definition is required. Therefore, when pointers or references to a class template are used, no instantiation is generated. Similarly, class operations are instantiated only when necessary, such as when they are called.

7.6.3 Default Template Parameters

You can provide default values for template parameters. For example, you can implement a template class for a stack that by default holds up to 100 integers:

```
template <typename T = int, size_t SIZE = 100>
class Stack {
...
```

You can use this definition as follows:

```
Stack s;                                    // Stack<int, 100>
```

You can also overwrite the default type parameter and create a stack of 100 characters without specifying the size explicitly

```
Stack<char> t;                              // Stack<char, 100>
```

or a stack of 50 characters:

```
Stack<char, 50> w;
```

7.6.4 Concepts and Models: Requirements for Type Parameters

Instantiation can *fail* if the actual template argument is a user-defined class that does not provide some operations required by the implementation of the template class. For example, consider the class Integer defined as:

```
class Integer {
public:
  explicit Integer(int);        // there is no no-arg constructor
  ...
};
```

and the template Stack (defined in Example 7.3) instantiated with Integer:

```
Stack<Integer, 100> s;                    // failed instantiation
```

This instantiation failed because the template uses an array of T:

```
T stack_[SIZE];
```

Therefore, it assumes that T has a no-arg constructor.

The code just shown did not compile because the instantiation failed. Sometimes there are more subtle reasons why the instantiation may be *logically* incorrect, even if it compiles. For example, if the type used to instantiate a Stack maintains a resource and uses a predefined overloaded assignment and a predefined copy constructor, then a shallow copy rather than a deep copy of objects will be used (to see that this is an error, recall Idiom 3.6). These kinds of errors are particularly nasty because programmers might be overconfident that the compiler will inform them that there is a problem, but the actual problem will show up much later, during the execution, when a template is instantiated. Therefore, I strongly recommend that you carefully verify whether the class used as an actual template argument satisfies all the requirements imposed by the code of this template. In the remainder of this section, I show some techniques that you can use for this verification.

First, there is a clear need for a good *documentation* of the template type parameters; for example:

```
template <typename T, int SIZE>
  // Template requirement for type T:
  //   must have a no-arg constructor
  //   ... more conditions
class Stack {
  ...
};
```

Two terms are used to precisely and consistently describe the requirements for template type parameters: a concept and a model. A **concept** is a list of requirements that the type has to satisfy; a **model** of the concept is a C++ type that satisfies all these requirements. For example, if a particular concept specifies that a no-arg constructor must be available, then a primitive data type such as int is the model, while the Integer type previously described is not. The int type is a model because C++ imitates no-arg constructors for primitive data types; for example, the expression int(3) represents the value 3, and int() represents the value 0. On the other hand, Integer is not a model because it does not have a no-arg constructor, so it does not meet the requirements specified by the concept.

From this point on, I use concepts and models to document all generic functions and classes. To help you differentiate in the text between the names of classes and the names of concepts, I use a bold monospace font for concepts and a regular monospace font for classes. STL defines many standard concepts, several of which I introduce in this book. While STL describes concepts in a more precise way, I do so more informally; for example:

Requires a no-arg constructor

Using this terminology, the documentation for the `Stack` template class looks like this:

```
template <typename T, int SIZE>
  // T is a model of Default Constructible
class Stack { ... };
```

The following example shows an array template class. There is an important difference between `Stack` from Example 7.3 and the previously shown `Array` in terms of how each class handles memory allocation: While `Stack` allocates memory statically on the runtime stack, `Array` allocates memory dynamically on the heap. The former solution is more efficient; the latter allows you to specify the size at runtime.

● EXAMPLE 7.4

Consider arrays defined in the namespace `ARRAY_NAMESPACE`. This namespace will be extended later on; for now, it contains one template class:

```
// File: ex7.4.array.h
namespace ARRAY_NAMESPACE {
  template <typename T>
    // T is a model of Default Constructible
  class Array {
  public:

    // canonical construction idiom 3.6
Array(size_t = 100);                        // size_t is predefined
    Array(const Array<T>&);
    Array<T>& operator=(const Array<T>&);
    virtual ~Array();

    // Overloading Subscripting and Function idiom 7.3
    virtual const T& operator[](int) const;
    virtual T& operator[](int);

    // auxiliary functions
    int size() const;
    typedef T element_type;
```

```
  protected:
    size_t size_;
    T* array_;
  };
}
```

There are two overloaded definitions of the `operator[]` because without the `const` version, you would not be able to access the elements of a constant array (see Idiom 7.3).

Finally, defining the type `element_type` using `typedef` is a useful technique if you want to be able to retrieve the type of a template's argument, for example, to declare local variables of that type:

```
// File: ex7.4.driver.cpp
Array<int> x(5);
cin >> x[1];
Array<int>::element_type y = x[1];
```

Instead of the type `Array<int>::element_type`, you can simply use `int`. There are advantages to using the current implementation, which will become more apparent in the next section.

Here is the implementation of the template operations:

```
// File: ex7.4.array.cpp
namespace ARRAY_NAMESPACE {

template <typename T>
Array<T>::Array(size_t size) : size_(size) {
  array_ = new T[size];
}

template <typename T>
Array<T>::Array(const Array<T>& ar) : size_(ar.size_) {
  array_ = new T[ar.size_];
  for(size_t i = 0; i < size_; ++i)
    array_[i] = ar.array_[i];
}

template <typename T>
Array<T>& Array<T>::operator=(const Array<T>& ar)  {
  if(this == &ar)
    return *this;
  if(size_ != ar.size_) {
    size_ = ar.size_;
    delete[] array_;
    array_ = new T[size_];
```

```
  }
  for(size_t i = 0; i < size_; ++i)
    array_[i] = ar.array_[i];
  return *this;
}

template <typename T>
Array<T>::~Array() {
  delete [] array_;
}

template <typename T>
int Array<T>::size() const {
  return size_;
}

template <typename T>
T& Array<T>::operator[](int i) {
  return array_[i];
}

template <typename T>
const T& Array<T>::operator[](int i) const {
  return array_[i];
}


}
```

──▶

7.6.5 Function Templates

As the previous sections have shown, class templates define parameterized classes
that can be instantiated (specialized) with actual classes at compile time. You can
also define **function templates** that have the same kind of parameters as class templates, including type parameters. In fact, all member operations of a template class
are function templates. You can also define stand-alone function templates. For example, a generic swap operation parameterized by the types of the elements to be
swapped looks like this:

```
template <typename T>
  // T is a model of ... (defined soon)
void swap(T& x, T& y) {
  T z = x;
  x = y;
  y = z;
}
```

A new concept is needed to describe the type requirements for this example:

Assignable **Concept 7.2**

Requires a copy constructor and an assignment operator so that it is possible to copy and assign objects

The documentation for `swap()` has the following form:

```
template <typename T>
   // T is a model of Assignable
void swap(T& x, T& y) {
   T z = x;
   x = y;
   y = z;
}
```

Function templates are instantiated by functions at compile time, but this process is different from the one used for template classes. To instantiate classes, you use the class template name and provide the actual parameters. On the other hand, to use a function template, you simply *call* the function, which results in the instantiation of the appropriate function. For the previous example, the client can use the function template like this:

```
int i = 2;
int j = 3;
swap(i, j);                              // first use of swap()
```

The last line generates the following instantiation:

```
void swap(int& x, int& y) { ... }
```

The `swap()` function can also be used with arguments that are user-defined types; for example:

```
Integer k(3);
Integer m(4);
swap(k, m);
```

The last line generates the instantiation of `swap()` with references to classes:

```
void swap(Integer& x, Integer& y) { ... }
```

Template classes often have associated function template helpers, which are usually defined in the corresponding namespaces (see Section 4.6.4). The next example defines two helpers for equality and inequality, respectively. It requires another concept:

Equality Comparable **Concept 7.3**

Requires == and != operations

Models of the Equality Comparable concept support !=; strictly speaking, this is not necessary because x != y can be expressed as !(x == y). A type is called a **regular type** if it is a model of these three concepts: Assignable, Default Constructible, and Equality Comparable. Predefined types are regular types.

The following code shows the promised declarations and definitions of the helpers for the arrays from Example 7.4 (note that they are stored in the same namespace as the template class):

```
// File: ex7.4.array1.h
namespace ARRAY_NAMESPACE {
  // helpers

  template <typename T>
    // T is a model of Equality Comparable
  bool operator==(const Array<T>&, const Array<T>&);

  template <typename T>
    // T is a model of Equality Comparable
  bool operator!=(const Array<T>&, const Array<T>&);
}

// File: ex7.4.array1.cpp
namespace ARRAY_NAMESPACE {

// helper
template <typename T>
bool operator==(const Array<T>& ar1, const Array<T>& ar2) {
  for(size_t i = 0; i < ar1.size(); ++i)
    if(!(ar1[i] == ar2.[i]))
      return false;
  return true;
}
```

```
// helper
template <typename T>
bool operator!=(const Array<T>& ar1, const Array<T>& ar2) {
  return !(ar1 == ar2);
}


}
```

A template class and its helper functions may have different requirements. In the example, it is possible to instantiate `Array<T>` even if T does not support ==, as long as you do not use helpers (since only the helpers require type T to support ==).

7.6.6   Combining Template Classes

Several template classes may be combined to create a new template class or a new concrete class. For example, the `Stack` and `Array` templates can be used to create a stack of arrays of `Integer`:

```
Stack<Array<Integer> > s;
```

This instantiation would fail if `Array` did not have a no-arg constructor. A space between the two occurrences of > is also required:

```
Stack<Array<Integer>> s;            // >> treated as right shift
```

As I mentioned before, you can use template class names whenever you use a regular class name; in particular, a template class can be used as a *base class;* for example:

```
template <typename T>
class MyStack : public Stack<T> { ... };
```

`MyStack` is a *template* class. You can also use an instantiated template as the base class; for example:

```
class IntStack : public Stack<int, 100> { ... };
```

In addition, you can create template classes by instantiating only some of the template parameters:

```
template <typename T>
class StackOfT : public Stack<100> { ... };
```

All types of inheritance are allowed, including public, private, and protected.
Although you cannot derive a concrete class from a template class, as in

```
class IntStack : public Stack<T, 100> { ... };
```

you can derive a template class from a concrete class:

```
template <typename T>
class Stack : public MyClass { ... };
```

In Section 7.9.2, I will show the application of this technique to the abstract factory design pattern.

Instantiations of templates are unrelated, even if classes for these instantiations are in an inheritance relation (that is, one is derived from the other). For example, given a general BankAccount class that has a derived class CheckingAccount, there is no inheritance relation between Stack<BankAccount> and Stack<CheckingAccount>.

The following code shows a template class CheckedArray derived from the class Array from Example 7.4, which adds exception handling. The definitions of virtual functions in derived classes can add exceptions to the definitions of these functions in the base class:

```
// File: ex7.4.checkedarray.h
namespace ARRAY_NAMESPACE {
  // declaration of the class and its helpers
  template <typename T>
  class CheckedArray : public Array<T> {
    // T is a model of Default Constructible
  public:

    CheckedArray(size_t = 100);
    CheckedArray(const CheckedArray<T>&);
    CheckedArray<T>& operator=(const CheckedArray<T>&)
      throw(std::out_of_range);
    virtual ~CheckedArray();

    virtual const T& operator[](int) const throw(std::out_of_range);
    virtual T& operator[](int) throw(std::out_of_range);
  };

// helpers

template <typename T>
  // T is a model of Equality Comparable
bool operator==(const CheckedArray<T>&, const CheckedArray<T>&)
  throw (std::out_of_range);

template <typename T>
  // T is a model of Equality Comparable
bool operator!=(const CheckedArray<T>&, const CheckedArray<T>&)
  throw (std::out_of_range);
```

```
// end of namespace
}

// File: ex7.4.checkedarray.cpp
namespace ARRAY_NAMESPACE {
  // definition of the class and its helpers
template <typename T>
CheckedArray<T>::CheckedArray(size_t size) : Array<T>(size) { }

template <typename T>
CheckedArray<T>::CheckedArray(const CheckedArray<T>& ar) :
   Array<T>(ar) { }

// perform error checking
//    if succeed then delegate to the base class operations

template <typename T>
CheckedArray<T>& CheckedArray<T>::operator=(const CheckedArray<T>& ar)
    throw (std::std::out_of_range) {
 if(this == &ar)
     return *this;
  if(size_ != ar.size())
     throw std::out_of_range("wrong sizes in operator=");
  Array<T>::operator=(ar);                   // base class operator=
  return *this;
}

template <typename T>
CheckedArray<T>::~CheckedArray() { }

template <typename T>
T& CheckedArray<T>::operator[](int i) throw(std::out_of_range) {
  if(i < 0 || i >= size_)
    throw out_of_range("wrong range in []");
  return array_[i];
}

template <typename T>
const T& CheckedArray<>T>::operator[](int i) const
     throw(std::out_of_range)  {
  if(i < 0 || i >= size_)
    throw out_of_range("wrong range in []");
  return array_[i];
}
```

```
// helper
template <typename T>
bool operator==(const CheckedArray<T>& ar1,
   const CheckedArray<T>& ar2) throw(std::out_of_range) {
  if(ar1.size() != ar2.size())
    throw std::out_of_range("wrong sizes in ==");
  return Array<T>::operator==(ar1, ar2);
}

// helper
template <typename T>
bool operator!=(const CheckedArray<T>& ar1,
   const CheckedArray<T>& ar2) throw(std::out_of_range) {
  return !(ar1 == ar2);
}

}
```

The client can use the `CheckedArray` class like this:

```
CheckedArray<int> c(1);
try {
  c[0] = 3;
  cout << c[0] << endl;
  c[1] = 5;                                // will throw out_of_range

} catch(out_of_range& e) {
  cerr << e.what() << endl;
}
```

7.6.7   Combining Template Classes and Functions

Template functions can have parameters whose type is a class template. Consider
the template class `Array` from Example 7.4, and the following functions used to input and output values into and from the array:

```
template <typename T>
  // T is a model of Default Constructible
void output(const Array<T>& array) {
  for(int j = 0; j < array.size(); ++j)
    cout << array[j] << " ";
  cout << endl;
}

template <typename T>
  // T is a model of Default Constructible
```

```
void input(Array<T>& array, const string& prompt) {
  cout << prompt;
  for(int j = 0; j < array.size(); ++j)
    cin >> array[j];
}
```

You can use these template functions to initialize an array and then display its contents; for example:

```
Array<int> intArray(10);
input(intArray, "input 10 values\n");
output(intArray);
```

The next example involves sorting an array. For this, another concept representing ordered types is needed. First, recall the definition of a **partial order**, which is a relation R that it is irreflexive (that is, it is never true that xRx), antisymmetric (that is, if xRy then it is not true that yRx), and transitive (that is, if xRy and yRz, then xRz):

LessThan Comparable **Concept 7.4**

Requires operator<, which defines partial order

Note that even though most models of the LessThan Comparable concept additionally support other relational operators, strictly speaking, this is not necessary because

- x > y can be expressed as y < x
- x >= y can be expressed as !(x < y)
- x <= y can be expressed as !(y < x)

● EXAMPLE 7.5

In this example, I show an implementation of insertion sort (see Aho, Hopcroft, and Ullman, 1983) which uses the Array template defined in Example 7.4.

```
// File: ex7.5.insertionsort.cpp
using namespace ARRAY_NAMESPACE;
template <typename T>
  // T is a model of LessThan Comparable and Default Constructible
void insertionSort(Array<T>& array) {
  int i;
  T key, comp;
```

```
        for(int j = 1; j < array.size(); ++j) {
            key = array[j];
            i = j - 1;
            comp = array[i];
            while(i >= 0 && key <= comp) {
              array[i+1] = comp;
              i--;
              if(i >= 0)
                comp = array[i];
            }
            array[i+1] = key;
        }
    }


// File ex7.5.driver.cpp
#include "ex7.5.insertionsort.cpp"
int main() {
    Array<int> x(5);
    input(x, "Enter 5 integer values:");
    insertionSort(x);
    output(x);
}
```

7.6.8   Deducing Template Function Arguments

This section looks at how the type of a template function's argument is determined.
Recall the template function used for swapping two values:

```
template <typename T>
void swap(T& x, T& y) {
    T z = x;
    x = y;
    y = z;
}
```

Suppose that the function is used as follows:

```
double x = 2.3;
double y = 3.7;
swap(x, y);
```

From the swap() function call, the compiler can deduce that the type T in the template definition is double. For instantiations of this template function, both

parameters have to be of the same type, because in general there is no standard type conversion for arguments:

```
unsigned p = 4;
int i = 44;
swap(i, p);                            // error: different types
```

The compiler's task of instantiating function templates is much harder than for the instantiating class templates, because the former instantiation is performed based only on the types of the actual parameters. This means that given a function call, the compiler has to *deduce* the types of the template arguments. This process of **template argument deduction** is fairly complicated (for details, see Lipmann and Lajoie, 1998) and is needed only for function templates, not for class templates.

The type of a function argument does not have to exactly match the type of the template function argument; in particular, an argument can be of a type that is *derived* from the template's argument type. For example, consider the template function `insertionSort()` from Example 7.5. This function can be called with the argument of type `Array` or a class that is derived from `Array`, such as `CheckedArray`:

```
CheckedArray<double> ca(10);
... // initialize
insertionSort(ca);
```

In addition to function and data members, a class can provide nested types; for example, all the containers in the standard library provide various types. In the remaining part of this section, I describe how a template class can provide a type the client can use, for example, to define variables of this type. Example 7.4 showed how to do this for a specific situation, where `Array` provided `element_type`. In that example, the template class was already instantiated, and the `element_type` was known to be `int`. In general, the client may want to use the provided type even before the instantiation takes place. To explain how you can support this, start with an insertion sort function template from Example 7.5, operating on an array:

```
template <typename T>
void insertionSort(Array<T>&);
```

To make this function more general, you can replace the specific `Array<T>` by a template argument `S`, which is an arbitrary representation of an array:

```
template <typename S>
void insertionSort(S& array);
```

The first version of the function used the template class `Array`, while the second version can use any class that satisfies certain requirements. These requirements can be determined by looking at the code for the function—for example, the need for an overloaded `[]` operator, the `size()` function, and so on. We must also be able to define a variable whose type is the same as the type of the elements of the array represented by the class S. Assume that the class S provides the type element_type. To define a local variable of this type, you cannot use the following definition:

```
S::element_type aux;                    // incorrect definition of aux
```

The qualification S::element_type is an identifier; by default, it refers to a construct that is not a type or a template. This definition is incorrect because during instantiation, when the compiler attempts to deduce template arguments, it will assume that S::element_type is *not* a type name. To get around this problem, you need to write the definition using special syntax:

```
typename S::element_type aux;
```

In this context, typename specifies that the attribute element_type of the template S is a *type*.

In general, it is useful to make types like element_type public so they can be provided by the template, as stated in the following idiom. (Example 8.1 will provide an example of an application of this idiom.)

Providing Types from a Template Idiom 7.6

When you define a general template class S, consider providing nested types, such as element_type for the elements of a container. To define a variable of this type, use the typename keyword:

```
typename S::element_type
```

7.6.9   Explicit Type Arguments for Template Functions

To avoid the failure of template function argument deduction, you can sometimes provide **explicit type arguments** using syntax that resembles the instantiation of class templates:

```
swap<int>                           // explicit instantiation of swap()
```

This example explicitly specifies the instantiation of swap() with an int type parameter, which means that no type deduction is needed in the following call to the function:

```
unsigned p = 4;
int i = 44;
swap<int>(i, p);                    // no deduction needed, explicit type
```

Here, unsigned p is converted to int p, and the call to swap() is correct.

Explicit type arguments can also be used if the template function has more than one type parameter. If there are fewer explicit type arguments than type parameters, only *leading* type parameters are instantiated. This technique is particularly useful for template functions that return the value of the type parameter, because you might not be able to deduce this type and may have to explicitly instantiate it. For example, consider the code borrowed from Stroustrup (1997):

```
template <typename ToType, typename fromType>
ToType cast(FromType f) {
  return f;
}

int i = 2;
char c = cast(i);                          // error: cast<?, ?>
double d = cast<double>(i);                // cast<double, int>
```

ToType is a leading type parameter, instantiated to double, and fromType is deduced to be int.

7.6.10 Template Explicit Specialization

A class or function template can be used to instantiate a number of classes or functions. In some cases, instead of using the very general functionality provided by the template, it is better to provide a specialized version. For example, a specialized version might provide a more efficient implementation than the general template.

To define a **template explicit specialization**, use the following syntax:

```
template<>                                 // empty <> brackets
... // here, function or class definition
```

To understand how to specialize template *functions,* first consider the helper template function from Example 7.4:

```
template <typename T>
  // T is a model of Equality Comparable
bool operator==(const Array<T>&, const Array<T>&);
```

Suppose you have a concrete class, Integer, that can be used with arrays, except it does not support ==, which you need to define the helper template function. Instead of adding the operator function operator==() to the existing template class, you can provide an explicit specialization of this helper:

```
namespace ARRAY_NAMESPACE {
  template<>
  bool operator==(const Array<Integer>&, const Array<Integer>&);
}
```

(The definitions of these functions are not shown here.) You can now use this helper for arrays of `Integer`:

```
using ARRAY_NAMESPACE::Array;
using ARRAY_NAMESPACE;
Array<Integer> ar1(10);
Array<Integer> ar2(10);
...
if(ar1 == ar2) ...
```

As another example, consider the `swap()` function again:

```
template <typename T>
void swap(T& x, T& y) {
  T temp = x;
  x = y;
  y = temp;
}
```

If you use this template to swap two pointers, as in

```
int i = 1;
int j = 2;
int* pi = &i;
int* pj = &j;
swap(pi, pj);
cout << i << " " <<  j << " " << *pi << " " << *pj <<  endl;
```

the output from this program would not be what you want:

```
1 2 2 1
```

The problem is that `T` is `int*`. Also, `swap()` changes the *values* of pointers `pi` and `pj` but does not swap the *values pointed to* by these pointers, so it does not swap the values of variables `i` and `j`. To help you understand this example, consider Figure 7.8. The parameters are passed by reference; therefore, `x` is an alias for `pi`, and `y` is an alias for `pj`.

You can implement a specialization of `swap()` that swaps the values pointed to by two integer pointers:

```
template <>
void swap(int*& x, int*& y) {
  int temp = *x;
  *x = *y;
  *y = temp;
}
```

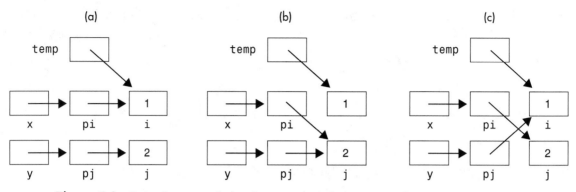

Figure 7.8   State of memory during the execution of `swap()`: (a) after the execution of `temp = x`; (b) after the execution of `x = y`; (c) after the execution of `y = temp`.

The output from this program is

```
2 1 2 1
```

which is what you want; the values pointed to by these pointers have been correctly swapped.

Template class features, including both attributes and operations, can also be specialized. Consider the template class `Array` from Example 7.4, modified to include a size attribute:

```
template <typename T>
class Array {
public:
    static const int Size;                          // data attribute
    ...
};

template <typename T>
const int Array<T>::Size = 10;                      // definition
```

You can overrule the initialization by providing a *specialization;* for example:

```
template <>
const int Array<long>::Size = 100;        // specialization for long
```

To understand how to specialize template *classes,* suppose you want to use the `Array` template for the class `Integer`, but for this specific class, you want to use your own implementation instead of an existing template. To accomplish this, you can define a specialization for Integer:

```
template<>
class Array<Integer> {
  ... // here the entire interface
};
```

You have to define all of the features of the Array class because the compiler will not try to generate them from the template. Although this is cumbersome, it does provide you with a *uniform interface*; you always refer to Array<T>, whether T is Integer or not.

If you use pointers, as in the swap() example, then there is a more general approach to specialization. Once you have defined a template with the type parameter T, you can specialize this template for *pointers* to T. Consider again the array template:

```
template <typename T>
class Array { ... };
```

To define a specialized version of a pointer, use the following syntax:

```
template <typename T>
class Array<T*> { ... };
```

To define an even more specialized version—for example, for type void*, use the syntax with empty <>:

```
template<>
class Array<void*> { ... };
```

All three versions may be present in the same program; the compiler prefers the more specialized version over a less specialized version. Therefore, if you have swap() specialized for pointers and another general version of swap(), a call to swap() with pointer arguments generates the specialized version.

If a template function or class has more than one parameter, you can specify a partial explicit specialization. For example, consider the Stack class from Example 7.3 again:

```
template <typename T, size_t SIZE>
class Stack { ... };
```

You can *partially* specialize this definition as follows:

```
template <typename T>
class Stack<T, 10> { ... };           // specialization for SIZE 10

template <size_t SIZE>
class Stack<Integer, SIZE> { ... };   // specialization for Integer
```

7.6.11   Member Templates

As I mentioned in Section 7.6.6, instantiations of two classes related by the inheritance relation are unrelated. To deal with this problem in some applications you can use classes and template classes that have nested **member templates**, which can be classes or functions (however, template functions cannot be virtual). The following example of a member template function, adapted from Stroustrup (1997), provides a template representing a pointer to the type T passed as a template parameter (therefore, it is a wrapper for a pointer to its template parameter). This example has a nested member template parameterized by another type, T2, used to support the conversion of Ptr<T> to Ptr<T2>.

```
template <typename T>
class Ptr {
public:
  Ptr(T*);

  template <typename T2>                       // nested template
  operator Ptr<T2>();        // overloaded type conversion operator

private:
  T* p;
};
```

To define the template member, you have to use the following syntax:

```
template <typename T>
  template <typename T2>
    Ptr<T>::operator Ptr<T2>() {
      return Ptr<T2>(p);
    }
```

The return statement invokes the constructor from the template, specialized with T2; specifically:

```
Ptr<T2>(T2)
```

Since the actual parameter p is of type T, the following conversion must be valid to compile the previous code:

```
T*   to   T2*
```

This is what you actually want, because the conversion Ptr<T> to Ptr<T2> should only be allowed if the conversion from T* to T2* is valid. For example, consider the class Student and a derived class StudentWithAccount:

```
Ptr<StudentWithAccount> pswa;
... // initialization
void foo(Ptr<Student>);

foo(pswa);                 // converts StudentWithAccount* to Student*

Ptr<Student>) ps = ...;
void goo(Ptr<StudentWithAccount>);
goo(ps);                   // can't convert Student* to StudentWithAccount*
```

As another example of a member template, consider a class Vector that is parameterized by the type Elem and supports an assignment that adds the contents of another container to the vector. This container is specified by two iterators that point to the beginning and beyond the end of the container, respectively. The function that defines this assignment must be a member template:

```
template <typename Elem>
class Vector {
public:

  template <typename Iter>                        // member template
  void assign(Iter, Iter);

  Vector();
  ~Vector();
  void insert(const Elem&);
  ...
private:
  ...
};

template <typename Elem>
  template <typename Iter>
    void Vector<Elem>::assign(Iter first, Iter last) {
```

```
    for(Iter aux = first; aux != last; ++aux)
        insert(*aux);
}
```

To see how `assign()` can be used, consider the instantiation of the class `Vector`:

```
Vector<int> v;
```

At this point, the member function `assign()` is not yet instantiated. You can use the class `List` from Example 7.1 to call `assign()` with the `Iterator` parameters:

```
List myList;
... // insert some elements
v.assign(myList.begin(), myList.end());
```

For the last line, the compiler uses template function argument deduction to determine that the type argument `Iter` of the template function `assign()` is instantiated with `List::ListIterator`. Since this class overloads `operator*()` to return an `int`, the `insert()` function gets the appropriate argument. This example demonstrates how to use the `assign()` function for the `List` class, which is not parameterized. However, in general, you can apply `assign()` to any class to copy elements from one container to another, as long as they support iterators. This technique is heavily used in the standard library.

7.6.12 Making Instantiation Possible

As I mentioned in Section 7.6.2, you may not be able to instantiate a template function or class because the type parameter does not satisfy the requirements imposed by the code of the function or class. In this section, I show that *sometimes* you can deal with this problem without changing the code of the existing class.

Consider the template class `Array` from Example 7.4. Is the following instantiation correct?

```
Array<Integer>
```

There are two requirements for the type `Integer`: it has to support both a no-arg constructor and the overloaded `==` operator. Not much can be done if the former function is missing, but the latter can be defined without modifying the class `Integer`, provided the class' interface is sufficient for the task at hand; specifically, it must provide an accessor, such as `get()`:

```
bool operator==(const Integer& i, const Integer& j) {        // helper
    return i.get() == j.get();
}
```

If the interface does not provide all of the necessary functionality to define a helper, you may want to resort to explicit instantiation (see Section 7.6.10).

In general, strong assumptions about type parameters make instantiation more difficult. Consider the following wrapper class:

```
template <typename WrappedType>                              // needs 0
class Wrapper {
public:
  Wrapper(WrappedType = 0);
  ...
private:
  WrappedType value_;
};

template <typename WrappedType>
Wrapper<WrappedType>::Wrapper(WrappedType v) : value_(v) { }
```

The intention of the default parameter of the constructor is to provide a simple wrapper for the 0 value:

```
Wrapper<int> w(3);
Wrapper<double> w1;                                          // w1(0);
```

Unfortunately, this code assumes that it is legal to say

```
WrappedType v = 0;
```

which may not be supported by all types. It is easy to remove this requirement by using a no-arg constructor instead of 0:

```
template <typename WrappedType>
// WrappedType is a model of Default Constructible
Wrapper<WrappedType>::Wrapper(WrappedType v = WrappedType()) :
  value_(v) {}
```

In general, template classes should be carefully designed; the larger the interface of the class, the more requirements exist for the parameter types.

7.6.13 Explicit Instantiation and Compilation of Templates

A compiler generates the code for a class template only when it is required. For example, the class template is instantiated as a result of code like this:

```
Array<Integer> x(5);
```

However, if you wish to gain control over the point at which the instantiation occurs, you can use an **explicit instantiation**, with the keyword `template` *not* followed by <:

```
template class Array<int>;           // instantiate array of int
template void swap<double>;          // instantiate swap for doubles
```

Instantiating a class implies instantiation of all its members. You can also instantiate specific members of a template class. The definition of the template function that is explicitly instantiated must be available in the same file as this instantiation. You can use explicit instantiation to force-test code that uses templates or to increase the efficiency of your program (for more details, see Stroustrup, 1997).

Unfortunately, templates create a lot of problems for compilers and linkers, and currently most compilers do not support all the features of templates defined for C++. Therefore, the safest way to organize template code is to avoid separate compilation of declarations and definitions; instead, put all template definitions in a header file that is included in each translation unit that instantiates the template. However, in terms of design, this is not a desirable option; the separate compilation version is clearly better. C++ standard supports it as follows:

- The template header file stores the template's *declaration*.
- The template implementation file includes the template header file and *defines* the template using the `export` keyword; for example:

```
export template<typename T> void swap(T& x, T& y) { ... }
```

Here is a quick-and-dirty solution that you can use when working with a compiler that does not support `export` and allows you to quickly update your source files when you start using a compiler that does support this keyword. The template implementation file, say `swap.cpp`, starts with a macro

```
#define export                              // expand to nothing
```

and contains all of the necessary definitions, such as `swap()`. The client code uses `#include "swap.cpp"`, but the file `swap.cpp` is not separately compiled. This way, all template definitions are available to the client code. To use the version that does use `export`, the definition of the macro is removed, and the `#include` statement from the client's code is also removed; finally, the file `swap.cpp` is separately compiled and then linked with the rest of the code.

7.7   *Resource Management, Part III*

This section describes more advanced issues related to resource management. In Section 5.14, you saw how you can use pointers to allocate a resource and what you should do when exceptions are thrown. Pointers are used so often that C++ provides a standard wrapper class, described in the following section.

7.7.1 `auto_ptr`

Using a pointer, in particular in conjunction with dynamic memory, often causes problems with resource management. Specifically, a memory leak occurs when a pointer goes out of scope but the destructor for the object pointed to by the pointer is not called. Previously, you looked at how to safeguard your pointers by putting user-defined wrappers around them. The C++ standard library defines a class to do just that—a template class `auto_ptr`, which is a wrapper class for pointers. To use `auto_ptr`, you must include the header file `<memory>`. Typically, you use `auto_ptr` as follows:

1. Allocate memory for a pointer, using `new`.
2. Create a wrapper object and initialize it with the pointer you just created. (Since `auto_ptr` is a template class, to create an object that is a wrapper for a pointer, you specify the type of *the value a pointer points to,* rather than the type of a pointer.)

Here is one example:

```
string* p = new string("C++");
auto_ptr<string> name(p);                    // not: auto_ptr<string*>
```

A simpler alternative is:

```
auto_ptr<string> name(new string("C++"));
```

`name` is wrapper object initialized with the pointer to string `"C++"`. We will say that a wrapper object is an **owner** of the object pointed to be the pointer; in the example, `name` is the owner of the string `"C++"` (see Figure 7.9).

The pointer is passed to the `auto_ptr` variable as a parameter of the constructor:

```
auto_ptr<string> name(new string("C++"));
```

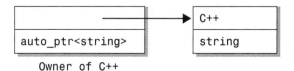

Figure 7.9 `auto_ptr`

You cannot use assignment:

```
auto_ptr<string> name = new string("C++");                    //error
```

Programming with `auto_ptr` requires that there should be at most one owner of any object; all class operations attempt to support this invariant, but as you will see later in this section, it is actually the programmer who is responsible for maintaining it.

The object of class `auto_ptr` acts like a pointer by overloading the dereference operations `*` and `->`. For example, you can write

```
cout << name->substr(0, 1);                              // output "C"
```

because the above call translates to

```
cout << name.operator->()->substr(0,1);
```

When the `auto_ptr` object goes out of scope, the object it owns is deallocated, for example:

```
void foo() {
  string* pname = new string("Java");

  auto_ptr<string> name(new string("C++"));

  *name += " after Java";        // *name is a string; concatenate
  cout << *name << endl;         // output: C++ after Java
}
```

Note that when the call of the `foo()` function terminates, the destructor for `pname` is not implicitly called, and in the previous example, this creates a memory leak. On the other hand, the use of the `auto_ptr` wrapper did result in a destructor call for `name`, which deallocated the string `"C++"`. The copy constructor and the assignment operator *change* the ownership of an object:

```
auto_ptr<string> name1(new string("C++"));      // name1 owns "C++"
auto_ptr<string> name2(name1);    // name2 owns "C++"; name1 doesn't
auto_ptr<string> name3 = name1;   // name3 owns "C++"; name2 doesn't
```

You should not pass an `auto_ptr` object as a function value parameter, because it results in a call to a copy constructor, which changes the ownership, for example:

```
void showName(auto_ptr<string> s) {
  ... // nice display of s
}
```

```
auto_ptr<string> name1(new string("C++"));

showName(name1);                    // now, name1 does not own any object
cout << *name1;
```

Since this function call invokes a copy constructor, it takes the ownership of the string object away from name1, and therefore name1 cannot be used to access the string.

Common Errors

Do not use auto_ptr as a function parameter passed by value.

To make it impossible to transfer ownership, you can use constant auto_ptr objects, which behave like constant pointers:

```
const auto_ptr<string> name2(new string("C++"));
showName(name2);                           // modifies constant
```

Constant auto_ptr objects have constant ownership, but the *value* of the object owned can be changed; for example:

```
*name2 += " after Java";
```

Note that it is possible to create an uninitialized auto_ptr object, which does not own any object, and later initialize it, for example

```
auto_ptr<string> ps;                            // uninitialized
```

The auto_ptr<T> class provides several useful operations in addition to the overloaded * and ->. A reset() function resets the state of the wrapped pointer by deleting all owned objects and assigning a new object to be owned; for example:

```
void reset(T* =0);
```

Here is another example:

```
auto_ptr<string> ps;
ps.reset(new string("C++"));         // ps owns "C++"
ps.reset();                          // delete "C++"; now ps
                                     // does not own any object
```

There is also an accessor `get()` function

```
T* get() const;
```

that returns a pointer to the owned object, or 0; for example:

```
if(ps.get() == 0)                                        // no owner
```

Unfortunately, it is possible to misuse `get()` and give ownership of the same object to *two* objects:

```
auto_ptr<string> ps(new string("C++"));
auto_ptr<string> ps1(ps.get());                         // two owners
```

It is an error to have more than one owner of an object, because the object will be deallocated more than once. The likely result is a program crash, and the error will not be found by the compiler.

To transfer ownership, you have to first release the ownership of the owned object by the `release()` operation:

```
X* release();
```

This operations works like `get()`, but it also releases ownership:

```
auto_ptr<string> ps(new string("C++"));
auto_ptr<string> ps1(ps.release());
```

The design of `auto_ptr` is supposed to provide a general wrapper class for pointers to help avoid memory leaks (for more on this topic, see Josattis, 2000). Unfortunately, it is possible to use the class incorrectly and generate programming errors. First, as I mentioned earlier, you should not pass an `auto_ptr` object as a function value parameter. Second, you must avoid creating an `auto_ptr` object that owns more than one object, which may happen if you incorrectly used `get()`, as previously shown, or if you use the following code:

```
string* s = new string("C++");
auto_ptr<string> ps1(s);                                // first owner
auto_ptr<string> ps2(s);                                // second owner
```

7.7.2 General Resource Management

In general, your code may use several different resources, such as memory, files, locks, and ports. To manage the design of such code, you can use a general three-step plan, which is formulated as the **resource management idiom** (this idiom is based on Stroustrup, 1997):

Resource Management Idiom 7.7

To use k resources, $r_1, r_2, ..., r_k$, divide your code into three steps:

1. Acquire all resources $r_1, r_2, ..., r_k$.
2. Use of resources.
3. Release resources $r_k, ..., r_2, r_1$.

Acquire resources by initializing objects representing these resources.

The execution of this plan is referred to by Stroustrup as "resource acquisition is initialization," because resources are acquired by invoking constructors and released *implicitly* by invoking destructors (releasing is done in reverse order of acquiring). All resources are implemented as classes, and all pointers have class wrappers around them. You can use the **resource wrapper idiom** to write wrapper classes not only for pointers but also for other resources. The use of wrapper classes is relevant because without them, resources such as pointers would not be automatically acquired and released.

Resource Wrapper Idiom 7.8

To create a wrapper for a resource R, implement a class `Wrapper` containing a private attribute of type R. Its interface should provide at least the following operations:

- Constructor that associates the resource with the private attribute
- Destructor that releases the resource
- Type conversion that converts the type of the wrapper class to the type of resource

To forbid making resource copies, make the copy constructor and the overloaded assignment operator private.

If you look at the example of the `ResourceHandle` class from Section 5.14, you will find that it has been designed according to the resource wrapper idiom. As another example, consider a wrapper class for a window (this example is based on the code from Meyers, 1998). To represent this class, you need the type `WINDOW_HANDLE`, which describes various windows in some windowing system, and the following operations:

- `createWindow()`, which returns a `WINDOW_HANDLE`
- `destroyWindow(WINDOW_HANDLE)`, which releases the window
- `display(string, WINDOW_HANDLE)`, which displays the string in the window

```
class WindowWrapper {
public:
  WindowWrapper(WINDOW_HANDLE);
  ~WindowWrapper() { }
  operator WINDOW_HANDLE();
private:
  WINDOW_HANDLE window_;
  WindowWrapper(const WindowWrapper&);
  WindowWrapper& operator=(const WindowWrapper&);
};

WindowWrapper::WindowWrapper(WINDOW_HANDLE handle): window_(handle) {}

WindowWrapper::~WindowWrapper(){
  destroyWindow(window_);
}

WindowWrapper::operator WINDOW_HANDLE() {
  return window_;
}
```

Now consider an application that uses two resources: a window and a stack of integers:

```
void foo() {
                                              // prolog, acquire
  WindowWrapper ww(createWindow());
  auto_ptr<IntStack> ps(new IntStack());
                                              // use
  ps->push(10);
  display("Hello", ww);
                          // implicit epilog:
                          // destructor for ps releases the stack
                          // destructor for ww deallocates the window

}
```

Even if an exception is thrown within foo(), both resources will be released.

7.8 *Inheritance and Delegation versus Parameterized Types*

So far, you have learned three techniques to compose objects: inheritance, delegation, and parameterized types. To compare them, consider a sorting routine. The ordering operation in the routine can be implemented using

- Inheritance—specifically, the template design pattern (see Section 5.15.1).
- Delegation—specifically, the reference to the object that implements the ordering.
- Template—specifically, by passing the ordering as a type parameter of a sorting routine (an ordering may be passed as a function or a functor).

Using both inheritance and virtual functions is sometimes called **runtime polymorphism**. On the other hand, using parameterized types is called **parametric** or **compile-time polymorphism**. These techniques can often be combined; for example, you can use both templates and inheritance to implement heterogeneous containers (see Section 9.10).

Inheritance (without virtual functions) and parameterized types are inherently compile-time techniques. Inheritance allows you to specify the default behavior in the base class and then specialize this behavior in derived classes. Templates allow you to change the types that parameterize the behavior of the template class. Both techniques are efficient, but they are compile-time operations and are thus less flexible than delegation, which allows you to modify the behavior at runtime. The overhead of indirection involved in delegation, which the proxy and bridge design patterns make use of, is the price you pay for this flexibility.

Two guidelines can help you choose between using inheritance and parameterized types. These guidelines are here exemplified by the class `Operator`, which operates on objects of `Element` type:

- Use parameterized types when `Element` does not affect its behavior and there is no hierarchical structure between `Element` objects.
- Use inheritance in all other instances.

For example, the behavior of containers, such as lists or stacks, does not depend on the behavior of the elements of this container and therefore should be implemented using parameterized types. On the other hand, suppose we are trying to design an account class, and different types of accounts need to be represented; in this situation, an object's behavior depends on the specific type of account and therefore should be implemented using inheritance.

Here are a couple of additional guidelines:

- Use inheritance if the types of objects being operated on are not known at compile time.
- Use parameterized types if efficiency is essential (to avoid the overhead of virtual functions).

7.8.1   Designing Iterators

To make the description from the previous section more concrete, I show two ways that iterators can be implemented: by using inheritance and templates (for a description of iterators, see Section 7.5).

Iterators designed using inheritance, like those in Java, rely on a common abstract base class; for example:

```
class Iterator { // abstract
public:
  virtual bool hasNext() = 0;
  virtual T next() = 0 throw(std::range_error);
};
```

You code to this abstract interface by using the functions that appear in the interface:

```
void traverse(Iterator& i) {
  while(i.hasNext()) {
    T aux = i.next();
    ... // use aux; may require RTTI
  }
}
```

Specific iterators are implemented in classes derived from Iterator. For example, a ListIterator is an iterator derived from Iterator, which implements this iterator for lists.

Iterators designed using *parameterized types* use concrete iterators as type parameters for implementing the traverse() operations:

```
template <typename Iterator>
  // Requirements for Iterator:
  // Supports: hasNext() and next()
void traverse(Iterator& i) {
  while(i.hasNext()) {
    T aux = i.next();
    ...  // use aux
  }
}
```

A specific iterator, such as the concrete class List::ListIterator is used as the template parameter:

```
traverse(List::ListIterator& i);
```

The standard library described in Chapter 8 is based on the idea of implementing iterators using parameterized types. These iterators are better than Java-style iterators because they do not involve runtime constructs, so they are more efficient.

7.8.2 Designing Reference Counting

In Section 6.6.2, I described the design of a reference counting technique that keeps track of the number of references to each object. This technique uses a bridge between the handle and the body, where each body has a reference counter. This design is often called a **smart pointer** class because it essentially describes a pointer wrapper.

The solution presented in this section uses parameterized types. It passes the type of the object that has a reference counter, here called Body, as the template parameter. The design is similar to the one provided by auto_ptr, but it does not maintain the ownership of pointers; instead, it supports the sharing of objects and maintains a count of the number of references made to the objects:

```cpp
// File: ch7.smartpointer.h
template <typename Body>
   // Template requirements for Body: None
class Handle {
public:
  explicit Handle(Body* = 0);
  Handle(const Handle&);
  ~Handle();

  Handle& operator=(const Handle&);
  Body* operator->();
  Body& operator*();
private:
  Body* bridge_;
  int* counter_;
};

// File: ch7.smartpointer.cpp
template <typename Body>
Handle<Body>::Handle(Body* b) : bridge_(b) {
  counter_ = new int(1);
}

template <typename Body>
Handle<Body>::Handle(const Handle<Body>& h) : bridge_(h.bridge_) {
  counter_ = h.counter_;
  (*counter_)++;
}

template <typename Body>
Handle<Body>::~Handle<Body>() {
  if(--(*counter_) == 0) {
```

```
      delete counter_;
      delete bridge_;
   }
}

template <typename Body>
Handle<Body>& Handle<Body>::operator=(const Handle<Body>& rhs)  {
   if(this == &rhs || bridge_ == rhs.bridge_)
      return *this;

   if(--(*counter_) == 0) {          // left-hand side has no references
      delete counter_;
      delete bridge_;
   }

   bridge_ = rhs.bridge_;
   counter_ = rhs.counter_;
   (*counter_)++;
   return *this;
}

template <typename Body>
Body* Handle<Body>::operator->() {
   return bridge_;
}

template <typename Body>
Body& Handle<Body>::operator*() {
   return *bridge_;
}
```

Now consider class Point:

```
// File: ch7.point.h
class Point {
public:
   Point(double = 0, double = 0);
   virtual ~Point();
   double getX() const;
   double getY() const;

   void setX(double) ;
   void setY(double) ;
private:
   double x_;
   double y_;
};
```

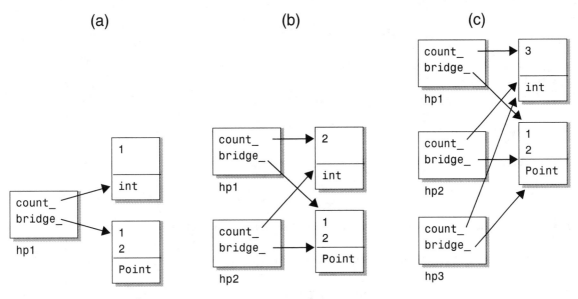

Figure 7.10   Reference counting for points

To add reference counting to points, you can do the following (see Figure 7.10):

```
Handle<Point> hp1(new Point(1, 2));      // Fig. 7-10 (a)
cout << hp1->getX() << endl;             // hp1.operator->()->getX();
Handle<Point> hp2(hp1);                   // share points; Fig. 7-10 (b)
Handle<Point> hp3(new Point(3, 4));
hp3 = hp2;                                // deallocate point (3, 4)
                                          // Fig. 7-10 (c)
cout << hp2->getY() << " " << hp3->getY() << endl;
```

7.9 *Applications of Templates to Design Patterns*

The first application of templates to design patterns was in the iterator design pattern (see Section 7.5.2). In this section, I show two more applications.

7.9.1 Singleton Design Pattern

Suppose you have two classes that need to be singletons. You could write separate code for these two classes following the singleton design pattern (see Section 4.5). However, a simpler solution is to use a single template class, which will give you the functionality of the singleton:

```
template <typename Type>
class Singleton {
```

```
public:
  static Type* instance();
};

template <typename Type>
 // Type is a model of Default Constructible
Type* Singleton<Type>::instance() {
 static Type* instance_;
 if(instance_ == 0)
   instance_ = new Type;
 return instance_;
}
```

If you have a class called `PrintSpooler`, it is easy to use it as a singleton:

```
Singleton<PrintSpooler>::instance()->print();
```

7.9.2   Abstract Factory Design Pattern

The abstract factory design pattern described in Section 6.2 suffers from the problem of having to create derived classes for each required type of product. Using templates, you can make the product a type parameter of the `StandardCreator` class:

```
template <typename TheProduct>
 // TheProduct is a model of Default Constructible
class StandardCreator : public Creator {
public:
  virtual TheProduct* factoryMethod();
};

template <typename TheProduct>
TheProduct* StandardCreator<TheProduct>:: factoryMethod() {
  return new TheProduct;
}
```

A specific product, `MyProduct`, is derived from the abstract class `Product` and can be supplied to the creator:

```
StandardCreator<MyProduct> sc;
```

7.10   *Exercises*

For all exercises in this chapter, you should carefully design the interface of each class; in particular, decide if you need to implement functions such as the copy constructor, destructor, and overloaded assignment operator. When an exercise calls for the creation of a namespace, you should design it carefully, and split it into files available to the client and the implementation. For each exercise, include a program that tests your code.

EXERCISE 7-1

Implement a wrapper class for double values. The interface of this class should include the following standard arithmetic operations, implemented by using overloaded operator functions: +, +=, -, -=, *, *=, /, /=, ++, --, I/O, type conversion to double. Use exception handling for all operators; for example, throw an exception if addition results in an overflow or in the case of division by zero. Use a namespace.

EXERCISE 7-2

Implement a class, Fractions, that represents fractions. This class should provide a constructor and overloaded operator functions to add, subtract, multiply, divide, and perform I/O for fractions. There should also be functions to compare fractions. Fractions should always be reduced to lowest terms. The operations do not need to perform any error checking. Use a single namespace, and design your classes so that they can be further extended (see Example 7-4).

EXERCISE 7-3

Implement a class, Point that represents a point in a three-dimensional space. Carefully design the interface for this class and include functions that appear to be useful for operating on points. Then use the proxy design pattern to implement a proxy class that provides access to points and accepts only points with positive coordinates.

EXERCISE 7-4

Extend the namespace from Exercise 7-2 by adding exception handling.

EXERCISE 7-5

Modify Example 7.1 by adding exception handling. In addition, add functions to insert elements before and after the value pointed to by the iterator and to delete the value pointed to by the iterator.

EXERCISE 7-6

Design and implement a robust iterator for Example 7.1 (try to avoid copying lists). You may have to find and read papers on this topic.

EXERCISE 7-7

Design and implement a class, Tree, that represents a binary tree of integers. Use the technique described in Example 7.1 to include iterators that iterate in pre-, in-, and postorder.

EXERCISE 7-8

Design and implement a class, Tree, which represents a binary tree of integers. Use the technique described in Example 7.2 to include polymorphic iterators that iterate in pre-, in-, and postorder.

EXERCISE 7-9

Modify Exercise 7.1 by implementing a list of strings with a filtered iterator, which filters out all strings that satisfy a condition, passed as a functor to the constructor of the list. For example, a functor may specify that a string does not contain any lowercase letters.

EXERCISE 7-10

Implement a template class, Queue, implemented using a circular array (hint: base your design on Examples 7.3 and 7.4). Do not use exception handling. Test your template with one primitive data type and the following two concrete types:

- Class Point (see Exercise 7-3)
- Class Segment, which has two pointers to points

EXERCISE 7-11

Implement a template class, List (hint: base your design on Examples 7.3 and 7.4). Do not use exception handling. Use the same testing criteria as in Exercise 7-10. In addition, test your class with a list of lists of integers.

EXERCISE 7-12

Extend the class Queue from Exercise 7-10 by adding exception handling. Use the same testing as in Exercise 7-10.

EXERCISE 7-13

Use arrays from Example 7.4 and implement a template function, sort(), that is implemented using bubble sort. Add functions to output sort-related statistics, such as the number of comparisons and swaps.

EXERCISE 7-14

Write a template function, reverse(), that uses the stack from Example 7.3 and the array from Example 7.4 and reverses an array.

EXERCISE 7-15

Use auto_ptr from Section 7.7.1 to implement a wrapper class for integers, which has a pointer to an integer value.

EXERCISE 7-16

Use the reference counting technique from Section 7.8.2 to maintain integer variables stored in a wrapper class. Use copy on writing when modifying the value of a constant. Add debugging messages that show the value of the reference counter for each constant—for example, when executing the following instructions:

create variable equal to 2
copy the above variable, using a copy constructor
create variable equal to 4
copy the above variable, using an assignment
change value of the first variable to 3
and so on

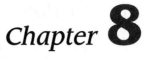

Chapter **8**

GENERIC PROGRAMMING USING STL

8.1 *Preview*

The standard template library was developed by Alex Stepanov. In 1997, it was accepted by the ANSI/ISO C++ Standards Committee as part of the standard C++ library. Like most libraries, the C++ standard library, often referred to as STL, is intended to provide standard tools for programmers to use for writing efficient and portable programs with high-level abstractions. In particular, STL supports various data types, such as vectors and lists, algorithms, such as sorting, I/O, strings, numeric algorithms, and internationalization. Since the design of STL supports *only* tools that can be efficiently implemented in a portable way, Java programmers will not find various tools they are used to in this library, such as graphics, GUI, and networking tools.

I begin this chapter with an introduction to the components used by STL, such as containers, iterators, and algorithms. I then provide examples of applications that use the standard STL components. Chapter 9 describes I/O streams defined in STL.

A complete understanding of STL is not an easy task. First, you need to understand the concepts introduced in Chapter 7—in particular, operator overloading and templates. Second, the flexibility provided by STL comes with a price: its complexity. This chapter is an introduction to STL and does not cover all its features. In particular, I do not cover numeric algorithms and internationalization; I also do not explain how to extend the library. For a detailed discussion of STL see Austern (1999), Breymann (1998), Musser and Saini (1996), and, in particular, a very detailed treatment in Josuttis (2000). The source code for STL is available from several sources, some of which are listed in Appendix H.

8.2 *Introduction*

STL provides three generic **components**:

- Containers, for holding *homogeneous* collections of values
- Algorithms, for operating on various containers
- Iterators, for iterating over containers

In addition, STL uses

- Functors, for using objects as if they were functions
- Adapters, for adapting a component to provide a different interface

An important consideration in the design and use of STL is *efficiency*. All STL algorithms have an associated **time complexity** and are implemented so that this complexity is roughly as good as you can get for the particular algorithm. To briefly summarize the concept of time complexity, programs that run in constant time are much faster than programs that run in linear time, which in turn are faster than those that run in quadratic time (a complete review of this topic can be found in Aho, Hopcroft, and Ullman, 1983). In addition, STL provides an **amortized time complexity** for some operations, which is the time complexity of an operation averaged over n executions of the operation. It is often useful to know both the time and the amortized complexity for an algorithm. For example, the worst-case time complexity for inserting into a vector is $O(n)$, but the amortized time complexity of this operation is constant, that is, $O(1)$. You can use this information to select the fastest components for a given application.

STL makes use of language-supported *compile-time* programming techniques and rarely uses encapsulation. Therefore, you will often see `struct` rather than `class` in STL constructs.

STL supports various kinds of **containers**, including lists and double-ended queues, or deques (rhymes with *checks*). Arrays are also supported for upward compatibility, but it is more efficient to use vectors, which are among the most popular STL containers.

Standard algorithms, called simply **algorithms** in STL, are template functions written in generic terms; they are parameterized by iterators to access the containers they operate on. This allows the algorithms to be decoupled from the containers, which in turn allows the *same* algorithm to work for different containers. For example, `sort()` works on built-in C++ data structures, such as arrays, and on library containers, such as the following:

```
vector<int> v;
... // initialize it

sort(v.begin(), v.end());                    // sort the range of vector

deque<double> d;
... // initialize it
```

```
sort(d.begin, d.end());                    // sort the range of deque
```

STL components are written according to certain guidelines. Components that adhere to the guidelines are referred to as **STL compliant**. You can write your own STL-compliant containers that will work with existing STL algorithms. You can also write STL-compliant algorithms that will work with all STL-compliant containers.

Efficiency (the time complexity of the various operations) should always be taken into consideration when using and designing STL components. The designers of STL have followed this philosophy and left out certain inefficient operations; the end result of this is that not *every* algorithm works on *every* container. For example, random access to a list element is not efficient (it is linear) and therefore is not supported by a general sorting STL algorithm. Similarly, sorting lists is inefficient and is also not supported. To make its components more flexible, STL designers came up with the following design scheme:

- *Containers* provide iterators; different containers provide different kinds of iterators.
- *Algorithms* take different kinds of iterators as parameters. To execute an algorithm on a container, this algorithm and the container must use the same kind of iterator.
- If a general algorithm, such as sorting, is not available for a specific container, the container provides its own *member operation* (whose time complexity does not necessarily conform to general standards and is usually higher than the time complexity of a general algorithm).

In this design, the iterators resemble cables that connect algorithms and containers; if a container does not provide the right kind of a cable, the algorithm cannot be connected to this container.

STL also provides *allocators* that allocate memory for containers, but since they are needed only for specialized applications, I will not discuss them in this book (for details, see Stroustrup, 1997).

The various generic components of STL are so closely interconnected that it is difficult to describe one component without making references to the others. Therefore, it is essential that you understand the design of my presentation before reading the remainder of this chapter. I assume that you have a good understanding of how to design iterators (see Section 7.5). First I give a very general description of iterators and containers and then more thoroughly describe iterators. Armed with this knowledge and the understanding of a few auxiliary concepts such as functors and predicates, you will be ready to look at several of the most important algorithms provided by STL. These algorithms work with various containers, with which you will not yet be familiar (I will describe the containers later). However, these algorithms use iterators rather than containers. I also provide several special examples of algorithms applied to the simplest containers available—arrays—and discuss general container operations and various kinds of specialized iterators. Finally, I describe the specific standard containers in more detail.

8.3 *Introduction to Iterators and Containers*

Recall from Example 7.1 that an iterator provides access to objects stored in a container; therefore, you can say that the iterator *points* to a value. There are three basic operations that every iterator (here called `iter`), has to support:

- `*iter`, to access the element currently pointed to by the iterator
- `++iter`, to move to the next element of the container
- `iter == iter1`, to compare two iterators

Every container provides one or more iterators; for example:

```
vector<string>::iterator                // iterator for a vector of strings
```

Each of these iterators must support at least the following two functions:

- `begin()` returns an iterator pointing to the first element of the container
- `end()` returns an iterator pointing beyond the end of the container (this iterator serves as a sentinel)

Standard iterators support *overwrite semantics*, which means that assigning a value to `*iter` overwrites the value to which `iter` was pointing. In addition, there are **iterator adapters** that support *insertion semantics*, which means that assigning a new value results in its insertion without overwriting any existing values.

The five operations just described (three iterator operations and two functions returning iterators) are sufficient for iterating over any container `c` of type `Container`:

```
for(Container::iterator iter = c.begin(); iter != c.end(); ++iter)
    ... *iter ...
```

All containers are template classes, parameterized by the element type. There are two kinds of containers:

- **Sequence containers** are used for representing *sequences* (in a sequence, each element is placed in a certain position):

  - `vector<ElementType>`, for vectors (sequences of varying length)
  - `deque<ElementType>`, for deques (queues with operations at either end)
  - `list<ElementType>`, for lists

- **Associative containers** are used for representing *sorted collections* (in a sorted collection, a position at which an element is placed depends on its value and a sorting method):

  - `set<KeyType>`, for sets with unique keys
  - `map<KeyType, ElementType>`, for maps with unique keys
  - `multiset<KeyType>`, for sets with duplicate keys
  - `multimap<KeyType, ElementType>`, for maps with duplicate keys

For a specific application, a container may be too general, and for the sake of efficiency and functionality, it should be further refined. For example, instead of simulating a stack using a list, it is better to have a stack container. Therefore, STL provides **container adapters**, which are containers adapted for the use of specific interfaces; for example, queues are adapters of lists.

Most standard containers are interchangeable—you can choose the one that is the most efficient for your needs. Different containers provide different iterators and different kinds of algorithms require different iterators. Therefore, once you choose a container, you can apply any algorithm that has a compatible iterator. In other words, you can use an algorithm as long as the iterator it requires is provided by the selected container.

The next section provides a detailed description of iterators. Once you understand how they work, you will be able to look at various algorithms, which you should be able to understand even before you have a detailed understanding of the specific kinds of containers.

8.4   *Iterators, Part I*

I start this section with a description of the notation used in conjunction with arrays: for an array x of size N, I use the range

```
[x, x+N)
```

to specify the entire array, that is x[0], x[1], ..., x[N-1], and for j>0, i<N, I use

```
[x+j, x+i)
```

to specify a subrange (slice) of this array consisting of x[j], x[j+1], ..., x[i-1]. For arrays, iterators are pointers to elements of the array; for example

```
x.begin()
```

points to the first element of x. Note that iterators—in particular, various arithmetic operations on iterators—are abstractions of pointers. However, as I mentioned earlier, the various C++ pointer operations that were inherited from C are now deprecated, so I do not describe them here. (An abstraction of a pointer is represented by a class that may have a constructor, a destructor, and other operations.)

I use the following array for the various examples in this section (see also Figure 8.1):

```
int x[4] = {0, 1, 2, 3};
```

As I indicated in Section 7.5.2, an iterator provides access to containers. Do not think of a general iterator as an pointer; it is an abstract concept. To explain this concept, it is useful to think about a container as a discrete set of values whose type

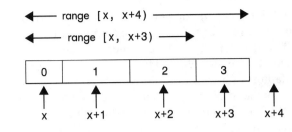

Figure 8.1   Arrays and ranges

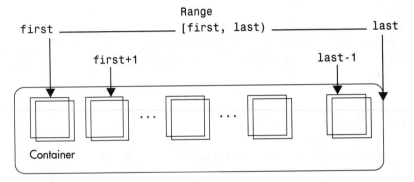

Figure 8.2   Iterators and ranges

is `value_type`. An iterator can be thought of as an object that can *point* to any value in the container (see Figure 8.2). An iterator `iter` associated with a container can point to either an element of this container or beyond it to special **past-the-end** value. In the former case, the iterator can be dereferenced by using the * operator (`*iter` is of the type `value_type`).

Two iterators can be compared for equality and inequality; they are considered equal if they point to the same element of the container.

An iterator can be incremented so it points to the next value in the container (assuming that such a value exists), using the ++ operator. Given one iterator, `iter1`, and another, `iter2`, that was initially equal to `iter1` and then incremented a number of times, it is often useful to determine the distance *between* `iter1` and `iter2`. Therefore, for each iterator type, there is a special type called `difference_type`; values of this type represent the distances between two iterator values.

A sequence of consecutive values in the container is determined by an **iterator range**, defined by two iterators—for example, `first` and `last`—and written as

```
[first, last)
```

This notation indicates that `last` is reachable from `first` by using the ++ operator, and all iterators, including `first` but excluding `last`, can be dereferenced. In other words, an iterator range determines a sequence of consecutive values, *including* the value pointed to by `first` and *excluding* the value pointed to by `last`.

As previously mentioned, each container provides the operations `begin()` and `end()`, which return the iterator pointing to the first value in the container and the value immediately past the end of the container, respectively. For example, consider a container that holds five elements, and let `first = begin()` and `last = end()` (see Figure 8.2). Iterators can be subtracted, so `last-first` is the distance between these two iterators, equal to the number of elements in this range. You can also add and subtract integers from iterators; for example, `first+1` points to the second element, and `last-1` points to the last element (see Figure 8.2). This type of arithmetic is useful for representing a range that does not include all the elements in the container; for example, for a container with five elements, `[first+1, last-1)` represents three elements: the second, the third, and the fourth. Sometimes you need the empty range, which, for example, can be specified as `[first, first)`.

To perform some operation on each value in a range, the range can be traversed. For example, the values can be reinitialized, or copied to another container. Ranges are useful for all kinds of traversals in which there is no modification of the container. Traversals that modify the container may invalidate the iterators (this depends on the kind of container and the kind of modification and is described in detail later).

The description just presented gives you an idea of what general iterators look like. However, in some cases, it is useful to consider iterators that have a more limited functionality. Recall that an algorithm is parameterized with iterators. Thus, an algorithm that has strong requirements for the kinds of iterators with which it can work is only useful in a limited number of situations. For this reason, many algorithms have looser requirements for their iterators. For example, consider a generic linear search:

```
template<typename Iterator, typename ElementType>
  // ElementType is a model of Equality Comparable
  // Iterator is a model of ... (to be defined soon)
Iterator find(Iterator first, Iterator last, const ElementType& v) {
  Iterator aux;
  for(aux = first; aux != last; ++aux)
    if(*aux == v)                                          // found
      break;
  return aux;
}
```

This is a typical example of a *generic algorithm:* it is a template function parameterized by the iterator and element types. In particular, the algorithm does not know the type of container it operates on. Instead of accessing container elements directly, it uses iterators to specify the range of values. Although technically speaking this example is just a template function, I refer to such code as an *algorithm*. For the sake of readability, I write most generic algorithms in this book using auxiliary variables (`aux` in the example just shown); the actual implementations may be made more efficient by reorganizing, or eliminating these variables.

The `find()` operation in the previous example needs to support a single-pass traversal only. The type of iterator required for it is called an **input iterator** because a single traversal resembles the *reading* of standard input, where a value that is read cannot be read again. With the input iterator, there is no guarantee that *writing* the values pointed to by the iterator is supported (writing to values means assigning something to the value pointed to by the iterator).

Examine the code for `find()` in the previous example to determine the minimum set of requirements that the `Iterator` type must satisfy and to define the `Input Iterator` concept for which `Iterator` is a model. You want to look for the *minimum set* of requirements because any algorithm that will work with this minimal iterator will also work with other, more powerful iterators. At a minimum, the input iterator type must support two operations:

- Dereferencing `operation*()`
- `operation++()`

In addition, the type of the value that the iterator works on must

- Have a no-arg constructor
- Support the assignment operation
- Compare for inequality

These three requirements can be stated using concepts introduced in Chapter 7 (specifically, `Assignable`, `Default Constructible`, and `Equality Comparable`); the first two requirements are new. Thus the `Iterator` type must be a model of the three concepts and must additionally satisfy certain requirements.

In general, when some concept `Ref` has all of a concept `Con`'s requirements, plus some additional ones of its own, you say that `Ref` is a **refinement** of `Con`. Of course, every model of `Ref` is a model of `Con` (`Ref` has more requirements); in other words, `Ref` has fewer models than `Con`. The `Input Iterator` concept that follows is a refinement of the `Assignable` concept, and every model of the `Input Iterator` concept is also a model of the `Assignable` concept. In addition, the concept is a refinement of the `Default Constructible` and `Equality Comparable` concepts:

`Input Iterator` **Concept 8.1**

Refinement of `Assignable`, `Default Constructible`, and `Equality Comparable`. In particular, two input iterators can be compared for equality. Additionally supports the dereferencing `operation*()`, the `operation->()`, and the prefix and postfix `operation++()`. Is not required to support writing of the value or more than one pass through the data.

The `Input Iterator` concept I provide is a simplified and somewhat informal version of iterator concepts. For a complete description, see Austern (1999).

You can use the `Input Iterator` concept to complete the documentation of `find()`:

```
template<typename Iterator, typename ElementType>
  // ElementType is a model of Equality Comparable
  // Iterator is a model of Input Iterator
  // Returns last if v not found
Iterator find(Iterator first, Iterator last, const ElementType& v);
```

This algorithm can be used for arrays (recall notations used at the beginning of this section):

```
if(find(x, x+4, 2) != x+4) ...        // 2 found in x

if(find(x+2, x+4, 2) != x+4) ...      // 2 found in last two elements

if(find(x+1, x+3, 2) != x+3) ...      // 2 found in the array slice
                                      // consisting of x[1] and x[2]
```

To find a value in a range, the "right end" of this range must be the past-the-end value, which is `x+4` in the arrays just shown and which points beyond the array `x`.

Now look at an algorithm that copies the range specified by two input iterators to a range that is indicated by another iterator:

```
template<typename FromIterator, typename ToIterator>
  // FromIterator is a model of Input Iterator
  // ToIterator is a model of ... (to be defined soon)
  // copy the range [first, last) to the range starting at firstTwo
ToIterator copy(FromIterator first, FromIterator last,
    ToIterator firstTwo) {
  FromIterator aux;
  for(aux = first; aux != last; ++aux, ++firstTwo)
    *firstTwo = *aux;                                    // copy
  return firstTwo;
}
```

Notice the difference between `find()` and `copy()`; `find()` uses a single range defined by two iterators, while `copy()` uses two ranges. The first range is defined by two iterators, `first` and `last`. The second range appears to be defined by only one iterator, `firstTwo`, but in this case the two ranges must contain the same number of elements.

The requirements on `ToIterator` are different from those on input iterators. Instead of having to read the values pointed to by this iterator, you have to be able to *write* them. Therefore, this kind of iterator is called an **output iterator**. In addition, you do not need to compare output iterators. Intuitively, this iterator resembles writing to a sequential device, like standard output.

Output Iterator **Concept 8.2**

Refinement of Assignable and Default Constructible. Additionally supports the dereferencing operation*(), the operation->(), and the prefix and postfix operation++(). Is not required to support the comparing of two iterators, the reading of a value, or more than one pass through the data.

We can use the Output Iterator concept to complete the documentation of copy():

```
template<typename FromIterator, typename ToIterator>
   // FromIterator is a model of Input Iterator
   // ToIterator is a model of Output Iterator
OutputIterator copy(FromIterator, FromIterator, ToIterator);
```

You can use the algorithm to copy the contents of an entire array x to an array y:

```
int y[4];
copy(x, x+4, y);
```

You can copy just part of it:

```
copy(x+1, x+3, y+1);            // copy x[1] to y[1] and x[2] to y[2]
```

The destination range must have enough memory allocated. For example, the following code is incorrect:

```
int x[4] = {0, 1, 2, 3};
int z[6];
... // initialize z
copy(z, z+6, x);               // error x does not have 6 elements
```

There are three more kinds of iterators: forward, bidirectional, and random access. The concepts for these iterators are refinements of the Input Iterator and Output Iterator concepts (see Figure 8.3).

In Figure 8.3, a concept that appears lower in the hierarchy than some other concept is a refinement of that concept C. In particular, a Random Access Iterator concept is the most powerful concept (it is a refinement of all other concepts), and every model of this concept is also a model of any other concept in the hierarchy.

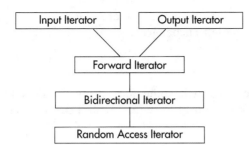

Figure 8.3   Hierarchy of iterators

Assignment to a value pointed to by the output iterator (as well as any refinement of it), such as

```
*iter = v;
```

overwrites the value previously pointed to by the iterator. There are other kinds of iterators, described later, that are used to insert a value rather than overwrite it.

Now consider yet another type of iterator. To *replace* each value in a certain range by another value, you need to be able to both read and write values; therefore, you need an iterator that is both an input iterator and an output iterator.

Forward Iterator **Concept 8.3**

Refinement of Input Iterator and Output Iterator. Additionally supports more than one pass through the data. Does not support reverse iteration (stepping backward).

You can use this iterator in an algorithm to replace a value:

```
template<typename Iterator, typename ElementType>
  // Iterator is a model of Forward Iterator
  // ElementType is a model of Equality Comparable and Assignable
  // Replace all occurrences of oldValue in the range [first, last)
  //   by the newValue
void replace(Iterator first, Iterator last,
    const ElementType& oldValue, const ElementType& newValue) {
  Iterator aux;
  for(aux = first; aux != last; ++aux)
    if(*aux == oldValue)
      *aux = newValue;
}
```

For example, the first *three* elements of the array x, which are equal to 0, can be replaced by 2 (elements not equal to 0 are left unchanged):

```
replace(x, x+3, 0, 2);
```

A forward iterator can only move forward; in some applications, you need an iterator that can also move *backward*. To support this requirement, I define the following concept:

Bidirectional Iterator **Concept 8.4**

Refinement of Forward Iterator. Can also be decremented using prefix and postfix versions of the -- operator.

The next example shows an algorithm used to copy a range *backward*. As for copy(), the second range is defined implicitly. Remember that this algorithms copies backward:

```
template <class Iterator1, class Iterator2>
  // Iterator1 and Iterator2 are models of Bidirectional Iterator
  // Copy the range [first, last) backward: the first element is
  //   copied just before result, and so on
Iterator2 copy_backward(Iterator1 first, Iterator1 last,
     Iterator2 result) {
  Iterator1 one, two;
  for(one = --last, two = --result; one != first; --one, --two)
    *two = *one;
  *two = *one;
  return result;
}
```

If the source and destination ranges do not overlap, copy() and backward_ copy() are identical, as shown in Figure 8.4(a). Otherwise, copy() copies the range to the *front*, and copy_backward() copies to the *back*; for example:

```
int x[] = {1,2,1,4,5,6,7,8};
int z[8];
copy(x, x+8, z);                          // z is a copy of x

copy(x+4, x+6, x+3);
copy_backward(z+4, z+6, z+3);
```

This copy() copies the range [x+4,x+6) to the front of [x+3,x+5); that is, it performs x[3]=x[4] and x[4]=x[5], so the array x is

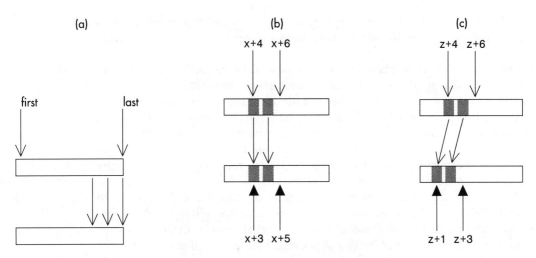

Figure 8.4 (a) Copying disjoint ranges; (b) copying overlapping ranges using copy(); (c) copying overlapping ranges using copy_backward()

```
1 2 1 5 6 6 7 8
```

as shown in Figure 8.4(b). On the other hand, copy_backward() copies the range [z+4,z+6) to the back of [z+1,z+3); that is, it performs z[2]=z[5] and z[1]=z[4], so the array z is:

```
1 5 6 4 5 6 7 8
```

as shown in Figure 8.4(c).

The destination range for copy_backward() is specified by the past-the-end value; for example:

```
copy_backward(x, x+4, y);            // overwrites memory before y
```

Now consider applications such as sorting, for which you need to be able to compare the values pointed to by the iterators. Consequently, you need another concept that describes types that can be compared.

Strict Weakly Comparable **Concept 8.5**

Refinement of LessThan Comparable. Requires that the relation defined as follows:

```
!(x < y) && !(y < x)
```

be transitive.

Notice that this concept does not say that x must be "equal" to y; indeed, it does not use an equality relation. Rather, it says that two elements are related if neither is less than the other.

The reason that the concepts of Equality Comparable and LessThan Compara-ble are not sufficient and the Strict Weakly Comparable concept is needed is that many applications have elements that are not identical but are *equivalent*. For example, consider a phone book, with entries containing first and last names and phone numbers. If entries are ordered by their last names, then two entries with identical last names, such as (John Smith 1234567) and (Mary Smith 9876543) are not equal, but they are equivalent in the sense of the relation described by the Strict Weakly Comparable concept.

General sorting algorithms require the ability to step forward and backward, to calculate the difference between two iterators, and to compare two iterators (this comparison must satisfy the requirement from the Strict Weakly Comparable con-cept). The most powerful type of iterator supports all these operations:

Random Access Iterator **Concept 8.6**

Refinement of Forward Iterator and Strict Weakly Comparable. Additionally supports the operation+=() and the operation-=() to make arbitrary-sized steps, as well as value comparisons and finding the difference between iterators.

● EXAMPLE 8.1

Here is an example of a sorting algorithm that uses various random access iterator operations—a shell sort (see Aho, Hopcroft, and Ullman, 1983). The following ver-sion is incomplete:

```
template <typename Iterator>
  // Iterator is a model of Random Access Iterator
void shellSort(Iterator first, Iterator last) {
  const difference_type size = last - first;
  for(difference_type gap = size/2; gap > 0; gap /= 2)
    for(difference_type j = i - gap; j >= 0; j -= gap)
      if(*(first+j+gap) < *(first+j)) {                    // swap
        value_type temp = *(first + j);
        *(v+j) = *(v + j + gap);
        *(v+j+gap) = temp;
      }
}
```

This code will not compile because types *difference_type* and *value_type* are not defined. The first type represents the difference between the two iterators, and the second type represent the values pointed to by the iterator. One solution is to recode the algorithm and use only iterators. However, there is a more general solution that takes advantage of the fact that an iterator type has *associated types* that can be retrieved and used in the code. To implement this solution, you have to use a helper class called `iterator_traits` (and remember to include `<iterator>`):

```
iterator_traits<Iterator>::difference_type size;
iterator_traits<Iterator>::value_type temp;
```

These definitions are not quite complete: using Idiom 7.6, you have to indicate that the *name*, such as `value_type`, represents a type by using the `typename` keyword; for example:

```
typename iterator_traits<Iterator>::value_type temp;
```

Here is the complete code for shell sort using the random access iterator:

```cpp
// File: ex8.1.shellsort.cpp
#include <iterator>
template <typename Iterator>
// Iterator is a model of Random Access Iterator
void shellSort(Iterator first, Iterator last) {

  typedef typename
    iterator_traits<Iterator>::difference_type Distance;

  const Distance size = last - first;
  for(Distance gap = size/2; gap > 0; gap /= 2)
   for(Distance i = gap; i < size; ++i)
    for(Distance j = i - gap; j >= 0; j -= gap)
      if(*(first+j+gap) < *(first+j)) {

        typename iterator_traits<Iterator>::value_type temp;

        temp = *(first + j);
        *(first+j) = *(first + j + gap);
        *(first+j+gap) = temp;
      }
}
```

To swap two values pointed to by iterators, you can also use the general `swap()` algorithm:

```
swap(*(first+j), *(first+j+gap));
```

Now you can use `shellSort()` to sort an entire array like this:

```
int x[5] = {3, 2, 1, 4, 5};
shellSort(x, x+5);
```

You can also sort just a slice of this array:

```
shellSort(x+1, x+4);                          // sort x[1],...x[3]
```

This completes the discussion of iterators. Before I present the various algorithms, I will describe techniques used to make these algorithms more general.

8.5 *Making Algorithms Generic*

It is often useful to generalize various algorithms by adding function parameters. For example, you may wish to execute the same function on each element of a container, or you may want to count the number of elements in the container that satisfy a certain predicate (a Boolean condition). To provide this functionality, generic programming uses functors and predicates.

8.5.1 Functions and Functors

Consider the task of accumulating the result of performing a certain action, such as addition, on an array of objects of the same type T:

```
T init;
... // initialize init

T array[size];
... // initialize array

for(int i = low; i != high; ++i)      // assume low and high are correct
  init = init + array[i];
```

A generic version for this code can be defined as a template function as follows:

```
template <typename T>
  // T is a model of Default Constructible, Assignable and supports +
```

```
T accum1(T init, T array[], int low, int high) {
  for(int i = low; i != high; ++i)
    init = init + array[i];
  return init;
}
```

You can use this version for arrays:

```
int x[5] = {3, 5, 2, 1, 8};
cout << accum1(0, x, 0, 3) << endl;                        // outputs 10
```

The problem with this algorithm is that it is not STL-compliant, because to be compliant, algorithms should be parameterized by iterators instead of containers (which, in this example, is the `T array []`). The following corrected version uses an iterator `i` over a general container instead of using `int i`:

```
template <typename T, typename Iterator>
  // T is a model of Default Constructible, Assignable and supports +
  // Iterator is a model of Input Iterator
  // Returns the sum of init and values in the range [first, last)
T accum2(T init, Iterator low, Iterator high) {
  Iterator i;
  for(i = low; i != high; ++i)
    init = init + *i;
  return init;
}
```

Here is its application:

```
cout << accum2(0, x, x+4) << endl;                         //outputs 11
```

It is possible to write a more generic version of the algorithm, which would allow it to be used for a variety of binary operations, such as addition, subtraction, and multiplication. Before you can do this, you need one more concept.

Binary and Unary Functions **Concept 8.7**

A `Binary Function` is a refinement of `Assignable` and additionally supports the `operator()` with two arguments, or it is a function with two arguments. A `Unary Function` is a refinement of `Assignable` and additionally supports the `operator()` with one argument, or it is a function with one argument.

For example, any *binary* function that is a function with two arguments is a model of the `Binary Function` concept. Any class `Fun` that is a model of `Binary Function` must have an overloaded binary `operator()`; for example, if `foo` is an object of this class, the expression `foo(arg1, arg2)` is legal and resembles a function call.

Now you can write a more generic version of `accum()`:

```
template <typename T, typename Iterator, typename BinaryOp>
  // T is a model of Default Constructible, Assignable and supports +
  // Iterator is a model of Input Iterator
  // BinaryOp is a model of Binary Function
  // For each element in the range [first, last) apply binOp
T accum3(T init, Iterator low, Iterator high, BinaryOp binOp) {
  Iterator i;
  for(i = low; i != high; ++i)
    init = binOp(init, *i);
  return init;
}
```

As one example of an application of this algorithm, you can use it to accumulate the result of multiplication. First, you define a function `multiply()` that this algorithm will use:

```
template <typename T>
  // T supports *
T multiply(const T& x, const T& y) {
  return x * y;
}
```

Now you can find the product of all of the elements of an integer array:

```
int x[5];
... // initialize x

int res = accum3(1, x, x+5, multiply<int>);
```

Notice that for this application, you had to use the specialization `multiply<int>`; otherwise, the compiler would not know how to instantiate the template function.

Instead of using a function such as `multiply()`, you can define a *functor*:

```
template <typename T>
  // T supports *
struct Multiplication {
  T operator()(const T& x, const T& y) const {
    return x * y;
  }
};
```

(You can use `struct` rather than `class` because `Multiplication` has no data elements.) This functor is a model of the `Binary Function` concept and can be used to find the product of all elements of the integer array:

```
int res = accum3(1, x, x+5, Multiplication<int>());
```

The last argument of this call to `accum3()` is the call to the default no-arg constructor of `Multiplication<int>`.

You may wonder why you would ever bother to define functors, if the same task can apparently be accomplished with functions. There are three reasons why, in general, functors are better:

- The use of functors is more efficient because functors are passed at compile time and calls to operator function `operator()` can be inlined (that is, optimized at compile time)
- Functors can maintain their internal state (see the next example)
- Two functors with the same signatures that overload `operator()` are still different (they have different class or structure names)

The following example of a more powerful functor redesigns the previous `accum3()` algorithm, moving the responsibility of performing the required operation and saving the result to the functor; the algorithm itself merely invokes this functor:

```
template <typename Iterator, typename UnaryOp>
  // Iterator is a model of Input Iterator
  // UnaryOp is a model of Unary Function
UnaryOp accum4(Iterator low, Iterator high, UnaryOp unOp) {
  for(Iterator i = low; i != high; ++i)
    unOp(*i);
  return unOp;
}
```

The following functor is designed to accumulate the product by maintaining its state:

```
template<typename T>
  // T can be initialized by 1 and supports *=
class Product {
public:
  Product(T = 1);
  void operator()(const T&);        // perform multiplication
  T result() const;                 // retrieve result
private:
  T value_;
};
```

```
template<typename T>
Product<T>::Product<T>(T value) : value_(value) {}

template<typename T>                    // binary function is needed
void Product<T>::operator()(const T& v) {
  value_ *= v;
}

template<typename T>
T Product<T>::result() const {
  return value_;
}
```

You can use this functor in the definition of accum4(), for example, to find the product of the first four elements in the array:

```
Product<int> p;
p = accum4(x, x+4, p);
int res = p.result();
```

accum4() does not change the value of the object unOp; instead, it returns a modified value. Thus, when using a functor, you need an assignment:

```
p = accum4(...);
```

Functors that return Boolean values are particularly useful because they can be used to express conditions. I describe these in the next section.

8.5.2   Predicates

Many applications use functors that return a Boolean value; these functors are called **predicates**. STL supports a full set of predicates, such as equal_to, less_equal, and so on.

Look again at the linear search algorithm from Section 8.4:

```
template<typename Iterator, typename ElementType>
  // ElementType is a model of Equality Comparable
  // Iterator is a model of Input Iterator
Iterator find(Iterator, Iterator, const ElementType& v);
```

It is possible to generalize this search, which finds the first element equal to v, to a more general *filtering* search that uses a unary predicate to find the first element that satisfies this predicate:

```
template<typename Iterator, typename Predicate>
  // ElementType is a model of Equality Comparable
  // Predicate is a model of a Boolean Unary Function
Iterator find_if(Iterator first, Iterator last,
      const Predicate& pred) {
  Iterator aux;
  for(aux = first; aux != last; ++aux)
    if(pred(*aux))                                             // found
      break;
  return aux;
}
```

You can also write our own predicate, for example, to find the first element whose absolute value is greater than a certain threshold:

```
class AbsGreaterThan {
public:
  AbsGreaterThan(double v) : limit_(v) {}
  bool operator()(double i) { return abs(i) > limit_;}
private:
  double limit_;
};
```

You can use this predicate, for example, to find the first element in the array that is greater than 100:

```
double x[3] = {3, 200, 4};

if(find_if(x, x+3, AbsGreaterThan(100)) == x+3)
  cout << "not found" << endl;
else cout << "found" << endl;
```

Recall the `Strict Weakly Comparable` concept. A class type is a model of this concept if this class' operator function `operator<()` satisfies certain criteria. In general, you can require that the same criteria are satisfied by an arbitrary STL binary predicate class—specifically, by one of its members, the overloaded `operator()()`. Rather than defining a separate concept for binary predicates, I use the same concept as for the `operator<()`; it should be clear from the context as to which version of this concept is used.

The C++ library provides a number of useful functors and predicates, as described in the next section.

8.5.3   Utilities

This section lists the various auxiliary classes provided by STL. First, the `pair` class:
Various applications need to use pairs of values; for example, as you will see later,
maps use pairs. These value pairs are defined in the header file `<utility>`:

```
template <typename T1, typename T2>
struct pair {
  T1 first;
  T2 second;
  pair(const T&, constT&);
  ... // details left out
};
```

Pairs can be compared for equality and inequality. Using lexicographical comparison, a pair (x1, y1) is less than the pair (x2, y2) if x1<x2, or x1=x2 and y1<y2; for
example:

```
pair<int, double> p(1, 12.5);
pair<int, double> q(p);                          // copy constructor
pair<int, double> r(1, 12.51);

if(p != q || p >= r)
  cout << "cannot happen" << endl;
```

The related helper template function `make_pair()` is used to make pairs:

```
pair<int, double> w = make_pair(1, 1.2);
```

The `<utility>` header file also provides the various comparisons that can be defined in terms of the two operators `<` and `==`. For example, the `!=` operator is defined
as a negation of the `==` operator. The related definitions are placed in the namespace `std::rel_ops`. If you want to use these comparisons, you have to specify the
following:

```
using namespace std::rel_ops;
```

On the other hand, if you want to define your *own* versions, you can still use the
standard namespace

```
using namespace std;
```

and these definitions will not be generated.

The following built-in functors and predicates are defined in the header file
`<functional>`.

- **Arithmetic functors:**

```
plus<T>
minus<T>
multiplies<T>
divides<T>
modulus<T>
negate<T>
```

These functors have self-explanatory names, and all of them return a value of type T. The first five functors are binary, and the last one is unary; for example:

```
plus<int> p;
int i = p(2, 3);                              // 2 + 3
```

- **Predicates:**

```
equal_to<T>
not_equal_to<T>
greater<T>
greater_equal<T>
less<T>
less_equal<T>
```

Again, these binary predicates have self-explanatory names, and all of them return a Boolean value; for example:

```
equal_to<double> p;
bool q = p(2, 3.5);                           // 2 == 3.5
```

- **Logical functors:**

```
logical_and<T>
logical_or<T>
logical_not<T>
```

For example, the Boolean expression

```
1 < 2 && 4 > 5
```

using built-in predicates looks like this:

```
logical_and(less<int>(1, 2), greater<int>(4, 5))
```

These examples are meant to give you an idea of how to compose functors; I will provide more useful applications in Section 8.6.

8.5.4   Functor Adapters

Instead of creating new functors, it is often easier to adapt existing ones. You can define a functor called an **adapter**, which takes functor parameters and *adapts* them to a new requirement (some people call these functors *adaptors*). The idea of adapters is borrowed from the adapter design pattern (see Section 6.6.5).

STL provides four kinds of adapters; I describe two of them here and the remaining two (used for pointers to functions and member functions) in Section 9.9. The first two adapters are **binders**, which bind specific arguments of binary functors, and **negaters**, which negate predicates. To recall what *binding* means, consider a binary function defined as

```
f(x, y) = x*y - x
```

Binding an argument of a binary function means fixing its value and thereby defining a unary function; for example, binding x to 3 defines a unary function:

```
ff(y) = 3*y - 3.
```

Consider the binary functor Fun and the object foo of this class. There are two kinds of binders, each of which produces a unary functor:

- bind1st(foo, constant)(x) binds the first argument of foo to constant, equivalent to foo(constant, x)
- bind2nd(foo, constant)(x) binds the second argument of foo to constant, equivalent to foo(x, constant)

For example:

```
bind1st(less<int>(), 7) is a unary predicate:

  less<int>(7, x), or 7 < x

bind2nd(less<int>(), 2) is a unary predicate:

  less<int>(x, 2), or x < 2

bind1st(times<double>(), 0.1) is a unary functor:

  times<double>(0.1, x), or 0.1 * x
```

We can use the find_if() algorithm with the binder to find if there are elements less than 7:

```
if (find_if(x, x+4, bind2nd(less<int>(), 7)) == x+4) . . .          //success
```

There are two *negaters*:

- not1 negates unary predicates
- not2 negates binary predicates

Negators operate on predicates and are required because you cannot apply the negation operator ! to an object. For example, you can use

```
not2(greater<double>())                              // not greater
```

or

```
not1(bind2nd(greater<double>(), 7))                  // not greater than 7
```

● EXAMPLE 8.2

Consider the following predicate used to check if a number is prime:

```
// File: ex8.2.isprime.cpp
struct isPrime {
  bool operator()(int) const;
};

#include <cmath>
bool isPrime::operator()(int n) const {
  int root, divisor;
  if(n < 4)
      return n > 1;

  if(n % 2 != 1)                                       // even
      return false;

  root = sqrt(static_cast<double>(n)) + 0.5;
  for(divisor = 3; divisor <= root && n % divisor != 0;)
    divisor += 2;
  return divisor > root;
}
```

You can use not1 to negate this predicate—for example, to find the first nonprime value in an array:

```
int x[4] = {2, 5, 7, 11};
if(find_if(x, x+4, not1(isPrime())) == x+4)
    cout << "not found in x" << endl;
```

Now you are ready to review the list of generic STL algorithms.

8.6 *Generic Algorithms*

An algorithm operates on a range of elements defined by a pair of iterators. It can be categorized as mutating or nonmutating, depending on whether it modifies the underlying data structures or not, respectively. To use generic algorithms, you must include ⟨algorithm⟩.

Table 8.1 lists most of the STL algorithms (for a complete list of algorithms, see Austern, 1999).

Understanding which algorithms are mutating and which are nonmutating is essential; for example, mutating algorithms cannot be used if the destination is an associative container. One algorithm, for_each, can be mutating or nonmutating, depending on the function applied to each element.

When reading the description of the various algorithms, you should remember the requirements for the associated iterator types. For example, an algorithm that requires an input iterator works with all iterators, except an output iterator (see Figure 8.3).

To explain these algorithms, I will show their application to regular arrays in the following sections. These are not the typical application for most generic algorithms, but I will use it to give you a chance to see some simple examples. In all subsequent examples in this chapter, I will use this array:

```
int x[N]; // N>4
... // initialize x
```

8.6.1 Nonmutating Algorithms

The first two algorithms perform a linear search over the range [first, last) of values looking for an element that is equal to the given value or that satisfies a unary predicate, respectively. The algorithms return the *first* iterator for which they are successful or end() if they fail:

```
template<typename Iterator, typename ElementType>
  // ElementType is a model of Equality Comparable
  // Iterator is a model of Input Iterator
Iterator find(Iterator first, Iterator last, const ElementType& v);

template<typename Iterator, typename Predicate>
  // ElementType is a model of Equality Comparable
  // Predicate is a model of a Boolean Unary Function
Iterator find_if(Iterator first, Iterator last, Predicate pred);
```

For example:

```
// look for value 3
if(find(x, x+N, 3) != x+N) ...                              // found
```

Table 8.1 List of algorithms

Name	Time Complexity	Use
Non-mutating algorithms		
find	O(n)	Perform linear search using ==
find_if	O(n)	Perform linear search using a predicate
search	O(n²)	Search for a subsequence using == or a predicate
count	O(n)	Return number of occurrences of a value using ==
count_if	O(n)	Return number of occurrences of a value using a predicate
for_each	O(n)	Apply a function to each element; can be either mutating or nonmutating
equal	O(n)	Compare two sequences using == or a predicate
lexicographical_ compare	O(n)	Compare using lexicographical comparison
min	O(1)	Find the smallest and the largest element using < or a predicate
max	O(1)	
min_element	O(1)	
max_element	O(1)	
is_sorted	O(n)	Check if a range is sorted
binary_search	O(log n)	Perform a binary search in a sorted range
Mutating algorithms		
copy	O(n)	Copy a range
copy_backward	O(n)	Copy a range backward
swap	O(1)	Swap two elements
swap_ranges	O(n)	Swap two ranges
transform	O(n)	Apply a function to each element and copy the result
replace	O(n)	Replace each element equal to a value, compare using ==
replace_if	O(n)	Replace each element equal to a value, compare using a predicate
replace_copy	O(n)	Replace each element equal to a value, store in a copy
replace_copy_if	O(n)	Replace each element equal to a value, compare using a predicate, store in a copy
fill	O(n)	Replace each value in a range with a copy of a value
fill_n	O(n)	Replace first n values with a copy of a value
generate	O(n)	Replace each value with a copy of a value generated by the functor
sort	O(nlogn) on average; O(n²) worst	Sort into ascending order using < or a function to compare
merge	O(nlogn)	Merge two sorted ranges

```
// look for the first value less than 7
if(find_if(x, x+N, bind2nd(less<int>(), 7)) != x+N) ...      // found
```

The next two algorithms perform a search over the range [first1, last1) of values, looking for a subrange in which every element is identical to the corresponding

element in the range [first2, last2]. They both return the first iterator in the former range if successful or last1 if they fail (for the first version, *identical* means
equal; for the second version, *identical* means that the binary predicate passed as a
parameter is true):

```
template <typename Iter1, typename Iter2>
   // Iter1 and Iter2 are models of Forward Iterator
Iter1 search(Iter1 first1, Iter1 last1, Iter2 first2, Iter2 last2);

 template <typename Iter1, typename Iter2, typename Predicate>
    // Iter1 and Iter2 are models of Forward Iterator
    // Predicate is a model of a Boolean Binary Function
Iter1 search(Iter1 first1, Iter1 last1, Iter2 first2, Iter2 last2,
    Predicate pred);
```

For example:

```
int y[3] = {1, 2, 3};

// look for the sequence {1,2,3} in x
if(search(x, x+N, y, y+3) != x+N) ...                    // found

// look for the sequence of 3 numbers whose values are
//    greater than 1, 2, and 3, respectively
if(search(x, x+N, y, y+3, greater<int>()) != x+N) ...    // found
```

To understand the last example, assume that the array x contains the following
numbers:

```
3, 4, -1, 5, 6, 7, -2
```

The call to search() returns a pointer to 5 because (5, 6, 7) is a sequence whose
respective elements are greater than the elements of the sequence (1, 2, 3).
    To count the number of elements equal to a certain value or satisfying a predi-
cate, you can use the following algorithms:

```
template<typename Iterator, typename ElementType, typename Size>
   // ElementType is a model of Equality Comparable
   // Iterator is a model of Input Iterator
   // Size is an unsigned integral type
void count(Iterator first, Iterator last, const ElementType& v,
    Size& n);
```

```
template<typename Iterator, typename ElementType,
    typename Size, typename Predicate>
  // Iterator is a model of Input Iterator
  // Predicate is a model of a Boolean Unary Function
  // Size is an unsigned integral type
void count_if(Iterator first, Iterator last, Predicate pred,
    Size& n);
```

Typically, Size is replaced by int. More generally, Size is represented by difference_
type (see Example 8.1). You have to remember to initialize the variable used to
return size; for example:

```
// count the number of 100's in the first 4 elements of the array x
int c = 0;
count(x, x+4, 100, c);

// count the number of elements are greater than 5
int d = 0;
count_if(x, x+N, bind2nd(greater<int>(), 5), d);

// count the number of prime numbers
int p = 0;
count_if(x, x+N, isPrime(), p);  //isPrime is defined in Example 8.2
```

```
template<typename Iterator, typename Function>
  // Iterator is a model of Input Iterator
  // Function is a model of a Unary Function
Function for_each(Iterator first, Iterator last, Function foo);
```

The next algorithm applies a unary functor to each element of the range; it is similar to accum4() defined earlier:

Consider the following function:

```
void out(int j) {
    cout << j << endl;
}
```

You can use this function to output all elements of the array:

```
for_each(x, x+N, out);
```

(For an example of a mutating for_each, see the next section.)

You can compare two ranges using either equality or a predicate:

```
template<typename Iterator1, typename Iterator2>
  // Iterator1 and Iterator2 are models of Input Iterator
bool equal(Iterator1 first, Iterator1 last, Iterator2 where);

template<typename Iterator1, typename Iterator2, typename Predicate>
  // Iterator1 and Iterator2 are models of Input Iterator
  // Predicate is a model of a Boolean Binary Functor
bool equal(Iterator1 first, Iterator1 last, Iterator2 where,
  Predicate pred);
```

The algorithms shown so far compare the range [first, last) and the range starting with where; for example:

```
int y[N];
... // initialize y

// check if x and y have identical first 5 elements
if(equal(x, x+5, y)) ...

// check if the elements of two arrays are equal modulo 7
if(equal(x, x+5, y, bind2nd(Modulus<int>, 7)))...
```

You can lexicographically compare two ranges using either equality or a predicate:

```
template<typename Iterator1, typename Iterator2>
  // Iterator1 and Iterator2 are models of Input Iterator
bool lexicographical_compare(Iterator1 first1, Iterator1 last1,
  Iterator2 first2, Iterator2 last2);

template<typename Iterator1, typename Iterator2, typename Predicate>
  // Iterator1 and Iterator2 are models of Input Iterator
  // Predicate is a model of a Boolean Binary Functor
bool lexicographical_compare(Iterator1 first1, Iterator1 last1,
  Iterator2 first2, Iterator2 last2, Predicate compare);
```

For example:

```
char w1[9] = {'w','o','l','f','v','i','l','l','e' };
char w2[9] = {'W','o','l','f','v','i','l','l','e' };

if(lexicographical_compare(w1, w1+9, w2, w2+9))...
```

```
bool noCase(char c, char d) {
    return toupper(c) == toupper(d);
}
if(lexicographical_compare(w1, w1+9, w2, w2+9, noCase))...
```

Finally, there is a group of algorithms you can use to find minimum and maximum values:

```
template<typename Element>
  // Element is a model of LessThan Comparable
const Element& min(const Element&, const Element&);

template<typename Element>
  // Element is a model of LessThan Comparable
const Element& max(const Element&, const Element&);

template<typename Element, typename Predicate>
  // Element is a model of LessThan Comparable
  // Predicate is a model of a Boolean Binary Function
const Element& min(const Element&, const Element&, Predicate);

template<typename Element, typename Predicate>
  // Element is a model of LessThan Comparable
  // Predicate is a model of a Boolean Binary Function
const Element& max(const Element&, const Element&, Predicate);

template<typename Iterator>
  // Iterator is a model of Forward Iterator
Iterator min_element(Iterator first, Iterator last);

template<typename Iterator>
  // Iterator is a model of Forward Iterator
  // Predicate is a model of a Boolean Binary Function
Iterator min_element(Iterator first, Iterator last, Predicate);

template<typename Iterator>
  // Iterator is a model of Forward Iterator
Iterator max_element(Iterator first, Iterator last);

template<typename Iterator>
  // Iterator is a model of Forward Iterator
  // Predicate is a model of a Boolean Binary Function
Iterator max_element(Iterator first, Iterator last, Predicate);
```

8.6.2   Mutating Algorithms

Mutating algorithms may change the values pointed to by the iterators, but they do not change the *iterators*. By convention, algorithms with `copy` in the name do not modify the values pointed to by the iterators; instead, they modify a copy of the range defined by these iterators (the destination may overlap with the source, which is why these algorithms are, in general, mutating). All mutating algorithms assume that there is enough memory allocated for the destination range; if this is not the case, their behavior is undefined.

To copy the range `[first, last)` to the range starting at `result`, use this algorithm:

```
template<typename Iterator1, typename Iterator2>
  // Iterator1 is a model of Input Iterator
  // Iterator2 is a model of Output Iterator
Iterator2 copy(Iterator1 first, Iterator1 last, Iterator2 result);
```

There is a similar algorithm to copy the range `[first, last)`, starting from the element preceding `result` and moving backward:

```
template<typename Iterator1, typename Iterator2>
  // Iterator1 is a model of Bidirectional Iterator
  // Iterator2 is a model of Bidirectional Iterator
Iterator2 copy_backward(Iterator1 first, Iterator1 last,
  Iterator2 result);
```

For examples of these algorithms, see Section 8.4.

There is an algorithm for performing a swap:

```
template <typename Element>
  // Element is a model of Assignable
void swap(Element&, Element&)
```

You can use the next algorithm to swap all elements in the range `[first, last)` with the elements in the range starting at `where`:

```
template<typename Iterator1, typename Iterator2>
  // Iterator1 is a model of Forward Iterator
  // Iterator2 is a model of Forward Iterator
Iterator2 swap_ranges(Iterator1 first, Iterator1 last,
  Iterator2 where);
```

For example:

```
int y[4] = {0, 1, 4, 3};
swap_ranges(x, x+4, y);              // swap first 4 elements of x and y
```

The next two algorithms are similar to for_each, except they copy the result of each application of a functor to the output range:

```
template<typename Iterator1, typename Iterator2, typename Function>
  // Iterator1 is a model of Input Iterator
  // Iterator2 is a model of Output Iterator
  // Function is a model of a Unary Function
  // Apply foo to every element in the range [first, last)
  //  and store results in the range starting at where
Iterator2 transform(Iterator1 first, Iterator1 last,
  Iterator2 where, Function foo);

template<typename Iterator1, typename Iterator2,
     typename Iterator3, typename Function>
  // Iterator1 and Iterator2 are models of Input Iterator
  // Iterator3 is a model of Output Iterator
  // Function is a model of a Binary Function
  // Apply foo to elements of [first, last) and [first1, last1)
  //   and store results in the range starting at where
Iterator3 transform(Iterator1 first, Iterator1 last,
  Iterator2 first2, Iterator3 where, Function foo);
```

For example:

```
transform(x, x+2, x, negate<int>());                // negate first 2 elements of x

int z[N];
// store in z[0] and z[1] products of first 2 elements of x and y
transform(x, x+2, y, z, multiplies<int>());
```

The next two algorithms perform replacements. To replace each occurrence of the old value in the range [first, last) by a new value, you can use the replace algorithm:

```
template<typename Iterator, typename Element>
  // Iterator is a model of Forward Iterator
  // Element is a model of Assignable
void replace(Iterator first, Iterator last,
  const Element& oldValue, const Element& newValue);
```

To replace each occurrence of a value that satisfies a predicate, you can use the replace_if algorithm:

```
template<typename Iterator, typename Element, typename Predicate>
  // Iterator is a model of Forward Iterator
  // Element is a model of Assignable
  // Predicate is a model of a Boolean Binary Function
void replace_if(Iterator first, Iterator last, Predicate pred,
  const Element& newValue);
```

Additional versions of these two algorithms—replace_copy and replace_copy_if—copy the input range:

```
template<typename Iterator1, typename Iterator2, typename Element>
  // Iterator1 is a model of Input Iterator
  // Iterator2 is a model of Output Iterator
  // Element is a model of Assignable
void replace_copy(Iterator1 first, Iterator1 last, Iterator2 where,
  const Element& oldValue, const Element& newValue);

template<typename Iterator1, typename Iterator2,
      typename Predicate, typename Element>
  // Iterator1 is a model of Input Iterator
  // Iterator2 is a model of Output Iterator
  // Predicate is a model of a Boolean Binary Function
  // Element is a model of Assignable
void replace_copy_if(Iterator1 first, Iterator1 last, Iterator2 where,
      Predicate pred, const Element& newValue);
```

Here are some examples.

```
replace(x, x+5, 1, 2);                             // replace 1 by 2,
                                                   // in first 5 elements

replace_if(x, x+N, bind2nd(less<int>(), 0), 0);    // set to 0
                                                   // negative elements

replace_copy(x, x+N, y, -1, +1);                   // copy x to y
                                                   // replace -1 by +1

replace_copy_if(x, x+N, y, bind1(greater<int>, 10), 0);  // copy
                                                   // replacing elements
                                                   // greater than 10 by 0
```

The next group of algorithms is used for filling ranges of values. The first two algorithms fill the range with the same value:

```
template<typename Iterator, typename Element>
  // Iterator is a model of Forward Iterator
  // Element is a model of Assignable
void fill(Iterator first, Iterator last, const Element& value);

template<typename Iterator, typename Size, typename Element>
  // Iterator is a model of Output Iterator
  // Size is an integral data type
  // Element is a model of Assignable
  // Fill n values in the range starting at first
void fill_n(Iterator first, Size n, const Element& value);
```

The next two algorithms fill the range with the value generated by the provided functor:

```
template<typename Iterator, typename Function>
  // Iterator is a model of Forward Iterator
  // Function is a model of Unary Function
void generate(Iterator first, Iterator last, Function gen);

template<typename Iterator, typename Size, typename Function>
  // Iterator is a model of Output Iterator
  // Size is an integral data type
  // Function is a model of Unary Function
void generate_n(Iterator first, size num, Function gen);
```

For example:

```
fill(x, x+N, -1);        // set all elements to -1

generate(x, x+N, rand);  // set all elements to random values
                         // rand is function returning random numbers
```

It is also possible to use the generate algorithm to initialize containers using functors. For example, if you want to initialize an array with values 1, 2, ..., N, you can define the following functor:

```
class Sequence {
public:
  Sequence(int start) : value_(start) {}
```

```
   int operator()() { int v = value_; ++value_; return v; }
private:
   int value_;
};
```

and use it as follows:

```
generate_n(x, N, Sequence(1));
```

As a final example, here is the mutating version of `for_each` that doubles every element of an array:

```
for_each(x, x+N, bind2nd(multiplies<int>(), 2));
```

8.6.3 Sorting and Searching Algorithms

The algorithms presented in this section are used for sorting and searching through the elements of a type that is a model of the `Strict Weakly Comparable` concept. Recall that with this concept, it is the equivalence of rather than of the equality of the two elements that is important; therefore, the search algorithm will look for an element equivalent to the one specified as its parameter. Equivalence is defined by the standard `operator<()` or by a user-defined comparison function.

The first algorithm sorts the range using the ordering relation <; the second algorithm uses the function `comp` to compare:

```
template<typename Iterator>
   // Iterator is a model of Random Access Iterator
void sort(Iterator first, Iterator last);

template<typename Iterator, typename Function>
   // Iterator is a model of Random Access Iterator
   // Function is a model of Strict Weakly Comparable
void sort(Iterator first, Iterator last, Function comp);
```

The algorithm `is_sorted` checks if the range is sorted:

```
template<typename Iterator>
   // Iterator is a model of Forward Iterator
bool is_sorted(Iterator first, Iterator last);

template<typename Iterator, typename Function>
   // Iterator is a model of Forward Iterator
   // Function is a model of Strict Weakly Comparable
bool is_sorted(Iterator first, Iterator last, Function comp);
```

For example:

```
if(!is_sorted(x, x+N))
  sort(x, x+N);                           // sort in ascending order

if(!is_sorted(x, x+N, greater<int>()))
  sort(x, x+N, greater<int>());           // sort in descending order
```

A group of algorithms is defined for operating on sorted ranges. First look at binary search:

```
template<typename Iterator, typename Element>
  // Iterator is a model of Forward Iterator
  // Element is a model of Strict Weakly Comparable
bool binary_search(Iterator first, Iterator last,
      const Element& value);

template<typename Iterator, typename Element, typename Function>
  // Iterator is a model of Forward Iterator
  // Function is a model of Strict Weakly Comparable
  // Element is a model of Assignable
bool binary_search(Iterator first, Iterator last,
      const Element& value, Function comp);
```

You can use binary search as follows:

```
if(is_sorted(x, x+N) && binary_search(x, x+N, 0))     ...
                        // is 0 in array sorted in ascending order

if(is_sorted(x, x+N, greater<int>()) &&
   binary_search(x, x+N, 0, greater<int>()))     ...
                        // is 0 in array sorted in descending order
```

To merge two sorted ranges, you can use either of the two following algorithms:

```
template<typename Iterator1, typename Iterator2,
    typename Iterator3>
  // Iterator1 and Iterator2 are models of Input Iterator
  // Iterator3 is a model of Output Iterator
Iterator3 merge(Iterator1 first1, Iterator1 last1,
  Iterator2 first2, Iterator2 last2, Iterator3 where);

template<typename Iterator1, typename Iterator2,
    typename Iterator3, typename Function>
```

```
// Iterator1 and Iterator2 are models of Input Iterator
// Iterator3 is a model of Output Iterator
// Function is a model of Strict Weakly Comparable
Iterator3 merge(Iterator1 first1, Iterator1 last1,
   Iterator2 first2, Iterator2 last2, Iterator3 where, Function fun);
```

For example, you can sort two arrays and then merge them:

```
int y[N];
fill(y, y+N, rand);
sort(x, x+N);
sort(y, y+N);
int z[2*N];                    // needs that much memory
merge(x, x+N, y, y+N, z);      // merge x and y; store results in z
```

This section showed you the most important algorithms. In the next section, I will describe containers. First I will describe containers in general and talk about the operations that are common for all kinds of containers. Then, I will describe operations that are available only for specific containers.

8.7 Containers and Their Common Types and Operations

A **container** is a class whose objects hold a *homogeneous* collection of values; these values are other elements or objects, possibly of the same type as the container itself. As I mentioned in Section 8.3, there are various kinds of containers: sequence containers, such as vectors, lists, and deques; and associative containers, such as maps and sets. A *heterogeneous* collection is represented as a container storing pointers to a base class; I discuss this type of container in Section 9.10. In this section, I cover homogeneous collections; I call the type of each object in a collection ElementType.

When you *insert* an object into a container, you actually insert a copy of the object. Therefore, it is important that ElementType support a copy constructor that performs a sufficiently deep copying of object attributes. If you do want to have a single object shared by more than one collection, you can insert a pointer to this object into the container.

To *access* an object stored in a container, you do not remove it from the container; instead, you get a reference to the object (there is a separate operation designed to do a removal).

Standard containers available in STL use parameterized classes rather than classes with inheritance or delegation. Therefore, there is no common base class for all containers. However, all containers implement the standard container interface.

Table 8.2 Types common to all containers

Type name	Description
iterator	Type of an iterator (random access for vectors and deques, and bi-directional for other containers)
reverse_iterator	Type of an iterator to iterate in reverse order (random access for vectors and deques, and bidirectional for other containers)
const_iterator	Type of a constant iterator
const_reverse_iterator	Type of a constant reverse iterator
value_type	Type of a container element
difference_type	Signed integral type to represent a difference between two iterators
size_type	Unsigned integral type to represent non-negative values from difference_type
reference	Typically, value_type&, that is, reference to value_type
const_reference	Like reference but constant

This interface typically does not support I/O operations, because iterators can be used to refer to the elements in the containers and perform the required input or output operations.

Rather than presenting formal concepts for various kinds of containers (see Austern, 1999), I provide a more informal list of requirements for type parameters of container templates. First, as previously mentioned, to insert an element, this element's type must be a model of Assignable. Second, many container operations use some kind of an ordering relation, which must be a model of LessThan Comparable.

The types provided by each container are described in Table 8.2. In this table, a constant iterator is the one that does not modify the value to which it points.

It is often useful to use typedef to simplify iterator type names; for example:

```
typedef list<int>::iterator IntIter;
typedef vector<Integer>::const_iterator ConstVecIter;
```

It is a matter of personal taste whether or not you use typedef to simplify types of various sorts, so I do not formulate it as a programming guideline.

The operations available for all containers are listed in the Table 8.3. In this table, Container stands for vector, deque, list, set, map, multiset, or multimap.

Here are a few examples of the operations shown in Table 8.3:

```
vector<string> s;                       // empty vector of strings
... // initialize s

vector<string> s1(s);                   // copy of s
```

Table 8.3 Operations common to all containers

Signature	Use
Access to iterators	
`iterator begin()` `const iterator begin()`	Point to the first element
`iterator end()` `const iterator end()`	Point to the past-the-end value
`reverse_iterator rbegin()` `const iterator rbegin()`	Point to the first element of the reverse sequence
`reverse_iterator rend()` `const iterator rend()`	Point to the past-the-end value of the reverse sequence
Constructors	
`explicit Container()`	No-arg constructor to create empty `Container`
`Container(const Container &)`	Copy constructor
`~Container()`	Destructor to empty `Container` and then destroy it
`Container(iterator first,` `  iterator last)`	Create a `Container` by inserting the range in another container defined by input iterators `first` and `last`
Auxiliary size functions	
`size()`	Number of elements
`empty()`	Check if container is empty
`max_size()`	The size of the largest possible `Container`
`swap(Container&, Container&)`	Swap with another `Container`
Comparisons between two `Containers`	
`==, !=, <, <=, >, >=`	Two containers are equal if they have the same number of elements and contain the same elements in the same order; the last four operators are based on a lexicographical comparison
Assignments	
`operator=(const Container&)`	Copy existing `Container`

The constructor operating on ranges is useful, for example, to copy the range in one container to another container:

```
list<string> head(s.begin(), s.end());      // list with a copy of s

if(!s.empty())
  cout << s.size() << endl;

list<string> head1;
... // initialize head1
swap(head, head1);                          // swap two lists
```

Before looking at operations specific to various containers, I will present various kinds of iterators.

8.8   *Iterators, Part II*

In this section, I describe specific kinds of iterators: constant and mutable, reverse, iterator adapters and utilities, and I/O.

8.8.1   Constant and Mutable Iterators

Forward, bidirectional, and random access iterators may be

- Constant; `operator*()` behaves as a constant reference
- Mutable; `operator*()` behaves as a reference

The implementation of constant iterators does not allow for changing the values in the containers, but the programmer can modify these iterators. For the sake of generality, algorithms that do not modify containers should use constant iterators.

As I described in Table 8.2, all containers provide the type `iterator` and `const_iterator`. A conversion between these types is also provided to allow assignment of a nonconstant iterator to a constant iterator; for example:

```
bool isFirst(list<string> h, const string& s) {
                                    // is it first on the list
  list<string>::iterator i = h.begin();
                    // *i == s; <- can't use for a constant string
  if(i == h.end())
    return false;
  list<string>::constant_iterator ci = h.begin();      // conversion
  return *ci == s;
}
```

8.8.2   Reverse Iterators

All containers provide iterators to traverse over collections in reverse order. These iterators implement their operations backward. For example, incrementing a reverse iterator means going backward by one step, and decrementing means going forward by one step.

Consider the range

```
[first, last)
```

defined by two forward iterators, `first` and `last`. To traverse this range backward, you *convert forward iterators to reverse iterators* using a type described in Table 8.2:

```
container::reverse_iterator
```

This class has a constructor that takes a parameter of a forward iterator type; therefore, for the range [first, last), if you define

```
container::reverse_iterator rfirst(last);
container::reverse_iterator rlast(first);
```

you have the range

```
[rlast, rfirst)
```

which contains the same set of values as those in the range [first, last) but can be traversed backward (see Figure 8.5). Note that rfirst points to the element just before the element pointed to by last, and rlast points to the element just before first.

A few examples of reverse iterators will help clarify the concept. Here is a helper function to print out a value:

```
template <typename Element>
  // Element can be output
void output(Element t) {
  cout << t << endl;
}
```

Now consider a vector v, its iterator types, and some common operations:

```
vector<double> v;
... // initialize v

typedef vector<double>::iterator Diter;
typedef vector<double>::reverse_iterator RevDiter;

Diter first =                 // look for the first value greater than 7
  find_if(v.begin(), v.end(), bind2nd(greater<double>(), 7));
```

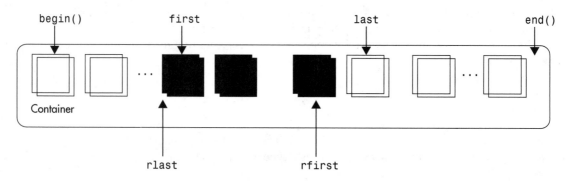

Figure 8.5 Range and reversed range

```
Diter last =                    // look for the first value greater than 17
   find_if(v.begin(), v.end(), bind2nd(greater<double>(), 7));

for_each(first, last, output<double>);          // print values between
                                                // 7 and 17 forward

RevDiter rfirst(last);                          // get reverse range
RevDiter rlast(first);

for_each(rfirst, rlast, output<double>);    // print the range backward
```

As I noted in Table 8.3, each container provides two functions:

- rbegin(), an iterator pointing to beyond the end of the container
- rend(), an iterator pointing to the element before the first element

It is possible to convert reverse iterators to forward iterators using the reverse iterator member function base(). For example, suppose you are looking for the last occurrence of an element in a vector and want to return a *forward* iterator to the place where it was found:

```
template<typename T>
vector<T>::iterator findLast(const vector<T>& v,
   const T& value) {
      vector<T>::reverse_iterator i = find(v.rbegin(), v.rend(), value);
      return i.base();
}
```

8.8.3   Iterator Adapters: Insert Iterators

When using standard iterators, you have to make sure that there is enough memory allocated to perform operations on the specified range. For example, the following code would result in a silent error that corrupts memory:

```
vector<int> v;                          // empty vector
int x[3] = {1, 2, 3};
copy(x, x+3, v.begin());                // no memory allocated for v
```

In some situations, you need an iterator to insert values. There are two iterator adapters, designed to *insert* rather than overwrite; both take a collection c as a parameter. This iterator adapter inserts at the front of container c in reverse order and is available for deques and lists:

```
front_inserter(c)
```

This iterator adapter inserts at the back of container c, preserving order, and is available for vectors, deques, and lists:

```
back_inserter(c)
```

One more general iterator inserts at position pos of container c, preserving order, and is available for all containers:

```
inserter(c, pos)
```

All insert iterators can appear on the left side of an assignment, for example, to insert a single element:

```
vector<string> vs;                              // empty vector
back_inserter(vs) = "C++";
```

Insert iterators are typically used with STL algorithms. For example, you can use the back_inserter iterator to fix the incorrect use of copy() from the beginning of this section and insert all elements of the array x into the vector v:

```
copy(x, x+3, back_inserter(v));         // preserve order; v ={1,2,3}
```

Similarly, to insert these elements into the list in reverse order, you can use the front_inserter iterator:

```
list<int> head;
copy(x, x+3, front_inserter(head));
```

As a final example, here is a general inserter:

```
list<string> vs;
inserter(vs, vs.begin()) = "Hello";
inserter(vs, vs.end()) = ", how are you";
// head = {Hello, how are you}

list<string> head;
copy(vs.begin(), vs.end(), inserter(head, head.begin()));  // copy vs
                                                           // to head
```

8.8.4   Iterator Utilities

Three functions can enhance your use of iterators (be sure to include <iterator>):

- advance(), to advance an iterator by an integral value:

```
<typename Iterator, typename Distance>
  // Iterator is a model of Input Iterator
void advance(Iterator& iter, Distance n);
```

- `distance()`, to find the distance between two iterators:

```
<typename Iterator, typename Distance>
  // Iterator is a model of Input Iterator
Distance distance(Iterator first, Iterator last);
```

- `iter_swap()`, to swap two iterator values:

```
<typename Iterator1, typename Iterator2>
  // Iterator1 and Iterator2 are models of Forward Iterator
void iter_swap(Iterator1 first, Iterator2 last);
```

For random access iterators, you can use +=, -=, or a difference between iterators instead of these functions.

8.8.5   Iterators and I/O

There are two kinds of iterators that perform I/O using the C++ stream I/O library:

- To perform input of an element of type T (`istream_iterator` is a model of Input Iterator):

```
istream_iterator<T>
```

- To perform output of an element of type T (`ostream_iterator` is a model of Output Iterator):

```
ostream_iterator<T>
```

The actual template definitions of both these iterators are more complicated (see Stroustrup, 1997), but the details are not essential to be able to use them. Both template classes have constructors that associate the iterator with the standard I/O streams cin and cout. For example, to perform I/O on strings, you can define the following two objects:

```
istream_iterator<string> input(cin);
ostream_iterator<string> output(cout);
```

There is an additional constructor for the latter class to output a delimiter after each value. For example:

```
ostream_iterator<string> output(cout, "\t"); // tab after each value
```

The two iterators described here are used just like any other I/O iterators; ++ is used to advance the iterator, and * is used to access the value pointed to by the iterator. For example, using the declarations just shown, you can read and write strings as follows:

```
string s = *input;              // read one string
*output = s;                    // write this string

++input;                        // get ready for another string
++output;
*output = *input;               // read and write another string
```

You can test for the end of input by using the *default* input iterator, for example:

```
istream_iterator<string>()
```

Usually, it is convenient to define a variable that represents the default input iterator. For example, the following defines a variable called eof:

```
istream_iterator<string> eof;
```

It is easy to copy the entire input stream to the output stream using the copy() algorithm:

```
copy(input, eof, output);
```

You can also read strings from the standard input and store them in a vector:

```
vector<string> v;
copy(istream_iterator<string>(cin), eof, back_inserter(v));
```

The code could have been written in a simpler way using the vector's constructor with two iterators:

```
vector<string> v(istream_iterator<string>(cin), eof);
```

To output all strings, each on a separate line, you can use again the copy() algorithm:

```
copy(v.begin(), v.end(), ostream_iterator<string>(cout, "\n"));
```

Here is how you can output all strings in reverse order:

```
copy(v.rbegin(), v.rend(), ostream_iterator<string>(cout, "\n"));
```

The input iterator can be moved using the `advance()` function (see Section 8.8.4). For example, consider a file `a.dat` that stores integer data:

```
3 4  6  7
8  6
-1
```

The following code finds the sum of every second integer value from this file:

```
ifstream inFile("a.dat");
if(!inFile) {
  cerr << "can't open " << endl;
  ...
}
int sum = 0;

istream_iterator<int> eof;
for(istream_iterator<int> i(inFile); i != eof; advance(i, 2))
  sum += *i;
```

8.9 *Sequence Operations*

Recall that a **sequence** is a collection of elements stored in linear order. There are three kinds of sequences: vectors, deques, and lists. The client of a sequence can

- Insert an element *before* the element pointed to by an iterator `iter`.
- Remove an element pointed to by an iterator `iter`.

Each sequence container provides the operations listed in Table 8.4. In the table, `Sequence` stands for either `vector`, `deque`, or `list`, and `T` stands for an element type. (Recall that a deque is a queue with operations at either end.) A default value of an element type `T` is the one available through a no-arg constructor `T()`.

In the examples that follow, I make use of these classes:

```
class Integer {
public:
  explicit Integer(int = -1);                 // no-arg constructor
  ...
};

class Double {
```

```
public:
  explicit Double(double);      // there is no no-arg constructor
  ...
};
```

Here are a few examples of operations that are common for all sequences:

```
deque<Double> d(10, Double(1.0));    // deque with 10 Double's, each 1.0

vector<Integer> v(10);               // vector with 10 Integer values; each -1
```

Table 8.4 Operations common to all sequences

Signature	Use
Constructor	
`explicit Sequence(size_type n,` `  const T& v = T())`	Create n copies of v. If the type T does not have a no-arg constructor, then use explicit call to the constructor.
Reconstruction	
`assign(first, last)`	Copy the range defined by input iterators `first` and `last`.
`assign(size_type n,` `  const T& v = T())`	Assign n copies of v.
Access	
`reference front()` `const reference front()`	Return first element. A `reference` type depends on the container; usually it is `T&`.
`reference back()` `const reference back()`	Return last element.
Insertions and deletions	
`iterator insert(iterator` `  p, T t)`	Insert a copy of t before the element pointed to by p and return the iterator pointing to the inserted copy.
`void insert(iterator p,` `  size_type n, T t)`	Insert n copies of t before p.

`void insert(iterator p,`
`  InputIterator i,`
`  InputIterator j)`
	Insert copies of elements from the range `[i,j)` before p.

`iterator erase(iterator p)`	Remove the element pointed to by p, return the iterator pointing to the next element if it exists; otherwise, `end()`.
`iterator erase(iterator i,` `  iterator j)`	Remove the range `[i,j)`, return the iterator pointing to the next element if it exists; otherwise, `end()`.
`clear()`	Remove all elements.

Note that the `assign()` function destroys the old contents of the sequence before inserting the new contents, and it allocates memory for the new contents; for example:

```
list<Integer> head1(10);
... // store some elements in head1

// create list head2 that has a copy of all elements from head1
list<Integer> head2(head1.begin(), head1.end());

//reinitialize all elements to Integer(2)
head2.assign(head2.size(), Integer(2));
```

You can access sequences using iterators; for example:

```
list<char> head;                                    // empty list

head.insert(head.end(), 'a');
head.insert(head.end(), 'b');                       // head has (a, b)

list<char> head1;                                   // empty list

head1.insert(head1.end(), head.begin(), head.end());    // copy head
                                                        // to head1

head.clear();                                       // empty list head

cout << head1.front();          // output the first element of head1

head1.erase(head1.begin());     // remove the first element of head1
```

The operations just shown are *undefined* if called with incorrect arguments (recall that an operation is called undefined if it compiles but its result is unpredictable); for example:

```
Sequence c;                                         // empty
... c.front()...                                    // undefined
```

There are several kinds of sequences. For the sake of efficiency, you should choose

- *Vectors* if
  - The number of elements does not vary widely over all executions of the program
  - There are random choice operations
  - Most insertions and removals are at the end of the container

- *Deques* if
  - There are frequent insertions and deletions at either end
  - There are random access operations

- *Lists* if
  - There are frequent insertions and deletions at positions other than at the end
  - There are few random access operations

Of course, sometimes there are conflicting requirements. For example, you may need to frequently insert and remove elements at positions other than at the end and also randomly access them. In such a situation, you can consider using profiling or switching between various representations at runtime using the bridge design pattern (see Section 6.6.1). Another very important consideration is the cost of executing a copy constructor, because the cost of performing a copy operation for large objects can be high.

8.9.1   Vectors

To use STL vectors, you must include `<vector>`. The vector template class represents a *resizable* array. Each vector has a **capacity**, which is the maximum number of elements it can currently contain, and a **size**, which is the current number of elements actually stored in the vector (see Figure 8.6). The capacity is initialized by the constructor and may be changed by the operations described in Table 8.5. The size is always less than or equal to the capacity. When you want to *insert* a new element and there is no more room—that is, the size is equal to the capacity—then the vector is resized. Care must be taken when using overwriting operations that do not resize vectors to avoid memory corruption.

All vector iterators are random access, and because the model for a random access iterator is the model for any other kind of iterator, all STL algorithms will work with vectors.

In addition to the operations available for all containers listed in Table 8.3 and sequence operations listed in Table 8.4, there are several additional operations available for `vector<T>` (see Table 8.5).

Remember that size and capacity are two different attributes (see Table 8.5), and note that `resize()` does not change the capacity of the vector. You can decrease the capacity by reinitializing the vector—for example, by using `assign()`. On the other hand, `reserve()` sets the capacity without resizing the vector. It is useful

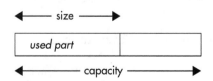

Figure 8.6   Size and capacity of vectors

Table 8.5   Vector operations

Signature	Use
Capacity	
`capacity()`	Return current capacity
`reserve(n)`	Allocate space for n elements
`resize(n, t = T())`	If n>size then add new n-size elements; otherwise, decrease size
Accessors	
`reference operator[]` `const reference operator[]`	Return element; unchecked access
`reference at() throw(out_of_range)` `const reference at() throw(out_of_range)`	Return element; checked access
Modifiers	
`push_back()`	Insert a new element at the end; expand vector if needed
`pop_back()`	Remove the last element; undefined if vector is empty

to preallocate a certain capacity to avoid expensive reallocations (each reallocation can result in two memory management operations: *allocating* a new larger block, copying of the old block into the new one, and then *deallocating* the memory allocated for the old block).

Here are some examples of vector operations:

```
vector<int> v;
v.reserve(100);                 // allocate space for 100 integers
                                // capacity 100, size 0

int i;
while(cin >> i)                 // read from the standard input
  v.push_back(i);               // will expand v if needed

for(i = 0; i < v.size(); ++i)   // output all using unchecked access
  cout << v[i] << endl;

try {                                   // use checked access
  cout << v.at(100);                    // will throw
} catch(std::out_of_range&) {
  cout << "doesn't have 100 elements" << endl;
}
```

```
for(int i = 0; i < v.size()/2.0; ++i)        // remove the second half
   v.pop_back();

vector<int> v1(v);                    // copy to v
v1.insert(v1.begin() + 1, 117);       // insert 117 after the first
```

● EXAMPLE 8.3

You can combine I/O operations with data filters. For example, assume that you
want to read even integer values, skipping odd values, and store the values in a vector; then you want to output all values divisible by 6. First, you need to define a vector
and I/O filters:

```
vector<int> v;
void filterIn(int i) {                    // input only even numbers
   if(i%2 == 0)
      v.push_back(i);                     // v is a global variable
}

void filterOut(int j) {           // output only numbers divisible by 6
   if(j%6 == 0)
      cout << j << endl;
}
```

Both functions must have a single integer parameter so that they can be called for
each data in the I/O stream. Therefore, the vector v in filterIn() could not be
passed as a parameter; instead, it is a global variable (later I will show an alternative solution).

   You can use these functions to read and filter input data, and then you can
write the data, again filtering data:

```
istream_iterator<int> i(cin);
istream_iterator eof<int>;

for_each(i, eof, filterIn);                  // read filtered data
for_each(v.begin(), v.end(), filterOut);     // write filtered data
```

You can also code the filterIn() function as a functor, with the vector as its
attribute. This allows you to avoid using a global variable:

```
class FilterVector {
public:
   void operator()(int i) {                             // input filter
      if(i%2 == 0)
```

```
      v_.push_back(i);
   }
   iterator begin() { return v_.begin(); }
   iterator end() { return v_.end(); }
private:
   vector<int> v_;
};

istream_iterator<int> i(cin);
FilterVector f;

f = for_each(i, eof, f);                    // read filtered data
for_each(f.begin(), f.end(), filterOut);
```

When for_each() is called with a functor, you need to save its return value, but when it is used with a function, you do not need to do so.

Insertions can result in reallocation of memory used for the vector. Not only is reallocation expensive in terms of time complexity, but it also can invalidate any iterators as well as any *references* to elements of the vector; for example:

```
vector<int> v(1);
int& r = v[0];
... // insert several elements causing reallocation
... // now, r may be invalid
```

Insertions and deletions that do not cause reallocation invalidate only those iterators and references that refer *to* or *after* the insertion point. You can avoid these problems if you know in advance how many elements are going to be inserted and use reserve() to allocate enough memory.

Vectors provide the following guarantees for time complexity of their operations:

- Constant time—that is, O(1)—random access to all elements, and insertions and deletions at the end of the vector
- Linear time—that is, O(n)—and insertions and deletions at other positions

8.9.2 Deques

To use deques, you must include <deque>. All deque iterators are random access. Recall that deques are lists that can operate on either end; in other words, they are "open-ended" in front and at the back. A deque is similar to a vector (see Table 8.5) but provides two additional operations to insert and remove elements in front of the deque (see Table 8.6).

Table 8.6 Deque operations (in addition to vector operations)

Operation	Use
push_front()	Add new first element
pop_front()	Remove the first element

Deques do not have a capacity; therefore, the functions capacity() and reserve() are not present. For deques, insertions and deletions may invalidate any references and iterators.

Deques provide the following guarantees for time complexity of their operations:

- Constant time—that is, O(1)—random access to all elements, and insertions and deletions at *either* end
- Linear time—that is, O(n)—and insertions and deletions at other positions

Therefore, as I pointed out earlier, deques should be used if there are frequent insertions and deletions at *either* end, and there are random access operations. On the other hand, you cannot preallocate deques to avoid future reallocations.

8.9.3 Lists

To use lists, you must include <list>. List operations include those supported by vectors (see Table 8.5) and those described in Table 8.7. Lists are optimized for insertions and deletions, and random access operations are not provided; in particular, there is no operator[].

All list iterators are *bidirectional* rather than random access. As a consequence, generic algorithms that require random access iterators—for example, sorting—cannot be used. This is why lists provide specialized member operations to perform some tasks that are accomplished by general algorithms for other containers.

Here I show a short code example in which ten integer values are inserted to a list, the largest value in the list is found, and then the list is spliced:

```
list<int> h;
int k;
for(int i = 0; i < 10; ++i) {
  cin >> k;
  h.insert(h.end(), k);
}

// find the largest element in h
list<int>::iterator m = h.begin();
for(list<int>::iterator j = m; j != h.end(); ++j)
  if(*m < *j)
    m = j;
```

Table 8.7 List operations

Operation	Use
Modifiers	
`push_front(t)`	Insert at back
`pop_front()`	Delete from front
Auxiliary (specialized for lists)	
`sort()`	Sort the list
`sort(cmp)`	Sort the list using the comparison `cmp`
`reverse()`	Reverse a list
`remove(const T& value)`	Use == to remove all elements equal to `v`
`remove_if(pred)`	Use the predicate `pred`
`unique()`	Remove consecutive duplicates using ==
`unique(pred)`	Use the predicate `pred`
`head.splice(i_head, head1)`	Move the contents of `head1` before iterator `i_head`, which must point to a position in `head`, and empty the list `head1`
`head.splice(i_head, head1, i_head1)`	Move the element pointed to by `i_head1`, which must point to a position in `head1`, before iterator `i_head`, which must point to a position in `head`
`head.splice(i_head, head1, i_head1, j_head1)`	Move the range `[i_head1, j_head1)`, which must be a valid range in `head1`, before iterator `i_head`, which must point to a position in `head`
`head.merge(head1)`	Merge two sorted lists into `head`, empty the list `head1`

```
list<int> h1;
// move the largest element and all elements that follow it
h1.splice(h1.end(), h, m, h.end());
```

● EXAMPLE 8.4

Consider a list of fractions from which you want to first eliminate all duplicates (for example, ¾ and ½) then simplify the fractions (for example, ⅜ should be simplified to ⅓), and finally to output the list sorted in ascending order. The following code uses STL lists to accomplish these three actions. First, you declare `Fraction` to be a pair of integers and the function `same()` to compare two fractions:

```
// File: ex8-3.cpp
typedef pair<int, int> Fraction;
```

```
bool same(const Fraction& one, const Fraction& two) {
  return one.first*two.second == one.second*two.first;
}
```

Next, you define a function to simplify fractions:

```
void simplify(Fraction& p) {
  // Use Euclid's algorithm to find gcd of p.first and p.second
  int gcd = abs(p.first);
  int b = abs(p.second);
  while(b) {
    int t = b;
    b = gcd % t;
    gcd = t;
  }
  p.first /= gcd;
  p.second /= gcd;
  if(p.second < 0) {
    p.second = -p.second;
    p.first = -p.first;
  }
}
```

Finally, you create a list, insert several fractions, eliminate duplicates, and simplify them. To insert fractions into the list, you use the function `make_pair()` defined in `<utility>`:

```
list<Fraction> h;
h.push_front(make_pair(1,2));
h.push_front(make_pair(4,2));
h.push_front(make_pair(1,2));
h.push_front(make_pair(4,2));
h.push_front(make_pair(6,3));
h.push_front(make_pair(3,2));
h.push_front(make_pair(24,4));
h.push_front(make_pair(12,15));
h.sort();
h.unique(same);                           // remove same fractions
for_each(h.begin(), h.end(), simplify);   // simplify each fraction
```

To output the list of remaining fractions, you need to define a helper function, because there is no predefined output for pairs:

```
ostream& operator<<(ostream& os, const Fraction& ip) {
  os << ip.first << "/" << ip.second << endl;
```

```
    return os;
}

ostream_iterator<Fraction> o(cout);
copy(h.begin(), h.end(), o);        // output all remaining fractions
```

Insertions into lists do *not* invalidate any references and iterators; deletions invalidate only those iterators that point to the element being deleted.

Lists provide the following guarantees for time complexity of their operations:

- Linear time—that is, $O(n)$—random access to all elements, and insertions and deletions at the end of the list
- Constant time—that is, $O(1)$—insertions and deletions at other positions

8.9.4 Container Adapters: Stacks, Queues, and Priority Queues

Container adapters use the adapter design pattern to change the interface. There are three container classes: stacks, queues, and priority queues. A priority queue is like a list except that the interface of the priority queue is limited to the operations specific to the class.

To use stacks, you must include `<stack>`. A stack is a container that supports the familiar stack operations (that follow the last-in, first-out policy):

```
void push(t)
void pop()
T& top()
bool empty()
size_type size()
```

A stack is defined as a container that, by default, uses deques:

```
template <typename T, typename Container = dequeue<T> >
class stack;
```

Therefore, to instantiate a stack, it is enough to provide the type of a stack's element:

```
stack<int> t;
```

For an example of a program that uses a stack, see Section 1.9.

To use queues and priority queues, you must include `<queue>`. A *queue* is a container that supports the following operations (that follow the first-in, first-out policy):

```
T& front()
const T& front()
```

```
T& back()
const T& back()
bool empty()
size_type size()
void push(const T& t)                        // insert at back
void pop()                                   // delete from front
```

A *priority queue* is a container that supports the following operations (recall that a priority queue comes with an ordering operation that defines a priority; this operation is used to find the element with the *highest* priority):

```
void push(const T& t)                                      // insert
void pop()              // remove the element with the highest priority
const T& top()         // return the element with the highest priority
bool empty()
size_type size()
```

A priority queue is defined as a container that, by default, uses vectors, and the priority is based on the `less` predicate:

```
template <typename T, typename Container = vector<T>,
  typename Compare = less<typename Container::value_type> >
class priority_queue;
```

Therefore, if you define

```
priority_queue<int> i;
```

then the largest element has the highest priority.

You can also instantiate a priority queue providing the priority relation, for example, so that the smallest element has the highest priority:

```
priority_queue<int, vector<int>, greater<int> > p;
```

Next, consider the application of priority queues to a time-shared system, with processes that have ID's and priorities. Processes are selected based on their priorities, and so you need an `operation<()` function in the class `Process`:

```
struct Process {
  int id;
  int priority;
  Process(int i, int p) : id(i), priority(p) {}
  bool operator<(const Process& r) const {
    return priority < r.priority;
  }
};
```

```
priority_queue<Process> waiting;
// simulate the execution of a process
Process p(100, 2);

waiting.push(p);                              // insert p

p = waiting.top();                            // get the top one
cout << p.id;                                 // output its id
waiting.pop();                                // remove from the queue
p.priority -= 1;                              // update priority
waiting.push(p);                              // re-insert
```

This completes the discussion of sequences; I now go on to discuss associative containers.

8.10 *Associative Containers: Sets, Maps, Multisets, and Multimaps*

To use sets and multisets, you must include <set>; to use maps and multimaps, you need to include <map>. Associative containers are used for representing *sorted collections;* therefore, they must have keys and be sorted on these keys (internally, associative containers are usually stored as balanced binary trees, and this sorting is transparent to the user).

A **map** is a good starting point for a description of associative iterators. The reason for the name *map* is that there is a mapping from keys to values. A map stores pairs in the form (key, value), with the constraint that there may be at most one pair with the *same* key. For example, if a key is an integer ID and a value is a string name, a map can consist of the pairs (123, "Smith") and (124, "Kowalski") but not the pairs: (123, "Smith") and (123, "Kowalski").

A **multimap** can have more than one pair with the same key; for example, it can consist of (123, "Smith") and (123, "Kowalski").

A **set** is a map for which the key and the value are identical; therefore, it stores single elements rather than pairs. For example, a set can consist of (123, 124). A **multiset**, sometimes called a *bag,* is like a set except the same element may occur more than once. For example, a multiset can consist of (123, 123, 124).

You may find it surprising that all associative containers are sorted—in particular, that a set is sorted—because in mathematics, sets do not come with the ordering relation. However, all STL containers must be stored efficiently, so associative containers need to be sorted. The most important concept for an associative container is that of a **key** of Key type; all elements in the containers are stored sorted by the value of the key. To compare elements, associative containers use a binary predicate less<Key>, which compares two Key elements using Key::operator<. The less predicate also determines the meaning of two keys being equivalent; more precisely, two keys of an associative container are equivalent if neither is less than the other. Recall the discussion of the Strict Weakly Comparable concept 8.5, and the example of a phone book with entries containing first and last names and phone numbers. If two entries are ordered by their last names—that is, the predicate less considers only last names—then two entries with identical last names are not necessarily equal, but they are equivalent.

You can define your own comparison predicate as long as it is a model of the Strict Weakly Comparable concept. For example, if you use strings as keys and you use *case-insensitive* string comparison, then strings that are the same but differ in case are considered equivalent. Note that this predicate defines a less-than comparison, and you are not required to define other comparisons, such as greater than, because they are derived from less than. In general, you can provide a comparison predicate either at compile time as a template parameter or at runtime as a constructor parameter. In the former case, the comparison is used for all objects of the template instantiation; in the latter case, you may have different objects that use different comparisons.

Since associative containers are sorted collections, there are no operations available to modify values in these collections (otherwise, they may not be sorted anymore). For the same reason, you can insert an element, but you cannot insert at a specific position. Therefore, all associative container iterators are designed in a way that makes it impossible to modify the value of the key. In particular, this means that set and map iterators are constant. For multisets and multimaps, iterators allow modification of collection values but not keys. All these cases are handled at compile time; for example, it is a compile-time error to modify the value of the key. As a result of these assumptions, you cannot apply mutating algorithms that modify collections to associative containers.

In addition, all associative container iterators are bidirectional rather than random access. In particular, you cannot forward these iterators by arbitrary steps or subtract two iterators to find the distance between them.

Sets and multisets are defined as template classes; for example:

```
template<typename Key, typename Compare = less<Key> >
class set;
```

As you can see from this definition, the first type parameter is mandatory and defines the key. The second type parameter is optional; by default, it uses the less predicate specialized for keys. It can also be defined by the user if another comparison is required.

Maps and multimaps are also defined as template classes; for example:

```
template<typename key, typename T, typename Compare = less<Key> >
class map;
```

In addition to providing the types and operations available for all sequences (see Table 8.4), each associative container provides the types and operations listed in Table 8.8. (AssocContainer stands for any associative container).

Table 8.8 Associative container types and operations

Type or Signature	Use
Types	
`value_type`	Type of each element
`key_type`	The same as `Key`
`key_compare`	The same as `Compare`
`value_compare`	The same as `key_compare` for sets and multisets; for maps and multimaps, compare `pair<Key, T>`
Constructors	
`AssocContainer()`	Empty container; with `Compare()`, used to compare
`AssocContainer(const Comparison& c)`	Container with a specialized comparison `c`
`AssocContainer(i, j)`	Container initially containing the range `[i, j]`
`AssocContainer(i, j, c)`	Container initially containing the range `[i, j]`, with a specialized comparison `c`
Accessors	
`iterator find(key)` `const_iterator find(key)`	Find the element with `key` and return an iterator pointing to this element
`iterator lower_bound(key)` `const_iterator lower_bound(key)`	Return the iterator to the first element with `key`
`iterator upper_bound(key)` `const_iterator upper_bound(key)`	Return the iterator to the element with key greater than `key`
`pair<iterator, iterator>` `equal_range(key)` `pair<const_iterator,const_iterator>` `equal_range(key)`	Return the pair of iterators; respectively, pointing to the first and to the last element equal to `key`
`size_t count(key)`	Return the number of elements with the key
Insertions and deletions	
`pair<iterator, bool> insert(t)`	Insert element t; return a pair (iterator to the element, success status); may fail for sets and maps
`void insert(i, j)`	Insert the range `[i, j]`
`void erase(pos)`	Erase element pointed to by `pos`
`size_t erase(key)`	Erase element equal to `key`
`void erase(i, j)`	Erase range `[i, j]`

The following examples show the use of sets and multisets:

```
set<double> sd;                         // sorted by less<double>

typedef set<double, greater<double> > Dset;
                                        // Comparison fixed at compile time

Dset ds1;                               // sorted by greater<double>

set<double, greater<double> > s;        // Comparison fixed at run time

fill(s.begin(), s.end(), 0);            // can't use mutating algorithms

s.insert(0);                            // insert 0 to s
s.insert(0);                            // correct, but does nothing

vector<int> v;

generate_n(back_inserter(v), 10, rand);    // store ten random value

s.insert(v.begin(), v.end());                   // copy to the set

multiset<double> ms(v.begin(), v.end());        // copy to multiset

if(s.find(5) != s.end())        // find if 5 is in a set; if so erase it
  s.erase(5);

int i = ms.count(5);            // find how many times 5 is in a multiset
cout << "5 found" << i << " times" << endl;

typedef multiset<double>::iterator MI;
pair<MI, MI> res = ms.equal_range(5);      // two iterators pointing to 5
ms.erase(res.first, res.second);           // erase the range
```

All set and map iterators are bidirectional, and all access and insert and delete operations have logarithmic time complexity.

For a map, the key and element can be of different data types. Recall its definition:

```
template<typename Key, typename T, typename Compare = less<Key> >
class map;
```

For a map<Key,MappedType>, value_type is the same as pair<Key, Mapped-Type> (the same is true for multimaps); for example:

```
map<string, double> salaries;
```

```
                    // map from string to doubles
                    // sorted by the default predicate less<string>

map<string, double, greater<string> > salaries1;
                              // map from string to doubles
                              // sorted by greater<string>
```

To access an element of a map, you can use an overloaded index operator:

`operator[](key)` , access the element with `key`

However, this operator can only be used if `MappedType` has a no-arg constructor; for example:

```
salaries1["John"] = 10000;
salaries1["Mary"] = 20000;
```

This operator cannot be used for multimaps; for example:

```
multimap<string, string> mm;
mm["color"] = "blue";                    // error, mm is a multimap
```

Instead, you have to use `insert()`:

```
mm.insert("color", "blue");
mm.insert("color", "green");
```

All operations for associative containers (see Table 8.8) can be applied to maps. When you iterate over maps and multimaps, you actually iterate over sequences of pairs; for example:

```
for(salaries1::iterator i = salaries1.begin(); i != salaries1.end();
    ++i)
  cout << "name:" << i->first << " salary:" << i->second << endl;
```

If you use `operator[]`, with a key which is not in a map, the pair consisting of the key and the default value, constructed using a no-arg constructor for the value, is inserted into the map; for example:

```
cout << salaries1["007"];                    // inserts ("007", 0);
```

Therefore, you should use `find()` before such an operation:

```
if(salaries1.find("007") == salaries1.end())          // not in map
  ...
```

Suppose you have a file `b.dat` containing some names and salaries (there may be duplicate names), and you want to read this file and output the salaries of people recorded in the file. First, you declare several auxiliary types:

```
typedef pair<string, double> STR_D;
typedef istream_iterator<STR_D> Input;
typedef multimap<string, double>::const_iterator MI;
```

To input pairs consisting of a string and a double, you need to declare a helper operator function that overloads the input `operator>>()`:

```
istream& operator>>(istream& os, STR_D& ip) {
  os >> ip.first;
  os >> ip.second;
  return os;
}
```

Now, you can write the code that reads data from the file and looks for names and salaries:

```
multimap<string, double> store;
ifstream ifs("b.dat");
Input eof;

for(Input i(ifs); i != eof; ++i)                    // store file in multimap
  store.insert(*i);

while(1) {
  cout << "enter name ";
  string name;
  if(!(cin >> name))
    break;

  pair<MI, MI> found = store.equal_range(name); // is name in multimap
  if(found.first == found.second)
    cout << "No " << name << " found" << endl;
  else {
    cout << "Name: " << name << endl;          // output all occurrences
    for(MI p = found.first; p != found.second; ++p)
      cout << p->second << endl;
  }
}
```

Following are two more examples of maps.

● EXAMPLE 8.5

This example shows a simplified version of Java's `Property` class (the example does not deal with Java's *default* property lists):

```
// File: ex8.5.property.cpp
typedef pair<string, string> STR;

// auxiliary I/O for pairs of strings
ostream& operator<<(ostream& os, const STR& ip) {
  os << ip.first << " " << ip.second << endl;
  return os;
}

istream& operator>>(istream& os, STR& ip) {
  os >> ip.first;
  os >> ip.second;
  return os;
}

// class representing a property
class Property {
public:
  // canonical construction
  Property();
  Property(const Property&);
  Property& operator=(const Property&);
  ~Property();

  // additional members
  bool getProperty(const string&, string&) const;   // get value
  void addProperty(const string&, const string&);   //add new property

  bool list(const string&) const;                   // output
  bool load(const string&);                         // input

  typedef map<string, string>::const_iterator MI;
private:
  map<string, string> property_;
};

bool Property::getProperty(const string& name, string& value) const {
  MI i = property_.find(name);
  if(i == property_.end())
    return false;
```

```
    value = i->second;
    return true;
}


void Property::addProperty(const string& s, const string& t) {
  property_[s] = t;
}

bool Property::load(const string& fname) {
    ifstream ifs(fname.c_str());
    if(!ifs)
      return false;

    istream_iterator<STR> eof;
    for(istream_iterator<STR> i(ifs); i != eof; ++i) {
      STR aux = *i;
      property_[aux.first] = aux.second;
    }
    return true;
}

bool Property::list(const string& fname) const {
    ofstream ofs(fname.c_str());
    if(!ofs)
      return false;

    ostream_iterator<STR> o(ofs);
    copy(property_.begin(), property_.end(), o);
    return true;
}
```

Here is a simple application of this class, in which the property file is specified on the command line. The user can search for properties in this file and save one additional property in another file:

```
int main(int argc, char** argv) {
  if(argc != 2) {
    cerr << "usage: " << argv[0] << " filename" << endl;
    return 1;
  }
  Property p;
  if(!p.load(argv[1])) {
    cerr << "can't load " << argv[1] << endl;
    return 2;
  }
```

```
  string name;
  string value;
  while(1) {
    cout << "enter name (. to finish) " << endl;
    cin >> name;
    if(name == ".")
      break;
    if(p.getProperty(name, value))
      cout << value << endl;
     else cout << "not found " << endl;
  }
  p.add(string("zz"), string("bb"));
  if(!p.list("junk.dat"))
    cout << "list failed" << endl;
}
```

● EXAMPLE 8.6

Recall the interface AttributedIfc for using attributes from Example 6.3. The following example shows an implementation of this interface that additionally provides iterators:

```
// File: ex8.6.attr.cpp
class AttributedImp : public AttributedIfc {  // implements
public:
  virtual void add(const Attr&);
  virtual bool find(const string& name, Attr&) const;
  virtual bool remove(const string& name, Attr&);

  typedef pair<string, Attr> PAIR;
  typedef map<string, Attr>::iterator ITER;           //mutable
  typedef map<string, Attr>::const_iterator C_ITER;    //constant

  ITER begin();
  ITER end();
private:
  map<string, Attr> impl_;
};

void AttributedImp::add(const Attr& a) {
  impl_[a.getName()] = a;
}
```

```
bool AttributedImp::find(const string& name, Attr& a) const {
  C_ITER i = impl_.find(name);              // needs a constant iterator
  if(i == impl_.end())
    return false;
  a = i->second;
  return true;
}

bool AttributedImp::remove(const string& name, Attr& a) {
  ITER i = impl_.find(name);                // needs a mutable iterator
  if(i == impl_.end())
    return false;
  a = i->second;
  impl_.erase(i);
  return true;
}

AttributedImp::ITER AttributedImp::begin() {
  return impl_.begin();
}

AttributedImp::ITER AttributedImp::end() {
  return impl_.end();
}
```

To iterate over the list of attributes, the user can proceed as follows:

```
AttributedIfc* at = new AttributedImpl;
for(AttributedIfc::ITER i = at->begin(); i != at->end(); ++i)
  cout << "attribute name " << i->first << end;
```

In a similar way, the iteration capability can be added to the class `Registrar-WithAttributes`.

8.11 *STL and Error Handling*

STL does not perform extensive checking for logical errors because the standard components are assumed to be heavily used, and error checking would result in decreased performance. Aside from the `at()` operation for vectors and deques, STL operations do not throw exceptions. Therefore, you have to be very careful when coding with STL. In the future, when compiler and system designers decide that additional error checking does not adversely affect performance, there may be a safe version of STL available. In the meantime, you can use one of the publicly available versions (see Appendix H) and add your own error checking as appropriate.

A different question is what happens when an exception is thrown by a function called by an STL operation. (For example, an STL algorithm may call a constructor that throws an exception.) Simply allowing the execution to proceed could leave a container in an ill-defined state, although in an ideal world, a full rollback would be performed (using database terminology, such an operation is referred to as a **safe transaction**; it either succeeds or has no effect whatsoever). For the sake of efficiency, STL makes this guarantee only in some cases and always based on the assumption that user-defined destructors never throw exceptions (see "Common Errors" in Section 3.4.2). STL always gives a basic guarantee that there will be no memory leaks and that the basic container invariants will be maintained. In addition, for lists, sets, maps, multisets, and multimaps, all operations that insert a *single* element are safe transactions (they either succeed or have no effect; in the latter case, a rollback is performed). For more details, see Josuttis (2000).

8.12   *Reference Counting and STL Containers*

The smart pointer class presented in Section 7.8.2 can be used with STL, for example, to implement reference counting by sharing objects stored in various collections. Recall the previously defined class Point:

```
// File: ch7.point.h
class Point {
public:
  Point(double = 0, double = 0);
  virtual ~Point();
  double getX() const;
  double getY() const;
  void setX(double);
  void setY(double);
private:
  double x_;
  double y_;
};
```

Here is the previously defined handle class:

```
// File: ch7.smartpointer.h
template <typename Body>
  // Template requirements for Body: None
class Handle {
public:
  explicit Handle(Body* = 0);
```

```
  Handle(const Handle&);
  ~Handle();
  Handle& operator=(const Handle&);
  Body* operator->();
  Body& operator*();
private:
  Body* bridge_;
  int* counter_;
};
```

Assume that you want to store points in a vector and in a list but that identical points are shared:

```
typedef Handle<Point> Hpoint;

void show(const Hpoint& h) {                              // output point
  cout << h->getX() << " " << h->getY() << endl;
}

vector<Hpoint> v;
list<Hpoint> h;

// insert two points to both the vector and the list
Hpoint p(new Point(1, 2));
v.push_back(p);
h.push_front(p);

Hpoint q(new Point(1, 3));
v.push_back(q);
h.push_front(q);

// output all points
show(v[0]); show(v[1]);
show(h.front()); show(h.back());

// modify
v[0]->setX(3);
h.back()->setY(5);

// output the vector and the list again
show(v[0]); show(v[1]);
show(h.front()); show(h.back());
```

8.13 *Exercises*

For all the exercises in this chapter, whenever possible, you should use the STL containers and algorithms. When an exercise calls for the creation of a namespace, you should design it carefully and split it into files available to the client and to the implementation. For each exercise, include a program that tests your code.

EXERCISE 8-1

Implement a class, `Employee`, that represents an employee with three attributes: name, salary, and ID. ID numbers for new employees are assigned values 1000, 1001, and so on. Carefully design the interface for this class. Then write the following classes:

- `Company1`, which represents a company that can hire up to ten employees
- `Company2`, which represents a company that can hire up to *n* employees, where the value of *n* is determined in the constructor

Both companies should be stored in abstract collections. Provide three implementations of these collections, using STL lists, vectors, and deques.

EXERCISE 8-2

Reimplement Exercise 5-7 using an STL `stack`.

EXERCISE 8-3

Reimplement Exercise 5-8 using an STL `stack`.

EXERCISE 8-4

Implement a class, `SafeStack`, that is derived from the STL class `stack` and uses exception handling.

EXERCISE 8-5

Implement a class, `SafeList`, that is derived from the STL class `list` and uses exception handling.

EXERCISE 8-6

Reimplement Exercise 6-5 using the STL class `list`.

EXERCISE 8-7

Reimplement Exercise 6-6 using the STL classes `stack` and `list`.

EXERCISE 8-8

Reimplement Exercise 6-8 using the STL classes `vector` and `list`.

EXERCISE 8-9

Implement a class, `Point`, that represents a point in a three-dimensional space. Carefully design the interface for this class, and include functions that appear to be useful for operating on points. Then use this class and the STL class `list` to write a class representing a list of points.

EXERCISE 8-10

Consider students taking courses. There is a many-to-many relationship between courses and students, because each student can take many courses and each course can be taken by many students. Implement a class, `Registrar`, whose interface includes at least the following operations:

- Insert or delete a student
- Insert or delete a student from a specific course
- Find out if a student is taking a specific course
- Find all courses taken by a specific student
- Find all students taking a specific course

EXERCISE 8-11

Implement a generic `BubbleSort` algorithm with the following signature:

```
template <typename Iterator>
void BubbleSort (Iterator first, Iterator last);
```

EXERCISE 8-12

Implement a predicate, with the Boolean function `operator()(const string&)`, that returns true if all characters in the string are in lowercase. Then, use this predicate to write a program that has a filename passed on the command line, and that outputs the number of words in the file that are in lowercase.

EXERCISE 8-13

Adapt the interface provided by the STL class list to implement the class `Another List` that has at least the following interface (x represents an element, p a position obtained using an iterator):

- `void insert(x, p)` to insert x at position p
- `iterator find(x)` to return a position of x (beyond the last value if not found)
- `void retrieve(p, &x)` to return through x an element at position p
- `void remove(p)` to remove the element at position p
- `clear()` to remove all elements from the list
- `iterator first()` to return a position of the first element
- `print()` to print the entire list
- Iterator functions (decide yourself what is needed)

Then write a helper function `purge(AnotherList& h)`, that removes duplicate elements from the list h. Use a namespace and exception handling.

EXERCISE 8-14

Implement a template function, `concatenate()`, that uses the STL `list` class and returns a list that is a concatenation of a list of lists passed as a parameter.

EXERCISE 8-15

Implement a template class, `Tree`, that represents *n*ary trees (that is, trees in which the nodes can have any number of children). Use a list-of-children representation (see Aho, Hopcroft, and Ullman, 1983) and the STL `list` class. Then use the STL stack class to write a nonrecursive function to perform a preorder traversal.

EXERCISE 8-16

Complete the code given in Example 4.3.

Chapter **9**

MISCELLANEOUS TOPICS

9.1 *Preview*

This chapter describes the following miscellaneous topics:

- Description of the I/O used in STL
- Separate compilation and linkage
- Generic pointers and pointers to functions
- Overloaded memory management
- General debugging and error-handling techniques
- `typeid` used for RTTI
- Multiple inheritance
- Pointers to members as well as member function adapters
- Heterogeneous containers
- Two more design patterns: composite and visitor

9.2 *Input/Output Library*

In Section 2.4.6, I briefly described basic I/O operations. In this section, I provide more details on these operations.

9.2.1 Common Input/Output Operations

C++ and Java I/O classes are designed quite differently; the **stream**, which is a sequence of characters, is the only shared concept. This section covers only the most important classes and operations. The complete *design* of the I/O library is rather complicated and is not discussed in this book; for details see Stroustrup (1997) or Josuttis (2000).

There are three kinds of I/O:

- Interactive I/O (described in this section and the next two sections)
- File I/O (described in Section 9.2.4)
- Stream I/O (described in Section 9.2.5)

To use interactive I/O, you need to include `<iostream>`. The three important classes used with this kind of I/O are

- `ios_base`, the common base for two classes described later in this section
- `istream` for input
- `ostream` for output

These classes are designed for streams of bytes (elements of type `char`). In addition, there are complementary classes and streams of *wide* characters (elements of type `wchar_t`). These classes and streams have the prefix w—for example, `wcin` for the wide input stream. You can use wide characters to represent Unicode or any other characters that require more than one byte (for details, see Lipmann and Lajoie 1998).

The class `ios_base` is actually a template class with two specializations:

- `ios`, a specialization for characters
- `wios`, a specialization for wide characters

Although I use the class `ios_base` here, some compilers may not support this class; for example, earlier versions of GNU g++ use the class `ios` instead of `ios_base`.

9.2.2   Output Operations

To output data, you use an overloaded `>>` operation. To output a single character, you can also use the member operation `put()`, as in `cout.put('a')`.

Output formatting is done through the so-called **format state**, which is operated on by objects called **manipulators**. Once a manipulator modifies the state of a stream, the state typically stays modified (with the notable exception of `setw`); this is why manipulators often come in pairs that toggle between the modified and unmodified state. Manipulators may be sent to the output stream; the examples shown in Table 9.1 include the most important ones. To use a manipulator that has a parameter, you need to include `<iomanip>`. There are also manipulators that are members, as described at the end of this section.

Examples of applications of these manipulators are shown in Table 9.2 (b stands for a blank character).

In addition to manipulators, you can use several stream *member functions* to format output; for example:

- `cout.width(i)`, to set the width to `i`, return the previous width
- `cout.precision(i)`, to set the precision to `i`, return the previous precision

Table 9.1 Most important manipulators

Signature	Use
flush	Flush the output buffer
endl	Send end-of-line, and then flush
dec	Display integers in base 10 (default)
hex	Display integers in base 16
oct	Display integers in base 8
showbase	Show prefix indicating numeric base
noshowbase	Hide prefix indicating numeric base
fixed	Display floats and doubles in fixed-point format (default)
scientific	Display floats and doubles in floating-point format
setprecision(i)	Set the total number of digits in a real value (by default 6)
showpoint	Display decimal point
noshowpoint	Display decimal point only when there is a fraction
showpos	Display + for non-negative numbers
noshowpos	Hide + for non-negative numbers (default)
setw(i)	Specify field width (does not modify the state of the stream)
setfill(c)	Specify fill character be c (by default, it is whitespace)
left	Specify left justification
right	Specify right justification (default)

Table 9.2 Applications of manipulators

Call	Output	Comment
cout << setw(5) << left << 12;	12bbb	12 left justified in a field of width 5
cout << setw(5) << showpos << setfill('0') << left << 12;	+0012	setfill adds leading 0s and +s
cout << setw(5) << setprecision(2) << 12.787;	bbb13	Precision is the *total* number of digits
cout << setw(10) << setprecision(2) << 12.787;	bbbbb12.79	
cout << hex << 12;	c	Converts to hexadecimal; to add leading 0 or
cout << showbase << hex << 12;	0xc	0x, use showbase
cout << 12.9876543;	12.9877	Default precision is 6
cout << scientific << 12.9876543;	1.298765e+001	Scientific notation

9.2.3 Input Operations

By default, the input operator >> skips whitespace characters. You can use the following manipulators: To modify the default, you can use `noskipws`, and to reset the default, you use `skipws`.

For example:

```
char c, d;
cin >> noskipws >> c >> d;
cout << c << d << endl;
```

For input consisting of a space and the characters x followed by y, the output is a space followed by x (without the `noskipws`, it would be the character x followed by y).

The member operation `cin.get(ch)` can be used to read a single character into its argument `ch`. This function does not skip whitespace, and it returns the input stream (and so can be chained):

```
cin.get(c).cin.get(d);                      // read two characters
```

To read an entire line, you can use the function `cin.getline()`. Unfortunately, this function requires a C-style string:

```
getline(char* buffer, streamsize size, char delimiter = '\n');
```

There is a related function `cin.gcount()` that returns the number of characters read with the most recent `get()` or `getline()`; for example:

```
char b[100];
cin.getline(b, 100);
cout << "read " << cin.gcount() << " characters" << endl;
```

Instead of using this version of `getline()`, it is better to use a stand-alone function that works with a string:

```
getline(istream&, string str&, char delimiter = '\n');
```

To perform I/O, you may wish to push back a character you have just read or peek at the current character without actually reading it. There are several input stream member functions that support this functionality:

```
cin.putback(ch);  // push back ch
cin.unget();      // unget last character read
c = cin.peek();   // return the next character, leave it in the input
```

For example:

```
char c;
cin >> c;
if(c == '/' && cin.peek() == '*')                    // start of comment
  ...
```

In place of `getline()`, you can use `ignore()` when you do not want to store the characters read but simply get to the next delimiter, such as a new line:

```
cin.ignore(s, delim); // ignore up to s characters or when delim is read
```

To recognize **end-of-file** and **error conditions**, you use the operation

```
cin >> var
```

which attempts to read a value of the type of the variable `var`. If it fails, it returns a value that is convertible to Boolean, and it changes the state of the input stream to an error state:

```
int i;
cin >> i;

if(cin) {                       // successful
  ...
} else {                        // failed, input is in the error state
  ...
}
```

`cin` returns false when an end-of-file has been reached or the input operation has failed. In either case, subsequent I/O operations will not be performed, unless the error state is *cleared* using `cin.clear()`.

The following four flags define the state of a stream:

- `ios_base::badbit`
- `ios_base::eofbit`
- `ios_base::failbit`
- `ios_base::goodbit`

The stream may be either in a good state or in an error state. There are several member functions that help you to deal with error states (note that these functions work both with interactive input and with files that are opened for input or input/output):

- `clear()`   Reset a stream to a *good* state
- `clear(ios_base::iostate io)`   Reset a stream to a state `io`

- eof()   Return true if end-of-file has been encoun-
                                          tered (see Example 9.1)
- bad()   Return true if the stream is in error state
- fail()   Return true if the previous operation failed
- good()   Return true if the stream is in a good state
- setstate(statebit)   Reset a particular state bit
- ios_base::iostate rdstate()   Return the current state

In most cases, eof() and fail() are all you need to use.

● EXAMPLE 9.1

This example includes code that reads integer values until the end-of-file or a non-integer value is encountered, and then outputs the sum of the read values:

```cpp
// File: ex9.1.cpp
int sum = 0;
int i;
bool ok = true;

while(1) {
  cin >> i;
  if(cin.eof())
    break;
  if(cin.fail()) {
    ok = false;
    break;
  }
  sum += i;
}
cout << (ok ? "" : "non-integer value encountered\n") <<
  " sum = " << sum << endl;
```

9.2.4   File Streams

To perform I/O operations on files you have to include <fstream>. There are two predefined file streams:

- ifstream, the input stream
- ofstream, the output stream

Once a file is opened, you can use the familiar operations << and >>. Both file-stream classes have constructors that take C-style string parameters representing filenames; for example:

```
ifstream inp("input.dat");
ofstream out("output.dat");
```

There are additional constructors of `ifstream` and `ofstream` that allow the programmer to specify how the file will open. This is done through the second parameter of the constructor, for which the following specifications are available:

`ios_base::in`	Open file for input. The file must exist (default for input).
`ios_base::out`	Open file for output. If the file exists, it will be overwritten; otherwise, a new file will be created (default for output).
`ios_base::ate`	Open file and move to the end.
`ios_base::app`	Open file for output. Whether or not the file exists, writing will *append* to this file.
`ios_base::trunc`	Open file and truncate it.
`ios_base::binary`	Open file for binary mode.

Two or more specifications may be combined using a bitwise *or*—that is, |; for example:

```
// open "io.dat" for input and output
ofstream fVar("io.dat", ios_base::in | ios_base::out);
```

When you use a file variable, as in this example, the constructor opens the file, and the file is automatically closed when the file variable goes out of scope and its destructor is executed. You can also explicitly open and close files using two member functions:

- `void open(const char* filename, openmode m);`
                         `// mm is one of the above specifications`
- `void close()`

Random access files are supported through functions that specify the offset relative to the *mode*, specified as one of the following three constants:

- `ios_base::cur`, the curent position
- `ios_base::beg`, from the beginning of the file
- `ios_base::end`, from the end of the file

In addition, the data type `ios_base::pos_type` is used for values that represent positions in the file.

A number of functions are available that allow the programmer to get and manipulate the current file position. In the following examples, the suffix g, which stands for *get,* is used for the input streams; the suffix p, which stands for *put,* is used for the output streams:

`seekg(ios_base::pos_type pos)`	Move to position `pos`
`seekg(ios_base::pos_type offset, mode)`	Move to position `offset` relative to `mode`

`ios_base::pos_type tellg()`	Return current position
`seekp(ios_base::pos_type offset, mode)`	Move to position `offset` relative to `mode`
`seekp(ios_base::pos_type offset, mode)`	Move to position `offset` relative to `mode`
`ios_base::pos_type tellp()`	Return current position

Here's an example of an application of the seek functions:

```
// find the size of file "a.dat"
ifstream f("a.dat");
f.seekg(0, ios_base::end);                          // move to the end
long size = f.tellg();

// replace in b.dat every occurrence of \t with a blank
stream g("b.dat", ios_base::in | ios_base::out);
f(!g) {
 cerr << "fail to find b.dat" << endl;
 return 1;
}
char ch;
while(g.get(ch)) {
 if(ch == '\t') {                                   // replace
   g.seekg(-1, ios_base::cur);
   g.put(' ');
 }
}
```

Remember that if an input operation falls into an error state, the program must clear this state before attempting any other input. In particular, if a program reads some file until it encounters the end-of-file and then wants to use `seekp()` to rewind to the beginning of the file, it must use `f.clear()` to clear the error state before rereading the file (the error state is set when the end-of-file is read).

9.2.5 String Streams

You can perform I/O operations on strings by including `<sstream>`. There are two predefined string streams:

- `istringstream`, the input stream
- `ostringstream`, the output stream

To write to a string stream, you use the familiar `<<` operator; for example:

```
ostringstream os;
os << "C++ " << "is my favorite language";
```

To retrieve the string from the string output stream, you use the `ostringstream` member function `str()`:

```
string s = os.str();
```

To read from a string stream, you use the `>>` operator; for example, the following code outputs each word from the string `s` on a separate line:

```
istringstream is(s);
string w;
while(is >> w)
  cout << w;
```

9.3 *Separate Compilation and Linkage*

A file is a unit of compilation, and typically, a program consists of several compilation units that can be separately compiled and then *linked* together to form executable code. Exactly one compilation unit must contain the `main()` function. This function must not appear in a namespace.

Various program *entities* may have the same identifier. When creating executable code, the linker must determine whether various occurrences of an identifier refer to the same entity or several different entities. To make this determination, the linker uses the information generated by the compiler. Specifically, the compiler associates various attributes with each name, one of which is the type of linkage performed for the identifier. There are two linkage types:

- **Internal linkage**, for which the name is accessible *only* in the compilation unit that defines the name
- **External linkage**, for which the name is accessible in compilation units *other* than the one which defines the name

In this section, I describe how these linkage types are assigned to entities, and then I explain how the linker uses them. The language defines various default rules that specify the type of linkage and the keyword `extern`, which can be used to change the default rules.

The default rules are

- Entities declared at the outermost level have external linkage.
- `const` identifiers, types defined by `typedef`, `class`, `struct` and `enum` types, and named namespaces have internal linkage. Similarly, members of an unnamed namespace (see Section 4.6.4) have internal linkage.

The `extern` keyword changes the linkage of entities to external and specifies that the definition of an entity will appear elsewhere, for example:

```
extern int i;      // i is defined in another file; can be used here
extern const j;    // j is defined in another file; can be used here
```

```
void f() {
  int if;
  static int sif;
  extern int eif;  // defined in another file
}
```

These constructs, in particular the use of extern, are very rarely needed in the object-oriented programs written in C++ because, typically, global variables are not used.

The process of dividing a program into multiple files and then separately compiling and linking them introduces a unique source of errors. In the context of a single file, the compiler can carefully check that every used identifier is defined and its use is consistent with its definition. For an external declaration of an identifier occurring in a separately compiled file, the compiler is not able to check that the identifier has been defined. It is the linker's responsibility to find matching definitions of all external identifiers. Error messages produced by the linker are usually quite easy to understand. For example, the message

```
undefined symbol  xxx
```

means that one file declares an identifier xxx but that no file being linked contains its definition. Unfortunately, linkers do not carry out foolproof error checking. It is possible to have a declaration and a matching definition that have conflicting data types. For example, if file a.c defines

```
int i;
```

and file b.c declares

```
extern long i;
```

the linker will likely not generate an error or even a warning about the fact that the variable i has two types, but the program's behavior will be undefined. Similarly, the linker may not recognize that a function is *defined* more than once. For example, if file a.c defines

```
int f() { ... }
```

and file b.c defines

```
double f() { ... }
```

the linker, instead of generating a warning, might arbitrarily choose one of the functions. This can lead to a great deal of confusion because you expect one function to be executed and a different one is actually used. As a result, code with inconsistent definitions of the same function should be treated as an error and avoided at all costs.

Note that inline functions must have identical definitions for *all* compilation units in which they are called. This is the case if these functions are not only declared but also defined in the header files.

9.3.1 Header Files

The main goal of using header files is to make function declarations available in such a way that various clients get consistent declarations and avoid duplicating declarations. The header files should never contain *definitions* of functions or variables (with the exception of inline functions). Also, they should not contain definitions of unnamed namespaces. The header file may contain *declarations* of any names that have internal linkage, including `const` identifiers; types defined by `typedef`, `class`, `struct`, and `enum`; inline functions; named namespaces; and template declarations and definitions.

C++ follows the **one definition rule (ODR)**, which states that a class or a template must have a unique definition. Consider two implementation files that require a single class definition—for example, a class called `Common`. If you place the definition of `Common` in a header file that is included in both implementation files, when the files are linked, there seem to be two definitions of the same class, seemingly in violation of ODR. However, the rule is not really violated because two definitions of a class are considered to be identical, provided they are *token-for-token identical*, which is obviously the case for this example.

ODR should also be used for members of namespaces, which should be declared in the header file and defined in the implementation file. Consider the example of the `Resource` namespace, and assume that for some unlikely reason, you do not want to hide the variable `value_` from the client. To accomplish this, the header file will have the following code:

```
namespace Resource {
// File: Resource.h
  int value();
  void value(int);
  extern int value_;                     // to declare you need extern
}
```

And the implementation file will have

```
namespace Resource {
// File: Resource.cpp
  int value_;                            // to define you do not use extern
  ... // definitions of value() functions
}
```

9.4 *Generic Pointers and Pointers to Functions*

C++ inherited various constructs related to pointers from C, such as pointer arithmetic. However, according to Stroustrup (1997), pointer arithmetic should *not* be used in C++ programs; therefore, I do not describe it in this book. In this section, I briefly describe two other pointer-related constructs, which are sometimes useful: generic pointers and pointers to functions.

9.4.1 Generic Pointers

Consider an application in which you want to have a reference to *any* kind of object. In Java, programmers would use a variable of type `Object` and would use the cast or `instanceOf` operator to work with the actual type of object this reference points to. C++ has a special pointer type, called a **generic pointer type**, that is declared using `void*` and can safely be converted to any other pointer type; for example, the following code defines a generic pointer p.

```
void *p;
```

Generic pointers are *typeless,* they cannot be dereferenced unless a cast indicating the type is used:

```
void* p;
... // initialize p
char* c = reinterpret_cast<char*>(p);
```

In general, generic pointers are useful mainly for low-level system programming.

9.4.2 Pointers to Functions

You can declare **pointers to functions**. The syntax of the declaration of a pointer to a function is:

```
returnType (*ptrName)(parameters);
```

For example, for

```
int (*fp)(void);
```

`fp` is a pointer to an integer function that has no parameters (the brackets around `*fp` are necessary; `int *fp()` would be a function returning a pointer to `int`).

A pointer to a function determines the prototype of the function but does not specify its implementation. You can assign an existing function to the pointer as long as both have identical parameter lists and return types. For example:

```
int (*fp)(void);       // pointer to int function with no parameters

double* (*gp)(int);            // pointer to a function that returns a
                               // pointer to double; this function has
                               // one int parameter

int f(void);            // function f() defined elsewhere

double* g(int);         // function g() defined elsewhere

fp = f;
gp = g;
```

You can call the function f() through the pointer fp and the function g() through the pointer gp:

```
int i = fp();
double* d = gp(i);
```

Pointers to functions may be used to pass **functions as parameters** to other functions. To do so, the formal parameter is explicitly specified as a pointer to a function. For example, suppose you want to write the function tabulate(), which has a function, say f(), as one of its parameters. The tabulate() function tabulates the values of f() within the specified range and the provided step. You can define tabulate() as follows:

```
void tabulate(double low, double high, double step,
     double (*f)(double)) {
  double x;
  for(x = low; x <= high; x += step)
    cout << x << ' ' << f(x) << endl;
}
```

The following code shows the tabulation of a functions $x^2 - 2$:

```
double pol(double x) {
   return x*x - 2;
}

tabulate(-1.0, 1.0, 0.01, pol);
```

9.5 *Overloading Memory Management (Advanced)*

In this section, I describe an advanced topic: the implementation of per-class memory management. While you may never end up writing this kind of the code, it is still useful to read this section because it shows the application of various programming techniques.

Standard memory management is provided through the functions declared in <new>. There are four basic functions: two manage memory for a single object:

```
void* operator new(size_t) throw (std::bad_alloc);
void operator delete(void*) throw();        // does not throw anything
```

Two functions manage memory for arrays of objects:

```
void* operator new[](size_t) throw(std::bad_alloc);
void operator delete[](void*) throw();
```

I do not discuss the last two functions here because they operate on arrays, which are less commonly used than vectors. For reasons of upward compatibility with previous implementations, there are four more memory management functions that do not throw exceptions and instead return 0; I also do not cover these here. For a complete description, see Stroustrup (1997).

For the class Student, call

```
new Student
```

is translated to

```
::operator new(sizeof(Student))                      // use global new
```

in which sizeof is a predefined compile-time operator that returns the size (in bytes) of its argument; recall that new invokes the class constructor. It is also possible to write a class-specific version of new to make the translation be as follows:

```
Student::operator new(sizeof(Student))
```

You may want to write this implementation to speed up memory management, because for some applications, it is much faster to manage your own heap rather than use the general heap. For example, your heap may consist of blocks of a fixed size, while the general heap has to deal with blocks of variable sizes and may suffer from fragmentation.

Your implementation should follow the general philosophy adopted by the global new. Recall that if new fails, it checks whether the global memory handler has been installed, and if so, it calls it; otherwise, it throws a `bad_alloc` exception. The following list summarizes the rules that you should follow when implementing your own memory management (this discussion is based on Meyers, 1998):

- Overloaded `new` and `delete` must be static operations.
- If you overload `new`, you should also overload `delete`. In addition, your class should have a static operation to set a new handler and a static attribute to store the current handler
- Design `operator new` to perform the following steps:
  1 Install the current handler as a global handler.
  2 If memory can be allocated, do so and return.
  3 If memory cannot be allocated and the current handler is not zero the handler will execute.
  4 If memory cannot be allocated and the current handler is zero, `bad_alloc` will be thrown and should be caught to restore the global handler.
- To overload `delete`, declare it as follows:

```
void operator delete(void*, size_t) throw()
```

Make sure you include a virtual destructor in the class; otherwise, `delete` will not work for its subclasses.

In the code that follows, I show a relatively simple way of defining class-specific memory management by allocating a chunk of memory using the global `new`, dividing it into a linked list, and then using the list to provide memory for the class objects. The design is broken into two classes: the client `Integer` class and the actual memory management class `MemoryPool` (for details, see Meyers, 1998). For the sake of simplicity, I use the example of a wrapper for integers, with the very basic interface:

```
typedef void (*HTYPE)();
class MemoryPool;
class Integer {                                    // integer wrapper
public:
  Integer(int = 0);
  int get() const;
  Integer& set(int);
  Integer& add(const Integer&);
  static void* operator new(size_t) throw (std::bad_alloc);
  static void operator delete(void*, size_t) throw();
  virtual ~Integer();
  static HTYPE set_new_handler(HTYPE);
private:
  int value_;
  static MemoryPool& memory_();
  static HTYPE& currentHandler_();
};
```

To avoid initialization problems, the two private functions are used according to the static nonlocal variable idiom. Specifically, each function has a local static variable and returns a reference to it:

```
MemoryPool& Integer::memory_() {
  static MemoryPool memory(sizeof(Integer));
  return memory;
}

HTYPE& Integer::currentHandler_() {
  static HTYPE currentHandler = 0;
  return currentHandler;
}
```

The implementation of the memory management functions is simple because it is delegated to the MemoryPool class:

```
void* Integer::operator new(size_t st) throw (std::bad_alloc) {
  return memory_().allocate(st, currentHandler_());
}

void Integer::operator delete(void* p, size_t st) throw () {
  memory_().free(p, st);
}

HTYPE Integer::set_new_handler(HTYPE h) {
  HTYPE old = currentHandler_();
  currentHandler_() = h;
  return old;
}
```

The implementation of set_new_handler() follows the standard method for initializing new handlers; also, it returns the old handler.

The client of the MemoryPool class uses it as follows:

```
void myHandler() {
  cerr << "oops\n";
  abort();
}

Integer::set_new_handler(myHandler);

Integer* p = new Integer(4);    // calls: Integer::operator new()
delete p;                       // calls: Integer::operator delete()

Integer::set_new_handler(0);        // no handler
```

```
try {
   p = new Integer(5);
} catch (std::bad_alloc&) {
   ...
}
```

Now look at the declaration of the memory management class:

```
class MemoryPool {
public:
  MemoryPool(size_t);
  void* allocate(size_t, HTYPE) throw(std::bad_alloc);
  void free(void*, size_t) throw();
private:
  static int const SIZE_;
  static int const CHUNKS_;
  size_t size_;
  void* free_;
  struct LowLevel {
    void* next_;
    void* initFree_();
    void deleteFreeFirst_();
    void insertFree_(void*);
  };
};
```

Memory is allocated in chunks. Each chunk consists of a number of memory blocks that are the same size, defined by the value of size_. The static constant SIZE_ specifies the size of a memory chunk, and it is initialized in the implementation file as follows:

```
const int MemoryPool::SIZE_ = 512;
```

The total number of memory chunks is determined by another static constant:

```
const int MemoryPool::CHUNKS_ = 100;
```

Whenever allocate() is asked to provide a block of memory, it gets it from the current chunk of memory; if this chunk is all used up, a new chunk is allocated. Therefore, up to SIZE_*CHUNKS_*size_ bytes can be allocated; if more memory is requested, then allocate() fails.

The two remaining private variables are used to maintain a free list in the memory chunk allocated by allocate(), and both are initialized in the constructor:

```
MemoryPool::MemoryPool(size_t st) {
  free_ = 0;
```

```
    size_ = st;
}
```

The functions `initFree_()`, `deleteFreeFirst_()`, and `insertFree_()` hide the
low-level implementation details; specifically, the operations on `void*` pointers are
hidden. These functions are not shown here.

The function `allocate()` allocates a large chunk of memory that is maintained
as a linked list, called the free list. We use lazy evaluation and allocate memory *only*
when it is requested for the first time:

```
void* MemoryPool::allocate(size_t st, HTYPE handler)
            throw (std::bad_alloc) {

  if(st != size_)
    throw std::bad_alloc();

  void* p = free_;
  if(p != 0) {                 // memory available on free list
    deleteFreeFirst_();      // remove this block from the free list
    return p;
  }

  // run out of memory, use the handler or exceptions
  if(handler == 0)
    throw std::bad_alloc();
  else {
    handler();
    // now, what? if the handler hasn't aborted, we shouldn't
    return 0;
  }
  // create a new list
  // first, make sure our handler is used
  HTYPE old = std::set_new_handler(handler);
  // use global allocation
  try {
    free_ = ::operator new(SIZE*st);
  } catch(std::bad_alloc&) {       // need to reinstall the old handler
    std::set_new_handler(old);
    throw;                      // rethrow bad_alloc
  }
  // if here, successful so restore the old handler
  std::set_new_handler(old);
  // create a free list, return the first element
  p = initFree_();
```

```
    return p;
}
```

This code is relatively complicated because it emulates the standard behavior of `new`. If the code fails, it tries to run the user-defined handler, but if the handler has not been installed, then `new` throws `std:bad_alloc`. Note that if the user-defined handler is installed and called, the control should not return to `allocate()`. For this code, I chose to return `0`; another solution would be to call `abort()`. More than one chunk of memory may be allocated, such as when the chunk that is currently used is empty. Here is the implementation of `free()`:

```
void MemoryPool::free(void* p, size_t st) throw() {
  if(p == 0)
    return;
  if(st != size_)
    ::operator delete(p);
  insertFree_(p);
}
```

The careful reader has probably noticed that the class `MemoryPool` has no destructor; indeed, chunks of memory are never deallocated (in this book, I do not describe how to deal with this problem; see Stroustrup, 1997).

9.6   *Debugging and Handling Errors*

In this section, I discuss several techniques for error handling. The general area of debugging and testing object-oriented systems is beyond the scope of this book; for details see Binder, (2000).

9.6.1   Debugging Techniques

Debugging often involves adding output statements or extra checks to verify that the program behaves correctly. The additional code is usually present only in the **testing version** and removed in the **production version**, although some crucial checks may be left even in the production version. Rather than removing the debugging and testing code by hand, you can use one of two techniques that automatically perform this task. The first technique, based on preprocessing and using conditional compilation, is described in the next section. The second technique is based on the fact that compilers exclude dead code, as in:

```
bool check = false;
if(check) {
```

```
    ... // dead code
  }
```

which causes a compiler to skip the entire if statement. In testing mode, check would be set to true. The disadvantage of this technique is that you are forced to modify the actual code.

9.6.2   Conditional Compilation

Conditional compilation, which is used for include guards (see Section 2.8.1), is also useful for debugging. C++ has two basic kinds of conditional compilation. One resembles the syntax of an if statement:

```
#if constantExpression1
    part1
#elif constantExpression2
    part2
#else
    part3
#endif
```

There may be any number of #elif parts, which, along with the else part, can be omitted. If the value of the constantExpression1 is true (nonzero), the text making up part1 of the file is included. If the value of the constantExpression2 is true (nonzero), the text making up part2 is included. Otherwise, part3 is included.

The second kind of conditional compilation is used to test whether a macro has been defined:

```
#ifdef macroName
    part1
#else
    part2
#endif
```

Here, part1 is included if macroName has been defined; otherwise, part2 is included. A similar command exists, which is the logical negation of #ifdef:

```
#ifndef macroName
    part1
#else
    part2
#endif
```

Finally, the `defined` operator can be used only in `#if` and `#elif` expressions. `defined(name)` evaluates to 1 if its parameter is defined; otherwise it evaluates to 0; for example:

```
#if defined(__STDC__)
   ...
#endif
```

You can use the predefined `#error` command to produce a compile time error message that includes `textMessage`:

```
#error textMessage
```

For example:

```
#if defined(IBM)
#error "can't use it"
#endif
```

During program development, it is often convenient to *exclude* portions of the code. The best way of doing so is by using an `#if #endif` syntax:

```
#if 0
   part to be excluded
#endif
```

A program typically has two versions: the *testing* version and the *production* version. In the testing version, the debugging information is produced; no such output should be produced in the production version. You can have both versions in the same source file and use a macro to make the compiler toggle between them. To implement this technique, you create a macro name—say, `DEB`—that when defined, turns debugging on and when undefined, turns it off:

```
#define DEB                            // empty, but defined

#ifdef DEB
   ... // some debugging statement, for example
   cout << "value of i =" << i << endl;
#endif
```

One way to turn debugging off and on is to edit the source file. A better way is to use the compiler command line. Many compilers allow the user to define or undefine a macro on the command line used to compile the program; for example, under Unix, the command

```
g++ -UDEB filename
```

undefines the macro `DEB` when `filename` is compiled, whereas

```
g++ -DDEB filename
```

defines the macro.

9.6.3   Assertions

To test and debug a program, you can use **assertions**, which are Boolean expressions defining conditions that should never fail. Because of the runtime cost associated with evaluating assertions, most of them are typically turned on in the testing version and turned off in the production version. C++ supports assertions by supplying the standard library `<cassert>`, which provides the macro

```
assert(int e)
```

This macro is used to print a message, and it calls `abort()` to stop program execution if a precondition `e` is not satisfied. In the context of this function, a precondition is represented by the argument of `assert()`; for example, for `assert(i>=0)`, the precondition is `i>=0`. To offer the programmer the choice of toggling between using and not using `assert()`, this function is used together with a macro called `NDEBUG`; when this macro is defined, `assert()` does nothing. If `NDEBUG` is *not* defined *and* the actual parameter of `assert()` evaluates to `0`, then the name of the source file and the number of the line on which `assert()` appears is displayed, and the execution of the program is aborted by calling `abort()`.

Assertions are often used to express conditions associated with operations and classes:

- A **precondition** for an operation is an assertion that must hold for the operation to be performed, and it should be checked by the caller; for example:

  ```
  assert(i >= 0);                 // precondition to computing the sqrt(i)
  d = sqrt(i);
  ```

- A **postcondition** for an operation is an assertion that describes the program state after this operation was performed. This assertion is implementation dependent; the postcondition is checked within the definition and holds if an implementation is correct. Here is an example:

```
int maxi(int x, int y, int z) {  // return the largest of three values
  int max;
  ... // the implementation, before return
  assert(max >= x && max >= y && max >= z);
  return max;
}
```

- An **invariant** is an assertion for a class that must always hold for every object of the class. Therefore, for each operation in the class, a complete precondition for the operation is a conjunction of the precondition for the operation and the class invariant. The same must be true for postconditions of class operations.

Exception handling and assertions do have different uses. When you use an assertion, the program always terminates when the assertion fails; when you use an exception, you can catch it and try to continue program execution. On the other hand, you can turn off an assertion but not an exception. Therefore, assertions are usually useful in the testing version, but in the production version, exception handling and possible recovery are more acceptable than simply aborting the execution. Instead of using `assert`, you can use exception handling:

```
if(!assertion)
  throw exception;
```

Following Stroustrup (1997), you can use template functions that take an exception class and an assertion as template parameters:

```
// a version for no-arg constructor for Exception
template<typename Assertion, typename Exception>
inline void Assert(Assertion e) {
  if(!a)
    throw Exception();
}

// a version for constructor with arguments for Exception
template<typename Assertion, typename Exception>
inline void Assert(Assertion a, Exception e) {
  if(!a)
    throw e;
}
```

For example, you can use the exception class `logic_error` to check a postcondition in the function `maxi()` as follows:

```
int maxi(int x, int y, int z) {
  // return the largest of three values
```

```
    int max;
    if(x>=y && x>=z) max = x;
    if(y>=x && y>=z) max = y;
    if(z>=x && z>=y) max = x;                         // wrong assignment
    Assert(max >= x && max >= y && max >= z,
           logic_error("maxi failed"));
    return max;
}
```

Note that this implementation of maxi() is logically incorrect. Now, let's look at the application of this function:

```
try{
  cout << maxi(1,2,3) << endl;
} catch(logic_error& e) {
  cout << e.what() << endl;
}
```

When the code is executed, the logic_error exception is thrown and produces the following output:

```
maxi failed
```

Checking class invariants is more involved because it should be performed both when entering an operation and, for an operation that modifies the state of the object, before exiting the operation. For example, consider a class Editor, which is an implementation of a list editor that stores lines of text in an array of a fixed size. The current and the maximum number of lines are maintained by variables current_ and maxUsed_, respectively. Assume that the Editor class has a nested exception class that looks like this:

```
class Editor::WrongLine : public logic_error {
public:
  WrongLine(long);                          // offending line number
  ...
private:
  long number_;
};
```

You can add a function that tests the invariant to the class Editor:

```
void Editor::inv() {
  Assert<(0 <= current_ && current_ <= maxUsed_,
    Editor::WrongLine(current_));
  }
```

The code for the editor functions, such as `insert()`, looks like this:

```
void insert(const string& s) {
  inv();
  ... // insert s
  inv();
}
```

This technique is not quite satisfactory because you cannot turn it off. This problem can be easily fixed by adding conditional compilation:

```
inline void Editor::inv() {
#ifndef NDEBUG
  Assert(0 <= current_ && current_ <= maxUsed_,
    Editor::WrongLine(current_));
#endif
}
```

If the macro `NDEBUG` is defined, there is no cost involved in calling `inv()`. The compiler can determine that the body of this function is empty and eliminate the call.

9.6.4   Program Termination

Usually, a program terminates when `main()` terminates, but a program can terminate rather than crash for a number of other reasons, including an exception that has been thrown but *not handled* or a call to one of two functions defined in `<cstdlib>`: `exit()` and `abort()`. For normal or abnormal termination, you can use `return` in the main function, or `exit()` in any other function. The `exit(n)` function returns the value of `n` to the environment. Using these functions can make it difficult to properly deallocate resources. Specifically, `abort()` does not invoke any destructors, and `exit()` invokes destructors for static objects but not for local objects of the calling function.

   If an exception is thrown and is *not handled,* the function `terminate()`, defined in the `std` namespace, is called. By default, this function calls `abort()`. Note that the default action of `terminate()` can be changed by installing the required handler (see the next section). When a program terminates because of an uncaught exception, it may or may not call destructors. Therefore, if it is essential to perform any cleanup actions, you should add the appropriate handlers to the main function:

```
int main() {
  ...
}
catch(whetever) {
  ...
}
```

```
catch( . . .) {                        // catch all remaining exceptions
  . . . // cleanup
}
```

This handler does not catch exceptions thrown when global variables are being constructed or destructed.

9.6.5 Setting Error Handlers

There are several functions that, by default, terminate the execution of the entire program, but their behavior can be modified by installing **error handlers** (these handlers should not be confused with exception handlers in the `catch` statements). In general, error handlers are functions with a signature that is best defined as follows:

```
typedef void (*HTYPE)();
```

Here `HTYPE` is a synonym for a parameterless procedure.
  Error handlers can be installed to modify the default behavior of

- `new` when it fails
- a call to `unexpected()`, because an unexpected exception is thrown (that is, an exception not listed in the function declaration)
- a call to `terminate()`

To set up an error handler for each of these cases, you use, respectively

- `HTYPE set_new_handler(HTYPE)`, which is defined in `<new>`
- `HTYPE set_unexpected(HTYPE)`
- `HTYPE set_terminate(HTYPE)`

Each of these functions returns the previously defined `HTYPE` handler and installs the handler passed as a parameter. By default, the current handler is 0. For example, to modify the behavior of the `new` handler, you can use

```
void myHandler() {
  cerr << "out of memory\n";
}

HTYPE old;
old = set_new_handler(myHandler);       // save old handler
                                        // and install new handler
. . . new . . .
set_new_handler(old);                   // restore old handler
```

If `new` fails, you get the message `out of memory`; regardless of whether or not this happens, the previous error handler will be reinstalled. If the user-defined handler is not installed—that is, the current handler is 0—then `new` throws `bad_alloc`.

Functions installed as handlers for `terminate()` and `unexpected()` should not return program control to the caller.

9.6.6   Exception Handling and Specifications

The most important purpose behind exception handling is to separate the detection of errors and the handling of them. In principle, C++ supports the same model as Java: It uses a **termination model** of exception handling, which means that, in general, the execution never returns to the point where an exception is thrown. Of course, you can always try to restart by looping around the `try` block. In this section, I continue the topic of exception handling that I introduced in sections 3.3 and 5.13.

Handling and throwing exceptions resemble declaring and calling functions. You should be careful when passing a handler parameter representing an exception by value, because if the exception handler has a parameter of the base class, and the throw statement creates an object of a derived class, then the latter object will be *sliced*. Therefore, in general it is better to use constant pass by reference.

As I mentioned in Section 3.3, a function may or may not specify exceptions in its signature. However, if it does specify exceptions in its *declaration*, it must repeat the same specification in its *definition*.

Like Java, C++ supports polymorphism by allowing a function to throw exceptions that are extensions of the type given in the exception specification; for example:

```
void foo() throw(std:runtime_error) {
  ...
  throw std::range_error("derived exception");
  ...
}
```

Unlike Java, C++ detects violations of a function's exception specifications only at runtime. If the function throws an exception that is *not* specified, the `unexpected()` function is called. By default, this function calls `terminate()`.

For example, consider the following function that throws an unexpected exception:

```
int add(int, int) throw(Overflow) {
  ...
  throw Underflow();
}
```

The call to this function calls `unexpected()`, which in turn calls `terminate()`. If you add `bad_exception` to the list of exceptions that may be thrown, as in

```
int add(int, int) throw(Overflow, std::bad_exception) {
  ...
  throw Underflow();
}
```

then the throw Underflow() statement results in throwing std::bad_exception
and does not call terminate(). For example, consider the following code:

```
void h() {                          // handler for unexpected
  cout << "unexpected" << endl;
  throw;  // re-throw the exception
}

void t() {                          // handler for terminate
  cout << "terminate" << endl;
  exit(1);
}

class X{ };                         // trivial exception class

void f() throw(logic_error , bad_exception) {
  throw X();
}
```

In the calling code, you first install handlers:

```
set_unexpected(h);
set_terminate(t);
```

Then you call f() in a try block:

```
try {
 f();
} catch(bad_exception& e) {
  cout << "bad" << endl;
}
cout << "ending" << endl;
```

The output is

```
unexpected
bad
ending
```

As I previously explained, the handler for terminate() has not been called. If the handler for unexpected() is not installed, then the program execution will be aborted.

   In Section 3.4.5, I described exception handling in a member initialization list.
You can use a similar syntax to replace the entire function body with the try block;
for example:

```
void testing()                                     // no { here
  try {
    int x, y;
    cin >> x;
    cin >> y;
    int result = add(x, y);
  }
  catch(const my_overflow_error& exc) {
    cerr < exc.what() << exc.getArg1() << " "
      << exc.getArg2() << endl;
  }
  catch(const my_underflow_error& exc) {
    cerr < exc.what() << exc.getArg1() << " "
      << exc.getArg2() << endl;
  }
```

9.7 typeid

In Section 5.5, I described the dynamic cast RTTI construct. In this section, I briefly describe another RTTI facility called typeid. This facility is needed only for more advanced programming, such as implementing debuggers; it is used to obtain information about the type of an object (compared to Java's reflection mechanism, the information provided is rather limited but can still be useful).

To use typeid, you must include <typeinfo>. The typeid operator returns an object of class typeinfo, which provides the following three operations: == and != to test for equality and name() to return the class name. There is an important difference between using typeid for a pointer to the object and for the dereferenced value of this pointer. Specifically, if the type of pointer p is the base class B, and the value of p is an object of the derived class D, then typeid(p) is B and typeid(*p) is D. In other words, for such a pointer, you can use typeid() to find the type of the current value of the pointer, which is a runtime information; for example:

```
class Student { ... };
class StudentWithAccount : public Student { ... };
Student* s = new Student;
...
cout << "<" << typeid(s).name() << ">" << endl;
cout << "<" << typeid(*s).name() << ">" << endl;
```

The output this code generates depends on whether or not the type of the argument to `typeid` is a class with *virtual functions*:

- If `Student` has at least one virtual function, then it prints:

```
<pointer to Student>
<StudentWithAccount>
```

- If `Student` does not have virtual functions, `typeid()` does not provide any useful information, and the code prints:

```
<pointer to Student>
<Student>
```

Unlike `dynamic_cast`, `typeid` can be used with the primitive data types; for example

```
const int* p;
cout << typeid(p).name() << endl;
```

prints

```
int * const
```

Some implementations print a brief symbolic representation, for example `PCi`, rather than the more readable version shown here.

You can use type information to write a generic prompting function to enter a value:

```
template<typename Type>
void prompt(T& value, const string& p = "Enter ") {
  cout << p << " of type " << typeinfo(Type).name() << endl;
  cin >> value;
}
```

You can then use the function as follows:

```
int i;
prompt("Enter a value", i);
```

This call prompts the user, "Enter a value of type integer" and then reads the value.

When using `typeid` in a comparison, the equality

```
typeid(exp1) == typeid(type1)
```

is true if, for a type `T` (either predefined or user-defined), the type of `exp1` is a *pointer* to `T`, and `type1` is `T*`; or `exp1` is of type `DT`, derived from `T`, and `type1` is `DT` (assuming that T has virtual functions). For example, assume that Student has at least one virtual function:

```
class Student { ... };
class StudentWithAccount : public Student { ... };
Student* s = new StudentWithAccount(...);

typeid(s) == typeid(Student*);     // both sides are of type Student*

typeid(*s) == typeid(StudentWithAccount);     // value of *s is
                                              // StudentWithAccount

typeid(*s) != typeid(Student);
```

9.8 *Multiple Inheritance*

Java supports single inheritance of classes and multiple inheritance of interfaces. On the other hand, C++ supports multiple inheritance of all classes, which I describe here and in Section 6.5.3 (for more details, see Stroustrup, 1997). There is a potential problem associated with using multiple inheritance: It can lead to *diamond inheritance* (see Figure 9.1), where a class may have two parents, both of whom inherit from a single class (note that this *diamond* is unrelated to the diamond used in UML):

```
class Ancestor { ... };
class Child1 : public Ancestor { ... };
class Child2 : public Ancestor { ... };
class Descendant : public Child1, public Child2 { ... };
```

In the presence of diamond inheritance, a single attribute, atr, from the Ancestor class appears in the Descendant class twice; once inherited through Child1 and a second time inherited through Child2.

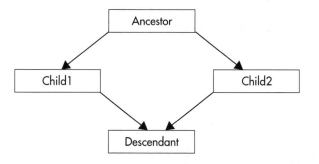

Figure 9.1 Multiple inheritance

In the previous example, the class `Descendant` does in fact have two instances of `atr`; therefore, a qualification is needed to refer to it:

```
atr;                                              // ambiguous
Child1::atr;
Child2::atr;
```

If only one instance is desired, the children of the `Ancestor` class are declared as virtual:

```
class Child1 : public virtual Ancestor { ... };
class Child2 : public virtual Ancestor { ... };
```

Here, `Ancestor` is called a **virtual base** for `Child1` or `Child2`. As Section 6.5.3 described, multiple inheritance can mix public and private inheritance (protected inheritance can be used as well). Note that an attribute is accessible if it is accessible through any path down the inheritance tree; for example, in

```
class Descendant : private Child1, public Child2 { ... };
```

public attributes of the class `Ancestor` are accessible in the class `Descendant`.

9.9 *Pointers to Members and Function Adapters*

In this section, I describe pointers to functions that are members of classes and their adapters for use in STL algorithms.

9.9.1   Pointers to Members

For some applications, instead of invoking class operations directly by using their names, it may be useful to invoke them indirectly through an intermediate layer of software. As described in Section 7.4, this intermediate layer is often known as a *proxy*. For such applications, C++ supports the concept of a **pointer to a member**. The name *pointer* is a bit misleading, because pointers to members differ from the general pointers to functions described in Section 9.4.2.

● EXAMPLE 9.2

Consider the following class used for representing two arithmetic operations:

```
// File : ex9.2.mathifc.h
class MathIfc { // interface
```

```
public:
  virtual double sum(double, double) const = 0;
  virtual double sqrt(double) const = 0;
};
```

To declare a pointer to a member operation of a class, you use the syntax `::*` (similarly, you can declare pointers to data members, but since they are less useful, they will not be discussed here). The required syntax is

```
type (ClassType::*name)(arguments);                    // watch brackets
```

For this class, you use

```
double (MathIfc::*twoP)(double, double);   // twoP is pointer to double
                                           // member operations with
                                           // two double parameters
```

Often, it is useful to define auxiliary types; for example:

```
typedef double (MathIfc::*TwoType)(double, double);
                    // TwoType represents a pointer to a double
                    // member operations with two double parameters

typedef double (MathIfc::*OneType)(double);
                    // OneType represents a pointer to a double
                    // member operations with one double parameter
```

You can use these types as follows:

```
TwoType sumP;
OneType sqrtP;
```

To assign a pointer to a member to a specific member operation, you use the following syntax:

```
&ClassType::member
```

For example, the following assignment uses previous declarations:

```
sumP = &MathIfc::sum;                     // no brackets; i.e. no sum()

sqrtP = &MathIfc::sqrt;
```

If p is a pointer to an object and m is an object, then member operations can be invoked through pointers to members using ->* and .*, respectively; for example (watch all brackets here):

```
MathClass* pm = new MathClass;
MathClass m;

double d = (pm->*sumP)(1, 3.4);          // access through pointer

double r = (m.*sqrtP)(2);                // access through object
```

Assignments between pointers to members are governed by the **contravariance rule**, which says that a pointer to a member of a base class cannot be assigned to a member operation of a derived class, but a pointer to a member of a derived class can be assigned to a member operation of a base class. (This rule is similar to an important rule that makes polymorphism possible: A pointer to the base class can be assigned an object of a derived class.) For example, consider the implementation of the interface just shown:

```
// File : ex9.2.math.h
class Math : public MathIfc { // implements
public:
  virtual double sum(double, double) const;
  virtual double sqrt(double) const;
};
```

Using this implementation, you can declare two pointers:

```
double (MathIfc::*twoP)(double, double);
double (Math::*twoMathP)(double, double);
```

You cannot write this assignment

```
twoP = &Math::sum;              // derived class may have more members
```

but you can fix it as follows:

```
twoMathP = &MathIfc::*sum;
```

From these examples, it should be apparent that the way to invoke members of the derived class through pointers to these members is to declare a pointer (or reference) variable of a base class and point it to the derived class; for example:

```
// File : ex9.2.math.cpp
double Math::sum(double x, double y) const {
```

```
    return x+y;
}
double Math::sqrt(double x) const {
    return ::sqrt(x);                           // call global sqrt
}


  // File : ex9.2.cpp
int main() {
    MathIfc* p = new Math;
    double (MathIfc::*twoP)(double, double) = &MathIfc::sum;
    cout << (p->*twoP)(2, 3) << endl;
}
```

I can use the previous example to show how you represent class operations and their arguments as strings and then invoke these operations (this is somewhat similar to the Java reflection mechanism). First you need a mapping from strings to pointers to the base class:

```
map<string, MathIfc*> objectPointer;
```

Next you need a mapping from strings to pointers to members. The members of the class MathIfc have two different signatures so you need two such mappings:

```
map<string, TwoType> binaryOps;          // TwoType defined above
map<string, OneType> unaryOps;           // OneType defined above
```

Now you can associate the string "math" with the implementation of MathIfc:

```
objectPointer["math"] = new Math;
```

You can also associate the string "sum" with the member function sum() of the MathOfc interface:

```
binaryOps["sum"] = &MathIfc::sum;
```

Finally, you can use the two strings to make a call to sum():

```
cout << (objectPointer["math"]->*binaryOps["sum"])(4, 5) << endl;
```

In a similar way, you can assign the string "sqrt" to a member function sqrt() and make the function call using strings:

```
unaryOps["sqrt"] = &MathIfc::sqrt;
cout << (objectPointer["math"]->*unaryOps["sqrt"])(4) << endl;
```

The technique shown in Example 9.2 makes it possible to create repositories of operations accessible through names that are strings. Such repositories are useful in various applications; for example, they can be used for remote execution of operations (names of operations are sent to the remote site as strings) or to implement a repositories of prototypes (see Section 6.6.4).

9.9.2   Member Function Adapters

In Section 8.5.4, I described various functor adapters. In this section, I describe several more adapters used for adapting pointers to functions and member functions. These adapters are particularly useful for heterogeneous containers of pointers, described in more detail in the next section.

Consider the class `Double`:

```
class Double {
public:
  Double(double);
  void show() const;
  void show2(double d) const;
  double get() const;
private:
 double value_;
};

Double::Double(double v) : value_(v) {}
void Double::show() const {
  cout << value_ << endl;
}
void Double::show2(double d) const {
  cout << value_*d << endl;
}
```

Assume that you want to perform some operations provided by this class on each element of a vector of `Double` values:

```
vector<Double> v;
... // initialize v
for_each(v.begin(), v.end(), invoke Double::show );   // pseudo-code
```

You must adapt the member function instead of invoking it. The header file `<functional>` defines six **member function adapters**: two for pointers to functions and four for member functions—two for pointers and two for references. Member function adapters are available only for *constant* member functions. For each kind of adapter, there is one for a parameterless function and one for a unary function:

- `mem_fun()`, to call a member function through a pointer
- `mem_fun_ref()`, to call a member function through a reference
- `ptr_fun()`, to call a pointer to a function

Since the vector v is an object rather than a pointer, the previously shown pseudo-code is translated using `mem_fun_ref`:

```
for_each(v.begin(), v.end(), mem_fun_ref(&Double::show));
```

The parameterless function `show()` is called here. A *unary* member function can be called by fixing its parameter using the `bind2nd` adapter:

```
for_each(v.begin(), v.end(), bind2nd(mem_fun_ref(&Double::show2), 2));
                                 // each element is multiplied by 2
```

Now consider a container of *pointers*. Adapters for both `Double` functions use `mem_fun()`:

```
vector<Double*> pv;
... // initialize pv
```

```
for_each(pv.begin(), pv.end(), mem_fun(&Double::show));
for_each(pv.begin(), pv.end(), bind2nd(mem_fun(&Double::show2), 2));
```

In the next section, I will show applications of these techniques. This section completes the topic of adapters by describing adapters for **pointers to functions**, which are useful if you need to use binders (binders cannot take functions as parameters). For example, consider the following function:

```
bool equal(const Double& d1, const Double& d2) {
   return d1.get() == d2.get();
}
```

Suppose you want to find the first occurrence of the value 1.3 in a vector:

```
find_if(v.begin(), v.end(), bind2nd(equal, 1.3));    // can't do this
```

You have to adapt the function so that it can be used with the binder:

```
find_if(v.begin(), v.end(), bind2nd(ptr_fun(equal), 1.3));
```

9.10 *Heterogeneous Containers and Composite and Visitor Design Patterns*

Containers that hold pointers can be used to implement **heterogeneous containers,** which store objects of various data types. In this section, I describe a heterogeneous container that stores pointers to objects of classes derived from a common base class—specifically, a list holding pointers to objects of the derived classes. I also describe two final design patterns: composite and visitor. These two patterns often appear together, which is why I describe both in the same section.

The **composite design pattern** is used in applications with a hierarchy of objects, some of which are composites of others. Three kinds of objects are defined:

- *Component objects*, which make up the interface the client interacts with
- *Composite objects*, which contain a number of children that are either other composites or leaves
- *Leaf objects*, which have no children

To understand the differences among these objects, consider a file system. A directory file is a composite object, and the regular and special files are the leaves (a special file is a device, such as a tape unit). As another example, think of graphical applications, where a picture is a composite and atoms, such as lines, circles, and so on, are the leaves. In both examples, the component is the client's interface, like the file system's API.

The structures involved in the composite design pattern are typically recursive and can be drawn as trees. The main advantage of this design pattern is that the clients can treat objects and compositions of objects in the same way (see Figure 9.2). A composite maintains a collection (for example, a list) of components; each component is either a leaf or a composite (which in turn can have children).

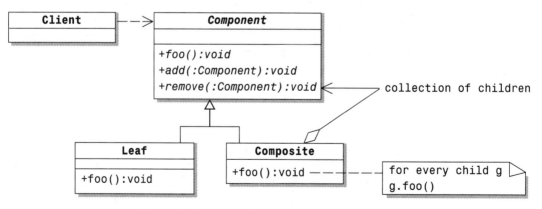

Figure 9.2 Composite design pattern

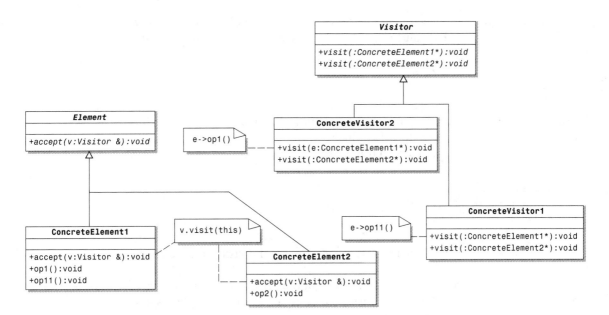

Figure 9.3   Visitor design pattern

The **Visitor design pattern** can be used to perform an operation on the elements of the existing aggregate, without changing the existing classes and avoiding a dynamic cast. This pattern is similar to the iterator design pattern, but it imposes only one requirement on each element of the hierarchy: It must support an accept(Visitor&) operation. This operation indicates that the element will accept a visitor operation that will perform some actions on the element. These actions are defined in the class Visitor, which provides overloaded operations visit (Element*) for every kind of element of the hierarchy. Figure 9.3 shows the general setup of the visitor design pattern. The client accesses the abstract classes Visitor and Element. The figure shows two sample implementations of the class Element and two implementations of the class Visitor. There are also two examples of the implementations of visit(ConcreteElement1*): one that calls op1() and one that calls op11().

A typical scenario for the client is to set up a visitor and then call accept() on a selected element.

The following sample execution (based on the design shown in Figure 9.3) will help explain the inner workings of this design:

```
ConcreteVisitor1 v;
Element* p = new ConcreteElement1;
p->accept(v);                         // element p accepts a visitation
```

p is a receiver of the message `accept(v)`. Since `accept()` is polymorphic, it is *dispatched* based on the current value of p, which here is `ConcreteElement1`. The function `accept(v)` is always implemented as follows:

```
v.visit(this)
```

Since `v` is passed by reference, and `visit()` is polymorphic, so this code is *dispatched* based on the current value of v, which is `ConcreteVisitor1`. Consequently, the operation `op1()` is invoked. If you use another visitor, such as

```
ConcreteVisitor2 v;
Element* p = new ConcreteElement1;
p->accept(v);
```

the operation `op11()` is invoked; in other words, the second visitation is different from the first one.

Notice that the word *dispatch* appears twice in the previous description; this is why this technique is called a **double dispatch**. Compare it with a single dispatch that is used in polymorphic programming

```
class B { ... };
class D : public B { ... };
B* p = new D;
p->foo();
```

where p is a receiver that dispatches `foo()` based on its value.

The visitor design pattern helps to avoid using a dynamic cast because you call `accept()`, which performs the required actions, rather than having to check the type of the node in the hierarchy using `dynamic_cast`.

You can design and use visitors for a composite hierarchy. For every leaf, the `accept()` function is implemented as follows:

```
void accept(Visitor& v) { v.visit(this); }
```

For composite objects, the code for `accept()` involves calling it for every child and then visiting this composite object. In the previous code, `Visitor` is the class that implements the visiting:

```
class Visitor {
public:
  virtual void visit(Leaf&);
  virtual void visit(Composite&);
};
```

● EXAMPLE 9.3

This example further explains the composite and visitor design patterns. It implements a directory that may store other directories, regular files, and special files (therefore, there are two kinds of leaves). A composite stores the list of children, which are represented by the File abstract class. There are three derived classes that represent directory, regular, and special files. Since the directory class stores the list of files as list<File*>, this example also shows how to use *heterogeneous containers*.

```
// File: ch9-file.h
class File {   // abstract element
public:
  virtual void accept(Visitor& v) = 0;
  virtual ~File();
  string name() const;
protected:
  File(const string&);
private:
  string name_;
};


// File: ch9-regularfile.h
class RegularFile : public File {
public:
  virtual void accept(Visitor& v);
  RegularFile(const string&);
  virtual ~RegularFile();
  void cat() const;                 // catenate file
  void insert(const string&);       // insert a string into a file
private:
  string contents_;
};


// File: ch9-directoryfile.h
class Directory : public File {
public:
  virtual void accept(Visitor&);
  virtual void add(File*) throw(domain_error);
  virtual void remove(File*) throw(domain_error);
  virtual ~Directory();
  typedef list<File*>::iterator FileIterator;
  Directory(const string&);
private:
```

```
    list<File*> children_;
};

// File: ch9-specialfile.h
class SpecialFile : public File {
public:
    virtual void accept(Visitor& v) { v.visit(this); }
    SpecialFile(const string&);
    virtual ~SpecialFile();
};
```

This design is somewhat simplistic. For example the SpecialFile class has no attributes, and the RegularFile class has a simple string attribute that represents the contents of the file. However, the design is sufficient to explain the inner working of the visitor design pattern and heterogeneous containers. For the UML description of this design, see Figure 9.4.

The remainder of this section briefly describes the implementation of the classes previously defined (as always, for the complete code, see the corresponding Web pages). You can add a new file if the directory does not have a file with the same name; to help implement this, you can define a predicate to be used by the find_if algorithm. Since every element of the container is of type File*, the operator() must have a parameter of the type File*&:

```
// File: ch9-directoryfile.cpp
class Same { // predicate class
public:
    Same(File*& f) : f_(f) {}
    bool operator()(File*& f) {
        return f->name() == f_->name();
    }
private:
    File* f_;
};

void Directory::add(File* f) throw(domain_error) {
    if(find_if(children_.begin(), children_.end(),
            Same(f)) != children_.end())
        throw domain_error("duplicate name");
    children_.insert(children_.end(), f);
}

    void Directory::accept(Visitor& v) {
    // first, visit every child
    for(FileIterator i = children_.begin(); i != children_.end(); ++i) {
        File* f = *i;
```

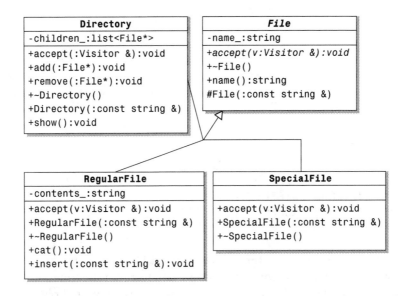

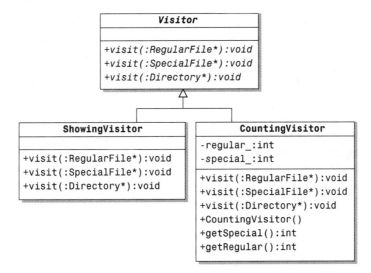

Figure 9.4   A simple file system

```
    f->accept(v);
  }

  v.visit(this);              // finally, visit this composite object
}
```

Here is the `Visitor` class implementation:

```
// File: ch9-visitor.h
class Visitor {  // abstract
public:
  virtual void visit(RegularFile*) = 0;
  virtual void visit(SpecialFile*) = 0;
  virtual void visit(Directory*) = 0;
};
```

The `Visitor` class accumulates information processed while visiting the hierarchy. The following code defines two concrete visitors: one to count the number of special and regular files, and the other to display the contents of all visited regular files:

```
// File: ch9-countingvisitor.h
  class CountingVisitor : public Visitor { // implements
  // counts the number of regular and special files
  public:
    virtual void visit(RegularFile*);
    virtual void visit(SpecialFile*);
    virtual void visit(Directory*);
    CountingVisitor() : regular_(0), special_(0) {}
    int getSpecial() const;
    int getRegular() const;
  private:
    int regular_;
    int special_;
  };

// File: ch9-showingvisitor.h
  class ShowingVisitor : public Visitor { // implements
  // shows the contents of all visited files
  public:
    virtual void visit(RegularFile*);
    virtual void visit(SpecialFile*);
    virtual void visit(Directory*);
  };
```

The implementations of these two visitors is straightforward:

```
// File: ch9-countingvisitor.cpp
  void CountingVisitor::visit(RegularFile* f) {
  ++regular_;
}
void CountingVisitor::visit(SpecialFile* f) {
  ++special_;
}

void CountingVisitor::visit(Directory* f) { }

int CountingVisitor::getSpecial() const {
  return special_;
}

int CountingVisitor::getRegular() const {
  return regular_;
}

// File: ch9-showingvisitor.cpp
void ShowingVisitor::visit(RegularFile* f) {
  f->cat();
}

void ShowingVisitor::visit(SpecialFile* f) { }

void ShowingVisitor::visit(Directory* f) { }
```

Finally, here is the code for an application program that creates a simple directory structure and uses both visitors:

```
// create a structure
Directory* root = new Directory("root");
RegularFile* f = new RegularFile("regA");
f->insert(string("reg regA"));
root->add(f);
f = new RegularFile("regB");
f->insert(string("reg regB"));
root->add(f);
root->add(new SpecialFile("spA"));
root->add(new SpecialFile("spB"));
Directory* r = new Directory("left");
root->add(r);
r->add(f);

// create and use visiitors
CountingVisitor cv;
root->accept(cv);
```

```
ShowingVisitor sw;
root->accept(sw);

cout << "There are " << cv.getRegular() << " regular files" << endl;
cout << "There are " << cv.getSpecial() << " special files" << endl;
```

---➤

9.11 *Exercises*

For all of the exercises in this chapter, whenever possible, you should use the STL containers and algorithms. When an exercise calls for the creation of a namespace, you should design it carefully, and split it into files available to the client and the implementation. For each exercise, include a program that tests your code.

EXERCISE 9-1

Write a filter program that replaces all sequences of consecutive whitespace characters by a single space.

EXERCISE 9-2

Write a filter program that replaces all occurrences of the tab character by two blanks.

EXERCISE 9-3

Write a program that can be executed either with a filename argument, such as

```
trans x y file.txt
```

or as a filter, such as

```
trans x y < file.txt > newfile.txt
```

In both cases, the program must write to the standard output a copy of file.txt in which all occurrences of the character x are replaced by the character y. For example, to convert all A characters in the file letter.msg to lowercase a, use

```
trans A a letter.msg
```

or

```
trans A a < letter.msg
```

Check whether the first two arguments (x and y) are single characters. For example, the execution

```
trans abba baba f1.txt
```

should produce an error message.

EXERCISE 9-4

Write a program that takes command-line arguments. There are two possible arguments for the number of lines displayed on the standard output:

```
program file1 -d
```

or

```
program file1
```

In the first case, the program displays the first d lines from file1. In the second case, it displays up to the first 20 lines from the file. If anything goes wrong (for example, the file file1 does not exist or d is not an integer value), an error message should be displayed.

EXERCISE 9-5

Use the reference counting technique from Section 6.6.2 to implement a program that maintains integer values stored in a wrapper class. Use the copy on writing technique when modifying the value of a constant. Use conditional compilation to write two versions of the code: a production version and a debugging version that shows the value of the reference counter for each constant. For example, here is a sample of what some of the debugging version's execution should look like:

```
create variable equal to 2
copy the above variable, using a copy constructor
create variable equal to 4
copy the above variable, using an assignment
change value of the first variable to 3
```

EXERCISE 9-6

Use STL vectors to implement a class, CircularQueue, that represents a bounded queue. Use assertions to verify all relevant preconditions and postconditions.

EXERCISE 9-7

Use heterogeneous containers to create a simple database of books. You can assume that there are two types of books: reference books and textbooks.

For each book, include its name (you can make assumptions about the maximum size of the name). For a reference book, include the subject of the book (math, computer science, physics, and so on). Use an enumerated type enum to represent the required information. For a textbook, also include the course associated with the book (represented as an integer). The database will be stored in a *list of pointers* to books. Implement a class hierarchy (with the class Book as a root) to represent this scenario. For testing, create a database with several books.

EXERCISE 9-8

Implement a class, Employee, that represents an employee with two attributes: name and ID. ID numbers for new employees are assigned values 1000, 1001, and so on. Write a derived class that represents full-time employees who have salaries and another derived class that represents part-time employees who have wages and assigned employment periods (for example, 30 days). Finally, write the following classes:

- Company1, which represents a company that can hire up to ten employees
- Company2, which represents a company that can hire up to *n* employees, where the value of *n* is determined in the constructor.

Store both companies in abstract collections. Use vectors and lists to provide two implementations of these collections as heterogeneous containers.

EXERCISE 9-9

Section 6.6.4 described the prototype design pattern and three classes: Account, SavingsAccount, and CheckingAccount. Implement a class, Bank, that uses a map to associate names with accounts. This class should have at least the following interface:

```
void addSavingsAccount(const string&) throw (domain_error);
void addCheckingAccount(const string&) throw (domain_error);
void removeAccount(const string&) throw (domain_error);
void deposit(const string&, double) throw (domain_error);
void withdraw(const string&, double) throw (domain_error);
void showBalance(const string&) const throw(domain_error);
void showAll() const;
```

EXERCISE 9-10

Modify Example 9.3 to implement the visitor, which finds all files with a given name.

Appendix A:

LIST OF TABLES, FIGURES, AND EXAMPLES

List of Tables

Table	Page
8.7. List operations	411
8.8. Associative container types and operations	417
9.1. Most important manipulators	433
9.2. Applications of manipulators	433

List of Figures

Figure	Page
2.1. State of memory immediately after the call to swap() with parameters passed by value	34
2.2. State of memory just before swap(), with parameters passed by value, terminates	34
2.3. State of memory immediately after the call to swap() with parameters passed by reference	35
2.4. State of memory after the execution of x = y in the call to swap() with parameters passed by reference	35
2.5. State of memory just before swap(), with parameters passed by reference, terminates	35
2.6. Heap, static memory and runtime stack	42
2.7. The state of the memory after executing p = &i	44
2.8. State of memory (a) before assignment *p = 5 and (b) after this assignment	45
3.1. Shallow and deep copy	83
3.2. Default assignment	85
3.3. Sharing resulting from use of the default copy constructor for a formal parameter	87
3.4. Copy constructor performing deep copy	88
3.5. Nested object	92
4.1. UML representation of class Student	134
4.2. Association between two classes	135
4.3. Aggregation between two classes	137
4.4. Composition between two classes	137
4.5. Combining interfaces	138
4.6. Two kinds of object composition	138
4.7. Instantiating operations	142
4.8. Singleton design pattern	147
4.9. UML diagram for namespace	150
4.10. UML diagram for two dependent namespaces	150
4.11. Classes for the part of namespace accessible to the client	159
4.12. Part of the namespace hidden in the implementation file	160
5.1. UML diagram for derived classes	164
5.2. UML diagram for a class derived from Student	166
5.3. Slicing	170
5.4. UML diagram for the overloaded assignment operator	178
5.5. Hierarchy of standard exceptions	184

Figure	**Page**

List of Examples

Appendix B:

LIST OF IDIOMS, PATTERNS, AND CONCEPTS

List of Idioms

List of Design Patterns

List of Concepts

Appendix C:

LIST OF C++ KEYWORDS

asm	do	if	return	typedef
auto	double	inline	short	typeid
bool	dynamic_cast	int	signed	typename
break	else	long	sizeof	union
case	enum	mutable	static	unsigned
catch	explicit	namespace	static_cast	using
char	export	new	struct	virtual
class	extern	operator	switch	void
const	false	private	template	volatile
const_cast	float	protected	this	wchar_t
continue	for	public	throw	while
default	friend	register	true	
delete	goto	reinterpret_cast	try	

Appendix D:

NUMERIC TYPES

To help you understand this section, I begin with a brief review of computer memory.

Computer memory consists of words, each word consists of a number of bytes, and a byte consists of a number of bits (usually 8 bits). In this book, I consider a byte-oriented memory architecture, in which the smallest addressable unit is one byte. (Other, less popular, memory architectures are word oriented.) During program execution, every data object is stored in some memory area consisting of several consecutive bytes. For example, an integer may be stored in four bytes of memory starting from the address 100 to the address 104. The size of a data object is the number of bytes it occupies. All data objects of the same type need the same amount of memory (although this amount of memory may not be the same between different platforms); therefore, it makes sense to talk about the size of a data type—for example the size of an integer.

Integer numbers (but not real numbers) come in two flavors: `signed` and `unsigned`. Signed integers use the leftmost bit, called the *sign bit,* to represent the sign (0 for non-negative values, 1 for negative values). Unsigned integers do not use the leftmost bit as the sign bit so their positive values can be larger than positive values represented as unsigned integers.

There is no guarantee that a specific amount of memory will be allocated to a particular data type. Instead, all implementations of C++ must follow certain rules (described later in this appendix). For example, the `int` type must always occupy at least 16 bits.

C++ provides the following numeric primitive data types: `char`, `int`, `float`, and `double`. In addition, there are several qualifiers (described later). Types `char` and `int` are called *integral types.*

Typically, signed characters are in the range –128 to 127, and unsigned characters are in the range 0 to 255. The most popular character set is ASCII (American Standard Code for Information Interchange). IBM computers use another character set called EBCDIC.

C++ guarantees the following:

- size(`short`) <= size(`int`) <= size(`long`)
- size(`float`) <= size(`double`) <= size(`long double`)

Constants

Literal integer constants may be specified as decimal, octal, or hexadecimal; for example:

```
123
04
0xAF3B
```

The actual type of a constant is the first from the following three types that is in the range of the type (does not cause an overflow):

- `int`
- `long`
- `unsigned long`

Adding the suffix to the constant can modify these types:

- `long`, with the suffix `l` or `L`, as in `1234555777L`
- `unsigned`, with the suffix `u` or `U`, as in `55u`
- `unsigned long`, with the suffix `lu` or `LU`, as in `2666LU`

Types of *octal* or *hexadecimal* constants are slightly different; the selected type is the first from the following four types that is in the range of the type (does not cause an overflow):

- `int`
- `unsigned int`
- `long`
- `unsigned long`

Floating-point constants can be written using either one of the following two notations:

- *Fixed-point notation;* for example, `3`, `3.14`, `.25`
- *Scientific notation;* for example, `3e+14`, `2.75E-20`

The type of a floating-point constant is *always* `double`, unless modified with a suffix:

- `f` or `F` to modify the type to `float`; for example, `3.23f` is of type `float`

- `l` or `L` to modify the type to `long double`; for example, `37668.668788L` is of type `long double`

Range of Values

For some applications, you may need to know the range of possible values for a specific data type. For example, to avoid integer underflow or overflow in arithmetic operations, you have to know the maximum possible integer value. For this reason, C++ provides the header file `<limits>` (see Josuttis, 2000).

Appendix E:

STRINGS OPERATIONS

Operation	Syntax
Return type used by many string operations	`string::size_type`
Value returned by find if it failed	`string::npos`
Length	`s.length()`
Assignments	`s1 = s2;` `s1 += s2;`
Concatenate	`s1 + s2`
Access to the *i*th character	`s[i]`
Insert	`s1.insert(location, s2)`
Remove	`s.remove(location, length)`
Replace	`s1.replace(location, length, s2)`
Substring	`s.substr(location, length)`
Return the index of a substring or npos	`s.find(s1, start=0)`
Return the index of the first character of s that matches any character in s1	`s.find_first_of(s1, start=0)`
Return the index of the first character in s equal to c	`s.find_first_of(c, start=0)`

Compare	`s1 < s2`
	`s1 == s2`
	`s1 > s2`

Conversion to C style	`s.c_str()`

Appendix F:

LIST OF GENERIC ALGORITHMS

The following is a list of algorithms discussed in the book; for a complete list of algorithms, see Lipmann (1998).

Name	Description
```template<typename Iter, typename T>``` ```T accumulate(Iter first, Iter last, T init);```	Add all values to the initial value
```template <typename Iter, typename T, typename Bin>``` ```T accumulate(Iter first, Iter last, T init, BinOp f);```	Use binary operation rather than addition
```template<typename Iter, typename T>``` ```bool binary_search(Iter first, Iter last, const T& v);```	Perform binary search in a sorted range

```template<typename Iter, typename T, typename Op>```
```bool binary_search(Iter first, Iter last, const T& v,```
``` Op comp);```	

```template<typename Iter1, typename Iter2>``` ```Iter2 copy(Iter1 first, Iter1 last, Iter2 res);```	Copy a range
```template<typename Iter1, typename Iter2>``` ```Iter2 copy_backward(Iter1 first, Iter1 last, Iter2 res);```	Copy a range backward
```template<typename Iter, typename T, typename S>``` ```void count(Iter first, Iter last, const T& v, S& n);```	Count number of occurrences of a value using ==

```template<typename Iter, typename T, typename S,```
``` typename Pred>```
```void count_if(Iter first, Iter last, Pred p, S& n);```
	Count number of occurrences of a value using a predicate

Name	Description

`template<typename Iter1, typename Iter2>`
`bool equal(Iter1 first, Iter1 last, Iter2 where);`
`template<typename Iter1, typename Iter2,`
`    typename Pred>`
`bool equal(Iter1 first, Iter1 last, Iter2 w, Pred p);`
	Compare two sequences using == or a predicate

`template<typename Iter, typename T>` `void fill(Iter first, Iter last, const T& v);`	Replace each value in a range with a copy of a value
`template<typename Iter, typename Size, typename T>` `void fill_n(Iter first, Size n, const T& value);`	Replace first n values with a copy of a value
`template<typename Iter, typename T>` `Iter find(Iter first, Iter last, const T& v);`	Perform linear search using ==
`template<typename Iter, typename Predicate>` `Iter find_if(Iter first, Iter last, Predicate p);`	Perform linear search using a predicate
`template<typename Iter, typename Op>` `Op for_each(Iter first, Iter last, Op foo);`	Apply a function to each element

`template<typename Iter, typename Op>`
`void generate(Iter first, Iter last, Gen g);`
`template<typename Iter, typename Size, typename Gen>`
`void generate_n(Iter first, Size num, Gen g);`
	Replace each value with a copy of a value generated by the functor

`template<typename Iter> bool is_sorted(Iter first,`
`    Iter last);`
`template<typename Iter, typename Op>`
`bool is_sorted(Iter first, Iter last, Op comp);`
	Test whether range is sorted

`template<typename Iter1, typename Iter2>`
`bool lexicographical_compare (Iter1 first1,`
`    Iter1 last1, Iter2 first2, Iter2 last2);`
`template<typename Iter1, typename Iter2,`
`    typename Pred>`
`bool lexicographical_compare(Iter1 first1,`
` Iter1 last1, Iter2 first2, Iter2 last2, Pred p);`
	Compare using lexicographical comparison

`template<typename Iter1, typename Iter2,`
`    typename Iter3>`
`Iter3 merge(Iter1 first1, Iter1 last1,`
`    Iter2 first2, Iter2 last2, Iter3 where);`
`template<typename Iter1, typename Iter2,`
`    typename Iter3, typename Op>`
`Iter3 merge(Iter1 first1, Iter1 last1,`
`    Iter2 first2, Iter2 last2, Iter3 where, Op fun);`
	Merge two sorted ranges

Name	**Description**

``template<typename T>
const T& min(const T&, const T&);```
 	
``template<typename T>
const T& max(const T&, const T&);```
 	
``template<typename T, typename Pred>
const T& min(const T&, const T&, Pred);```
 	
``template<typename T, typename Pred>
const T& max(const T&, const T&, Pred);```
 	
``template<typename Iter>
Iter min_element(Iter first, Iter last);```
 	
``template<typename Iter>
Iter min_element(Iter first, Iter last, Pred);```
 	
``template<typename Iter>
Iter max_element(Iter first, Iter last);```
 	
``template<typename Iter>
Iter max_element(Iter first, Iter last, Pred);```
	Find smallest and largest elements using < or a predicate

```template<typename Iter, typename T> void replace(Iter first, Iter last, const T& oldValue, const T& newValue);```	Replace each element equal to a value, compare using ==
```template<typename Iter1, typename Iter2, typename T> void replace_copy(Iter1 first, Iter1 last, Iter2 w, const T& oldValue, const T& newValue);```	Replace each element equal to a value, store in a copy

``template<typename Iter1, typename Iter2,
   typename Pred, typename T>
void replace_copy_if(Iter1 first, Iter1 last,
    Iter2 where, Pred p, const T& newValue);```
	Replace each element equal to a value using a predicate, store in a copy

```template<typename Iter, typename T, typename Pred> void replace_if(Iter first, Iter last, Pred pred, const T& newValue);```	Replace each element equal to a value, compare using a predicate

``template <typename Iter1, typename Iter2>
Iter1 search(Iter1 first1, Iter1 last1,
    Iter2 first2, Iter2 last2);```
 	
``template <typename Iter1, typename Iter2,
   typename Pred>
Iter1 search(Iter1 first1, Iter1 last1,
    Iter2 first2, Iter2 last2, Pred pred);```
	Search for a subsequence using == or a predicate

``template<typename Iter>
void sort(Iter first, Iter last);```
 	
``template<typename Iter, typename Op>
void sort(Iter first, Iter last, Op comp);```
	Sort into ascending order using < or a function to compare

Name	Description
`template <typename T>` `void swap(T&, T&)`	Swap two elements
`template<typename Iter1, typename Iter2>` `Iter2 swap_ranges(Iter1 first, Iter1 last, Iter2 w);`	Swap two ranges

`template<typename Iter1, typename Iter2, typename Op>`
`Iter2 transform(Iter1 first, Iter1 last,`
`    Iter2 where, Op foo);`
	Apply a function to each element and copy result

`template<typename Iter1, typename Iter2,`
`    typename Iter3, typename Op>`
`Iter3 transform(Iter1 first, Iter1 last,`
`    Iter2 first2, Iter3 where, Op foo);`	

Appendix G:

LIST OF STANDARD HEADER FILES

For the description of the standard header files not covered in this book, see Stroustrup (1997).

Name	Application	Examples
`<algorithm>`	STL algorithms	`find()`, `for_each()`
`<bitset>`	Template class for bitsets (not covered in this book)	
`<cassert>`	Assert macros	`assert()`
`<cctype>`	Character classification	`islower()`, `toupper()`
`<cmath>`	Standard mathematical functions	`sqrt()`, `sin()`
`<complex>`	Complex numbers (not covered in this book)	
`<cstring>`	C-style strings	`strlen()`
`<ctime>`	Date and time (not covered in this book)	`time()`
`<deque>`	Template class for double-ended queues	
`<fstream>`	File stream I/O	`ifstream`, `ofstream`
`<functional>`	Template functors and adapters	`equal_to`, `less`, `bind2nd`, `ptr_fun`
`<iomanip>`	I/O manipulators	`setprecision(i)`
`<ios>`	I/O stream base	`ios_base`
`<iosfwd>`	Forward declarations of I/O (not covered in this book)	
`<iostream>`	Standard I/O	`cout`, `cin`
`<istream>`	Input stream template	`operator>>()` for primitive types
`<iterator>`	STL iterator auxiliary functions	`back_insert_iterator`, `advance()`

Name	Application	Examples
`<limits>`	Numeric limits	`numeric_limits<int>::max()`
`<list>`	Template class for lists	
`<locale>`	Local setups (not covered in this book)	
`<map>`	Template class for maps and multimaps	
`<memory>`	Allocators for containers (not covered in this book), and `auto_ptr`	
`<new>`	Memory management	`new, delete`
`<numerics>`	Numeric operations (not covered in this book)	
`<ostream>`	Output stream template	`operator<<()` for primitive types
`<set>`	Template class for sets and multisets	
`<sstream>`	String stream I/O	`istringstream, ostringstream`
`<stack>`	Template class for stacks	
`<stdexcept>`	Standard exceptions	`range_error`
`<streambuf>`	Stream buffers (not covered in this book)	
`<string>`	STL strings	`substr()`
`<utility>`	Template pairs	`make_pair()`
`<valarray>`	Numeric vectors (not covered in this book)	
`<vector>`	Template class for vectors	

Appendix H:

LIST OF C++ COMPILERS
AND STL LIBRARIES

Compilers

KAI C++ compiler: http://www.kai.com/C_plus_plus/index.html
Intel C++ compiler: http://developer.intel.com/software/products/compilers/c50/
Cygnus g++ compiler from: http://gcc.gnu.org/
Borland C++ compiler from: http://www.inprise.com/about/press/2000/
  bcppcompiler.html

STL Libraries

STL Programmer's Guide from Silicon Graphics: http://www.sgi.com/tech/stl/
STLport standard library from http://www.stlport.org/download.html
Safe STL developed by Horstmann Software Design Corp.: http://www.mathcs.
  sjsu.edu/faculty/horstmann/safest.html

BIBLIOGRAPHY

Aho, A. V., J. E. Hopcroft, and J. D. Ullman. 1983. *Data structures and algorithms.* Reading, Mass.: Addison-Wesley.

Alexander, C., 1979. *The timeless way of building.* New York: Oxford University Press.

Alpert, S., K. Brown, and B. Wolf. 1998. *Design patterns smalltalk companion.* Reading, Mass.: Addison-Wesley.

Arnold, K., and J. Gosling. 1998. *The Java programming language.* 3d. ed. Reading, Mass.: Addison-Wesley.

Austern, M. H. 1999. *Generic programming and the STL: Using and extending the C++ standard template library.* Reading, Mass.: Addison-Wesley.

Binder, R. 2000. *Testing object-oriented systems.* Reading, Mass.: Addison-Wesley.

Breymann, U. 1998. *Designing components with the C++ STL.* Reading, Mass.: Addison-Wesley.

Cline, M., P. Greg, A. Lomow, and M. Girou. 1999. *C++ FAQs.* 2d ed. Reading, Mass.: Addison-Wesley.

Cooper, J. W. 1997. *Principles of object-oriented programming in Java 1.1: The practical guide to effective, efficient program design.* Research Triangle Park, N.C.: Ventana.

Cooper, J. W. 2000. *Java design patterns: A Tutorial.* Reading, Mass.: Addison-Wesley.

Coplien J. O. 1992. *Advanced C++: Programming styles and idioms.* Reading, Mass.: Addison-Wesley.

Coplien, J. O., and D. C. Schmidt. 1995. *Pattern languages of program design.* Reading, Mass.: Addison-Wesley.

Coplien, J. O. 1998. Software design patterns: Common questions and answers. In *The patterns handbook: Techniques, strategies, and applications*, edited by L. Rising. 1998. New York: Cambridge University Press.

Duell, M. 1997. Non-software examples of software design patterns. *Object Magazine* (July): 54.

Fowler, M. 1999. *Refactoring: Improving the design of existing code.* Reading, Mass.: Addison-Wesley.

Fowler, M. 2000. *UML distilled.* 2d. ed.. Reading, Mass.: Addison-Wesley.

Gamma, E., R. Helm, R. Johnson, and J. Vlissides. 1995. *Design patterns: Elements of reusable object-oriented software.* Reading, Mass.: Addison-Wesley.

Grand, M. 1998. *Patterns in Java: A catalog of reusable design patterns illustrated with UML.* Vol. 1. New York: Wiley.

Josuttis, N. M. 2000. *The C++ standard library: A tutorial and reference.* Reading, Mass.: Addison-Wesley.

Koenig, A., and B. Moo. 1997. *Ruminations on C++.* Reading, Mass.: Addison-Wesley.

Lipmann, S. B., and J. Lajoie. 1998. *C++ primer.* 3d ed. Reading, Mass.: Addison-Wesley.

Martin, C., D. Riehle, and F. Buschmann, eds. 1998. *Pattern languages of program design 3.* Reading, Mass.: Addison-Wesley.

Meyers, S. 1998. *Effective C++.* 2d. ed. Reading, Mass.: Addison-Wesley.

Musser, D. R., and A. Saini. 1996. *STL tutorial and reference guide: C++ programming with the standard template library,* Reading, Mass.: Addison-Wesley.

Pree, W. 1995. *Design patterns for object-oriented software development.* Reading, Mass.: Addison-Wesley.

Reiss, S. P. 1999. *A practical introduction to software design with C++.* New York: Wiley.

Stroustrup, B. 1997. *The C++ programming language.* 3d ed. Reading, Mass.: Addison-Wesley.

Vlissides, J. 1998. *Pattern hatching: Design patterns applied.* Reading, Mass.: Addison-Wesley.

INDEX